D0887059

WITHDRAWN
UTSA LIBRARIES

The Rise of Opera

by the same author

THE INTERPRETATION OF EARLY MUSIC

WAGNER'S 'RING' AND ITS SYMBOLS

A PERFORMER'S GUIDE TO BAROQUE MUSIC

STRING PLAYING IN BAROQUE MUSIC

THE OPERA
(Harcourt Brace Jovanovich)

THE
RISE OF OPERA

Robert Donington

CHARLES SCRIBNER'S SONS

New York

© Robert Donington, 1981

This book published simultaneously in the
United States of America and in Canada—
Copyright under the Berne Convention

All rights reserved. No part of this book
may be reproduced in any form without the
permission of Charles Scribner's Sons.

1 3 5 7 9 11 13 15 17 19   I/C   20 18 16 14 12 10 8 6 4 2

Printed in Great Britain
ISBN: 0-684-17165-1
Library of Congress Catalogue Number: 81 50730

LIBRARY
The University of Texas
At San Antonio

Contents

❧❧❧

Contents

PART THREE · THE BROADENING OF OPERA

PART FOUR · THE DIVIDING OF OPERA

APPENDIX

Illustrations

❦

between pages 256 and 257

Acknowledgements

It is my great pleasure to thank here some of the chief at least of the very many people who in varying measures and manners have helped me with this present book, the preparing and writing of which accompanied my other duties during a dozen years of teaching in American universities and, by now, several further years since I returned to England.

I should like first to thank the University of Iowa, and especially two of my most valued colleagues there: Albert Luper, on whose initiative as head of musicology I was brought along, to say nothing of his subsequent advice and friendship; and Himie Voxman, whose vision and diplomacy and unobtrusive humanity as chairman I rate no less highly. I was always allowed my summers off, and was in addition given an Old Gold Research Fellowship in 1966, and a Research Assignment in 1970, for two European sojourns very necessary in that so many of the operas here studied were (and for the most part still are) to be found only in their original sources spread around the leading libraries. Herald Stark, the director of operatic studies, and a most exceptional master—these days—of *bel canto* voice-production, was another valued colleague; and so also was Eugene Helm, my partner in the Collegium Musicum, as well as his successor, Edward Kottick; that admirable music librarian and scholar, Rita Benton, was unfailingly skilful and supportive; and indeed the entire faculty has my affection and respect.

So many were friendly and helpful to me on campus at Stanford, at Yale, at New York City and at Buffalo, and of course in briefer encounters at meetings both local and national of the American Musicological Society, that I should not know how to list them all here; but perhaps I may put in an especial word of gratitude to Howard Mayer Brown, George Buelow, Albert Cohen, Barbara Hanning, Wiley Hitchcock, Jerrold Northrop Moore, Claude Palisca, Muriel Wolf, and in England Winton Dean and Nigel Fortune. More than to any am I indebted to Paul Seligman and to Thomas Walker for reading and annotating my typescript in the most painstaking detail: the former on whatever concerned his distinguished learning in Platonic and related philosophy; the latter on that exact knowledge of seventeenth-century opera to which he is making so outstanding a contribution. My late wife Gloria Rose was the utmost of help and joy to me in our inexhaustible shop-talk, not to mention the hours we spent in the great libraries sharing our several discoveries in the closely related fields of early opera and cantata. Many students have brought many good thoughts in my graduate seminars on opera both at Iowa and at Buffalo. And many hands have typed many drafts, my thanks being particularly due to Jerry Nyall, and more recently to Redwood Fryxell and Judy Mott. For advice and encouragement of the rarest value, my cordial thanks go to Patrick Carnegy. For editorial assistance far beyond the normal, and many valuable discussions, I am most warmly grateful to Judith Osborne, my present wife. For the visual beauty of this book to its designers, Sally Lane and Shirley Tucker. A final scrutiny of my proofs was made by Howard Mayer Brown, and that a scholar of his distinction should accept this exacting under-taking is so generous a tribute that I do not know how to thank him enough. By all these people I have been helped so very much. Terence Miller is an indexer whose rare persistence, skill and imagination have brought great pleasure to me and great benefit to my book, and I thank him most gratefully.

The American Council of Learned Societies, by a greatly appreci-ated grant-in-aid, made possible the most extended and productive of my several journeys around the libraries of Europe where early oper-atic scores and librettos can (in many cases uniquely) be consulted. The accumulated notes and other material which I collected then have been distilling in my mind and getting into my drafts and my teaching for a very long time now; I could not have prepared this book without them, and for this indispensable assistance I should like to offer my regrettably belated but very heartfelt thanks.

London. Spring, 1980   ROBERT DONINGTON

PART ONE

The Approach to Opera

I
Defining Opera

DRAMA AS THE ESSENCE OF OPERA

My purpose in this book is to describe the rise of opera within a field of reference broad enough to suggest something of its working methods. My subject is how and why opera arose when it did, and no earlier in the long story of our human arts; my counter-subject is how opera works, since the nature of opera was certainly implicit in its origins and, I suppose, cannot radically alter without becoming a different form.

I want to ask what new turn the late Italian renaissance gave to old traditions in poetry and in music and in social and philosophical inclinations generally, since it would not as I think be realistic to look for anything quite like opera either before, or elsewhere as yet. I shall go in some detail to the death of Monteverdi in 1643, by which time the rise of opera—Italian opera—was an established fact. The sequel —still Italian—will be traced more concisely, by using a few operas as samples for many others, until I take up in rather more detail again for the rise of French opera with Lully: out of previous Italian opera, it is true; yet retaining more of the original conception of opera as a flexible drama in words and music than did current Italian opera, evolving as that already was towards the stabler patternings of number opera.

I share the view[1] that drama is the essence of opera. Not, indeed, as drama happens (without benefit of music) in the great world outside; but as drama unfolds in those inner moods which so condition our experience of the outer world. Not the naturalistic representation of outer facts, then, so much as the stylized representation of those inner feelings and responses which are also facts; for in the artistic convention which comprises opera, it may not so much matter how improbably the outer story is getting across, provided the inner story is coming through true and clear. Our inner realities are just as valid as our outer realities, and much more accessible to musical communication.

Broadly, the words of an opera are written before the music is composed. The structure of the libretto outlines the structure of the score. The plot, the characterization and with some exceptions the points of climax are laid down verbally, before being amplified musically. There is the sound and the sense and the entire linguistic craftsmanship of the verse, or of the prose where this is substituted in whole or part. There are the many enchanting conceits of poetic imagery, often highly appropriate for musical embroidery; and it is certain that no genuine poetic images are meaningless. In some though not in all cases, the music may be of a higher (and perhaps a much higher) quality than the words. Yet in no case should we underestimate the importance of the words and the music to one another. Mozart did not, nor Verdi, nor Wagner who made sure of the matter by being his own librettist, nor Richard Strauss whose correspondence with Hugo von Hofmannsthal on the subject is so informative.

It is in fact the characteristic advantage of opera that neither its words alone nor its music alone can express all that its drama requires. The images of music are just as communicative as the images of poetry; and the two arts may often combine with one another best when the sound and the sense of the poetry are either neutral enough or incomplete enough not to be unduly contorted by the difficult but rewarding compromises of pitch, rhythm and tempo involved in their combination: especially difficult and rewarding in opera, where the requirements of the drama have equally to be served.

To stage human characters in human situations so that they develop through their own inherent tensions and conflicts towards some sort of an inevitable resolution: this is drama. It is not drama to read or narrate an epic; it is drama to enact in our very presence certain of those perennial hopes and fears, loves and hates, joys and sufferings, mingled fortunes and misfortunes which grip us in a work of art because they are in one form or another the common themes of our ordinary existence. Nowhere do we identify more vividly than in drama with our vicarious representatives, which is perhaps why Bernard Shaw once called every theatre a church and every audience a congregation, leaving the performance not altogether the same as when we entered in.

The stage-production should also be serving the same numinous experience, by visual images drawn in the spirit although not necessarily in the letter from the same artistic idiom. The only images on stage which are in the spirit of Monteverdi's *Orfeo*, Mozart's *Magic Flute*, Weber's *Freischütz*, Wagner's *Ring*, Debussy's *Pelléas et Mélisande* or Berg's *Wozzeck* are images more or less baroque, or classical, or romantic, or symbolist or expressionistic as the case may be: broad idioms, no doubt, and capable of very free interpretation; but not interchangeable. No genuine image is an arbitrary invention or interpolation; it is much more like something already implicit in the given conditions of human nature, and waiting to be found within the boundaries of the style.

Thus Wagner's stage-directions, for example, are numerous, explicit and mostly quite workable in productions neither too literal for modern acceptance nor too incongruous to go with the verbal images from Nordic mythology[2] already in the poetry, and already provided with an explicitly romantic embodiment in the music. In early opera the stage-directions are apt to be sparse but challenging, as when hell or heaven is to open in full and costly spectacle before our eyes; while contemporary descriptions of such ambitious scenes and of the stage machinery for producing them are vivid in the extreme. Stage-spectacle took a prominent share in the rise of opera, among so many other fashionable extravagances of the day. We need to recreate some imaginative equivalent to their kind of spectacle, reconciled with our kind but not replaced by it. That is what I mean by a stage-production which is not incongruous.

A TOTALITY OF STAGED WORDS AND MUSIC

There are of course many other ways besides opera of making good theatrical use of music. In ballet, for example, there may be no words, but there may be drama joined to music by mime and gesture. In some modern music-theatre there may be words, but used for sonorous and not for semantic effect. In classical Greek and Roman drama, in medieval and renaissance mysteries and moralities and sacred representations, in various oriental traditions and indeed in drama generally, incidental music can be of great importance. But incidental music is not the same as opera. Only music which shares integrally with the words in unfolding the drama can make an opera.

There can, it is true, be various degrees and combinations. Operetta, including many fine American musicals, can be opera just in so far as the music does not merely diversify but carries forward the drama. Oratorio, in so far as theatrical illusion does not form part of the intention, is not opera, notwithstanding that some oratorios can be (and at various periods have been) staged to good operatic effect, and that any opera can be given a concert performance with something of the effect of an oratorio. It is opera when a verbal text articulates a drama intended to be staged with full theatrical décor, to music which does as much as the words to develop the characters and situations all the way through to their final resolution. It is still opera when the more active words are spoken without music, or against music in the superimposed texture known technically as melodrama (rare in opera though habitual in films), provided that the characters and situations are so caught up into the music that they would not be at all the same without it, as in such wonderful examples as Mozart's *Magic Flute* or Beethoven's *Fidelio*.

There can be wider definitions of opera, which might, for example, bring in some of what I shall be discussing here as pre-operatic and not as opera. But on my definition here, there was and I think there could have been no opera prior to the very end of the sixteenth century at Florence. My definition is as follows: opera is staged drama unfolding integrally in words and music.

II
The Philosophical Ingredient

THE LONG ARM OF NEOPLATONISM

Behind the rise of opera there lies a view of art inherited, like so much else of value in the renaissance, from Plato, and more especially through that recurrent tradition now known to us as Neoplatonism. On this view, art is a veil which half reveals, in the very act of half concealing, deeper meanings than its surface shows. Just as a statue might be veiled yet suggest its shape without actually disclosing it, so a work of art may at the same time be outwardly enjoyable and inwardly suggestive. The instructed are well aware of this; the uninstructed sense it in the measure of their native perceptiveness.

Plato implied this view in some famous passages (especially in Books III and X of the *Republic*), and exemplified it by reverting to mythical comparisons at just those points in his argument where he felt that reason and logic could carry him no farther. It is of course the ancient and universal method of myth and ritual to suggest inner meanings through outer representations. At Eleusis, not far from Plato's Athens, one of the greatest mysteries of classical antiquity flourished well into the Christian era. Yet so closely were its inmost secrets kept, notwithstanding their many enigmatic depictions in ancient art, that we know very little about them; for its early Christian opponents, from whom our attempted reconstructions mostly derive, are now thought to have had very much less inside knowledge of what they were opposing than they wished us to believe.[1] We are not much better informed about the Orphic mysteries, though we are about the Orphic doctrines, related as these were to the relatively familiar Pythagorean teaching.[2] The early history of opera was crossed by Orpheus at several points, and we shall need to inquire somewhat into his reputed significance at the time when opera arose, little as this may have really had to do with the legendary musician and initiator of his pristine mythology. The Orphic rites of classical antiquity were themselves connected in some degree of intimacy with the Eleusinian and more distantly with the Egyptian mysteries. One famous Platonist of the second century A.D., Lucius Apuleius, described in his highly allegorical *Metamorphoses* (more popularly known as *The Golden Ass*) his own eventual initiations into the mysteries of Isis and Osiris; but having done so in what he obviously feared was somewhat too open a manner, he added with belated misgiving: 'I have related to you that which, although heard, nevertheless it is necessary for you not to know.'[3]

It was, of course, forbidden to reveal the mysteries. But the same distinction was also drawn more generally between levels near the surface of a work of art which can be accepted at face value in popular appreciation, and levels best kept from those who might only be confused and disturbed by direct exposure to the deeper truths. This is fundamentally a Platonic attitude, and Plato was taken as very high authority by those poets and musicians of the sixteenth century who were making their way towards opera without as yet knowing that it was opera towards which they were making their way.

The tenacity both of Plato's thought and of Aristotle's through so many centuries is one of the astonishing facts of Western history. There was a particularly productive period when much of Plato and something of Aristotle merged by the third century A.D. into that remarkable outburst of philosophical energy and metaphysical elaboration now known to us as Hellenistic Neoplatonism. This flourished especially at Alexandria, and also at Athens until the Emperor Justinian closed the Platonic Academy there in A.D. 529. The line ran strongly from Plotinus through Porphyry and Proclus, Iamblichus and Boethius (well known to musicians); the regular teaching of philosophy by pagan instructors was not ended until the second half of the sixth century and that was in no sense, of course, the end of pagan philosophy. The writings by an unknown author once attributed to St Paul's famous convert, Dionysius the Areopagite (now more cautiously ascribed as pseudo-Dionysius or pseudo-Areopagiticus) are Neoplatonic texts of the late fifth or early sixth century; and there we find reiterated that typical insistence on using 'misleading symbols for sacred matters, so that divine matters may not be easily accessible'.[4] It would still be possible to apply some such considerations to *The Magic Flute*, where the Masonic meanings are certainly not all visible on the surface.

These writings by the pseudo-Dionysius were particularly prominent in that great movement of ideas by which Christianity, in overcoming the pagan religions broadly associated with Neoplatonism, was itself virtually taken over by Neoplatonic theology, cosmology, philosophy and morality, in all respects but the cardinal Christian dogmas of the creation, the incarnation and the resurrection of the flesh. The philosophical system of Plotinus was not a religion; but it proved so compatible with Christian religion that St Augustine, even after his conversion, continued to attribute a main share in his own spiritual development to that great founder of Hellenistic Neoplatonism. Nine centuries later, St Thomas Aquinas again reconciled revelation with reason in a philosophy based primarily on Aristotle and Aristotle's Arabian transmitters and commentators; but we have to remember that Aristotle, too, was something of a Platonist, and so indeed was Aquinas in addition to his admiration for the Hellenistic Neoplatonists. It was not possible to be an educated man without being something of a Platonist during the formative centuries of our modern Western civilization.

Dante, whose lifetime overlapped with that of Aquinas, was as indebted to this philosophical tradition for his Neoplatonic cosmology (with extensions from Aristotle[5]) as he was to Christian orthodoxy for his learned theology. Man is in little what the universe is in large: that was the broad Neoplatonic metaphor or comparison. Man is a microcosm corresponding to the macrocosm of eight spinning spheres for the seven planets and the fixed stars, with the ninth as the transparent *primum mobile* and above that the fixed Empyrean where the One dwells motionless yet moving all. However much or little this elaborate construction may have been credited at the time with outer reality, as an astronomical explanation of the earth and the heavens (antiquity already had a fair grasp of the actual solar system), it was certainly credited with inner reality as a symbolical map of the psyche. When 'in the middle of the journey of our life' Dante found himself 'in a dark wood, because the straight way was lost', he did not mean a literal journey or an actual wood: he meant a state of mind, through which, aided by a certain artistic identification of his own genius with his forerunner Virgil, he had to work out his devious but healing route in course of the great poem of which these are the wonderful opening lines.[6] Having lost his loved Beatrice in outer reality, he described in his *Vita Nuova*[7] how she appeared to him, more as muse than as mistress, in a sort of visionary embodiment of his own most creatively feminine and poetic aspect, urging him to that search which she herself rewarded at the distant end of it. For in exploring his Neoplatonic cosmos from its bottom to its top, Dante was (no less than Goethe almost a millennium later in *Faust*) exploring his own depths and heights; and surely for Dante this was a transforming experience no less human for being also experienced as an image for the divine ordering of things. 'You who have sound understandings, consider the doctrine concealed beneath the veil of the strange verses' —so Dante put it to us;[8] and this again is typical of the Neoplatonic view of art which eventually found its way into opera. The art is the veil; the doctrine is the truth half revealed in the very imagery by which it is half concealed.

THE START OF RENAISSANCE NEOPLATONISM

As Dante's medieval Christendom dissolved into the adventurous tumult and classical aspirations of the early renaissance, Petrarch's passion for purer Latin studies and pioneering Greek studies well signified that emerging mood which we know as humanism, no doubt because of a certain renewed regard for human individuality in contrast to collective authority. It is true that human reason and divine revelation had always been taken as complementary by the best ecclesiastics; and it is also true that the tolerance of the renaissance was always limited, and subsequently declined; yet there is no mistaking the liberation accompanying the classical revival nor the flood of pagan thoughts and pagan images released by it into general circulation. Above all, pagan images are conspicuous in renaissance art; and they were by no means used there merely as art for art's sake, but rather for the allegorical and symbolical implications which were Neoplatonically assumed to comprise the veiled significance of art.

It was Petrarch's remarkable friend Boccaccio who, having himself (unlike Petrarch) at least some command of the Greek language, spread the widest net for pagan images and pagan mythology. His vast and learned *Genealogia deorum gentilium* (Genealogy of the Pagan Gods), at quite an opposite extreme of his versatile talent from the popular *Decameron* upon which rests his modern fame, drew not only on Hellenic and Hellenistic but also on distinctively Egyptian and other ancient or reputedly ancient sources, together with more recent material from a great diversity of authors. The lost autograph has been ascribed to around 1350; there were extensive revisions and augmentations; copies seem to have gone into considerable circulation shortly after 1370; there was a printed edition at Venice in 1472, which remained the best; a choice of editions was available in the sixteenth century, when the artistic preparations were going forward which, although not yet opera, soon led into opera.

Itself an assembly of very many sources, the *Genealogy* became in turn a source of text-books by which pagan images became yet further diffused, and upon which some of the most direct precursors of opera depended for their scenarios and even for their scenery. The entire disposition and interpretation of these pagan images, and of the beliefs and the fables into which they enter mythologically, falls within the Neoplatonic tradition, and came to be so regarded by the strong school of 'Platonists' (*Platonici*) who dominated much of the thinking and most of the serious art of the fifteenth and the sixteenth centuries. But here we must draw an important distinction between the different phases of the Neoplatonic tradition.

There were Platonists from antiquity downwards, one of them

being that lively author and deliberate allegorist Apuleius in the
second century A.D., whose thinly veiled account of his own initiations has already been mentioned and whose charming narration of
the old fable of Cupid and Psyche we shall find among the pre-
operatic scenarios of the sixteenth century. But the substantial modifications of Platonic thought which have come to be known as Neoplatonism, though interestingly anticipated by Philo Judaeus early
in the first century among others, were pre-eminently the work of
Plotinus in the third century, and of those followers such as Porphyry
and Proclus and Iamblichus who stood most closely indebted to
Plotinus. This was the school of Hellenistic Neoplatonism, centred in
the main upon Alexandria and Athens, which is ordinarily intended by
the term Neoplatonism in modern usage.

But the same term is also applied to the great revival of Neoplatonic
tradition in Italy and elsewhere during the fifteenth and sixteenth
centuries, and rightly so, since it was indeed the same tradition at a
different stage. Plato and the earlier Neoplatonists were then equally
revered, and they were most sincerely studied, however diffracted
through the tacit assumptions of what was after all quite another
period. For this revived school we use the term Renaissance Neoplatonism, and it is this variety which unless otherwise indicated or
implied will be intended by the words Neoplatonic and Neoplatonism
in the remainder of the present book. We shall be talking at times quite
generally about Neoplatonism, since this has been a continuous tradition through Western civilization; but we shall more specifically be
talking about Neoplatonism in the renaissance context.

The Neoplatonism of Plotinus impresses us alike by its imaginative
range and by its intellectual exactness. The distinctive vision of Hellenistic Neoplatonism is certainly exalted; but its boundaries are exceptionally clear. This clarity of outline was by no means generally
maintained. Even at the time, there were plenty of marginal Neoplatonists who welcomed almost any reinforcement from emotional
cults and philosophical doctrines (with the chief exception of the
Epicureans, for some reason felt to be irreconcilably antagonistic) in
the losing battle of pagan religions against the Christian religion. So
soon as Christianity conclusively prevailed, this tactical inducement
to syncretic amalgamation disappeared; but there remained ample
opportunities for exploiting pagan images under allegorical and symbolical justifications which could be stretched to almost indefinite
lengths. Pagan teachings had been and continued to be endorsed as
premonitions and intimations, attained by reason or by intuition, of
Christian revelation and Christian doctrine. Pagan art even of the
most sensuous kinds could be enjoyed on the respectable assumption
that the sensuous veil was merely there to render palatable the
virtuous instruction; and while this assumption was undoubtedly

convenient, we have no reason for supposing that it was basically insincere. Yet certainly the door was left wide open, and the classical restraint and philosophic discipline which commend the pure Hellenistic Neoplatonism of Plotinus and his school became subjected to great artistic and intellectual dilution.

If the classical images could be legitimately taken as the allegorical or symbolical representations of our human impulses in all their inner variety and conflict, why not a few further animal-headed deities from ancient Egypt, or some additional esoteric mysteries from cabalistic or hermetic sources? Why not Moses and Hermes Trismegistus as well as Orpheus? And of course always Aristotle as well as Plato, since the renaissance Neoplatonists did not regard these founding fathers of our Western philosophy as by any means necessarily antagonistic to one another? Syncretism could hardly go farther than in these latter developments of the Neoplatonic argument. Yet the underlying vision of an inner reality half concealed and half revealed by outer reality persisted; the basic genius for introversion which was Plato's contribution to our understanding of this bewildering universe runs through it all; and in fifteenth-century Florence, much of the necessary philosophical discipline and artistic selectiveness was brought back again, if not by every perfunctory practitioner, at least by many of the best and most influential minds of the day.

In Boccaccio's *Genealogy* the selection was already wide, but the treatment was anything but perfunctory. It would be hard to exaggerate the authority attributed throughout the renaissance to this once celebrated book. Obviously it is intended to be at least as instructive as it is entertaining; but the whole point is that the instruction is taken to be implicit in the entertainment, not merely superimposed by the interpretations provided. The most primitive Hellenic or pre-Hellenic deities; the far more elegant and less primitive Olympians, and the wilder survivors or newer arrivals who were not Olympians; the demi-gods and demi-goddesses; the heroes and heroines; the nymphs and shepherds; the ogres and witches and monsters and dragons; the many strange denizens of river and fountain and sea and woodland: all the splendid or alarming or enchanting creatures of mythic fantasy from ancient Greece or Rome, with others from the Near East partially assimilated to their alleged classical cousins, jostle and compete in that multitudinous company.

It says much for the enlightened humanism of the renaissance, before the harsher fears and renewed guilts of the Reformation and the Counter-Reformation hardened into a more defensive intolerance, just how much richly mythological imagery could be assimilated from the vivid pages of Boccaccio, or enjoyed in the best of the pagan poets, such as Ovid, who provided Boccaccio's originals. Boccaccio was not, as his successors sometimes became, promiscuous in his comprehensiveness to the point of diminishing returns; and unlike some of the bolder humanists of the subsequent centuries, he left it in no doubt that his own faith was as orthodox as his scholarly aims were reputable. But comprehensive he certainly was, and open-minded. If he knew an image, he described it. If he was aware of divergent traditions (and no vital myths are static) he reported all the information available to him. If there were alternative classical or post-classical interpretations, he compared them, before providing contemporary glosses of his own. He was seldom at a loss for some explanation of an attribute, an emblem or a mythological episode. Some of these explanations seem very far-fetched, many are perhaps rather more ingenious than persuasive, many others are perceptive in a conventional manner and a few come quite disconcertingly near to what a modern depth-psychologist might hazard. This last is a feature which recurs in certain of the derived text-books of the sixteenth century, in connection with which we shall return to it.

Yet it is ultimately none of these explanations which give Boccaccio's book its solid convincingness. The universal relevance of the mythological material itself glows through the somewhat fitful rationalizations, and the ancient symbols project their own suggestiveness to our feelings and our intuitions. No wonder this massive volume, with its medieval exhaustiveness and its renaissance curiosity and its eminently readable humanist Latin, became a sort of Neoplatonic bible for generations of artists, including those artists in poetry and music and stage-spectacle whose work made opera possible by the end of the renaissance. For Boccaccio made it plainer than ever that he taught mythology not just for its own sake, but in order to teach 'how to conceal truth in a fabled and seemly covering'.[9] And once more, as with Dante, Boccaccio did not mean truth about the outer world. He meant truth about the inner man.

THE SPREAD OF RENAISSANCE NEOPLATONISM

In fifteenth-century Florence, with the full flood of the classical revival, the distinctive discipline of renaissance Neoplatonism[10] emerged with Marsilio Ficino,[11] a quiet scholar and philosopher at the court of Cosimo de' Medici, who set him up in a villa outside Florence to direct an academy of the arts and sciences in wishful imitation of Plato's Athens. And there Ficino continued under Lorenzo de' Medici, translating Plato and the Hellenistic Neoplatonists, and paying a special regard to the spurious but much valued Neoplatonic writings then attributed to Hermes Trismegistus ('thrice-great', and supposedly equated with Thoth the Egyptian god of wisdom); and also to certain of the cabalistic speculations (said to be traditionally derived from

Moses); and very particularly to the so-called *Orphic Poems*, the Hymns, the didactic and narrative poetry surviving under the purported authorship of Orpheus, for whom the academy set up a curious cult, half playful but half serious. There were recitations and musical performances and rites and ceremonies all associated with the annual celebrations of Plato, and with the philosophical debates on those and other festive occasions. Some Pythagorean doctrine concerned with the symbolism of numbers also found its way in (as it had in Plato himself). There were in addition some very refined and symbolical astrological and alchemical activities, as well as some fairly cautious experimenting with the less dangerous and heretical areas of 'white' as opposed to 'black' magic (but certain Neoplatonists such as Giordano Bruno did venture unwisely into the forbidden regions).[12] Renaissance Neoplatonism was indeed a heterogeneous assortment; but the basis of it was still Plato's own creative intuition, and by and large it was a noble vision.

Ficino was evidently a conspicuous example of what his age called the *vir contemplativus*, the contemplative man, such as Michelangelo (himself an eager participant in the Platonic debates) depicted in his statue of Ficino's patron, Lorenzo de' Medici: astrologically saturnine, a 'child of Saturn': as we might say, an introvert in our modern sense of a man more involved with, and more perceptive of, the inner than the outer aspects of reality. His opposite, the *vir activus* or active man, was depicted by Michelangelo in his statue of Giuliano de' Medici: astrologically jovial, a 'child of Jove' (i.e. Jupiter), an extrovert. A Platonist might well tend to have somewhat more of the introvert and an Aristotelian somewhat more of the extrovert; and certain it is that people of these opposite dispositions can find it remarkably difficult to understand one another, whether in religion, philosophy, politics, science or art.

For Plato, the essential realities were the universal forms existing independently of the particular things we experience outwardly. For Aristotle, the essential realities were the particular things, in which he considered that the forms are merely immanent, having no independent reality of their own. But he too agreed that forms must be thought of universally, because thought itself is essentially of universals. It was for this reason that Aristotle considered statements in tragedy to be about universals, that is to say about a kind of man, even though imitating an individual. Plato put it that art, except for music, is no more than the imitation of an imitation, and quite low down in our perception of reality. But Aristotle, while conceding that art can only imitate the individual instance, nevertheless held that it must do so in universal terms, since that is how our minds work. This seems much nearer to the Neoplatonic view of art, and may perhaps be a valuable example of cross-fertilization between the Platonic and the Aristotelian traditions.

For Plato, a form meant a pattern laid up in heaven, perfect of its kind as no individual instance within our earthly experience can be. Since we nevertheless can think of it, without having experienced it in this life, Plato argued that we must have experienced it in a previous existence of the soul; for our judgements to the effect that such-and-such is good or beautiful imply an ideal standard of comparison which we certainly do not encounter in this mortal state. We can only, Plato suggested, be in some manner remembering what once we knew: hence his doctrine that knowledge is recollection.

We do not need to take this doctrine literally in order to find it perceptive. For there can be more or less deliberate allegory, of which the crude terms at least may be a sort of code mutually and perhaps traditionally understood. But there can also be intuitive symbolism, of which our recognition seems to be innate, passing as it does beyond what tradition and context can sufficiently explain. One suggested explanation in the Platonic line of descent, which I have found useful in understanding the Neoplatonic contribution to opera, is C. G. Jung's concept of archetypal images.[13] It was as a result of wide and even esoteric reading of Neoplatonic writings that Jung was confirmed in some of the thoughts which took him beyond his initially Freudian psychology. Where Plato spoke of patterns laid up in heaven, Jung spoke of archetypes laid down in the unconscious. Among our innate behaviour patterns there appear to be psychological as well as physiological predispositions—if indeed it ultimately makes sense thus to separate our psycho-somatic manifestations at all. An archetype might be thought of as a concentration of converging signals: a dynamic focus within a network of inner promptings, variously operative, but nevertheless somehow characteristic for our species.

Archetypes would necessarily lie (as instincts were always thought to lie) too deep within the unconscious for direct awareness. Rather as iron filings scattered across a magnetic field reveal its lines of force, our conscious behaviour suggests the archetypal dispositions which condition us from the unconscious. Our intuitions about them appear both collectively, in the recurrent themes of myths and fairy-tales and many forms of art, and individually, in the dreams and fantasies which in part relate to those recurrent themes. It is the dynamic centres behind the recurrent themes that can be described as archetypes. It is the images upon which we project these intuitions that can be described as archetypal.

The word archetype (Gk. ἀρχέτυπον, sc. παράδειγμα; Lat. *archetypum*, sc. *exemplum*) was classical, but rare, and does not appear in Plato. However, it was used by Philo Judaeus in a very Platonic context; by Dionysius Halicarnassiensis (as opposed to ἀπόγραφον, copy); in Cicero, Juvenal and Martial; Neoplatonically in Plotinus, in

Proclus (commenting on Plato's *Republic*), and in the pseudo-Dionysius (as opposed to ἀντίτυπον, image) where it seems that Jung encountered it, as he also did in the so-called *Corpus Hermeticum*.[14] Jung, moreover, was particularly struck by St Augustine's Neoplatonic description of *ideae principales* or *formae*, primary ideas or forms, 'which cannot perish', but from which 'is derived everything which does arise and perish'; and these forms, St Augustine added, 'it is possible for the soul to intuit (*intueri*)'.[15]

But what are we intuiting? What are we perceiving beneath an artistic veil? Even more than Plato[16] did Aristotle teach[17] that 'poetry tends to convey the universal', and that 'the ideal form' thus invoked 'must surpass the particular'. We can quite see why, in the context of the sixteenth century, G. B. Gelli[18] thought poetry 'very difficult to understand perfectly without knowledge of the philosophy both of Plato and of Aristotle.' For to invoke the universal by means of the particular seems a very acceptable statement of the case. Art is certainly some sort of communication on the subject of what it feels like to be a human being. But not just a particular human being: rather a kind (or even in a measure any kind) of human being. Not the outer reality: rather the inner reality to which the outer image draws our attention by a sort of inspired indirection. That was the Neoplatonic view of art; that was the philosophical assumption which went into opera. And perhaps opera more than most forms depends on this kind of artistic indirection, trading as it so often does a minimum of outer plausibility for a maximum of inner credibility.

FICINO'S PLATONIC INWARDNESS

And so we are back with that essential inwardness which Ficino taught and which the earliest librettists of opera both learnt and practised. 'We have to penetrate the inward depths of the mind', Ficino taught. 'The soul has to leave outer things and withdraw into itself'; for 'in a certain sense the soul of man (*anima hominis*) is all things', since 'the inner perception and mind judge all things through certain formulations, which are stimulated by outer realities.' Whether in dreams or in art, Ficino concluded (and it is interesting to find him thus comparing them), we can recognize true images from false just in so far as 'our spirit (*animus*) possesses and produces true patterns (*formas*).' Then, using a biologically inherited behaviour-pattern for comparison (the cuckoo which can acquire nothing by imitation from the parents it never sees would have made his point still better): 'just as every swallow builds its nest in the same way, so every intellect conceives in the same way first principles of art and morals, which are known to everyone by nature.' For 'we have in our minds a certain common model of values (*commune quodam bonorum exemplar*)', so that our living consists in bringing our innate patterns 'from a certain potentiality into activity'. But 'all things have two actions, an inner and an outer'; and 'by what means will you ever grasp outer realities (*exteriora*), if you have lost [touch with] inner realities (*interiora*)?'[19]

Ficino's brilliantly recalcitrant disciple, Pico della Mirandola, urged once again that 'divine matters, when written at all, must be covered beneath enigmatic veils and poetical dissimulations', thus 'showing only the crust of the mysteries to the ordinary people, while reserving the marrow of the true sense for higher and more developed spirits.' And as an example, Pico instanced the Orphic Hymns: in appearance, 'the merest fables and trifles (*fabulas nugasque meracissimas*)'; but in reality, veils for the deepest of inner meanings.[20]

III
The Poetical Ingredient
꒰ᵒ꒳ᵒ꒱

NEOPLATONIC POETRY IN ITALY

Another of Ficino's young disciples with a great future before him was Angelo Ambrogini, called Poliziano (Politianus, Politian) after the town of Montepulciano in Tuscany where he had been born in 1454. Poliziano was brought to Florence as a precocious boy of ten. He learnt Latin as a matter of course, and Greek because of that Medici enthusiasm for classical studies which was opening up such new insights in fifteenth-century Florence. For philosophy, Poliziano proved one of the liveliest and most erudite of Ficino's many pupils; he rapidly acquired a reputation as a linguist and a scholar; he was brought in high favour into Lorenzo de' Medici's ducal household, and presently established in a teaching post at the University. His poetry in Latin, in Greek and in the Italian vernacular was of the greatest fluency and charm, full of classical images whose allegorical intentions were of the Neoplatonic significance expected from a pupil of Ficino and a Florentine courtier of the day. Poliziano was actually commissioned by Lorenzo de' Medici to instruct the yet more gifted Botticelli, ten years his senior, how to put a proper Neoplatonic significance into his paintings, some of which are visual depictions of Poliziano's own Neoplatonic poetry (as for example in the famous *Primavera*, more or less based on Poliziano's *La Giostra*, with Apuleius in the background and Ficino in person as the link).[1]

Among Poliziano's large and distinguished output of poetry, there is a small verse drama in the Tuscan vernacular of which the style and construction set a somewhat novel model for what became known as the pastoral drama. This is his *Orfeo*,[2] performed not apparently at Florence but at Mantua, probably in 1478 (rather than in 1472 as previously supposed, but certainly no later than 1483). Its connection with the Florentine cult of Orpheus nevertheless seems evident. Least of all on the subject of Orpheus could Poliziano forget his Neoplatonic inclinations: Orpheus, whom the Florentine academy took to have been a kind of proto-Platonist by anticipation. On the other hand, there was never any intention, whether in painting or poetry or anywhere else, for the Neoplatonic significance to show ostentatiously. It is merely set there inconspicuously below the enchanting surface, for those who understand to recognize approvingly, and for those who do not to pick up intuitively just so far as they have eyes to see and ears to hear.

For us today, there glows through the enchanting surface of Neoplatonically inspired art an impression of underlying meaningfulness which moves us to especial delight, even if we have not been brought up to translate it. If we do learn to translate it, perhaps from the fine studies by Warburg, Gombrich, Panofsky or Edgar Wind[3] of renaissance and early baroque painting, we may be yet further moved; and it is part of my intention here to comment in this way on certain early librettos of which the Neoplatonic meanings appear to be specific. For the earliest librettos are pastoral dramas in direct line from Poliziano, and along this line among others the lucid imagination and multiple levels of Neoplatonic poetry passed into opera.

As an enchanting entertainment at its surface level, Poliziano's *Orfeo* sets out in dramatic form the legend variously recounted in Ovid, Virgil and other classical sources.[4] Orpheus lost his beloved Euridice by the bite of a snake hidden in the grass, and recovered her by the charm of his legendary musicianship from the dark underworld; but only on condition of not looking round at her until he had brought her up again into the bright upper world of daylight. Through some overmastering compulsion of his eager spirit, he did look round, and lost her for ever, after which he was himself torn to pieces by a group of infuriated women, followers of Dionysus (Bacchus) the god of wine and of manic inspiration, and variously known as Bacchae or Maenads or Bassarids (Fox-maidens).[5]

For a Neoplatonic listener, the keys to this most familiar of classical legends would have been, first, the contrast between the dark underworld and the bright light of day; and second, the relationship of Orpheus the archetypal musician to Euridice his beloved companion and feminine complement. No cultivated listener of the renaissance could be confronted with a dramatized descent into the underworld without thinking of Dante lost 'in the middle of the journey of our life' and finding his way out of his 'dark wood' only through the yet darker regions of the *Inferno*; nor watch a beloved lost and regained and lost again without recalling Beatrice whom Dante lost and sought and in a manner regained. It was a current Neoplatonic interpretation[6] of Euridice that she was to Orpheus very much what Dante's Beatrice by his own account became to Dante:[7] his soul (*anima*); his muse; as we might put it, the carrier of his own complementary component of inner femininity, projected onto the woman in the case as we so often do. There were alternative interpretations in Plato's *Symposium*[8] and in the Neoplatonic commentators of the cause and symbolism of her second disappearance, and of the subsequent melancholy fate of Orpheus. We may turn to these sources when the whole story comes up again in early opera, especially in the wonderful *Orfeo* of Striggio and Monteverdi at Mantua in 1607: a work certainly written and very possibly composed in full cognizance of Poliziano's *Orfeo*. But that the underworld connects with the unconscious, and that the day and the sun connect with the light of conscious reason, seems evident throughout the traditional and above all the Neoplatonic use of these transcendent images.[9] They hardly need interpreting; they interpret themselves, as archetypal imagery habitually will.

PASTORAL DRAMA

The construction of the pastoral drama was based, as we might expect, on the classical Greek and Roman drama. In manner, the resemblance is rather to the tragedies of Aeschylus, Sophocles and Euripides than to the ribald comedies of Aristophanes or Terence or Plautus—and still less does the lyric charm and graciousness of the pastoral drama remind us of the weight and pompousness of Seneca. But in subject, there is little of the sombre legend of the tragic Greek dramatists, or of the grandeur of Homer, or of the cosmic sweep of Hesiod; and there is much of the idyllic enchantment of Theocritus or of Ovid or of Virgil in his more lyrical passages. As the pastoral drama quickly evolved and settled to an accepted idiom, we can trace it down with few substantial changes through Bernardo Bellocini's *Il Paradiso* (performed at Milan in 1483), Nicolò da Correggio's *Il Cefalo* (performed at Ferrara in 1486), Matteo Maria Boiardo's *Il Timone* (performed at Ferrara in 1492) and on into the sixteenth century, until two famous specimens set a standard which was not again equalled although sometimes attempted: Torquato Tasso's *Aminta* (performed and published at Ferrara in 1573), and Giovanni Battista Guarini's *Il pastor fido* (The Faithful Shepherd, written at Ferrara in evolving versions between 1581 and 1590, probably performed at Turin in 1583, and published at Venice in 1590)—a work so apt for music that it became one of the richest sources of texts for madrigals.

However, in one substantial respect the pastoral drama did change before it came to provide the dramatic form and the poetic structure for the earliest librettos. A typical renaissance discussion arose as to whether it was really necessary to have anything so sad and ill-omened as a tragic ending, especially since the usual occasions for these lively performances were weddings and other celebrations of rejoicing and good will. Aristotle had of course argued very weightily for the purging of our feelings through pity and fear;[10] but on the other hand, as Guarini ingeniously contended[11] when defending his *Pastor Fido*, the consolations of Christianity were by his time happily available, as they had not been in the old pagan times, to purify the soul and combat fear. So he called his great poem a *tragicommedia pastorale*, not meaning comic, but with a happy ending; and it came to be generally understood, in spite of occasional misgivings, that the purposes of serious drama might be even better served by this agreeable relaxation of the classical proprieties. We shall find that it was quite against the accepted conventions for early opera to end in tragedy.

The poetry of the pastoral drama, as already exemplified in Poliziano's *Orfeo*, falls into a most effectual alternation of symmetrical line-lengths without metrical variation, on the one hand, and symmetrical stanzas having a pattern of varied metres and line-lengths, on the other hand. These are features taken from classical Greek drama, where continuous metre is used for the action and the dialogue and the narratives of messengers, but mixed metres are used for the lyrical or contemplative or moralizing or agitated commentary offered from a more collective viewpoint by the choruses. The most important distinction in prosody is that Greek poetry does not rhyme, whereas the stanzas of Italian vernacular poetry do rhyme, and in the pastoral drama they may have rhyme-schemes of considerable complexity, variety and ingenuity. The continuous portions of the pastoral drama, mainly unrhymed, are suitable for dialogue and narrative such as was subsequently composed in recitative. The strophic stanzas, with their sophisticated rhyme schemes, proved equally suitable for choruses or for solo arias; and indeed they were already sung, or partly sung, in Poliziano's *Orfeo*, since the term *cantare* occurs in the stage-directions.

For Agostino Beccari's *Il sacrificio d'Abramo* (The Sacrifice of Abraham, performed at Ferrara in 1554), we actually have a little surviving music, composed by Alfonso della Viola. It includes a strophic variation for a priest in a sort of stately recitation interspersed with choruses in a rhythmically unmeasured style anticipating the direction later taken by recitative, towards which it was perhaps, as John Bettley interestingly suggests, a contributory factor.[12] However, neither recitative nor any other form of music capable of unfolding a drama cumulatively was as yet available, and these pastoral dramas, though enlivened by much incidental music, were not operas.

Meanwhile, the same Neoplatonic impulse which inspired Poliziano's *Orfeo* found influential admirers and practitioners wherever the strong tides of the Italian renaissance reached. Poliziano's own pupils alone were a distinguished company: many Italians; a few from Germany, Portugal and England, including names so famous as Linacre and Grocyn; while the least writings of Poliziano in scholarship

or literature became prized for their ripe embodiment of a relaxed
yet learned humanism half way between that of Boccaccio or of
Petrarch on the one side and that of Erasmus or of Ariosto on the other
side. One early centre of Italian influence was the French city of
Lyons, whose cultured Italian archbishop, Cardinal Ippolito d'Este,
was a distinguished patron of the arts; and altogether the French poets
became increasingly interested in Neoplatonic artistic theory during
the first half of the sixteenth century—all the more so when, in 1547,
Catherine de' Medici became Queen of France and surrounded herself
with Florentines and other Italians. The group of French poets with
humanist ideals whose original leader was Jean Dorat had formed
themselves into a sort of unofficial academy at court already in about
1549, under the subsequently familiar name of the Pleiad, whose
Neoplatonic inclinations came over very clearly when Ronsard, the
greatest of them, described almost in the same words as Boccaccio
'how one must dissemble and conceal fables, fitly, and disguise well
the truth of things with a fabulous cloak in which they are enclosed',
so as to 'make enter into the minds of ordinary people, by agreeable
and colourful fables, the secrets which they could not understand
when the truth is too openly disclosed.'[13]

There we have it again: the fabulous semblance on the outside; the
veiled truth within, not to be too openly disclosed, yet not to be
omitted either. The philosophical assumptions and the poetical
assumptions which went into opera came very close together at this
point; for Rinuccini, the Florentine poet who wrote the first libretto,
exchanged a mutual influence with Chiabrera, who wrote the second
or the third; and Chiabrera was the most avowed and famous Italian
follower of Ronsard. Striggio, the librettist for Monteverdi's *Orfeo* in
1607, came next in line. And it would seem that one of the most
characteristic elements in all this exchange of influence was the allegorical and symbolical intention.

ALLEGORY AND SYMBOLISM

A Neoplatonic account of the use of allegory, contemporary with the
rise of opera, was given by Sir John Harrington in the preface to his
English translation (London, 1591) of Ariosto's chivalric epic, *Orlando
Furioso*,[14] which was begun in 1539, and which later became a much
favoured source for the scenarios of early operas:

> The Ancient Poets have indeed wrapped as it were in their writings
> diverse and sundry meanings, which they call the senses or myster-
> ies thereof. First of all for the litterall sense (as it were the utmost
> [outmost] barke or ryme) they set downe in manner of an historie

the acts and notable exploits of some persons worthy memorie: then in the same fiction, as in a second rime [bark] and somewhat more fine, as it were nearer to the pith and marrow, they place the Morall sence profitable for the active life of man, approving vertuous actions and condemning the contrarie. Many times also under the self same words they comprehend some true understanding of Naturall Philosophie, or sometimes of politik governement, and now and then of divinitie: and these same sences that comprehend so excellent knowledge we call the Allegorie, which Plutarch defineth to be when one thing is told, and by that another is understood.

And so, it is implied, did those renaissance poets, including Ariosto, whose models were the 'Ancient Poets'. We have already noticed this metaphor of the outer crust contrasted with the inner marrow in that impetuous Neoplatonist Pico della Mirandola, whom Sir John Harrington could well have been reading, since he thus echoes not only his views but also his language. The most noted contemporary English example of the allegorical method is Spenser's *Faerie Queene*, of which the first three books were published at London in 1590. The setting is another of those dark woods familiar from the opening lines of Dante's *Divine Comedy*, and representing a darkness and indeed a mystery of the spirit as well as of the forest; the sequel in all its romantic (but unfinished) complications is as deliberately allegorical as ever a romance could be. Yet however deliberate the allegory, it can never supply more than a proportion of the veiled content. If there were no more content to the *Faerie Queene* than its advertised allegory of Queen Elizabeth and her Anglican religion, with the virtues of chastity and friendship and courtesy and for good measure a concise history to date of the British monarchy, these worthy objectives might offer more poetical impediment than inspiration; but in so far as the archetypal attributes of masculinity and femininity and heroism in search of greater consciousness and maturity shine through, the poetry radiates a symbolism far beyond its deliberately allegorical intention, and the poem lives—neither so vividly nor so consistently, perhaps, as the *Orlando Furioso* of Ariosto which was its chief model; but in the same kind.[15]

It is in this kind, allegorically intended and Neoplatonically derived, that we have to place the earliest librettos of opera. Nevertheless, there can be very great differences in the rigour with which an allegorical intention is introduced. Manni's libretto for Cavalieri's *Rappresentatione* of 1600, the second opera in history if we class it as an opera rather than as a morality with operatic features, is so deliberate an allegory that its human interest nearly disappears—which is why we do not quite know how to class it. This is not the case with those others of the earliest operas which really established the form. The human interest there is intensely moving—and none the less so for being represented by such very archetypal characters and situations. There are certainly some deliberately allegorical intentions to be considered; but we hardly experience them as allegory in the theatre, since the symbolism is so largely of that elusive order which works directly on our feelings and our intuitions.

How deliberate is an allegory when it takes over and begins to tell itself, like *The Pilgrim's Progress* of which Bunyan wrote that he 'fell suddenly into an allegory', and 'having now my method by the end, still, as I pulled, it came'?[16] How much was deliberate and how much was spontaneous in *The Magic Flute*, of which some of the Masonic symbols (especially the illuminating sun over against the obscuring night) were actually derived, by way of Rosicrucian and other channels, from Neoplatonic originals? There is always some blend of conscious and unconscious purpose in our human affairs; and perhaps the arts work best when neither takes on too dominant a share. An artist as such is less concerned with concepts than with symbols. Conceptual consciousness shines so far as possible in the clear light of reason; but we might also perhaps speak of symbolic consciousness, as of some strange but glowing twilight where images are symbols and symbols are themselves a kind of consciousness.[17]

It was in some such sense as this, I think, that Wagner[18] wrote of using 'mythological symbols' for their 'deep and hidden truth' in order 'to bring the unconscious part of human nature into consciousness', yet insisted that to reveal too openly what he himself experienced as something of a 'riddle' might only 'get in the way of a genuine understanding.' It was in this same introverted spirit that Goethe[19] countered Eckermann's rather insensitive questioning as to what was the veiled meaning of *Faust* by replying that he did not know himself, and that 'the more impossible for reason to assimilate a work of poetry is, the better'. Carlyle[20] went so far as to put it that 'it is in and through *symbols* that man, consciously or unconsciously, lives, works and has his being'; and that 'in a Symbol, there is concealment and yet revelation.' That indeed is Neoplatonism in a nineteenth-century formulation.

And so we may feel that while only certain of the earliest operas were deliberately Neoplatonic, opera did not cease to be symbolical when it ceased to be Neoplatonic. There is no form of art better suited than opera to carry inner meanings. Some of these meanings are connected with that human duality (of which Plato himself[21] was so well aware, partly through the prior influence of Heraclitus), that divided nature underlying so many of the problems of our human, yet also animal, existence. The dark and the light, the instinctual and the cultural, the feminine principle and the masculine: take it up where we may, and quite regardless of our biological sex, we are all of us dual, functioning as we do with greater or lesser awareness from either pole. Ambivalence is the very price of being human. We are unavoidably in conflict, and intuitively in search of reconciliation.

The Neoplatonic librettos of the earliest operas are full of images for that conflict and that reconciliation, drawn as they are from a familiar tradition which itself draws upon archetypal material still as open as ever it was to our subliminal recognition. Many are the gods and the goddesses, the heroes and the heroines, the impossible monsters by land and sea and air to delight us throughout the renewed classical artistry of the renaissance; and diverse are the human characteristics and situations thus shown to us not openly, but as in a glass darkly. For the fables in which Boccaccio or Ficino, Pico or Poliziano or Ronsard instructed their fellow-artists 'to disguise well the truth of things'[22] are the legends of pagan and above all of classical mythology. But the truth is the truth about ourselves.

IV
The Musical Ingredient

MUSIC AND DRAMA

There was no novelty in that intimate association between music and drama of which the pastoral drama was so relevant an instance. Feasts and banquets; welcomes and farewells; processions and progresses; disguises and tourneys; births and birthdays; weddings and funerals; visits and victories—if it could be celebrated with any touch of the dramatic, celebrated it was; and if it was celebrated, then it was celebrated with music. For ballets and for dancing, music was a necessary accompaniment; for the half-serious, half-playful pretendings of good society, an invaluable support.[1]

The pretence was commonly that the grand people had somehow a mythological significance. In sixteenth- and seventeenth-century France, for example, the king was presented as the sun, or as Apollo god of the sun, with an originally Neoplatonic signification behind the obvious flattery. The dancers and the musicians and even the whole distinguished company might be in fancy dress, pastoral or allegorical. The part taken by music in all this informal posturing must have made it much easier to accept the formal stylizations of opera when the time for opera arrived.

The regular drama was also amply supported and enriched by music. Fanfares and curtain tunes; marches and dumb shows; dirges and serenades; mad scenes and drinking scenes; dances and sonnets; interludes and postludes:[2] any excuse, or no excuse, and the music sounded. Yet none of this is really very near to opera. Not even in Shakespeare can isolated scenes made atmospheric by music fuse into drama unfolding through music. Not even the famous production at Vincenza in 1585 of Sophocles' *Oedipus Rex*,[3] with its sung choruses by Andrea Gabrieli, anticipated opera, though no doubt it contributed indirectly towards the preparation of opera. There were professional singers, instrumentalists, producers, costumiers, engineers, carpenters and many others available to take their skills straight over into opera; but for opera to arise, two further developments in the resources of music itself were required. One was modulation. The other was monody.

MODULATION AND MONODY

Modulation is a progression through the tonal field by the chromatic alteration of notes previously diatonic. The keys thus reached are alike in their disposition of tones and semitones, different only in their relative positions; hence they offer no resistance to modulation. Modes are unlike, and their difference is absolute; they resist sustained modulation, since too much chromatic alteration destroys them. It was already happening in Josquin, in fact though not in name;[4] and Glareanus himself could not reverse the tendency.[5] For a sharp or sharpened third above a bass which then drops a fifth or rises a fourth will always exert a tonal pull from dominant to tonic, call them what we may, just as a plagal cadence will pull from a sub-dominant and remoter pulls will link the eight major or minor mediants and submediants. Concurrently with the rise of opera, to adventure full cycle round the keys was not unknown;[6] and indeed the normal adventurousness of Marenzio, Gesualdo, Monteverdi, Frescobaldi, Dowland or John Bull far exceeded the later refinements of Corelli or Alessandro Scarlatti. It is this journey through the keys, called modulation, which above all endowed our music with the capacity for progressive development needed to unfold a staged drama as much in the music as in the words.

Monody is melody flexible enough to combine dramatic action with musical expression. Polyphony has for this purpose too structured a texture: Orazio Vecchi called his madrigal comedy *L'Amfiparnaso*, which is not an opera, merely a 'musical play' at which 'one looks with the mind, where it enters through the ears and not through the eyes.'[7] Opera can include dramatic ensembles; but opera could not arise except through the monody, the single song, of individuals in personal conflict and development. The claims of personal individuality took over from those of collective authority more conspicuously in renaissance humanism than at any other period since antiquity. We might almost put it that the predisposing cause of opera was humanism.

Monody was chiefly novel in being so dramatically conditioned by its harmonies. Harmony for coloration is world-wide; harmony progressing as vertical chords for two hands on the Celtic harp may possibly be as ancient as medieval counterpoint;[8] but harmony modulating through distant areas of the tonal field had surely no precedents. Modulation was the most consequential of all renaissance innovations in music. Monody depended upon it; for whereas in equal-voiced polyphony, melody and harmony more or less balance, and whereas in later polyphony, harmony itself works out as counter-point, in monody a solo melody enlists a subsidiary accompaniment on a modulating bass. Monody is a tune with harmonies, supported by a bass which itself implies those harmonies. Monody without its progressions could express nothing, and without its modulations, could express nothing continuously dramatic. Modulation and monody together brought sufficient novelty into the resources of music for opera to arise.

The grand strategy which shaped up as modulation seems to have been one of those evolutionary changes rather attributable to the climate of the times than to the specific enterprise of individuals or groups. The brilliant tactics which resulted in monody, on the other hand, can be credited to highly individual intentions and to groups whose constitution can be largely specified; but there are still certain preliminaries to opera which can best be considered before we turn to the details of that fascinating campaign.

V

The Threshold

NEOPLATONIC SPECTACLES IN ITALY

Just before the rise of opera, there were several nearly operatic forms such as the interlude (*intermedio, intermezzo, intermède*),[1] the ballet and the masque (*balletto, ballet de cour, masquerade*),[2] showing a varying amount of drama diversified rather than unfolded by their plentiful music. Thus a five-act spoken drama might be framed and divided by six interludes, the curtain remaining open (if present, dropped rather than raised[3]). There might merely be madrigals sung and danced and instrumentally accompanied; there might be some slight or not so slight dramatic thread, with or without relation to the main drama; there might well be some allegorical pretext flattering to the ruling dynasty and often politically topical. Recitation and song, mime and dancing might alternate or combine. To support the customary light polyphony of the voices, the orchestra might be extremely colourful and various; the scenery elaborate; the costumes picturesque; the stage machinery ingenious; the aerial manoeuvrings breath-taking; the transformations of scene, the opening of heaven or hell, the monsters by sea and land and air, the simulated sieges and conflicts and conflagrations ruinously expensive and not a little hazardous. The more ambitious of the ballets shared similar professional resources, though often with much distinguished amateur participation, and commonly with general dancing at the evening's end. In addition, there were the many allegorical occasions ranging from what we might call floor-shows at formal banquets to every sort of public procession or reception. In all this decor and in all this allegory, we encounter Neoplatonic assumptions and Neoplatonic sources.

Among the many spectacles at Florence in 1565 for the wedding of Francesco de' Medici with Giovanna of Austria, there was a five-act comedy, *La Cofanaria*, by Francesco d' Ambra.[4] For this, six interludes were written by Giovanni Battista Gini, with dances and madrigals composed for three of them by Francesco Corteccia and for the other three by Alessandro Striggio the Elder, a Mantuan then in the service of Cosimo de' Medici and already famous for his publications of madrigals. The orchestra included lutes, harpsichords, viols and a variety of brass and wood-wind. The subjects were linked episodes from the beautiful fable, probably drawn from a traditional tale, of Cupid and Psyche, in the well-known version given by Apuleius in his *Golden Ass.*[5] Apuleius was a significant figure in the early history of fiction, if only for his long popularity and influence, and for his veiled but deliberately Platonic intentions. His method, which became relevant eventually to the rise of opera, is here seen at its symbolic best.

Psyche, so the story runs, was a mortal woman, but so exceedingly beautiful that men worshipped her for a second Venus, and none of them could pluck up the courage to approach her in courtship. The goddess Venus herself saw her shrines neglected and her godhead slighted. She called on her own mischievous little son Cupid to avenge her, which he did, but with unexpected consequences for all concerned. First the parents of Psyche, well aware that something untoward was threatening, decided to consult the oracle of Apollo; indeed in one version of the tale, reported by the indefatigable Boccaccio, Apollo was Psyche's real father, which would certainly account for much that was unusual in the situation. It was the terrifying command of the oracle that Psyche should be exposed on a mountaintop for a snake-dragon (and of course we remember that brutal Python which it was part of Apollo's own legend to have destroyed) to take as his bride. So the mournful bridal procession set out, to melancholy music in the Lydian mode, and with the torches of love lit, indeed, but burning smoky and low, perhaps as we see them in some funeral reliefs where Cupid himself becomes a god of death with his torch held not up but down. Then as she stood alone and in fear, a great wind from the West swept her away, not to the serpent-dragon she dreaded, but to a fairy palace where unseen hands served her, and an unseen lover visited her at night to her perfect rapture, subject only to the condition that she must never see him in the light. What the goddess Venus thus set up, two wicked elder sisters of Psyche next interrupted, by getting themselves invited to her palace in seeming admiration, but cunningly sowing the suspicion that perhaps her lover was after all a monstrous serpent who would not let himself be seen because he was so hateful to be seen. So now Psyche, courageously though shockingly, approached her lover with a lighted lamp in one hand and a sharp razor in the other. And there lay Cupid himself in all his celestial beauty. A drop of hot oil fell from the lamp and woke him. Immediately he flew away, leaving Psyche to a long and arduous series of ordeals, as she went everywhere in search of him. Her troubles brought her to the verge of suicide, before the tower from which she was about to throw herself gave her magical advice. Like

Orpheus, Psyche had to descend undaunted into the underworld. From there she was to bring back, but on no account to open, a casket containing a share of Proserpina's beauty as a present for Venus. Disobeying this prohibition (as what true woman would not?) she opened the casket to look inside, and like Pandora, let out that which she could not control. An infernal sleep fell upon her; but as in so many crises of the human spirit, it proved to be the darkest hour which comes before the dawn. Jupiter, rewarding her for her steadfast courage, reconciled her with Venus, gave her immortality, and married her to Cupid not just in the dark clandestinely but in the full light of heavenly apotheosis.

Now of course there is nothing in the least surprising about this famous little story being drawn upon for the scenes of an Italian interlude of the second half of the sixteenth century, at Florence and upon the direct highway to opera. It is touching, it is picturesque, it afforded admirable opportunities for the spectacular stage-craft which was so essential an ingredient of these fashionable and popular entertainments. Nevertheless, this is what Boccaccio[6] has to say about the heroine, post-classical as she is in this particular treatment of her story, but having behind her a folk history of unknown extent: 'Psyche then is to be interpreted as the soul (*anima*). She however is said to be daughter to Apollo, that is the sun, of him namely who is the true light [and] god of the world.' We are a long way here from any folk origins, indeed; but then so was Apuleius, who would have been more in touch with Plato's own imagery of the sun as knowledge and the dark as ignorance. That which Apollo's oracle began, brought Psyche (like Apollo's son Orpheus her putative half-brother) down into the darkest underworld, as the climax of her hard journey from the mere night-time dark (in which Cupid first came to her) right up to the celestial light (in which she was united with him as lawful partner). The Neoplatonic implication lay in that upward journey, which Pico della Mirandola described,[7] from 'desire without knowledge (*senza cognitione*)' to 'desire with knowledge (*con cognitione*)'. The modern implication might be that necessary growth of character away from the real or imaginary bliss of child-like innocence towards the adult responsibility, for better or worse, of greater consciousness and maturity. But growth is apt to feel wrong and dangerous at first; and a fairy-tale usually gets it going through some initiator in the role of villain, like the wicked sisters here who induce the heroine to break the first prohibition, so that she brings (literally and symbolically) light on the scene—and she has evidently gone far enough to break the second prohibition against opening Proserpina's casket of her own accord. For in a fairy-tale, prohibitions are surely put there in order to be disobeyed: nothing begins to happen until they are. The prohibition is the test of character.

There was something matriarchally instinctive about Venus, who had no objection to Psyche being visited by Cupid in the elemental dark, but only to her seeing him in the revealing light. There was something patriarchally approving about Jupiter, who rewarded her constancy through her trials in the darker underworld by reuniting her with Cupid in the brighter light of heaven. The Neoplatonic implication probably included an inner enlightenment and reconciliation between those masculine and feminine components of our nature which could, in some contexts, be distinguished as *animus* (spirit) and *anima* (soul).[8] The theme is that commonly known as the 'sacred marriage', and I shall return to it in connection with certain early operas which may at an underlying level be thought to hint at it.

A much more crude and popular display of Neoplatonic imagery was mounted early in the following year. This year, 1566 as we reckon the calendar, was still counted as 1565, because at this period in Florence, the new year began not on 1 January, as it does everywhere today, but on 25 March, under a system now known to us as Florentine Old Style dating. The complications resulting from this and numerous other discrepancies in the use of the calendar at different times and places can be of crucial importance to historians, including historians of early opera; and particularly in Florence do small margins of dating become of frequent importance. For a more general discussion of those problems of dating most likely to interest the readers of this present book, please turn to the Appendix on p. 307.

The entertainment early in 1565, Florentine Old Style, was an immense procession or mobile pageant, called *Mascarata della genealogia degli dei de' gentile* (Masquerade of the Genealogy of the Gods of the Pagans):[9] the very title, translated into the vernacular, of Boccaccio's *Genealogia deorum gentilium.* The idea of the pageant seems to have been to mount on wagons and horseback as much material from this learned treatise as the crowded streets would hold, blended with other material from certain more recent authors who had been starting to explore the potentialities of a wider market for Neoplatonic information and interpretation.

There was, for example, Lilio Gregorio Giraldi with his groundbreaking *De deis gentium* (Concerning the Pagan Gods, published at Basel in 1548): a much less encyclopedic and for that very reason more accessible compilation than Boccaccio's, as well as a little more up to date in scholarship (but not much). There was Vincenzo Cartari with his greatly consulted *Imagini . . . de i dei de gli antichi* (Images of the Gods of the Ancients, published at Venice in 1556): particularly convenient because many of its editions, from the second edition of Venice 1571 on, were so copiously provided with pictorial illustrations. Natale Conti's *Mythologiae sive explicationis fabularum libri decem* (Ten Books of Mythology or Explanation of Fables, published at

Venice in 1567) could not have been consulted in 1566 unless an alleged but uncertain prior edition of 1551 did actually exist. The two extant books of Egyptian *Hieroglyphica* then mis-ascribed to the fourth-century Horapollo Nialiticus bear so few signs of genuine tradition and so many of late interpolations that they may be no older than the fifteenth century; but at least they were in high renaissance favour. So too was Giovanni Pierio Valeriano's *Hieroglyphica* (published at Basel in 1556), and at a later date Pierre L'Anglois' *Discours des hiéroglyphes égyptiens, emblêmes, devises et armoiries* (Treatise of Egyptian Hieroglyphics, Emblems, Devices and Armorial Bearings, published at Paris in 1583 or 1584), and Cesare Ripa's much-used *Iconologia* (Rome, 1593), the title of which in its French redaction by Boudin, published in Paris in 1637, promises 'many images, emblems and other Hieroglyphical figures of the Virtues, the Vices, the Arts, the Sciences, the natural Causes, the different Humours, and the human Passions.' All these are allegorized in personifications designed to supplement the conventional classical and Near-Eastern deities as models 'especially for those who aspire to be, whether Orators, Poets, Sculptors, Painters, Engineers [of stage machinery], authors of Medals, of Devices, of Ballets, and of Dramatic Poems.' This remarkable compendium was still regarded as worthy of an English translation by P. Tempest, published in London in 1709; and it is part of a tradition of confused but suggestive Egyptian imagery which surfaced again, less than a century farther on, in *The Magic Flute*.[10]

The great pageant on wheels at Florence in 1566 was of little artistic significance: Neoplatonic images reduced to the level of a popular guessing-game. One contemporary observer[11] evidently regarded the game as not quite fair; for how could a masquerade 'so abounding in figures' (more than four hundred, and many of them extremely alike in their costumes and emblematic attributes) be taken in by everyone as it passed by? How much jumbled-up mythology can be packed, so to speak, into one glorified Lord Mayor's Show? But as a symptom of the prevailing artistic disposition the pageant is significant. Allegorical personification was everywhere the rage; and some of it, although not all, carried real symbolical suggestiveness.

It had long been a distinctive feature of Neoplatonism, and one which especially marked it off from pure Platonism, to draw upon a wide range of religious experiences, metaphors, ideas and images, as all illustrating from different points of view the central doctrine of a world permeated by the divine intelligence. Plato and the Platonici; Orpheus and the Orphica; Hermes and the Hermetica; Isis and Osiris, and more Near-Eastern cults with their attendant fantasies than Boccaccio himself could have envisaged: anything emblematic was allowable, and we may well ask to what condition such an unrestrained borrowing and unbridled imagination had brought the noble traditions of Neoplatonic artistry. Perhaps the answer is that it all washed over the surface, whether it meant anything underneath or not, and that the great artists of the day were not much involved in these shallow tides of fashion. Thus the more fanciful Egyptian material served for a brisk trade in coats of arms and personal or family emblems, and also for a substantial traffic in mainly quite innocuous and altogether illusory magic, rather than for the serious purposes of thought and poetry and visual art. Much magical play was made with the ancient Egyptian hieroglyphics, for example, but the first genuine transliteration of these was Champollion's[12] in 1821. To so strict a classicist and so practical a humanist as Erasmus, even Ficino or Pico della Mirandola seemed mere learned schoolmen, and closer to Aquinas than to Plato himself. And indeed it is quite true that even at its purest, Neoplatonism was not at all the same thing as simply Plato renewed. Nevertheless, Plato was the foundation, and we shall find Plato's own myths, as set out in various of his dialogues, exploited as themes for some of those very interludes at Florence which led on most directly into opera.

A UNION OF THE ARTS IN FRANCE

Meanwhile it was in France, under the dynastic alliance by which Catherine de' Medici ruled as Queen of France from 1547 to 1559, that some of the most interesting developments were occurring, both in Neoplatonic poetry, and in that mutual approach of words and music later consummated by the rise of opera. Distinguished Italian men of letters became established at the French court. The great Tasso himself paid a short visit to Paris in 1571. There were Italian actors, of whom one famous troupe, settled in Paris, the *Comici Gelosi*, had worked with Tasso in Italy; their extensive repertory required a great deal of music, and included Italian interludes of music and dancing. There were dancing masters from Milan teaching Italian steps and figures, as well as loosely dramatized *balletti* in the Italian manner. There was an entire band of Piedmontese violinists. There were Italian virtuosos of the viols, the lutes, the cornettos, the shawms and the sackbuts, judged by many to be as superior to the French instrumentalists as, at this date, the French and Belgian singers were still judged by many to be superior to the Italian. The Italian lutanists, in particular, among whom Alberto da Ripa was an early and very distinguished arrival, had a favourable influence on the solo performance of vocal music with instrumental accompaniment; and also on those idiomatically instrumental figurations which the French lutanists of the seventeenth century took up to such good effect, passing them down to the French harpsichordists in their turn. More important from our present point of view, an idiom now known as the Parisian Chanson was under particularly direct Italian influence, and has been valuably studied against its general background by Lawrence Bernstein.[13]

As early as 1548, the Italian archbishop at Lyons, Cardinal Ippolito d'Este, mounted there, in honour of a visit by the French royal family, a full Italian-style performance of Cardinal Bibbiena's humanist play, *Calandra*, complete with music, dances, scenery and interludes in the prevailing Italian manner. The impression made was very strong; but French poets were already familiar with the antique deities of Olympus and the Infernal Regions, the nymphs and shepherds of pastoral Arcadia, the satyrs and the centaurs, the nereids and the nyads, the sirens and the tritons, the enchanters and the enchantresses of the abounding classical revival. That particularly distinguished poet and teacher, Jean Dorat (Daurat, Auratus) was already training up his young disciples in the principles of Neoplatonic symbolism and the aspiring emulation of classical techniques.[14] Five of these (Pierre Ronsard, subsequently shown to be the greatest; Jean-Antoine de Baïf, later invaluable as organizer-in-chief; Pontus de Tyard, especially capable as a theorist; Joachim du Bellay; and Remy Belleau) deliberately recruited a sixth, Etienne de Jodelle, in order to complete, with their acknowledged master, Dorat, the mystical number of seven luminaries of the poetic art (the list is not always named quite consistently, however). Following seven previous poets under Charlemagne, and before that seven Alexandrian poets of the third century B.C., they called themselves the *Pléiade* (Pleiad) after the seven stars, seven sisters in Greek mythology, of the constellation Pleiades. Together with some other poets, artists and musicians, the Pleiad addressed themselves systematically to the problem uppermost in the humanist discussions of art throughout the sixteenth century: the recovery of that intimate union of all the arts to which was attributed their celebrated mastery in classical times over strong and specific emotions.

It was more particularly the ambition of this school, first to reform French poetry under the system of classical Greek and Roman prosody; and then, on the basis of that reform, to renew the classical relationship (or what was assumed to be the classical relationship) of poetry and music. Already by 1560 Ronsard published in Paris his *Abrégé de l'art poétique français* (Summary of the French Poetic Art).[15] In a still more determined and explicit attempt to press French poetry into a classical mould, Jacques de la Taille wrote in 1562 (though it was not printed until 1573) his *Manière de faire des vers en français comme en grec et en latin* (Manner of making Poetry in French as in Greek and in Latin).

The procedure envisaged was to make French poetry scan by quantity (that is to say, by the varied duration of the syllables) instead of by stress (that is to say, by the varied accentuation of the syllables, as of course it actually does). The result of this arbitrary contrivance was called *vers mesuré à l'antique* (verse measured, i.e. scanned, on the ancient method). That in turn was then subjected to a further arbitrary contrivance, by which a long syllable was set in music to a long note, and a short syllable to a short note usually of half the duration. The result, a grotesque curtailment of the vast rhythmic resources which music possesses, was called *musique mesurée à l'antique* (music measured, i.e. rhythmically spaced, on the ancient method). For in classical prosody, only two durations are structurally recognized: long and short. In modern prosody, only two accentuations are structurally recognized: stressed and unstressed. But in all poetry, it is the subtle variations of the structural metre which give the real vitality—including the unpredictable clashes between the postulated structural rhythms and the actual verbal rhythms which the poet irregularly superimposes. The strict application of classical prosody and its supposedly classical setting in music was an enterprise gravely misconceived, and not much continued; the free application had some wider influence, which can be traced perceptibly through a succession of chansons and court airs (*airs de cour*), particularly in court ballets (*ballets de cour*), right down to the symmetrical but noble operatic choruses of Lully.

A solo texture is not employed in this form of measured music; but there is a homophonic texture which preserves a similar uniformity of rhythm. We know from Mersenne's admiration of it in his rambling but encyclopedic *Harmonie universelle*, published at Paris, 1636, that some strict use of the method remained into the seventeenth century. But Mersenne, though conceding that composers could very easily 'reduce their Airs to the Rhythm of the Greeks', argued from experience that 'they do not adapt themselves well to this art', and that 'French Music requires a complete liberty, without tying itself to any sort of regimented Poetry.'[16] Thus while there is indeed a certain austere beauty, for example, in the *chansons mesurées à l'antique* of Claude Le Jeune, much the most fruitful effect of such 'measured' models was the encouragement of a certain spacious dignity in more flexible ensembles and choruses of predominantly though not exclusively chordal construction.[17]

Just as in poetry, stressed and unstressed syllables were deemed to be the equivalents of longs and shorts, and just as in music, notes of two durations were deemed to be the equivalents of longs and shorts, so also in dancing one long step (double) was deemed to be the equivalent of a poetic long, and one short step (single) was deemed to be the equivalent of a poetic short. Thus even dancing could be made to scan, as Mersenne[18] described with approval under the style of *ballet mesuré*. How far this allegedly classical measuring of the steps of the dance was taken in practice remains extremely questionable; we only know that such Neoplatonic conceptions as the cosmic motions of the spheres and their harmonious relationships were regarded as patterns which dancing by its steps and figures could represent on the human scale. Thus Sir Thomas Elyot's influential treatise of courtly manners, *The Boke named the Governour*, which was published at London in 1531 and ran to many subsequent editions, described dancing as:

> of an excellent utilitie, comprehendinge in it wonderfull figures, or, as the grekes do call them, *Ideae*, of vertues and noble qualities, and especially of the commodiouse vertue called prudence, whom Tulli defineth to be the knowledge of thinges which ought to be desired and followed, and also of them which ought to be fledde from or exchewed.[19]

The reference to Plato's Ideal Forms is direct here.

For the detailed technique of court dancing in the late renaissance, one of our chief sources is Fabritio Caroso, whose *Nobiltà di Dame* (published at Venice in 1600) is essentially a reworking of his *Il Ballarino* (published, also at Venice, in 1581); he is enthusiastic but vague about relating classically measured dance with classically measured verse and music. We get no more practical assistance from Sir John Davies' versified treatise of dancing, *Orchestra or a Poeme of Dauncing Judicially proving the true observation of time and measure, in the Authenticall and laudable use of Dauncing*, published at London in 1596, since what he seems mainly intent upon 'proving' is that all the harmonious processes of nature share in the character of a well-proportioned dance, and that to dance harmoniously is to encourage moral virtue and inner harmony. Mersenne in his *Harmonie universelle* further lived up to his ambitious title by suggesting that not only poetry, music, dancing and theatre but all the arts and sciences move within the orbit of harmonious measure as properly (which is to say classically) understood. And by that time, the English masques of Ben Jonson were uniting at least the first four of these in a particularly sophisticated compound for those capable of a proper (which is to say a Neoplatonic) understanding.[20]

Painting has rhythms of its own, but they can hardly be made to scan, and offer less scope than poetry, music or dancing for relating to a common measure. Yet painters could be asked to illustrate the images of a poem, allotted to corresponding positions on the canvas. For example, Tyard actually included instructions for the painted decorations (not extant) at the Château d'Anet in his *Douze Fables des Fleuves ou Fontaines, avec la description pour la peinture* (Twelve Fables for the Streams or Fountains, with the description for painting) published under that title by Etienne Tabouret in 1586; and we have already noticed the more celebrated example of Botticelli being instructed in Neoplatonic symbolism by Poliziano, and painting detailed images from his poetry.

Thus by the middle years of the sixteenth century, the classical union of the arts was not only a much-discussed proposal but to some extent a practicable proposition. In France, there was a substantial group of artists associated with the Pleiad and dedicated to working out the implications of that union. Their groupings and re-groupings remain hard to disentangle, and for a time they were merely known informally as Ronsard's *académie*, or as Baïf's *académie* when his house became the usual meeting-place. But by 1567, a short-lived but influential Académie de Poésie et de Musique had formally come together under the combined leadership of Baïf (probably the most committed of the Pleiad to the strict equation of longs and shorts with stressed and unstressed syllables, notes of double and single length in setting them to music, and doubles and singles in dancing) and of the not very distinguished but evidently amenable composer, Thibault de Courville.

The middle party was best represented by Ronsard himself. Ronsard's interest in reuniting the arts was shown by his insistent desire to have his poetry sung rather than read; he deliberately suited his line-lengths, his metrical patterns and his rhyme-schemes for setting to music. In these poems, however, his prosody is not classical: there is no forced scansion by longs and shorts; and (contrary to classical precedent) rhymes are used. The poems of this free method, as well as of the strict method, might at the time simply be called *vers mesurés*; or they might be distinguished as *vers mesurés à la lyre* instead of *à l'antique*—recalling Ronsard's own stated intention of 'sweetly marrying the lyre to the voice'.[21] Composers so excellent as Orlando di Lasso and Goudimel responded to this more freely classical kind of humanist poetry with admirable settings. Jacques Mauduit was perhaps especially close to Baïf. Eustache du Caurroy, Adrian le Roy and Claude Le Jeune also became associated with the work and aims of the Académie, as thus defined in its Statutes upon its official inauguration in 1570:

> In order to bring back Music into use according to its perfection, which is to present speech (*parole*) in song (*chant*) completed with its harmony and melody, which consist in the choice, [and] order (*règle*) of the voices, sounds and chords well suited to make their effect according as the sense of the words (*de la lettre*) requires, either constricting (*resserant*) or relaxing (*desserant*), or enlarging the spirit, and thus renewing the ancient manner of composing Verse measured to fit song equally measured according to the ancient Metric Art.

One gets the point. Measured. And measured according to an

ancient manner, on the ancient principle (stated earlier in the Statutes) that 'where Music is disordered, there frequently morals are depraved, and where it is well ordered, there men are well mannered.' The Académie and its exalted patron, Charles IX of France, took most seriously the prospect of renewing tranquillity in that troubled kingdom by the benign power of art restored to its classical efficacy, and joined with science, philosophy and religion in a harmonious hierarchy of which poetry and music were put very near the top. But to be thus artistically powerful and morally beneficial, poetry and music must, it was everywhere agreed, be again united in all their ancient fidelity to one another, and to their common purpose of arousing and guiding strong and specific emotion in the hearts of men.

CIRCE: A FRENCH COURT BALLET

Though the first French Academy soon succumbed to the renewed civil wars towards the close of the sixteenth century, its members (including its leader Baïf until his death in 1589) kept their favour at court. A sequel called the Académie du Palais also failed to survive, though after several vicissitudes it led on to the great Académie Française itself. The chief memorial, however, of Baïf's circle was a famous entertainment which, while not officially in their charge, was a substantial embodiment of their principles. This was *Circe*, the *Balet comique de la royne* (The Dramatic—not the comic—Ballet of the Queen), a spectacular affair which, without being an opera or leading directly into opera, was in certain aspects a particularly interesting precursor of opera. The inspiration of *Circe* recalls the Pleiad at every point. The organization and (as we are given to suppose) the initiative are to the credit of that somewhat vainglorious Italian immigrant — violinist, impresario and courtier — Baldassare de Belgiojoso, otherwise known as Baltazarini, or by the French name he adopted in course of his twenty-five years at court prior to *Circe*, Balthasar de Beaujoyeulx.[22] The performance was at Paris on 15 October 1581; there is a printed souvenir version, which was edited by Beaujoyeulx, and published at Paris in 1582.[23] (See Plate I.)

The interest of *Circe* lies in its union of poetry and music, spectacle and dancing for just such a classical allegory as the French Neoplatonists desired and the Academy of Poetry and Music existed to encourage. The scenario is mythological; the setting is pastoral; the cast is the usual legendary complement of classical Greek divinities, sirens, tritons, dryads, satyrs, nymphs, shepherds, and the sinister enchantress Circe herself, who nevertheless cherishes no very sustained power of malice, and submits with a good grace to the eventual reconciliation. There were, as was usual in the *ballet de cour*, successive 'entries' by actors some of whom combined dancing with reciting and singing. They included both amateur and professional performers, though the orchestra itself was professional. Forty musicians in all are stated (at the descent of Jupiter) to have joined forces. The entertainment began at ten in the evening, and with the customary general dancing in conclusion, went on until half past three in the morning.

The drama itself is slight, but continuous. There is a potential clash of opposites not very imaginatively acted out, though the reconciliation with which it ends has a certain archetypal suggestiveness. Unfortunately the music is almost entirely devoid of dramatic quality. There are a few solo songs, but they are ornamental rather than eloquent. There is one duet, and some vocal ensembles in homophonic part-writing which have a stiffness imparted though not strictly controlled by the principles of *musique mesurée*. There are instrumental ensembles in five unambitious parts. Though the score as notated is typically sketchy, we are given imprecise but interesting indications for a fairly large and very colourful orchestra including 'oboes, cornets, sackbuts and other sweet instruments of music' (f7v); 'lyras, lutes, harps, flutes and other instruments' (f17r); 'ten violins, five on one side, and as many on the other' (f36r etc.); 'eight Satyrs, seven of whom play flutes, and one sings alone' (f32r); 'voices and instruments' (f36r etc.); Pan playing 'his flageolet' (panpipes), and 'a sweet, pleasant and harmonious music of organs, in the grotto' (f39r); 'singing with new instruments, and different from the preceding' (f49r); and for the grand ballet at the end, 'the violins' (either the entire bowed strings or, rather more probably, the entire orchestra) 'change the sound' (f55v). The printed version is notable for its full and fascinating, not to say glowing descriptions of the scenario, the décor, the spectacle and the machinery, all of which obviously attracted considerably more attention than the music, as was very usual on such occasions. The poetry, by La Chesnaye, is a competent rather than inspired example of its French humanist school. The music, by various undistinguished musicians of the king's chamber under de Beaulieu and Salmon, cannot really be scanned by quantity, and is not particularly well accented on any scansion.

If that were the best that humanism could do for the union of music and poetry, we should not be very much impressed. In fact, our main interest in *Circe* concerns the scenario. Each of the numerous mythological characters painstakingly explains his own traditional attributes and functions, while insisting with gross flattery that these functions are now taken over still more beneficently by the King, the Queen and the Queen Mother. Circe, that same legendary enchantress whose dealings with Ulysses (Odysseus) and his companions were so familiar from Homer's *Odyssey*, has ensnared some French prisoners, one of whom escapes, and throws himself for assistance upon the King as he sits there conspicuously in the audience. Greatly to her chagrin, Circe has to let her prisoner get away for now; and as she departs frustrated, the whole scene comes to life with an entry and ballet. She returns, and immobilizes dancers and musicians with her magic wand. It is good theatre, but not in any other sense good drama, since none of these happenings has been dramatically prepared. Now Mercury (Hermes) descends in a cloud: a familiar renaissance stage-effect for which the machinery was well understood. It is Mercury's idea to renew his old Homeric triumph in immunizing Ulysses against Circe by the legendary herb Moly; and as he reanimates the dancers and the musicians, the scene once more comes vividly to life in sound and movement. He boasts of his mythological capabilities; but he boasts too soon. Circe, more angry than ever, comes back to immobilize the scene again, and at the same time to explain even more philosophically her own power and function in the mythological sphere of operations. She makes an interesting comparison with the golden age when nature controlled men by their instincts like the animals, until Jupiter planted at one and the same time understanding and care in their hearts, so that change became the law of life, spurred on by desire. And 'I alone', she tells us, 'am cause of all this change', under the ceaseless movement and revolution of her father, the Sun. She has no fear of Mercury, who is merely clever and vainglorious without the support (which he had in Homer) of Minerva (Athene). It is Minerva whose wisdom is genuinely potent, and whom alone Circe fears. The Goddess of Reason is a more formidable antagonist for a sensuous enchantress than mere tricky Mercury.

Now Circe uses her wand on Mercury, still hovering in his cloud, which at once floats him helplessly to the ground. She leads him to her garden, suddenly revealed, with all the animals into which the men have been changed who were her previous victims. Another stirring entry comes on, of seven Satyrs with flutes, and one singing (but in the score, words are given to all five parts of their music); they encounter four Dryads, costumed as a living wood (so that something immobile in nature here takes on movement); and all approach the King, to whom the leading Dryad offers further philosophical instruction about the gullibility of mankind in face of false images of good such as Circe represents. The Dryad next finds Pan in his thicket; and after being welcomed by his piping, she tells him that as a power of nature he should be rescuing the victims of nature's seductiveness from their slavery to Circe. As he responds with the greatest good will but not the least apparent effect, the third entry brings on four Virtues, who explain themselves as familiar nurturers of the King, and invoke Minerva to appear as the King's appropriate companion.

Minerva does appear, on a large chariot pulled by a serpent or dragon, and bearing her traditional shield with the head of Medusa upon it (with which Minerva, too, can immobilize her enemies by turning them to stone). Her explanation of herself becomes something of a Neoplatonic sermon when, having described her miraculous birth from the head of Jupiter (Zeus) and his gift to her of Reason, she claims superiority over Mercury, to whom Jupiter merely gave the Senses, yet lighter and more changeable than Mercury's natural element, the air; and the senses, she tells us, lead the will through desire and imagination now to true virtue, now to vain pleasure. Yet those drowned in pleasure do not die of it, for the soul cannot die: they merely undergo the living death of staying imprisoned in sin, without understanding; and it is such as these that Circe seduces to her palace and there holds prisoner. But now Minerva obeys the summons of the King of France to combat Circe, who alone in all the world, so they optimistically claim, remains to be combated.

On that piece of wishful thinking, Minerva in her turn invokes her father Jupiter, who, having descended in great splendour both scenic and musical, contents himself with a brief but equally Neoplatonic homily on the immortality of the soul and its transformability (like Circe's victims) into various shapes until, released from the body, it is with his help translated to a better existence. He flatteringly equates Minerva with the King's sister (Mademoiselle de Voudement, whose marriage to the Duc de Joyeuse is being honoured by these entertainments), and joins the rescue party, as Minerva chides Pan with allowing his father, Mercury, to languish under shameful enchantment. Circe, undaunted, announces that she will admit subservience, as they all should do, but only to the King of France. In the fierce contest then mimed and danced, Circe is gradually overcome by Minerva, and led captive in her turn before the King, to whom Minerva hands over both Circe and Circe's magic wand, so that every prisoner is freed. The action is over; but two further impressive entries follow, the second of which is for the customary Grand Ballet, here comprised of forty individual figures of geometrical design. General dancing follows.

But that, interesting as it is, does not quite conclude the printed description; for there follows a substantial appendix entitled: 'Allegory of Circe which Natalis Comes has taken from the interpretations of the Greek poets.' This name is the Latin form of Natale Conti, whose *Mythology*[24] of 1567 we have already noticed among the small outcrop of popular Neoplatonic treatises around the middle of the sixteenth century—successors to the voluminous *Genealogy* of Boccaccio. We know, therefore, what was the source of the scenario; and this knowledge is confirmed by some verbal correspondences. The sources for Boccaccio and his successors themselves were extremely various: some of them classical authors, among whom Homer, Hesiod and Ovid were chiefly prominent; some of them post-classical; and all of them expanded with many glosses from the intervening centuries. The primary source in this case was certainly Homer; but Homer would doubtless have been astonished at what his latest interpreters had read into him. As usual with renaissance works in the humanist tradition, we have to allow for that typical approach instanced by Boccaccio's instruction 'to conceal the truth in a fabled and seemly veil (*velamento fabuloso atque decenti veritatem contegere*)',[25] which Ronsard recalled when he described having learned from Dorat 'how one must dissemble and conceal fables seemingly, and disguise well the truth of things with a fabulous cloak in which they are enclosed.'[26] The veil or cloak was indeed a splendid entertainment which all present enjoyed far into the night. The truth has to be discovered on several underlying levels, visible only to some of those present, and to them doubtless in varying degrees.

One quite important level at the time, which a number of those present saw well enough because they were expecting it, was the political level. It was no secret that one purpose of this very showy and expensive evening's entertainment was to convey the impression (all the more emphatically since it was not in accordance with the facts) that a prosperous and beneficent and perfectly stable monarchy was giving freely of its bounty to a contented court and populace; that all outstanding enemies other than the purely mythological Circe had already been satisfactorily defeated; and that when she, too, yielded, general reconciliation must needs be achieved. For we have seen it clearly stated in Baïf's Statutes that the union of the arts was expected to contribute to the unity of the nation by sheer force of example. There was, indeed an entire tradition of such politically oriented court ballets, certain of which in the late sixteenth century presented Henry IV in the image of Apollo, god of the sun, with his rays but temporarily clouded by civil dissension, and besought him to scatter the clouds and restore the peace of the realm with his sunshine triumphant. It was this very real aspiration which helped Mazarin in the seventeenth century to turn men's utter weariness with civil war into tolerance for absolute monarchy, with Louis XIV, *le Roi Soleil*, the sun-king, at last firmly entrenched in power as well as in flattery. But the flattery worked all the better for having its roots in Neoplatonic symbolism.

The political ballet of 2 August 1592 goes the symbolic limit, which makes an interesting comparison.[27] We read in the poetry these extraordinary words: 'Let us sing of the divine union which can make a hermaphrodite (*Androgine*) of this hero and you.' The reference is apparently to Plato's *Symposium*, where there occurs an elaborate parable of a primordial hermaphrodite (androgyne or man-woman) who symbolizes the totality of our masculine and feminine components, represented as now painfully severed but still in perpetual search for one another. This like other hermaphrodites in Hellenic art can be taken on one level as a reflection of Greek bisexuality (homosexual as well as heterosexual), but on another level as a reference to the 'sacred marriage', the ritual (or divine or royal) union already mentioned as an ubiquitous symbol for inner reconciliation and a common element in mysteries and initiations aimed toward psychological integration or individuation: in short, a token for wholeness, as which it featured repeatedly in Neoplatonic and more particularly in Hermetic literature.[28] But any poet who could in all seriousness recommend a politically expedient marriage under quite so recondite an image was a philosophical poet indeed, and one in no way afraid to plumb the psychological depths under the occasion even of so purely social and topical an assignment.

The political level is now of more historical than artistic interest to us; but we might hint at it in performance, for example by fleurs-de-lis in the décor and costumes. More important, of course, are the mythological attributes. We can look them up, as the organizers of *Circe* did, in Conti's descriptions, or we can copy them, as the organizers of some Florentine interludes seem to have done, from the pictures in Cartari's second edition of 1571 and onwards. The visual symbolism in any such staged performance must be got right, or it will not work. The costumes and the décor are part of the symbolic image. A further part, which must also be got right, consists of the steps and the figures of the court dances prominent in *Circe* and similar entertainments. We are told of the forty figures which made up the concluding grand ballet of *Circe* that they were of geometrical design, thus demonstrating on the actual floor of the hall that harmonious symmetry and orderly motion Neoplatonically attributed to the heavenly bodies, and hopefully to be induced within both the state and the individual: an earthly harmoniousness corresponding with the heavenly music of the spheres. That would indeed be a high tribute to the power of the arts united; but many writings of the period testify to the naïve earnestness with which it was anticipated.

CONTI'S CONTEMPORARY EXPLANATION

There is in the appendix to *Circe* a very condensed summary of Conti's own narrative and explanation. It is quite complicated, but valuable because it gives us a rare description by an actual contemporary— indeed, by the actual author from whom the scenario was taken—of the allegorical intentions and some of the symbolical implications of an entertainment which lay parallel to those leading on, in Italy, to the earliest operas. We are told by Conti to interpret Circe herself as a sort of mingling of elements, being as she is 'a daughter of the sun, which is heat, and a daughter of the sea, which is moisture'. This combination arises through the movement of her father the sun, in his 'masculine' capacity as form, and of her mother the sea's daughter, in her 'feminine' capacity as matter. And when Circe 'changed men into monstrous and varied shapes', obviously (well, obviously) that was because 'the corruption of one thing becomes the generation of another thing formed out of it, but not in the first shape'; whereas Ulysses was not changed at all, because 'the human soul is immortal and divine, the body corruptible and earthly.' So compressed an account of orthodox Neoplatonic thought could only have enlightened a reader already familiar with it; but Conti himself, in his own book, is very much more expansive on the subject, and extremely revealing.

Next follows 'another allegory, by the Sieur de la Chesnaye', who was the poet employed as author of *Circe*, and as such entitled to have his opinion weighed. His words confirm that he was intimately aware of Conti, and that he drew at least in part on Conti's material, as the speeches of the characters in his text themselves suggest. But in order to be more specific than the summary of Conti just given, he adds a level of interpretation not drawn from Conti. This offers a curious anticipation of the scientific materialism of the ensuing age, by interpreting Circe and Ulysses as what would later have been called a seasonal or vegetation myth. Circe stands for 'the revolution of the year, following the revolution of the sun'; the four nymphs are four forms of vegetation; Ulysses on his wanderings is 'time, which never stops'; his companions are 'the past and the present'; his four children by Circe are 'the four seasons'; and his eventual death by a fish-bone arrow-head shows the sun passing through Sagittarius to end the year at the sign of the zodiac 'half fish and half ram'. This last seems somewhat idiosyncratic astrology; but it leads on smoothly enough into a 'moral allegory' on the same Neoplatonic lines as Conti, with Circe as 'man's nature' (because 'desire and lust come to animals through heat and moisture') and with Ulysses as 'that part of the soul capable of reason'. Not, we may feel, a very satisfactory specimen of Neoplatonic rationalization, though the species is recognizable.

Finally, there is printed 'another allegory of Circe, according to the view of Sieur Gordon, a Scotsman, chamberlain to the King'. It proves to be not so much another view as another gloss upon Conti, whom it mainly follows, and to some extent translates in almost exactly corresponding words. It makes much better use of Conti, however; and, moreover, when Sieur Gordon departs from Conti, as he sometimes does, his departures are themselves suggestive. We read in Conti[29] that 'Circe was the daughter of the sun and of Perseis daughter of the ocean. . .because from moisture and the heat of the sun all things are born (*quia ex humore et calore solis omnia nascuntur*).' Sieur Gordon[30] has 'daughter of the sun and of Perseis daughter of the ocean' because 'truly from the mixture of the Sun which is the cause of all heat, and of the sea which is the source of all moisture, all things are generated.' (This genealogy, although not of course its Neoplatonic interpretation, is correctly drawn from Book X of Homer's *Odyssey*.) Conti continues: 'because in generation (*generatione*) it is necessary that what are called elements are mixed (*misceantur*), which cannot happen except by the movement of the sun (*per motum solis*)' and of 'the moisture of the ocean (*oceani humor*), which stands in place either of matter or of femininity (*vel materiae vel foeminae*): the sun [is on the contrary] formative or masculine (*artifex aut mas*), because it is the author of form in the generation of natural things: wherefore generation and that mingling which occurs in the generation of natural bodies was rightly called Circe, and daughter of the sun and of the daughter of the ocean.' So far, so plausible, on a more or less ostensibly physiological dimension.

But Conti then states explicitly the Neoplatonic assumption that beneath the outer appearance of every such physical reality, we have to understand an inner substance of psychological reality. He writes: 'so gifted were the ancient authors of the fables which are celebrated by poets, that not only physical things were encompassed beneath them by some, but also the most useful precepts concerning universal human life. And various were the causes by which the ancients were impelled to the feigning of fables: first because many things will be understood in few words',[31] and again because fables are easily remembered, pleasantly assimilated, morally valuable, and capable of revealing secrets of divine nature, all of which are preserved and transmitted to posterity 'under fabled barks (*sub fabulosis corticibus*)' more securely than if handed down by open philosophy, which an unworthy recipient will all too readily corrupt.

Conti now tells us all over again that 'Circe is said to have been the daughter of the sun, and of Perseis daughter of Ocean, because desire (*libido*) occurs in animals from moisture and heat'; and 'if this dominates us, it imprints the vices of beasts in our souls, and acts together with the aspect of the stars, and conspires with them, of which some draw us to Venus and to copulations, others to anger, cruelty and every depravity, whence if anyone submits to these passions (*cupiditatibus*), he is fabled as changed by Circe into some animal form by means of sorcery' according as his stars ordain, and unless divine mercy intervenes.

Sieur Gordon adds to this that 'the sea naturally nourishes and produces that which maintains and excites sensuality: and from that the poets have feigned that Venus rose from the sea.' Venus and Circe were frequently equated by Neoplatonists, both in positive aspect as desire for virtue, and in negative aspect as desire for sensuality (or rather, as entanglement with inordinate sensuality, since in Platonic doctrine, sensuality itself is in no way vicious, but is merely a stage of development on the journey from earthly to heavenly preoccupations, with which, though it is not in itself harmful, one should not get caught up indefinitely). Furthermore, the sun, properly understood, is not only 'the cause of all heat' but also 'signifies allegorically the clarity and light of the truth and the divine gleam which glitters in our souls.'

Conti[32] sums it up that 'the wise man ought in whatever fortune to rule himself moderately, and to stand unconquered against all difficulties, while the remaining multitude are carried here and there by the current like the lightest of vessels, and are impelled by any vicissitude of the winds: wherefore the companions of Ulysses were changed into beasts, while he himself remained unconquered through his wisdom, which is truly the gift of God. I would believe Ulysses to be the part of reason participant in our soul (*animae*): Circe to be nature: the companions of Ulysses to be faculties of the spirit (*animi*) when in collusion with the dispositions of the body (*corporis*), and not subject to reason.' But here is Sieur Gordon, going right on from there with what appears to be an intuitive recognition of that ambivalence within the psyche which both Freud and Jung later systematized in the concept of 'libido' (the same word as in Conti's account): 'from these considerations it seems that it will not pass the bounds of reason to take Circe for the desire in general which rules and dominates over all that has life and is mixed from the divine and the sensible, and makes very different effects, and leads some to virtue, others to vice.' And in this Sieur Gordon also stands close to Aristotle[33] with his famous doctrine of emotion as itself neutral in a moral sense, but always powerful whether for good or bad, virtue or vice.

So directly shall we find the earliest operas inheriting the Neoplatonic vision of which *Circe* is thus demonstrably an instance that we must be a little careful not to dismiss its surface images as mere antiquated superstition. The spheres and the stars, with their fateful influence upon the souls of men; the souls of the stars themselves, and the soul of the world; the intellect and the body of man; the angels above him and the beasts below; the plants lower again and inanimate matter at the bottom; God at the top infusing all and in a manner embracing all—none of this would have been taken literally as scientific astronomy or cosmology by any informed Neoplatonist of the late renaissance. But as a kind of intuitively expressed psychology, it was taken seriously. The symbolism in *Circe* is rather crudely handled and naïvely expounded; but it has points of interest. The idea of Circe as an image for that primal energy of life which can take any direction good or bad is certainly an instance of the sort of truth which Neoplatonists like Conti, Ronsard, Chiabrera or Rinuccini expected to introduce half revealed in the very act of half concealing it beneath the fabled veil.

BARDI'S FLORENTINE INTERLUDES

We may return to Italy through an example of the customary international movement of scholars and scholarship during the period of humanist literature: the distinguished French Latinist Marc-Antoine Muret (Muretus, 1526–85) who made such powerful friends and enemies with his fashionable lectures at Paris that he found himself thrown into prison and fetched out again in rapid succession, after which he wandered somewhat restlessly around Italy until Cardinal Ippolito d'Este settled him at Rome in 1559. He visited France in 1561, but was back at Rome in 1563, where he was persuaded by Pope Gregory XIII to remain (in spite of a tempting invitation to Cracow from the King of Poland in 1578), and where he died in 1585.

An international traveller indeed. And like so many artistically inclined humanists of his day, Muret was keenly interested in poetry and music as sister arts needing to be brought back into more intimate relationship with one another. Muret in France was closely associated with the Pleiad; he even set some of Ronsard's classicizing poetry to music. Muret in Rome became an immediate model for a considerably younger and eventually more important poet: Gabriello Chiabrera (1552–1638), who was born at Savona, near Genoa, but educated at a Jesuit college in Rome. Chiabrera also incurred enmities early in his literary career, and had to leave Rome. He spent some time in his native Savona; he spent some time in Florence; he had Mantuan connections, which brought him into contact with Monteverdi. In Florence, Chiabrera became the friend and associate of his somewhat younger contemporary, Ottavio Rinuccini (1562–1621). Both poets were in due course pioneer librettists for several of the earliest operas. Chiabrera passed on to Rinuccini the influence of Ronsard, whom he himself greatly admired and imitated; the influence of Tasso and Guarini on Rinuccini brought to bear the great tradition of pastoral drama, behind which stood Poliziano; Tasso himself paid his visit to Paris, already mentioned, in 1571; and from this rich blend of poetic influences, we shall presently find Rinuccini producing the earliest of all opera librettos, and thereby contributing more to the origins of opera than had been realized until Barbara Russano Hanning, in a notable Ph.D. thesis,[34] gave him fuller credit.

And so we are back in Florence, where lay the direct road into opera, although a few more years of preparation were still to come. In February of 1585, Florentine Old Style Dating (that is to say in 1586 as we reckon the calendar), as part of the celebrations at Florence for the dynastic marriage of Cesare d'Este and Virginia de' Medici, there was performed very lavishly the comedy, *L'amico fido* (The Faithful Friend), by Giovanni de' Bardi, Count of Vernio. The interludes, under Bardi's personal direction, were by several poets, one of them being Rinuccini; they represented disconnected scenes of the usual mythological order, with various divine or legendary figures finding one pretext or another to flatter eloquently (rather than dramatically) the noble couple. A most interesting study by Cesare Molinare has confirmed the direct connection in this instance with Neoplatonic material.[35] The music for the first, the second and the third interludes was by Alessandro Striggio the Elder; for the third and fourth, by Cristofano Malvezzi; for the sixth by Bardi himself, with an elaborate Ballata sung and danced by shepherds and shepherdesses in fancy Tuscan costume to the accompaniment of a sizeable orchestra which included cornettos, flutes, recorders, viols, rebecs, dolcians, shawms, lutes and harps.

So brilliant and so popular was the success of this spectacular affair, replete as it was with stage machinery and showy décor, that Bardi was again put in charge as 'inventor' of a yet more ambitious undertaking in 1589, for the wedding of Ferdinando de' Medici and Christiana di Loreno (Christine de Lorraine). Of the three plays then given, Girolamo Bargagli's comedy, *La Pelegrina*, concerns us here.[36] Rinuccini was again commissioned: at first, to supply the poetry for all six interludes; but there were intrigues at court. Seemingly at the direct intervention of the recently elevated Duke Ferdinando, this Duke's newly appointed supervisor of the arts, Cavalieri, set to music some substituted verses by Laura Guidiccioni, used for at least some performances (two were with *La Pelegrina*, two with the other two comedies). Bernardo Buontalenti, who was by now a very celebrated architect and engineer, and who had taken a share in the scenery, costumes and stage machinery of 1586, was given full responsibility for the production in 1589. Cavalieri was, however, designated 'organizer' of the spectacle, and the extent of his actual interferences is not now known. The music, much of which is extant, was by Malvezzi, Marenzio, Caccini, Peri and Cavalieri; Bardi himself had some small part in the poetry, and rather more in the music. Quite a combination of the talents, perhaps not altogether voluntary, but at least entirely customary on these great occasions of so much expenditure, so much prestige, and so much rivalry and intrigue.[37]

The first interlude was an ambitious staging of the upper cosmos and its chief inhabitants, carefully based on the famous Myth of Er given by Plato in Book X of the *Republic*,[38] with Neoplatonic amplifications. After an introduction by a personification of the Doric Mode, the goddess Necessity was revealed on a high cloud, holding between her knees that enormous spindle whose turning is the symbolic centre of the cosmos. The three Fates (*Parcae* or *Moirae*) clustered around her; and splayed out on clouds at the sides came Plato's eight sirens of the spheres, with two others, whose harmony was supposed to combine into the music of the spheres. Still lower came the seven Planets, with Astraea, that goddess of Justice whom Ovid[39] relates to have lived on earth during the Golden Age, but to have retired to heaven in outraged disapproval thereafter. Twelve heroes and heroines poised up at the back, standing for six virtues, were a more mixed collection, as for example the Roman Numa Pompilius and the Egyptian Isis jointly representing Justice (in addition to Astraea).

Buontalenti's original sketch for this scene is preserved,[40] as well as an engraving (clearer, if a little less suggestive) by Agostino Caracci. (See Plate II.) With the starry heavens behind, and the celestial beings (not all are shown) disposed before, the scene lacks nothing for imagination, although the contemporary descriptions show that by no means everybody gave to all of the allegory that erudite recognition for which Bardi worked so conscientiously. But this would not have unduly distressed him, for the spectacle was greatly admired, and it was always the Neoplatonic expectation that the many would see only the glittering surface, whereas the few could profitably look deeper in.

The spindle held traditionally by the goddess Necessity has an inherent phallic suggestiveness, perhaps reflecting some primitive fantasy of matriarchal domination. The immediate model may be a picture in Cartari[41] which so resembles Buontalenti's that he seems likely to have copied it. (See Plates IV and V.) For while we can usually identify the classical references for the décor, the costumes and the stage properties in these Neoplatonic spectacles, and while the more sophisticated members of their contemporary audiences could identify them at least in part, it does not follow that the designers took them from their sources at first hand, nor the audiences either. Erudition was made easy by just such popular textbooks of mythology as Giraldi's, Cartari's, Conti's and the rest; and we have seen that of all these, Cartari's (in most editions, though not in its first edition of Venice, 1556) had the advantage of the most numerous and resourceful pictures.[42]

The many who enjoyed the spectacle without looking into the meaning were of course aware that the whole ingenious and astonishing production stood for something classical, and some of these would have taken the reference to Plato's *Republic*. Of the few who could follow the Platonic and Ovidian references in more detail, some would have taken the Neoplatonic intention in a general sense, and some in a specific sense. Bardi's implications have every appearance of being specific. The figure of Necessity now enthroned before us with her formidable spindle has the outer semblance of a woman for the same sort of reason which Dante gave when he explained[43] that 'Scripture condescends to your capacity, and attributes feet and hands to God, and means otherwise', because 'only through what is sensed (*sensato*) does your mind take in what it afterwards makes suited for

I. Le Balet comique de la royne: *audience and actors in the Salle de Bourbon, from the souvenir edition of Paris, 1582.*

II. The Neoplatonic décor for the
Florentine interludes of 1589:
Necessity holds her cosmic spindle,
with the three Fates beneath her
and representatives of the harmony
of the spheres and others deployed
around, above and below. This
engraving is by Agostino Caracci
more or less after the original
design by Bernardo Buontalenti.

III. The stage-dragon (a fine and typical specimen) for the third Florentine interlude of 1589; he may have served again for the related episode in Dafne, the first opera, at Florence in 1598 (modern style dating). A puppet Apollo is seen attacking from the air; it was imperceptibly replaced by a dancer for the actual combat. The engraving is by Agostino Caracci after the original design by Bernardo Buontalenti.

IV. Necessity with her cosmic spindle and the three Fates, as they appear on p. 304 of Vincenzo Cartari's popular Neoplatonic text-book, Le imagini . . . de i dei antichi (Venice, 1556) in its much illustrated second edition of Venice, 1571: compare Plate V below, of which this or a similar illustration (those in Cartari are considerably different though basically similar in various editions) would seem to be the source.

V. Bernardo Buontalenti's own beautiful design for Necessity with her cosmic spindle and the three Fates, as they appeared in the first Florentine interlude of 1589: compare Plate IV for the crude but undoubtedly Neoplatonic source which may have been drawn upon.

VI. Giulio Caccini's most famous song in arioso style, 'Amarilli', as it appears quite undeveloped in Florence, Biblioteca Nazionale Centrale, MS. Magl. XIX. 66, p. 36: compare Plate VII.

VII. Caccini's 'Amarilli' as it appears, fully developed, in his Nuove Musiche, Florence, 1602, p. 12: compare Plate VI.

VIII. Titian's Neoplatonic painting known as 'Venus Blindfolding Cupid', though in fact there are two Cupids, the sensuous one who is being blindfolded and the spiritual one who is not.

intelligence (*intelletto degno*)'. The outer image is the vehicle for the inner truth.

The music preserved from this first interlude consists of various madrigals, of which the first is described as having been sung solo with 'one large lute and two archlutes', and is preserved both in a plain and in an ornamented version; the others for several choruses, with varied instrumental accompaniment. In the middle, for a change of scene, came a Sinfonia using lutes (at least eight), harps and other plucked instruments, lyras, viols (at least seven), a flute, a cornetto and four trombones. At the close, all these vocal and instrumental forces joined to accompany a united ascent to heaven.

The second interlude presented (as in Ovid[44]) a rivalry of the Muses and the Muse-named daughters of Pieros, judged by a chorus of Nymphs in favour of the real Muses, the rival claimants being turned derisively into magpies and hopping about the stage in this bizarre guise. A Sinfonia then accompanied a scene-change, from the town of Pisa to a garden in which arose a mountain with two opposing caves. The ensuing madrigals increased from three voices to eighteen; the instruments supported them in various colourful combinations.

The third interlude changed to a forest having a desolate cave, with signs of scorching in the undergrowth: the abode of that fiery dragon and legendary representative of massive unconsciousness, the serpent called Python. After some madrigalian lamentation from opposed choruses of Delphic inhabitants (whose costumes Bardi learnedly insisted must show something of the maritime, *cose marine*, in token of Delphus founder of Delphi having been a son of Neptune), the elaborately constructed beast came on stage, flapping its wings and breathing fire. Apollo flew down in the form of a puppet on a wire, imperceptibly replaced by a dancer who mimed the combat with the monster in a series of highly formalized sequences, to the sound of viols, flutes and trombones; his victory was then acclaimed in joyful chorus and ballet. (See Plate III.)

The fourth interlude showed the new Golden Age prophetically in contrast to a vision of hell, which was indebted in many details to Dante, and was colourfully represented in the orchestra by the trombones already familiarly associated with the underworld. A virtuoso solo composed and sung by Caccini called down celestial spirits, who arrived to the sound of lyras, lutes, double harps, viols, a violin, bass trombones and chamber organs of wood. The infernal spirits noisily but vainly opposed them, lamenting 'to a melancholy music' the prophesied though surely not very probable shortage of new souls to torment.

The fifth interlude took a still more maritime turn, with the famous Vittoria Archilei as Queen of the Sea singing, alone, the top line of a five-part madrigal, accompanied by herself on the lute, with further support from an archlute and a lyra da gamba. Tritons and Nymphs responded in various vocal and instrumental combinations: and the famous virtuoso tenor and composer Peri, as Arion, sang a song of his own composing, accompanying himself on an archlute, and introducing florid embellishments very much in the character of Arion as a legendary singer. These survive in one version for a tenor '*Parte Principale*', with '*Prima Risposta*' and '*Seconda Risposta*', also in the tenor clef, and singing mainly a kind of double echo; but there is another version set out in normal four-part writing with hardly any figuration. The traditional rescue of Arion on a dolphin's back was then greeted by a seven-part chorus of sailors instrumentally accompanied.

The sixth interlude brought the characteristically Neoplatonic reconciliation of opposites, here represented by gods and mortals. An entire Council of the gods was accommodated on five celestial clouds, with Apollo, Bacchus, the Muses, the Graces, Cupids, Rhythm and Harmony. Their vocal combinations were yet more various, their instrumental accompaniments yet more diverse. The gods, just as it was related in Plato's *Laws*,[45] have taken pity on the human race. To console mortals for their manifold miseries, Jupiter has graciously commanded Apollo, Bacchus and the Muses to endow the earth with Rhythm and Harmony. In response, mortals in pastoral costume appear by pairs from all four directions, until a total ensemble of sixty voices is present, together with all the available instruments. The fruits of Rhythm and Harmony are then made apparent as the gods and goddesses, descending, lead the assembled mortals into a particularly grand concluding *ballo*, sung and danced to a very elaborate choreography illustrative of the union of the opposites thus visibly depicted.

Many of these details are differently reported in the available sources and may have varied considerably at the three successive performances. We do not know how much interest Bardi himself took in Neoplatonic theory. It was not necessary to be a speculative philosopher in order to follow the descriptions and copy the pictures of the many Neoplatonic popularizations available. But these outstanding interludes show every sign of genuine classical erudition. They are not, like the masquerade of 1566, mere showy exploitations of the current fashion; they are deliberate presentations of actual Platonic themes and images, and may well have been largely taken from Plato's dialogues with some pictorial assistance from the current treatises. As spectacle, as tableau, as vivid divertissement, everything which they had to offer passed straight over into opera very shortly afterwards. As drama, they were farther off than some other interludes, such as those which presented the developing story of Cupid and Psyche in 1565; for in 1589, there was little story and virtually no connected drama. They were further off, for the same reasons, than *Circe* in 1581. As music, they were much better than *Circe*, but they were no more operatic. In spite of the extent of the music in 1589, and in spite of a few solo songs of a virtuoso brilliance such as later found some reflection in opera, there was little attempt to unfold character and situation in the music, most of which consists of either dances or madrigals. The fact that some madrigals were sung by a soloist with instruments supplying the rest of the counterpoint did nothing to make them into a dramatic form. Their polyphony is of that lightly imitative texture in which Giovanni Gabrieli, for example, made himself so adept; for there is often a show of very many real parts, but on such triadic harmonies that the skill in avoiding unisons and forbidden consecutives, though requiring considerable ingenuity, is less remarkable than it seems—and even so, some awkward rhythms and linear intervals are unavoidable, together with all the verbal confusion of overlapping words. Musically it is something of a learned trick; but in any case, it takes the melody still farther from any such eloquent flexibility as could carry the more impassioned developments of opera.

For impassioned development in opera, a form of on-going melody with harmonic support was required which did not in 1589 exist. Yet it was well on the way to existing in that general style of monody which Bardi himself and his friends had already opened out, although, for whatever reason, they made hardly any use of it in these famous interludes: perhaps the popular conventions were too strongly established there for Bardi to risk too much refined and cultured novelty. This newly evolving style of monody, within which the on-going recitative for dramatic development shortly afterwards emerged, is best distinguished as the reciting style. Its very interesting background and history must be considered next.

VI
The Reciting Style

❧❧

DECLAMATION THE CENTRAL PROBLEM

The central problem of opera is declamation. There can be many passages in a drama where the action moves slowly if at all, and the characters can be allowed to express their reflections or their feelings or their anticipations, pleasant or unpleasant, at the usual more or less leisurely pace of song. It may even be of advantage to the drama for such episodes of relaxation or preparation to punctuate the onward impetus of events; and here the customary arts of song may be brought to bear without losing any of the intensity of the story, but on the contrary adding the grace and atmosphere of a musical form to the felicity and explicitness of a verbal text.

It is where the drama requires a greater swiftness and flexibility that the central problem of opera comes up. For there the dialogue can no longer afford to linger while the shapely patterns of an aria, an ensemble or a chorus develop. Anger is unruly; love cannot wait; fear distracts and courage presses on. It is in the very nature of our passions that we express them in urgent words and intemperate deeds; we should not be human if we were not liable to mental and physical violence, and drama would not be drama if it were not human. Music is perfectly capable of being as impassioned as we are ourselves, and of moving as swiftly and as flexibly as our most impetuous utterances; but in order to achieve this, something of its more formal symmetry has to be let go. Without neglecting to be song, music must contrive to be declamation. This was the crucial achievement reached before the end of the sixteenth century within that style which can best be known in general as the reciting style.

The reciting style in general may be described as a form of vocal melody essentially for one singer; standing on a modulating harmonic bass which supports a subordinate instrumental accompaniment; and composed for the explicit purpose of expressing as faithfully and as vividly as possible a more or less dramatic verbal text. The reciting style does not only belong to the theatre, and indeed it began, and largely continued, as a chamber form, one of whose important later consequences was the chamber cantata. Its theatrical importance nevertheless appears greatest, in as much as it included the historical development which made opera possible. Even those texts which it carries more lyrically than dramatically have some element of human drama, often setting out some sort of a little scene if not an actual scenario. It is in the nature of the reciting style to be theatrical, if only in the sense of dramatizing a passing feeling for whatever it is worth of rhetoric and effect. And above all it is in the nature of the reciting style to be individual. It is the direct expression of a personal emotion, whether projected on the stage or in church or in a private drawing-room. Much of the transition from the renaissance to the baroque is reflected in the evolution of the reciting style.

There were, up to a point, plenty of historic precedents. Wherever there has been song, there have been elements in it of individual virtuosity and personal expression. In some primitive societies, a song may be not only a solo performance but a private enterprise, jealously guarded or commercially marketed in fair exchange: monody in the sense of one man's property! Some quality of display is inherent in all solo performances; but there are phases of fashion, and we get the impression that solo displays of vocal virtuosity were markedly on the increase for at least a century before the rise of opera. We are beginning to appreciate how flexibly even the polyphony (not to mention the courtly melody) of the middle ages and the renaissance may always have been intended. The very same chansons of Guillaume de Machaut, for example, have been shown by Sarah Jane Williams to survive in such varying numbers of parts with or without words that no one version can be regarded as more definitive than any other.[1] The chansons, the frottole, the ayres and even the madrigals of the sixteenth century were hardly less liable to this variety of options, including solo performance with an instrument or instruments filling in or doubling or replacing or adding to some or all of the existing parts. An element of improvisation and ornamentation and spontaneous variation was regularly associated with such performances.

Howard Mayer Brown[2] has studied, so far as the slight extant repertory permits, the practice in good Florentine society of singing monophonic songs (*canzone*, which were for singing, and *ballate*, which might be though they were not necessarily danced as well), as described by Boccaccio in the *Decameron*, that series of one hundred stories written over a period from 1344, and first combined for publication in 1353. The songs are strophic with refrain; the melody is occasionally quite melismatic, though never really declamatory or dramatic, and it might be accompanied by a lute or a bowed

instrument (especially a fiddle, it would seem probable from contemporary pictures).

Over a century later, we find another and rather more explicit
account of the same sort of practice in Pietro Bembo's fashionable
narrative of courtly conversation and elegant entertainment, his *Dialoghi degli Asolani* (Talks of the People of Asolo—cultivated people
encountered on his visit there—probably begun in 1495, and published at Venice in 1505). A well-born young lady took up her lute,
and 'preluding very masterfully, after some time to the pleasant sound
of which, blending her soft voice with it and sweetly singing, she
uttered' the poem in dispraise of love then printed. 'When she had
uttered this song', and made 'a brief passage of music leading back to
her first notes again', another, younger girl 'to the strain (*tenor*) of
those [notes] in the same way as she, sweetly loosening her tongue,
replied to her' in a second stanza opening with the same words, and
using the same line and rhyme scheme, but neatly reversing the
sentiment to be in praise of love. Thereupon the Queen brought
forward a companion of her own who, 'taking a viol of hers of
marvellous sound', modestly 'sang this song with such delightfulness
and with such a new style of melody, that beside the sweet flame
which her notes left in the hearts of the hearers', the other two were
outdone; and she still more skilfully reconciled their opposite sentiments in a deeper sentiment which acknowledged both. A very Neoplatonic reconciliation; and to its more sophisticated readers, but thinly
veiling the allegorical reference to Platonic love of the divine, beneath
the graceful surface of courtly love of the human.[3]

Baldassare Castiglione's similar and even more popular *Libro del
Cortegiano* (written by 1514, and published at Venice in 1528), was
certainly influenced and probably criticized in manuscript by Bembo,
who is made to appear very eloquently in its later pages. Among other
passages describing such music at the princely courts, Castiglione
echoed Bembo, in making mention of the professional singer Bido, at
whose singing 'the spirites of the hearers move all and are inflamed,
and so listing, a man would ween they were lift up into heaven. And
no lesse doth our Marchetto Cara move in his singing, but with a
more soft harmony, that by a delectable way and full of mourning
sweetness maketh tender and perceth the mind, and sweetly imprin-
teth in it a passion full of great delite.' Still more prophetic of the
reciting style, Castiglione confessed that 'all the sweetness consists
almost in a solo, and one notices and understands the fine manner and
the melody with much greater attention when the ears are not occupied with more than one solo voice.' And (as with Bembo's third
young lady), 'above all singing to the viol by way of reciting (*cantare
alla viola per recitare*) seems to me the most pleasing.'[4] The use here of
the word *recitare* is particularly striking.

Yet more striking, coming as it does from the greatest champion of vocal polyphony in the mid-sixteenth century, is the passage in Gioseffo Zarlino where he wrote that 'one hears with greater delight a solo sung to the Organ, the Lira, the Lute, or another such Instrument', this approaching 'more to the usage of the ancients', which he elsewhere equated with the much-cited opinion of Plato that 'harmony and rhythm ought to follow speech'.[5]

The improvising element in this sixteenth-century tradition of impassioned solo singing may well account for a larger part of it than ever got into notation. We are aware, at least, of a very widespread custom in sixteenth-century Italy of half-memorizing and half-improvising vocal melodies, with subordinate accompaniment, to poetry such as that of Ariosto and Tasso, sophisticated indeed, yet symmetrical enough to fall readily into a spontaneous compound of habitual formulas and ready invention. Apparently this custom has never died out. Michael Kelly[6] reported encountering it in 1781. Diego Carpitella[7] reported it as vigorously continuing in the middle of the present century; while Paul Collaer[8] mentioned certain very archaic features in melodic formulas still used for verses of Ariosto and Tasso in some rural areas of Italy.

It was a feature of this flourishing art of solo improvisation in sixteenth-century Italy that it rested on familiar ground-basses, or merely on the simple harmonic progressions implied by them, which were repeated while the melody varied. This is the pattern which in the reciting style became strophic variation form; and there can be no doubt that the link was a direct one. From there, this same form subsequently took its place in early opera. Another strange though less substantial antecedent may be noticed in the type of more or less polyphonic madrigals which Einstein[9] called pseudo-monody (they are not 'false' anything, however, and all he meant was quasi-monody). Here one part stands out from the others almost like a solo from its accompaniment, and sometimes with a curious and untypical suggestion of what later became recitative.

But that precisely is the point. It was not recitative. The reciting style itself, at its inception, was not recitative. It was a graceful and lyrical idiom with declamatory potentialities, from which recitative subsequently emerged in one and the same creative impulse as opera. For all essential purposes, early recitative was early opera. There were, of course, adjuncts: overtures, dances, ensembles with or without dancing, a few brief arias; but there was no special novelty in any of these, and very much less importance as yet attached to them in opera than was subsequently the case. For opera, the problem of declamation itself had to be solved; and the solution was, as we shall see in due course, that declamatory aspect of the reciting style in general which can best be described in particular as recitative.

SOUND AND SENSE IN POETRY

There could be no question in the sixteenth century of adapting the sense to the sound, as may happen in some modern music-theatre. To bring words and music into closer union meant adapting the sound to the sense, in deliberate compliance with Plato's advice: 'the notes and the rhythm ought to follow the speech' (καὶ μὴν τήν γὲ ἁρμονίαν καὶ ῥυθμὸν ἀκολουθεῖν δεῖ τῷ λόγῳ).[10] Literature, statues, buildings, even late paintings survive as models from classical antiquity; but music, beyond a handful of belated and controversial fragments, does not. Thus it is not surprising that the basic discussions of the sixteenth century about the technical relationship of sound and sense should have begun from the poetic end.

We have a workmanlike treatise by Pietro Bembo, a distinguished practitioner of the Tuscan vernacular, generally regarded as a true heir to Dante and more directly to Petrarch, whose lyrical gift he was felt to approach most nearly of all poets then living. The treatise is called *Prose della volgar lingua* (Essays on the Vernacular Language), and it was published at Venice in 1525. Bembo was noted for having up-dated even the revered image of Petrarch, not only in his own poetry but in his reading of Petrarch's poetry, by exploiting every possibility for sonorous contrast or for cross-rhythm counterpointed against the underlying metre; and it has been interestingly suggested by Dean T. Mace[11] that the intricate rhythms and complex polyphony of the mid-sixteenth-century madrigal may have been developed to accommodate in music these poetic intricacies, which the more homophonic rhythms of the frottola or chanson could no longer follow.

It was argued by Bembo[12] and his circle that words have not only semantic meanings, conveyed by grammar and syntax and linguistic convention generally, but also sonorous meanings, conveyed by pitch and rhythm and aural associations generally. It is not just that the sound of the words enhances the sense; the sound is part of the sense. Fluctuations in the length, speed, accentuation, gravity and acuteness of succeeding syllables evoke strong and specific responses. Verbal sounds have meanings, of course; but also, on this theory, verbal sounds are meanings. The sound and the sense have to match in order not to negate but to reinforce one another.

A verbal sound may be swift or sluggish, light or heavy, elating or depressing, from the distribution of its accents among its syllables. Thus a word accented on its last syllable but two (so that it ends with two unaccented syllables following an accented syllable) will be experienced as slipping off the tongue and falling on the ear in a rapid, light and elusive manner. It can therefore be classified technically, in modern Italian, as a *parola sdrucciola*, a slippery word (Bembo has *sdrucciolosa*). The word *sdrucciola* is itself a slippery word, accented on its first syllable, unaccented on its second (double but elided) syllable, and unaccented on its third (last) syllable. And in English, too, slippery is itself a slippery word. The sonority of a slippery word is felt to convey an emotion, or at least a hint, of liveliness, mobility, eagerness or the like.

But a word accented on the last syllable (so that it ends with its accent) was regarded as coming from the tongue, and falling on the ear, in a ponderous, abrupt and truncated manner. It can therefore be classified as a *parola tronca*, a truncated word (Bembo speaks of its weight, *peso*). The word *tronca* is not itself a truncated word; but *pietà* (pity) is a truncated word, unaccented on its first two syllables and accented on its third (last) syllable. In English pronunciation truncate is a truncated word. The sonority of a truncated word is felt to convey an emotion or a hint of solidity, grief, deliberation, immovability or the like.

And a word accented on the last syllable but one (so that it ends with one unaccented syllable following an accented syllable) was regarded as coming from the tongue, and falling on the ear, in a level, unexcitable and ordinary manner. It could therefore be classified as a *parola piana*, a level word (Bembo calls it medium, *mezzana*). The word *piana* is itself a level word, accented on its second (middle) syllable and unaccented on its third (last) syllable. The sonority of a level word is felt to convey an emotion or a hint of equability, moderation, indeterminateness or the like, somewhere between the two extremes.

These connections between semantic meaning and sonorous meaning do not have to be regarded merely as arbitrary linguistic conventions. There must be many autonomous associations reinforcing them beneath the threshold of consciousness. Vernacular poets had been discussing the mechanism of language since Dante's own unfinished *De vulgari eloquentia*,[13] and as one might expect, inconclusively; but there are or should be no arbitrary connections in art, merely hidden connections. There is something in the sonority, for example, of *piacevolezza* (a level word made especially lingering by the double consonant) which causes it not merely to mean charm in the dictionary, but to fall charmingly on our poetic sensibilities. There is something in the sonority of *gravità* (a truncated word made especially massive by the light syllable before the heavy last syllable) which causes it not merely to mean gravity in the dictionary, but to fall gravely on our poetic sensibilities. Sound and sense are functions of one another; and it is hardly necessary to stress the importance of this fact as a working principle of opera, where verbal sonorities are further matched to musical sonorities.

Besides the sonorous meanings of individual words, there are their subtle combinations and arrangements, especially at line-endings where their prominence may be greatest. Again, line lengths can be protracted and sluggish, or short and volatile. Lines extensively continued at moderate length and in an inconspicuous metre, steadily maintained, especially when unrhymed or rhymed only at occasional concluding couplets, make for an easy flow of narrative or description. Lines of variable lengths and metres, subtly interchanged, especially when grouped into recurring stanzas, make for a more artful and sophisticated texture, lyrical or urgent, felicitous or forceful as the case may be. Both the metrical schemes and the rhyme schemes can be regular or irregular. There can be internal rhymes as well as end rhymes. There can be interlocking rhymes in an endless chain, as in Dante's astonishing *terza rima*. Syllables can be packed more tightly or more loosely into lines of the same underlying metre. Thus through the elision of two adjacent vowels not separated by a consonant, additional syllables can be inserted, which weight the flow; while a line ending with a slippery word can readily, as Bembo pointed out, have one syllable the more by way of compensation, if so desired, and conversely, a line ending with a truncated word may have one syllable the less—but not necessarily so. Or a syllable can be just irregularly dropped here or there, which lightens the flow; or added, which again weightens the flow. The caesura expected as a regular break in the line may be displaced unexpectedly, which disturbs the flow. In these and other ways, the natural lilt of the metre can be accepted or it can be exaggerated or it can be deliberately contradicted, so that the rise and the fall and the speed and the rhythm of the actual words sometimes accords with the metrical expectation and sometimes counterpoints against it.

The sonorous resources of poetry are of infinite variety and adaptability; and it is these resources which Bembo required to be fitted to the semantic sense which the poetry is making. He would not have accepted or even understood that there could be poetry without semantic sense. He was not being original in requiring the sound and the sense to go together: that is the normal course in anything conventionally regarded as poetry. But he was setting out these requirements with unusual awareness, examining deliberately what poets do habitually. In this he made an early and significant contribution to that thoughtful reassessment of the relationship of words and music which poets and musicians of the sixteenth century were undertaking in their search for a classical union of the arts, and for the strong and specific power over the emotions which they ascribed to such a union. It was all part of the preparation, although not as yet the conscious preparation, for opera.

It cannot of course escape our attention that different languages have different sonorities. Greek is more volatile; Latin is more compact. Italian abounds in feminine endings, having a preponderance of what Bembo analysed as the 'medium' (i.e. level) rhythm, which tends to flexibility (the feminine ending can be memorized by the phrase 'I am a woman'). The Italian consonants are soft (though well articulated in *bel canto* singing); the vowels are pure and open; the flow is voluble and passionate. French has fairly soft consonants and pure vowels, but less open and somewhat nasal; German has hard consonants with conspicuous gutterals; English has moderate consonants, impure vowels and a preponderance of masculine endings in Bembo's 'weighty' (i.e. truncated) rhythm (the masculine ending can be memorized by the phrase 'I am a man').[14] And these, too, are aspects of the sonorous sense. No wonder translation is a problem in opera; for the semantic meanings are too important for a mere singable paraphrase really to serve; yet the sonorous meanings have somehow to be retained, or an acceptable substitute found. So much in opera is inevitably a compromise between sound and sense that this problem also can only be handled with tact as best we can (for example, we might ask ourselves how many of a given audience would know a foreign language if retained). Nevertheless Bembo did well to isolate for us certain samples of sonorous meaning in poetry, and to stress the importance of matching the sonorous meaning with the semantic meaning.

POETRY IN MUSIC

The next contribution towards the great sixteenth-century reappraisal of the relationship between words and music came on the musical side. Gioseffo Zarlino, in common esteem the leading musical theorist of his day, and himself a reputable though not an outstanding composer of the middle school, drew freely (and, after the manner of the time with little acknowledgement) on previous and current writers; but he certainly brought into open discussion, in his great *Istitutioni armoniche* (Principles of Music, published at Venice in 1558), a theory of sonorous meaning in music resembling Bembo's in poetry. The length, the speed, the accentuation and the pitch of notes, successively and in combination; the rhythms which they set up; the directions in which their pitches move: these and other factors produce an ongoing pattern of musical sonority of which the meaning is just as definite as Bembo found in poetic sonority. The principle is the same which Mendelssohn[15] later explained when he replied to Marc-André Souchay's question about the meaning of some of the *Songs Without Words*: namely, that music expresses thoughts not too indefinite (*unbestimmte*) to be translated into words, but too definite (*bestimmte*). Music has no directly semantic meanings; thus no problem of matching its sonorous meanings to its semantic meanings can arise. But music can be united with poetry; and then the problem does arise of matching the sonorous meanings of the notes both to the sonorous and to the semantic meanings of the words.

This, in effect, was the problem which Zarlino set himself to elucidate, so successfully that half a century afterwards Thomas Morley in his *Plaine and Easie Introduction to Practicall Musicke* paid him the tribute of translating without acknowledgement, but with only slight modifications, expansions and abridgements, his crucial sentences, as a still adequate instruction in 'how to dispose your musicke according to the nature of the words which you are therein to expresse, as whatsoever matter it be which you have in hand, such a kind of musicke must you frame to it.'[16] Only a few years later came Byrd's splendid testimony:[17] 'Moreover, there rests indeed in the very meanings themselves (as I have learnt from experience) a hidden and profound power; so that to one thinking about divine matters, and diligently and seriously attending to them; I know not in what manner, the very aptest notes(*aptissimi quiqui numeri*), come up as if of their own accord.' No one, be it observed, ever raised a doubt as to whether the words ought to be given this unqualified supremacy over the music. It was what Plato thought, and in spite of the vast differences both of technique and of context, it was taken as an axiom that so it was thought by any cultivated person of the sixteenth century.

It was only a very shallow application of this principle when, for example, 'black' notation (as opposed to 'white' notation) was used for words of darkness or despair; such mere eye-music, which the ear does not hear, was censured as severely by Zarlino as by his most noted antagonist, Vincenzo Galilei. On the other hand, it is a valid and perfectly audible association, although still quite elementary, when (as Zarlino recommended and Morley repeated, but Galilei ridiculed) rapid movement accompanies happy words, and slow movement accompanies unhappy words; or when we are told to 'have a care that when your matter signifieth ascending, high heaven, and such like, you make your musicke ascend: and by the contrarie where your dittie [text] speaketh of descending loweness, depth, hell and others such, you must make your musicke descend.' Other associations are not only audible but very far from elementary: 'when you would express any word signifying hardnesse, crueltie, bitternesse, and other such like, make the harmonie like unto it, that is, somewhat harsh and hard but yet so it offend not.' And more explicitly: 'the naturall [i.e. diatonic] motions are those which are naturallie made between the keyes without the mixture of any accidentall signe or corde, be it either flat or sharpe, and these motions be more masculine causing in the song more virilitie than those accidentall [i.e. chromatic progressions which] make the song as it were more effeminate and languishing.'[18]

These are subtle relationships indeed; but they are not merely conventions. They depend upon a most complicated network of acoustic phenomena, physiological reaction and psychological conditioning. Discord actually beats within the mechanism of the ear so as to feel subliminally more uncomfortable than concord, which beats less or does not beat; thus discords sound to us intrinsically harsher, acclimatize ourselves to that harshness as we may. Diatonic intervals are more closely defined in the tonal spectrum than chromatic intervals; thus diatonic progressions sound intrinsically stabler, habituated though we may become to following their chromatic alterations without losing our sense of tonal direction. Tonality and modulation alike derive however indirectly from the natural harmonic series, which is an objective property of matter having subjective implications for mind. The links between mind and matter are always hard to trace beyond the most elementary connections; yet we cannot really doubt, for example, that rapid rhythms make for excitement, and slow rhythms make for repose, in some manner relating our bodily to our mental functions; or that the rapid vibrations of high-pitched sounds and the slow vibrations of low-pitched sounds somehow account for the mental effects on us of their physical acuteness and gravity. Our associations may be elusive but they are not arbitrary. Associations both conscious and unconscious are a primary means of artistic communication; and Zarlino's discussion of the sonorous associations between words and music made a further valuable contribution towards the preparations for opera.

Zarlino in his First Book also got extensively but inconclusively involved in the symbolism of numbers, of which there were some obscure traditions current, partly Neo-Pythagorean, partly Cabalistic, and mostly assimilated like so much else into the fringe-areas of Neoplatonism. The most familiar example is the association of triple metre and other triple combinations with the Holy Trinity in all that supreme perfection for which three was the traditional number-symbol, and the perfect circle was the graphic emblem — and thus the circle was the notational sign for triple (perfect) time. It may sometimes be difficult to detect whether a composer is using systematic number-symbolism, since the symbolism was as usual intended to be at least half-concealed; and it is sometimes still more difficult to feel convinced of any vital artistic significance, even when it is detected. Number-symbolism does not appear to have had much if any direct significance for the growth of opera, though Zarlino's discussion of proportion and symmetry, in music as in man himself, is typically Neoplatonic and of the broadest interest.

Most of what Zarlino had to say about those sonorous meanings which give to music its capacity for expression is actually as relevant to instrumental music as it is to vocal music. It was typical of his age that he discussed these meanings primarily in relation to vocal polyphony, being himself of that school of adventurous Italian madrigalists whose preoccupation with expression, and with 'word-painting' in music as a vivid means of expression, built one of the main bridges from the renaissance into baroque music. But not specifically into opera. It has been shown that opera itself eventually made considerable use of 'word-painting' directly inherited from this madrigalian idiom.[19] But opera was not arrived at by way of any polyphonic idioms, however adventurous. Opera was arrived at in opposition to polyphony. Bembo's clarification of poetic sonority, and Zarlino's clarification of musical sonority in relation to poetry, were significant for opera; but for opera itself we must return once more to Florence.

GROUPS AND PERSONALITIES AT FLORENCE

Discussing many learned discussion-groups of the late renaissance, Claude Palisca in a most valuable article[20] has drawn our attention to no fewer than four officially organized academies at Florence during the middle years of the sixteenth century. Their membership overlapped, and so no doubt did their interests; but Claude Palisca has shown that one of them, the Accademia degli Alterati, had a particular interest in the topical issue of uniting words and music for dramatic purposes. Palisca has also shown that Bardi (from 1574), Corsi (from 1586), Chiabrera (also from 1586) and Rinuccini were among its members.

Greek music, and modern music; poetry, and the relationship of music to poetry; the opinions on this matter of Plato and more particularly of Aristotle: such subjects were early included among the discussions of the Alterati. Of all learned scholars of the Greek language and its literature in the sixteenth century, one of the most distinguished was the Florentine Girolamo Mei, then living in Rome: the Alterati honoured him in 1585 with membership although he was not in Florence to take a personal part in their proceedings. But from 1572 on, Mei was in correspondence with some of the Florentines most interested in the union of poetry and music.[21] These were Giovanni de' Bardi and the group informally associated with him, known subsequently as Bardi's Camerata.

This word *camerata*, which has become so familiar in modern usage, is not to be found in the Italian dictionaries of the sixteenth century, such as Alberto Accarigo's *Vocabulario* (published at Cento in 1543 and in a revised edition at Cento in 1550), or Francesco Alumno's *Della fabbrica del mondo* (published at Venice in 1548 and in a revised edition at Venice in 1612). But in the first edition (published at Venice in 1612) of the celebrated *Vocabulario degli Accademici della Crusca*, we read (p. 145): 'CAMERATA. see CAMERA'. And there in turn we read: 'From CAMERA we say CAMERATA, that is to say an assembly of people, who dwell, and associate together (*adunanza di gente, che vivano, e conversano insieme*). Lat. *contubernium*.' The *Cambridge Italian Dictionary* of 1962 gives 'converse' as a current meaning and 'associate' as an obsolete meaning for *conversare*; but Lewis and Short has for *contubernium* at the nearest 'the accompanying, attendance (of teachers, friends etc.).' There is no necessary implication of discussions, and no possible implication of organization: *camerata* cannot mean an organized academy nor any other sort of formal body. The second edition of the *Vocabulario degli Accademici della Crusca* (Venice, 1623) has the same entry as the first. The third edition (Florence, 1691), has the same as the first (and so indeed does the 'fifth impression' of Florence, 1866), except that CAMERATA has this same definition under its own heading as well as under CAMERA, and that its own heading adds an illustration with the comment '(*qui compagnia*)', '(here [meaning] company)'. Perhaps on the strength of that, the *Cambridge Italian Dictionary* gives 'sharing quarters' as a modern meaning but 'company' as an obsolete meaning for *camerata*. We might speak of 'Bardi's company', in the ordinary social sense of 'having company'. Or we might speak of 'Bardi's circle'. It was Caccini who in the preface to his *Euridice* (published at Florence in 1600, Florentine old-style dating, i.e. in modern dating 1601) and again in the preface to his *Nuove musiche* (published at Florence in 1602), seems to have had the idea of describing it as *virtuosissima camerata*, a most brilliant company: with Caccini, by strong implication, as its most brilliant ornament. Pietro de' Bardi, son of Giovanni, in a letter written to G. B. Doni at Doni's request in 1634, also spoke of 'the Camerata of my father (*camerata di mio padre*)' as being 'almost a pleasing and continual academy (*quasi una dilettevole e continua accademia*).'[22] This is the only use of the word 'camerata' which has historical justification: i.e. for Bardi's circle.

From some time before 1570 until some time after 1580, over a period of perhaps some twelve or fifteen years, Giovanni di' Bardi, Count of Vernio, had distinguished 'company' at his palace in Florence. No membership was listed; no dues were paid; no right of entry was bestowed; there were as far as we are aware no officials, nor any other features of a formal organization. But there were evidently habits of attendance, and the company kept was very interesting company. Bardi himself wrote poetry, and a little music. His guests were enthusiasts for anything that cultured society of the late renaissance in Florence might have been expected to regard with enthusiasm in philosophy, in the sciences, in the arts, and in their relationship with one another. Among much else, music was discussed, and the fashionable commonplaces as to why music should be restored to its classical capacity for arousing and guiding strong and specific emotions. As to how it could be restored, however, conclusions were reached and experiments were made which were not merely the fashionable commonplaces, but which made a significant contribution towards the theory and practice of the reciting style.

Two notable musicians demonstrably frequented Bardi's circle. One was Vincenzo Galilei (*c.*1520–91), who was an amateur performer and composer but a theorist professionally trained (ironically enough) under Zarlino. The other was the Roman-born Giulio Caccini (*c.*1550–1618), habitually called Giulio Romano or just Romano although he became acclimatized in Florence: talented precociously as a virtuoso tenor singer and soon also as a composer; already a distinguished servant of the Medici court through the last decades of the sixteenth century; and very eminent though not the first to be eminent for the rise of opera.

Jacopo Corsi (*c.*1560–1602), meanwhile, was a younger social equal, and social rival, of Bardi.[23] There can be no doubt of their close acquaintanceship and habitual intercourse. But Corsi, too, had his own informal circle, never called Camerata nor merged with Bardi's Camerata. Their circles greatly overlapped; but they were divided by mutual jealousy as well as related by common interests. We should not, perhaps, really be talking at all, as our habit is, about a Florentine Camerata, although we may well talk about a Florentine environment; and, of course, perfectly correctly, about Bardi's Camerata as opposed to Corsi's circle.

Corsi's circle regularly included the poets, who presently became the librettists, Chiabrera and Rinuccini; and there it seems that these two literary figures cemented their mutual regard and friendship, so significant for the rise of opera. And whereas Bardi patronized Caccini, Corsi patronized the still younger Jacopo Peri (1561–1633), also born in Rome (but of noble family), also acclimatized in Florence, also a virtuoso tenor singer and soon also a composer of growing reputation. These two were unavoidably in competition, and often associated in the same performances, as singers, composers or both.

A yet further complication was introduced into this already tense situation when in 1587 Ferdinando de' Medici succeeded to the hereditary Florentine rulership, as Grand Duke of Tuscany. He did so on the rapidly successive deaths (the rather too conveniently successive deaths, some hinted) of his brother Francesco and his brother's wife. One of his earliest actions was, in 1588, to appoint as his official director of public spectacles yet another Roman then recently come to Florence, like Peri of good family although certainly no amateur: Emilio de' Cavalieri (*c.*1550–1602). This appointment must have seemed to be and may actually have been an intentional rebuff to the two established patrons.[24] Corsi got on to rather better terms than Bardi with Cavalieri: neither Peri nor Caccini themselves suffered any apparent setback. Bardi, who had been asked to organize the noted festivities for the marriage of Cesare d'Este and Virginia de' Medici in 1586 (modern-style dating), and who remained important enough to be again asked to organize those for the marriage of Ferdinando and Christine of Lorraine in 1589, was nevertheless so obviously in decline that he may not have been sorry to leave the scene of his previous eminence, when in 1592 he accepted an invitation to go to Rome as secretary to Pope Clement VIII.

THE START OF THE RECITING STYLE

The most significant contribution of Bardi's Camerata towards opera was in connection with the reciting style. Mei's letters to Bardi and to Galilei were virtually the start of it, from 1572 onwards. Claude Palisca has suggested that Mei, coming to the problem unprejudiced, may have been all the quicker to appreciate a historical fact of which the most precise study had convinced him. This is that Greek music, even in the choruses of Greek drama, was not only without polyphony but without harmony; for while the term harmony was often employed, it meant something different from chords (tonality or tonal disposition might be approximately the meaning). Not even Zarlino, who was aware that solo song approached 'more to the usage of the ancients', had Mei's exact perception of what that ancient usage might imply. It considerably astonished Bardi and Galilei, who were opposed to polyphony but had no intention of dispensing with harmony; however, they felt generally encouraged in the enterprise which earned them their place in history, since it resulted in the reciting style.

As Bembo for poetry and Zarlino for music, so Mei defined 'acuteness and gravity (*acutezza e gravità*)' of pitch, together with a 'middle (*mezzana*) quality' in between, in combination with 'swiftness and slowness of measure or rhythm (*prestezza e lentezza de numero ò ritmo*)'. But if, as Mei argued, these factors, and these alone, are the primary determinants of musical expression, then the power of Greek music over strong and specific emotions actually came from its being unharmonized. Voices either solo or in unison concentrate the effects of pitch and rhythm which contrapuntal parts confuse and dissipate; hence the alleged powerlessness of 'modern music' thus to 'move the emotions (*movere gli affetti*)'.[25] A conclusion so extreme might never have occurred to a professional in the musical field; but having occurred to the ruthless Mei (who, after all, was every inch a professional in his own linguistic field), it proved stimulating and even a little intoxicating to Bardi, who was a very serious amateur, and to Galilei, who had had the best of professional trainings under Zarlino, and showed it in his writings. The originality of the thoughts discussed by the participants in Bardi's Camerata thus came essentially from Mei. The working out of the theory, and the practice of it in the beginnings of the reciting style, was their own achievement.

We have an open letter of around 1580 addressed by Bardi nominally to Caccini, and included by G. B. Doni around 1635 among the writings later edited by A. F. Gori, where it appears as a 'Discourse on Ancient Music and Good Singing addressed to Giulio Caccini, called Romano'.[26] This letter does not get far beyond recalling (after Mei) the famous statements of Plato[27] that the music ought always to follow the speech, and of Aristotle[28] that music is only good when it can move a man's mind to strong and specific emotions of a suitably moral quality.

Then followed the first extended deployment of the argument. This was Vincenzo Galilei's impressive and lucid, though fairly short and very controversial *Dialogo della musica antica, e della moderna* (Discussion of Ancient and Modern Music, Venice, 1581). Galilei's book is substantially and sometimes verbally indebted to Mei's letters, with general though not detailed acknowledgement to this invaluable counsellor. Regarding 'modern music' in its existing condition as fundamentally unable 'to express the words with the passion which they require', Galilei (p. 89) recommended composers to learn at the theatre 'in what manner, with what voice regarding acuteness and gravity [i.e. higher and lower pitches], with what quantity [i.e. duration] of sound, with what sort of accents and gestures, with how much speed and slowness they talk' when acting the parts of different characters in different situations.

'What', exclaimed the powerful and respected Zarlino,[29] 'what has the musician to do with those who recite tragedies and comedies?' But theatrical recitation in music is indeed what opera has to do with; and Galilei's polemical preparation for the reciting style, and the attack on counterpoint by which he buttressed it, were indeed on the way to opera. Under the heady stimulus of Mei's letters, Galilei attacked counterpoint, not for its admitted skill and elegance as an abstract construction suitable to instruments, but for its imputed obscurity and self-contradictoriness as an expressive medium in setting words. It must be admitted that in the context of the sixteenth century that was not so very different from an attack on counterpoint itself. We have seen, however, that the poets of the sixteenth century were themselves paying a particular attention to the theory of sonorous meanings in words, needing to be matched to the semantic meanings. It was, therefore, quite in the spirit of the age for the musicians to pay a particular attention to balancing this poetic compound of sound and sense with matching notes. The composers of 'modern madrigals'[30] who followed Zarlino (no reactionary himself) considered that they were doing just this in their own highly expressive polyphony.

But because with polyphony the same word does not come at the same time in different parts, and because the notes carrying the words likewise do not come at the same time in different parts, there is, as Mei perceived and Galilei reiterated, a problem of overlapping. The words overlap: this makes it hard to catch them and to understand their semantic meaning (the very worst defect for the devoted linguist Mei). The notes carrying the words overlap: that makes it impossible, on this argument, to convey their sonorous meanings without self-contradiction and inconsistency (the alleged defect on which the musician Galilei laid most stress). For at any given time, the notes of one part may be rising while the notes of another part are falling; or the notes of one part may be long and slow, while the notes of another part are short and fast; or the notes of one part may be in heavy rhythm, carrying truncated words, while the notes of another part are in light rhythm, carrying slippery words, or again in medium rhythm, carrying level words. Themes dovetail with themselves by imitation, and words dovetail with them. A new theme, with new words, may dovetail into the end of the old theme, with its old words; for it is normal in sixteenth-century polyphony to start a new contrapuntal section before quite finishing the old. Even the fit of the notes to their own words is conditioned by having to make the theme melodically a good one for contrapuntal working, that is to say sufficiently regular in rhythm and in harmonic implication. We can readily see this if we compare the free and eloquent recitative of Monteverdi's famous 'Lament of Ariadne' with the symmetrical and almost four-square madrigals which Monteverdi himself arranged from it: beautiful music in its own freely contrapuntal texture, but (except perhaps for the first) by no manner of means so subservient to the words.

The argument against vocal counterpoint advanced by Mei and elaborated by Galilei is thus in certain respects a reasonable argument; but not in all respects. The notes of a monody are single as to pitch, speed and rhythm, whereas in polyphony they are multiple as to pitch, speed and rhythm, and even in homophony they are multiple as to pitch. Thus it was reasonable to argue that solo song may give the words the most direct opportunity of moving our feelings in combination with the music, and that this was necessary for the purposes sought in the reciting style. It was, however, unreasonable to argue that polyphonic vocal music has no power to move our feelings, which of course it obviously has in its own quite different manner of combining words and music.

Mei, with his limited musical experience, may really have found

vocal counterpoint a mere confusion; but Galilei must have been
carried away by his own argument quite against the evidence of his
senses to suggest any such thing. In fact, after the reciting style had led
into opera, it seemed a perfectly acceptable compromise to contrast it
with ensembles and choruses in the lightly polyphonic style of contemporary madrigals. The case for monody as the main substance of
opera is valid in itself; but the case against vocal counterpoint as such
rests on certain rather disingenuous fallacies. For example, it assumes
that poetry has a simple contour which solo melody has only to
follow; but this is not true of sophisticated poems, which already set
up a kind of implied counterpoint between the stresses and durations
expected from the metre and those actually resulting from the poet's
deliberate liberties. Many are the small surprises of displaced accent,
added or subtracted syllables, sprung rhythms and the like, which too
literal a manner of reading or too simple a solo setting in music will
equally destroy. It might as plausibly be argued that nothing short of a
contrapuntal setting could do musical justice to such poetic subtlety.

In practice, what outweighs that possible advantage is the absolute
necessity in opera of having a solo melody to convey the emotions of
an individual character; and it may well be said, therefore, that the
renunciation of counterpoint was the right choice for the wrong
reason. For the case against vocal counterpoint as such quite wrongly
assumes that different sonorous meanings heard simultaneously,
through the normal course of contrapuntal combination, must set up
opposing messages which cancel out. That is not how experienced
hearers respond to counterpoint. Vaughan Williams used to maintain
rather defiantly that no one can attend even to so many as three
contrapuntal parts independently, which may possibly be true; but
what in fact we attend to is not the parts independently, but their
relationship as a compound whole. It is the *Gestalt*, the pattern entire,
which we perceive by a kind of masterly overview: not the contrapuntal parts; but the counterpoint. The whole subsumes and reconciles
the parts. Nevertheless, to renounce the resources of counterpoint was
a necessary step along the path towards opera.

To renounce certain resources in order to develop others is a voluntary limitation of the means of an artistic enterprise in order the better
to serve the ends. It is always in the nature of artistic material to set its
own limits, and it is always part of good artistry to accept these limits
in such a way as to turn them into advantages; for the limits of the
material are part of the material. The very earliest operas are so limited
as to be a little austere; but this may have been not only due to the
novelty of the experiment but also to the need at first to concentrate on
essentials. Already Monteverdi, ten years after the earliest opera,
could relax and enrich the growing form; and his greater genius took
immediate care of that.

The contribution of Bardi's Camerata, in the years leading up to the earliest opera, was to initiate the reciting style before it became an operatic idiom. We learn something of this contribution from the letter[31] (already mentioned) written by Pietro de' Bardi, the son of Giovanni de' Bardi, to the Roman musicologist G. B. Doni, at his request, and dated Florence, 16 December 1634:

My father signor Giovanni having great pleasure in music, of which, in his time, he was a composer of some note, always had around him the most celebrated men of the city, learned in such a profession, and inviting them to his house, formed almost a pleasing and continual academy (*quasi una dilettevole e continua accademia*), from which vice standing far away, and especially every sort of game [*giuoco*, ?gaming] the noble Florentine youth came enticed to their great profit, entertaining themselves not only with music, but also in discussions and teachings of poetry, astrology, and other sciences, which brought mutual advantage to such fine conversation.

Vincenzo Galilei. . .was the first to make us hear singing in the representative style (*in istile rappresentativo*). . .over an ensemble (*corpo*) of viols exactly played, a tenor singing in a fine voice, and understandable, he made us hear the lament of Count Ugolino from Dante. Such novelty, just as it aroused envy in a considerable part of the practitioners of music, so it gave pleasure to those who were true lovers of it. Galilei following so fine an undertaking composed part of the Lamentations, and responses of Holy Week, sung, of the same material (*nella stessa materia*), in devout company. There was then in the company of my father (*nella camerata di mio padre*) Giulio Caccini, at a very young age, but considered an exceptional singer, and of good taste, who feeling himself inclined to this new music, under the complete instruction of my father, started to sing over a single instrument various little arias (*ariette*), sonnets and other poems, suited to be understood (*intese*), to the amazement of those who heard them. There was also in Florence then Jacopo Peri, who, as the foremost scholar of Cristofano Malvezzi, and playing and composing to his own great credit on the organ and [plucked] keyboard instruments and in counterpoint, and among the singers of this city was without fail considered to be second to none. This man in competition (*a competenza* [a meaning then current though now obsolete]) with Giulio [Caccini] found out the undertaking of the representative style, and avoiding a certain roughness and excessive antiquity, which one heard in the music of Galilei, sweetened together with Caccini this style, and rendered it fit to move the emotions rarely, as in course of time came to be done by both one and the other.

By the which things these men acquired the name of the first singers, and inventors of this manner of composing and singing.

Peri had more science, and having found a manner of imitating common speech by touching few strings (*ricercar poche corde* [a meaning then current though now obsolete]), and with other exact care, acquired great fame. Giulio had more grace in his inventions.

This passage, of which the accuracy and fairness are confirmed by other evidence, credits Galilei with some not very well defined new departure, and Caccini and Peri, in that order, with some more positive achievement in the same direction. The music of Galilei's first pioneer experiments in this style does not survive;[32] but since it was sung solo with an ensemble of viols, it can hardly have been greatly different from the solo performance of one part and the instrumental performance of the other parts of some simple frottola, chanson or madrigal, in the familiar manner of the time. In that case, it may have been nearer to most of the music for the French dramatic ballet *Circe* (i.e. mainly homophonic part-writing) than it was to the genuinely monodic melody, with sparse accompaniment for lute etc., here credited to Caccini and Peri.

We are told that Caccini 'started to sing over a single instrument various little arias'; and while the 'amazement of those who heard them' may have been largely for his rare vocal artistry and *bel canto* virtuosity, we have the impression that the music itself was substantially novel; and that this may indeed be the effective start of the reciting style in so far as any one moment can be, or any one man's work. Then Peri (from the rival camp socially though not artistically), 'in competition with Giulio [Caccini]', so furthered the reciting style that these two men, 'the one and the other', became known as 'the first singers, and inventors of this manner of composing and singing', of which it was counted a crucial feature that the accompaniment was not in part-writing, however simple and however homophonic, but 'by touching few strings' on a lute or similar plucked instrument alone.

This manner differed, then, from the familiar performances of lightly polyphonic or mainly homophonic songs with one part sung and other parts played; for there were no other, independent parts to be played, but only a bass with chords, and sparse chords at that. And although much fuller accompaniments came later to be associated with some aspects of the reciting style, especially in opera, nevertheless this concentration upon a single melody supported by a bass with chordal realization was what led to opera.

VARIETIES OF THE RECITING STYLE

Fully developed examples of the reciting style as found in manuscripts from the latter years of the sixteenth century, and also in Caccini's celebrated collection called *Nuove musiche* (New Musics, i.e. compositions, Florence, 1602)[33] have it in common that the melody is simple in the main, a little diversified by melismatic figuration, shaped closely and expressively to the words, and supported by a quietly independent bass-line on which a subordinate harmonic accompaniment is to be improvised on the lute or otherwise. Some further ornamentation can be supplied by the singer, but with considerable restraint and only on suitably affective syllables (never the last syllable, but often the last but one), as the celebrated preface to the *Nuove musiche* explains. Within these common elements of the reciting style, however, we find three distinct though closely allied forms.

There are unpretentious little strophic arias on poems of somewhat deceptive simplicity. These poems are graceful and symmetrical, notable for their verbal conceits and felicity of language, in a vein more elegant than passionate; but they are turned with much linguistic cunning and poetic ingenuity. The music matches the words with equal elegance, flowing from the heart, but not very deeply from the heart. As befits an essentially strophic arrangement of balanced line-schemes and rhyme-schemes in the poetry, we have in the music mainly a bass which repeats virtually unchanged, supporting a melody also repeating substantially, but rather more apt to be slightly changed; and these written variations between the melodies of successive stanzas were certainly increased a little by the improvised ornamentation. When the variation in the melody is considerable, the bass remaining constant, we speak of strophic variation form. But elaborate variation was never the intention, since anything too showy would destroy the unambitious charm which marks the idiom. There is a certain dewy freshness for which Caccini no doubt deserves much credit; but we may be very close here to the popular practice of singing verses by Tasso, Ariosto and the like with a blend of traditional formulas and improvised variants, particularly on well-known basses or harmonic progressions several of which survive in dance collections and other sources. Evocative as these little songs in the reciting style may be, and suggestive of the simple sentiments in which the poetry deals, they are in themselves far less dramatic, for example, than the polyphonic madrigals in advanced style with which they are contemporary. They represent the most lyrical aspect of the reciting style; and while they presently found a very useful place in opera, they were not the aspect from which the musical rhetoric necessary for opera arose. Nor have they the power and virtuosity subsequently associated with dramatic aria. They can, perhaps, best be called songs in simple aria style.

Next there are songs which are not strophic, but more or less through-composed on poems of one elaborate stanza. Here we find the 'solo madrigals' of Caccini and others, so-called from their poetic structure and not from any resemblance to the musical texture of the polyphonic madrigal. There may be a couplet treated musically as a refrain. As befits the stronger poetry, there is not quite the tuneful elegance which we expect from the little arias, but rather a fuller passion and a more evident sophistication. There are fewer ingratiating curves in the melody, and more wide leaps, sharp angles, reiterated notes, above a bass less active but with tenser harmonic implications. The forward impetus is left more to the vocal line, and this in turn derives more of its force from the energy of words dramatically enunciated. Here we are approaching the more declamatory aspect of the reciting style. We are not yet in the free and open idiom of recitative; but we do have some of the transitional flexibility of arioso. It would perhaps be suitable to call these songs in arioso style.

Still further from the lyrical side and still nearer to the declamatory side, we meet with a few songs which are so rhetorical that if it were not for their rounded-off structure we should certainly regard them as recitative. Some are through-composed, others are in strophic variation form; and these last acquired historical significance as a standard recourse for the prologue in very early opera. Those we can perhaps call songs in recitative style.

Actual recitative differs from these songs in recitative style primarily in having not a rounded-off structure, but an open-ended structure. In this respect, recitative almost certainly originated not with Caccini, but with Peri; and recitative was quite certainly the innovation in and through which opera arose. Not Bardi's Camerata but Corsi's circle must be credited with this crucial step, to which so much had led and from which so much followed. It was the flexibility and adaptability and open-endedness of early recitative which enabled it to solve the central problem of opera: the problem of declamation.

Early recitative, for all its flexibility, or more truly, perhaps, because of its flexibility, is a splendidly eloquent idiom of vocal virtuosity. The virtuosity lay not in the sort of spectacular agility which later baroque *bel canto* acquired, but of which there are far fewer examples in early baroque opera. The virtuosity lay rather in sustaining a finely moulded line of melody with complete finesse and never an involuntarily wavering of the tone: *bel canto* in just as exacting and advanced a sense, but for the purposes of unfolding a drama, much more subtly adaptable. Where the cadences in aria are shapely in themselves and timely to the music, the cadences in any recitative are timely in sole relation to the words. Whole speeches or brief interjections; soliloquies in monologue or exchanges in dialogue; prose, or verse regular or irregular, rhymed or unrhymed, smooth or disjointed: it can all be accommodated in recitative. There is no musical texture more apt to the service of the words, nor more susceptible of sudden felicities where the words invite them.

As in speech, the range of pitch in recitative is mainly narrow, and the variety of rhythm by no means extreme. One note to a syllable is an ordinary method of setting, often with many rapid repetitions of one note culminating in a higher note of longer duration. But as passion mounts, so wider leaps and fiercer rhythms reflect it. And in general, the pitch is liable to rise with emotion, fall with relaxation. The rhythm is at no time so regular in performance as it may appear to be in notation, but follows the natural inflections of the spoken word with the greatest liberty. Meanwhile, the bass remains solid and supportive, mostly in long notes, almost like a succession of pedal-notes, with a slow rate of harmonic change through a few chords above which the voice may fling passing dissonances until the next change of chord brings it into momentary consonance. But here the difference between early baroque recitative (as in Monteverdi) and subsequent recitative (as in Handel) becomes very marked. For in subsequent recitative, the melody is scarcely a thing of beauty in itself, but just keeps music in the picture while action develops; and by far the main musical substance of the opera lies in the arias. But in early recitative, the melody carries both beauty and action, and itself holds the main musical substance of the opera, lying as it does much nearer to arioso and blending with it intermittently. For just as early librettos are more spontaneous, so early recitative is more fluid. Hardly anything is predetermined in very early opera: words and music alike take their structure from the immediate needs of the continuously unfolding drama.

The relationship of words and music in recitative, though it is close, is not so much naturalistic as stylized. It is closer to the theatrical enunciation of the Comédie Française, which sounds natural but is not, than to any speech of the street-corner (except perhaps in comic opera) or of the drawing-room. Recitative is not nature; it is a convention for suggesting nature by quite unnaturalistic contrivance. Above all, the primary consideration of recitative is dramatic expressiveness.

When the vocal melody, though still open-ended and timed substantially to the requirements of the words rather than of the music, nevertheless begins to flow more liltingly; when the bass pulses more evenly and tunefully; when the changes of harmony are more frequent and less distracted by random dissonances in the melody: then recitative has given place to arioso, where dramatic expressiveness and musical expressiveness stand on a more equal footing.

And when there is a predominance of musical symmetry over

verbal pronunciation; when there is a closed ending, timed and rounded to the musical rather than to the verbal requirements of the case (though hopefully felicitous for both); when the bass takes a still more active and cooperative part; when the changes of harmony are still more lucid and distinctive and significantly progressive: then aria is occurring. However aptly the music of an aria is suited to its words, it cannot be unreservedly accommodated to them as it goes along. On the contrary, a pattern of musical development has been set up which carries its own implications. A late baroque aria may actually contort the words and obscure their clarity by repeating incomplete sentences or isolated words or even syllables to accommodate the music. An early baroque aria seldom makes any such inroads into the verbal priorities, and still less so does early baroque recitative. Verbal repetitions, when they do occur, are of complete sentences or phrases, sometimes used as an elegant refrain. When the words are strophic, the music tends to repetition with or without slight written or improvised adjustments to improve the fit. A repeating bass with a substantially varied melody is strophic variation form, or rondo strophic variation if there is also a vocal refrain. A repeating instrumental ritornello may frame and separate the strophic units.

Other common arrangements in early opera include *abb*, repeating the second section of the music to the same or different words; *abb´*, repeating the second section with some (not necessarily much) musical variation; and *aba*, which is *da capo* aria, though in early baroque opera usually short and relatively infrequent. In later baroque opera, the *da capo* aria was longer, and was almost or entirely preferred, some improvised variation of the *da capo* repeat being expected so as to provide a certain element of surprise in what might otherwise seem too extensively repetitive a form.

The primary consideration of aria is musical expressiveness. Yet this, too, can serve the drama. If the long and elaborate aria 'Possente spirto' at the centre of Monteverdi's *Orfeo* had not been so musically expressive that it lulled Charon to sleep, Orfeo could not have made his dramatically necessary way across the river Styx into the underworld. If the duet of Nero and Poppea were not so enchanting that it sums up the entire feeling at the end of *Poppea*, it could not, as it does, form a dramatic climax in the very fact of providing a musical climax.[34] Thus even in aria, words before music remains the working principle of the reciting style.

VII
The Modern Style

❦

THE RECITING STYLE AS MODERN STYLE

Monody[1] is not a term used by its actual originators, nor often by its seventeenth-century historians; but it has been much misused since for any solo song (which at least is etymologically correct) or even for any instrumental solo (which is not). The Greek μονῳδία (monodia) was rare, but found in Plato[2] (as opposed to χορῳδία (chorodia) for a choral unison); the diminutive μονῴδιον (Lat. *monodium*) occurs in the fourth century A.D. with the grammarian Diomedes,[3] and the Latin *monodia* with the seventh century in Isidorus.[4] The Italian *monodia* does not seem to occur until Giovanni Battista Doni, in his *Compendio* (published at Rome in 1635),[5] described *monodie*, 'monodies', as songs for a soloist, in contrast with *chorodie*, 'chorodies', as unison choruses; and in this he not only picked up Plato's distinction, but correctly assumed that even the choruses in classical Greek drama were without harmony. Pietro della Valle, in a letter dated 16 January 1640, slipped the word *monodie*, 'monodies', without comment or definition, into a discussion of early opera and the reciting style.[6] These early uses, though infrequent, were correct, either for the reciting style in general, or for that particular aspect of it here called early recitative. The most frequent historical term for the reciting style, however, was always *stile recitativo* (which is perhaps better not translated 'recitative style', because what we call recitative was only one aspect of it). A less frequent alternative was· *stile rappresentativo* ('representative style', although it was not confined to theatrical representations). G.B. Doni[7] gave the following definitions around 1635:

Stile Recitativo, Rappresentativo e Espressivo is not entirely the same, although commonly no difference is made in it. By *stile Recitativo*, then, we understand today that sort of melody, which can suitably, and gracefully be recited, that is, be sung by one alone in such manner, that the words are understood, whether this is done on the boards of the stage (*sul palco delle scene*), or in Churches, and Oratorios in the manner of dialogues, or indeed in private Chambers, or elsewhere; and finally, by this name we understand every sort of Music, which is sung by one alone to the sound of some instrument, with little duration of the notes, and in such manner, that it approaches common speech; but however with feeling. [If the terms were used precisely, which they were not] by *Rappresentativa* we ought to mean that sort of melody, which is truly appropriate to the stage, that is, for every sort of dramatic action, which one wishes to represent. . .with singing.

In this passage, 'that sort of melody, which can suitably, and gracefully be recited' suggests the lyrical aspect of the reciting style; 'every sort of Music which is sung. . .in such manner, that it approaches common speech' suggests the declamatory aspect of the reciting style. But the emphasis is not on that distinction. The emphasis is on the shared element of recitation. To speak poetry out loud (a familiar experience of the times) was recitation. To body out the recitation in notes was the deliberate purpose of the reciting style.

Then, as we saw, a regular and strophic poem might yield some lyrical, strophic aria such as Giulio Caccini (*c.*1545–1618) composed for perhaps some fifteen years before printing specimens in his *Nuove musiche* (Florence, 1602):[8] i.e. a song in aria style. There is vocal grace and felicity here such as early opera found invaluable in averting the monotony of too continuous a recitative. And a less regular poem in a single stanza might yield some more or less declamatory solo madrigal such as Caccini also included in his *Nuove musiche* (his famous 'Amarilli' is a wonderful example, for which see Plates VI and VII): i.e. a song in arioso style; or again, it might yield a song in recitative style. It was by extending such textures beyond the formal bounds of song that opera gained its crucial novelty: early recitative. Thus there is music in the reciting style which, not being in recitative style, was not crucially novel. And there is music in the reciting style which, being in recitative style, was crucially novel. But from the historical viewpoint of its contemporaries who achieved or witnessed it, all this was recitation in music. *Recitare* is the operative word.

Recitare, to recite, or *cantare per recitare*, to sing in reciting, or *recitar cantando*, to recite singing; terms such as these, rather than merely *cantare*, to sing, are the commonest descriptions. Whatever is properly thus described, from the 1580s when the style recognizably emerged, until somewhere around the 1680s, when the transition into number opera began to gather momentum, is meant here by the reciting style. But we have also to consider what was meant by the *stile antico*, the old style; and by the *prima prattica*, the first practice, as contrasted with the *seconda prattica*, the second practice.

In that adventurous generation which saw the rise of opera there were some great instrumentalists, like Frescobaldi or John Bull or Sweelink, who were undoubted practitioners of the modern style, but not of the reciting style; and others essentially preoccupied with vocal music, like Peri or Caccini or Monteverdi, who were practitioners of the modern style and also of the reciting style. But not everything by Monteverdi in the modern style was also in the reciting style: his polyphonic madrigals, for example, were not. And some adventurous composers of polyphonic madrigals, from Cipriano de Rore through Giaches de Wert, Luzzasco Luzzaschi, Carlo Gesualdo and on, were not practitioners of the reciting style, although Frescobaldi rightly called their works 'modern madrigals'.[9] The 'modern style' is therefore the broader term, within which the 'reciting style' becomes the narrower term.

THE SECOND PRACTICE

It was when he was under attack by Artusi[10] for his polyphonic modern madrigals that Monteverdi seems to have introduced the terms 'first practice' and 'second practice', as explained in an appendix to his *Scherzi musicali* of Venice, 1607, by his brother Giulio Cesare Monteverdi. To illustrate the first practice, there is instanced the still to be respected polyphony in old style, as in Ockeghem, Josquin etc., and 'finally perfected' (*perfectionata ultimamente*) by Adriano Willaert; and this first practice of polyphony is seen as making music 'not the servant, but the mistress of the words'. And to illustrate the second practice there is instanced the now to be preferred polyphony in the modern style, as instigated by its 'first restorer' (*primo rinovatore*, i.e. presumably restoring from classical antiquity), Cipriano de Rore, and continued by Ingegneri (Monteverdi's teacher), Marenzio, Giaches de Wert and Luzzaschi; and this second practice of polyphony is seen as making 'the words the mistress of the music'.

So far, so good: an old practice of polyphony, giving music the priority, is distinguished from a modern practice of polyphony, giving words the priority. That is to contrast two opposites which are different but comparable, and is the natural and only logical interpretation of Monteverdi's terms. But next we read that the second practice was continued 'equally (*parimente*) by Jacopo Peri, by Giulio Caccini, and finally by more exalted spirits' (i.e. presumably Monteverdi and his brother) bent on the 'perfecting of melody (*perfectione de la melodia*)'. This is to bring in what is not a practice of polyphony at all, i.e. the reciting style; this is therefore to contrast two opposites which are not only different, but not comparable in terms of Monteverdi's argument with Artusi. For that which is not counterpoint cannot be either good or bad counterpoint; and an argument which began by being about whether liberties can be taken with counterpoint for the better expression of the words has turned into an argument about whether any counterpoint can be a good expression of the words.

We learn that Monteverdi had a book in hand, or in mind; he never managed to get it out, but he referred to it again in a letter of 22 October 1633.[11] Here Monteverdi merely defined first practice as 'in old kind (*in ordine all'antica*)' and second practice as 'in modern kind (*in ordine alla moderna*)'. Some seventeenth-century writers equated first practice with the music being mistress of the words, second practice with the words being mistress of the music, in no matter what texture of composition: for example, Marco Scacchi in his *Breve discorse sopra la musica moderna*, published at Warsaw in 1649.[12] But others (and perhaps Monteverdi himself at other times) have taken first practice and second practice, more usefully, as a distinction between an old style of counterpoint and a modern style of counterpoint. So understood, the first practice is one narrower division within the broader category of the old style; and the second practice is one narrower division within the broader category of the modern style.

We should distinguish here, it seems, between an issue of principle, which is primary, and an issue of technique, which is secondary although of great practical importance. The issue of principle is whether the words of vocal composition should come before the music. The issue of technique is whether liberties may be taken with counterpoint for the sake of the words; or more radically, whether counterpoint should be replaced by monody for the sake of the words.

On the issue of principle, it was as we have seen thought obvious that the words should come before the music. Why so? Because it was the purpose of art to improve the mind, as Plato taught, and Aristotle in advocating a good musical education since 'young people will not, if they can avoid it, tolerate anything which is not made sweet by pleasure, and music has a natural sweetness.'[13] For some, only the pill of virtuous words could warrant the sugar, like Miles Coverdale[14] who wished 'young men also that have the gift of synging' to 'take their pleasure' in his own not very inspiringly 'wholesome balettes' rather than their usual 'wanton ditties'. For others, even such wanton authors as Ovid could be brought in under the resolute excuse of allegory. Then again, Erasmus deplored 'modern church music' for obscuring the sacred word with too many notes and counterpoints.[15] The English reformers likewise stipulated 'a modest distinct songe, that the same may be as playnely understood, as yf it were read without syngyng.'[16] One and all put words before music in principle.

On the issue of technique, Zarlino defended and Galilei attacked vocal polyphony on exactly the same test of its expressive service to the words. On both sides, the argument was how to match the sound to the sense. Monteverdi was merely summing up a century or more of humanist propaganda in his famous epigram: *L'oratione sia padrona dell' armonia e non serva*, 'speech should be the mistress of the music and not the servant'.[17] The technical issue was merely the issue of how this principle could be most effectively secured; and the real answer, of course, is that there are more ways than one. However, that was not quite how the matter looked in the heat of current controversy.

On the one hand, polyphony of the first practice, i.e. in the old style, was assumed to follow the rules of counterpoint regardless of the words. This is not quite a true and still less a sufficient account of Ockeghem or Josquin or Willaert; but it became retrospectively an idealized model for the baroque learned style or strict style. That in turn produced either rather sterile imitations of Palestrina's supposedly lofty purity, or else splendid baroque works in a tradition which may have been learned and strict but had very little to do with Palestrina.

On the other hand, when polyphony of the late renaissance was of the second practice, and therefore fell within the modern style, it was criticized by conservatives but admired by modernists for taking liberties with the laws of counterpoint. It was the deliberate intention to express wry feelings in wry progressions, anguished feelings in anguished progressions, wild feelings in wild progressions, and the like. The very incorrectness of the counterpoint might be the one factor most expressive of the intemperance of the feeling, and therefore the most correct for the words. Artusi stands on this point for the conservative critic; Monteverdi for the criticized modernist. But who, for Monteverdi,[18] was the ideal theorist, and who the perfect composer, of the first practice of counterpoint? 'The most excellent Zarlino', and Willaert by whom it was 'finally perfected'. And who started the second practice? 'The divine Cipriano Rore', followed among others by Giaches de Wert. But who, for Artusi, was the ideal theorist and who the representative composers of the only true practice of counterpoint? The ideal theorist, Artusi had to admit,[19] was Artusi; representative composers included Willaert, Cipriano de Rore and Giaches de Wert.

Where, then, was this notable difference between counterpoint of the first practice and counterpoint of the second practice, if two of the main composers (Cipriano and de Wert) could be claimed by either camp? And when Zarlino (Monteverdi's choice of theorist for the first practice) gave instructions which are at least as applicable to the second practice, and which in fact read very like guide-lines (as Morley evidently considered forty years later) for the modern madrigal? There was no notable difference; there was merely a normal development of style and technique, with some like Monteverdi more boldly pressing ahead, and others like Artusi more conservatively lagging behind. And even Artusi was not such a laggard as this controversy, taken in isolation, has made him seem. Artusi placed his confidence in reason as he saw it, and derived his reasoning from the acoustic properties of actual sonorous sound, just as Zarlino did. Artusi, too, appealed to classical Greek authority on the paramount importance of expressing the words appropriately in music, and did not see himself as reactionary, or his views as conflicting with the proper humanist service by the music to the words. It is merely that he would not tolerate concrete instances of what he too unadventurously regarded as disservice to the music. He would not consent to an absolute priority of the words over the music; but neither, in practice, of course, would Monteverdi.

It is easy for us, on the long perspective of history, to see that Monteverdi's harmony at its harshest meets Zarlino's and Morley's test of how to make music express the wilder emotions of its verbal text: 'make the harmonie like unto it, that is, somewhat harsh and hard but yet so it offend not.' It was more difficult for his conservative contemporaries, who could see the offence against strict counterpoint (voice-leading in particular), but not the inoffensiveness of using strong techniques for strong emotions, nor the inspiration which made great music out of this unconventional but faithful service to the words. Hence the Monteverdi storm in the Artusi teacup. For seen in perspective, it was a mere storm in a teacup whether Monteverdi's irregular progressions were to be justified by their expressiveness of the words. They are expressive of the words; but history has justified them on still surer grounds. They are expressive both verbally and musically: they are expressive in the absolute; after all these centuries, they bloom for us with living beauty, and on any grounds of argument, 'offend not'.

But, meanwhile, another storm was brewing of which the significance has not thus dwindled in the perspective of history. This was the storm over whether counterpoint is inherently damaging to the words, so that for genuine verbal expressiveness it cannot be mended, but can only be replaced by solo song with subordinate accompaniment—in short, by the reciting style.

History, once again, has decided the argument. In effect, the reciting style was the necessary step forward into the creative future, and more particularly towards the rise of opera. But, of course, it was not the end of vocal counterpoint, which never really stopped (or Monteverdi and his successors would have had to stop composing polyphonic madrigals—as did not happen altogether even through the seventeenth century[20]); and which subsequently renewed itself in the most powerful of late baroque forms. Nor did the pioneers of the reciting style themselves hesitate to include ensembles, madrigals and choruses in their earliest operas. Indeed, we may notice how much their early recitative itself shares with the contemporary madrigals that poignant harshness and chromatic exacerbation of harmony, those fierce modulations and fiercer sideslips into remote chords, that obsessiveness of melody and assertiveness of rhythm which were the marks of modern style around the year 1600, as they were not subsequently in the consolidating generation of Corelli and Alessandro Scarlatti. For to plunge from E major to G major, or from A major to E flat major, or from E flat major to E major, and as abruptly back: these are startling musical experiences some of which would be impossible in Lully or Vivaldi and are not even quite to be matched in Purcell; but Caccini and Peri dared such passages, and above all, as we shall see, Monteverdi dared. Such progressions are drama in themselves, and carry their dramatic words with correspondingly musical conviction. Drama and music move as one adventurous happening there. And such adventurousness was altogether in the modern style.

THE EMULATING STYLE

We have still to consider one further aspect of the modern style, which had a considerable effect on early opera, although hardly on the very earliest. This goes by the historical term: *stile concertato*. To translate this term literally as the 'concerted style' is not quite satisfactory, since that renders only one of two meanings attached to the earliest usages of the term in a musical significance. One meaning is concerting. The other meaning is contending. A rendering which though not quite literal perhaps combines these two meanings acceptably is: the emulating style.

Bottrigari[21] in 1594 was already amusing himself very learnedly over the possible derivation of *concerto* from its Latin meaning 'dispute', whence he gives rather ironically, as his own opinion, *contentione, ò contrasto*, 'contention or contrast'; or alternatively from the Latin *consero*, meaning 'join', by way of the Italian *conserto*, 'intertwined'. Praetorius[22] equated *concerto* (It.) with *concertatio* (Lat., 'contention', from Lat. *concertare*, defined in Lewis and Short as 'to contend with anyone zealously or warmly; esp. to dispute, debate'); but Praetorius failed to add that in Italian the meaning is different, since *concertare* (It.) means not 'to contend' but 'to concert'. *Consertare* (It.) means 'to intertwine'; *consorte* (It.), or *consorto* (It., obsolete), mean as noun 'consort', as adjective 'consorted'.

Concitare (It.) means 'to arouse', hence the *stile concitato*, the agitated style: the term which Monteverdi[23] claimed to have introduced for the use of insistent rhythms, and in particular for rapid reiterations of the

same note, as allegedly first employed in his *Combattimento di Tancredi
e Clorinda* (perf. Venice, 1624). The agitated style can be regarded as
one particular idiom falling within the emulating style; but it is a lesser
classification which had limited historical importance apart from
Monteverdi's proprietary interest in it. The measured tremolo (i.e. the
rapid reiterations of the same note) for which Monteverdi claimed
novelty was by no means without precedents, and subsequently
became a normal resource of instrumental music in various styles. It
became important as a resource, however, and not as a basis for
classification.

The emulating style is itself a division of the modern style, but one
of considerable importance as a basis for classification. The emulating
style—the *stile concertato*—is recognized by the same blend of characteristics to which its ambiguous etymology pointed from the start.
For both the two complementary implications of contending and of
concerting were original and inherent components of the emulating
style. There was a virtuoso contention, among concerted performers.

Thus Giovanni Gabrieli (1557–1612) flung together his massive
contrasts of sonority from groups of singers and instrumentalists, in
parts ostensibly polyphonic but actually chordal more or less tricked
out as polyphonic. Monteverdi wove his radiant duets over a continuo
bass, with the two vocal lines as mutually interwoven as they are
competitively dazzling; and here the emulating style bordered directly
upon the reciting style, with valuable consequences for opera. Again,
the contrast between individual and corporate instruments of the
orchestra, later so well exploited in the *concerto grosso*, the grand
concerto of soloists and ripienists, also appears in opera, rather earlier,
as a product of the emulating style. The trio sonata, too, has relationships both with the vocal duet and with the grand concerto. Most
trio sonatas show the influence of the emulating style by some competitive virtuosity as well as much harmonious balance between the
parts.

The emulating style is thus a reconciliation of opposites quite in the
baroque manner: on the one hand, flamboyant; on the other hand,
affecting. The reciting style shares something of the same ambivalence: on the one hand, simple feeling, from the heart to the heart;
on the other hand, showy display, from the virtuoso to the connoisseur. Opera came to make good use of either quality.

A BLEND OF STYLES IN EARLY OPERA

The originators of opera regarded their works as prime examples of
the modern style. This was true enough; but the elements of modern
style which they used were mixed from the start. Not even the very

earliest operas were wholly in the reciting style, although as wholes they are in the reciting style. There was, indeed, a higher proportion in the reciting style at the very start, and more of that was in actual recitative, than even a few years afterwards (i.e. more in Peri and Caccini than in Monteverdi); but even at the very start there were supplementary elements.

Of these supplementary elements, the many duets and the occasional trios are closest to the reciting style. Their polyphonic touches are of the slightest; so often do they simply move along in thirds, sixths and tenths that the single-mindedness of solo melody is hardly diminished, while at the same time the vocal pleasure and human interest of a concerted sound and sentiment is gained. Four, five or more voices add the contrast of larger ensembles, but these get farther away from the reciting style, and become in effect modern madrigals of the lightly polyphonic and largely homophonic texture usual at this period. It is not always clear whether solo ensembles or actual choruses are meant, and it may even to some extent be optional. The number, however, of madrigalian or choral ensembles declined very steeply even so early as Monteverdi's later operas, except that Roman opera retained more of them, and French opera presently began and continued with many more. The very early operas inherited their ensembles, and the dances which often accompanied them, from the established traditions of ballets and interludes. These ensembles are valuable for the artistic contrast they afford of texture and sonority; but they can also be justified dramatically, since the words are usually apt to the action, and often make shrewd commentary upon it, like the choruses in classical Greek drama on which they were evidently modelled. The service of the words is still the object; and to this extent, the choruses still honour the principle of the reciting style although not its idioms.

There are next the instrumental toccatas and fanfares, the overtures and sinfonias, the preludes and the ritornellos and the non-vocal dances, all of which are technically unconnected with the reciting style, yet artistically are more than ever necessary as a supplement to it, without which the vocal substance of an opera would lack a proper frame and a proper spacing. Both as a varied accompaniment for the voices, and as an independent contrast to the voices, instrumental sonorities are an integral and not an incidental ingredient in a drama unfolding as much in the music as in the words. Opera needs an orchestra as well as singers.

The orchestras for the very early operas were taken over from the ballets, interludes and other colourful entertainments which in this as in other respects were the immediate background to opera. Throughout the seventeenth century, orchestras of somewhat larger scope and variety than the manuscripts reveal may have continued to support

some performances of opera, although the surviving evidence is too
incomplete to confirm more than very occasional details, and the
probability is that small string orchestras predominated through most
of that century. There was never any instrumental doubling of solo
voices, which would be quite contrary to both the spirit and the
technique of the reciting style. But the larger vocal ensembles (though
not the duets nor perhaps the trios) were very likely to have been
doubled by instruments, and the choruses (both those danced and
those not danced) were almost certain to have been doubled by instruments. Even the solos, though not doubled, might have instrumental
obbligatos: hardly at all, if ever, in pure recitative; but perhaps, with
reticence and tact, in passages of arioso character; and more certainly
and extensively in aria. There is that magnificent specimen, 'Possente
spirto', which makes as we shall see the musical and dramatic centre-
piece of Monteverdi's *Orfeo* (Mantua, 1607), and in which a pair of
violins, a pair of cornettos, and an immense double harp take it in
turns to provide an accompaniment and a ritornello to successive
stanzas. Such elaboration was probably unusual and perhaps unknown in opera for some decades thereafter, though possibly not so
unusual in the more extravagant court ballets and interludes. What is
certainly unusual is to find the elaboration written out. If or when it
did occur, habitual techniques of improvisation must ordinarily have
taken care of it,[24] until the orchestration of operas began to fill out
again in the closing years of the seventeenth century.

In all such supporting and enriching uses of the orchestra or of
individual instruments, the artistic justification is that the unfolding of
the drama is amplified and diversified and intensified, but not distracted or obscured. On that condition, the instrumental contribution
also in a manner serves the words. It does not serve them directly, like
the singing; but it serves them indirectly, and it serves them well, since
it too follows out a succession of moods and carries forward an
unspoken commentary. It is not only in Wagner, but already in
Monteverdi, and at least to some extent in most opera worthy of the
name, that the orchestra is capable of taking part almost like another
actor in the drama.

The supplementary elements which were carried over from interludes and other theatre music into opera, and which took fresh forms
there, are not parts of the reciting style. But they are parts of the
modern style; and the whole entertainment to which they contribute,
namely opera, came into history under the influence of the reciting
style. We may turn next to the historic events by which early recitative
and early opera made their joint and inseparable appearance at
Florence in the very last years of the sixteenth century.

PART TWO

The Achievement of Opera

VIII
Across the Threshold
꒰•᷇ᵕ•᷆꒱

THREE PASTORALS NEAR TO OPERA

Early in 1590, Florentine old-style dating, i.e. in 1591 modern dating, two pastorals by Laura Guidiccioni, to music by Emilio de' Cavalieri (who is discussed later), were performed in Florence. One of these was *Il satiro*; the other was *La disperazione di Fileno*. Angelo Solerti[1] described *Il satiro* as having vanished without trace, and *La disperazione di Fileno* as only known to have had the characters: Pastore, Fileno, Ninfa, Venere, Cupido, Spiriti, Clori, Negromante. A thoroughly pastoral company, we conclude; and in all probability their deeds and utterances were not less pastoral. But we should very much like to see for ourselves, and to know how Cavalieri handled them in music.

In the year 1595, a third pastoral by the same authors was performed in Florence: *Il Giuoco della cieca* (i.e. Blind-man's-Buff, or more strictly, Blind-woman's). The source for Laura Guidiccioni's text was that favourite recourse of early baroque imitators, Giovanni Battista Guarini's pastoral drama *Il pastor fido* (first perf. 1585, first publ. 1590). Solerti actually found a poetic text, which being modified from Guarini's he very much hoped might be taken to be Laura Guidiccioni's; and with this in mind, he printed it. But unfortunately he was unable to confirm his supposition in any way. Solerti also wished very much to claim for Laura Guidiccioni and Cavalieri, on the strength of these three lost pastorals, the priority for the earliest operas; but while we lack the pastorals themselves, on which to make a definite judgement, we have enough indirect information about them to render this claim almost certainly inadmissible.

Our information, as we shall shortly see, is that the music of these three lost pastorals was, indeed, continuous throughout the action, a fact which relates them to opera; but that this music comprised not recitative but aria, which precludes their having carried the action forward as much in the music as in the words. Thus on the definition maintained throughout this present book, they were not operas. This view is confirmed by the barely operatic nature, a few years later, of Cavalieri's *Rappresentatione di anima, et di corpo* (perf. and publ. Rome, 1600), which has some but not much dramatic characterization and dramatic development. It may perhaps be accepted as an opera, but only just; and indeed there are good modern authorities who do not accept it as an opera. The three lost pastorals cannot be accepted as operas at all. Much credit is due to Cavalieri for his contribution, and it was given to him freely by his own contemporaries; but not the credit for the earliest opera.

DAFNE: THE EARLIEST OPERA

During the Carnival at Florence, early in 1597, Florentine old-style dating, that is to say 1598, the first performance was presented of a pastoral drama, *Dafne*, under the patronage of Corsi, on a libretto by Rinuccini, to music in some part by Corsi but mainly by Peri. We have every reason to believe that this was the earliest opera. We do not know quite what manner of poetic text Laura Guidiccioni provided for Cavalieri in their three lost pastorals, nor do we know whether the arias to which he composed it included any degree of the declamatory aspect appropriate to opera. We only know that *Dafne* was shortly afterwards put forward by its authors and accepted by its contemporaries as something different; and that this difference was ascribed above all to Rinuccini under Corsi's instigation, with Peri as their musical executant.

We gain the impression that the last narrow but crucial step into opera was taken through a deliberate courtship, not of poetry by music, but of music by poetry. Plenty of later composers have courted plenty of later dramatists for librettos; but at the origins of opera, we do not read of a musician soliciting a poet for poetry practicable as a libretto; we do read of a poet soliciting a musician, or at the least indebted to a musician, for music practicable as drama. The poet was Rinuccini, and the musician was Peri. The order of events is reasonably well established by Rinuccini's account, not long afterwards, in the dedication to his next libretto, *L'Euridice* (publ. Florence, 1600; and since the dedication is dated 4 October 1600, that was the actual year in modern-style dating):

> It has been the opinion of many, Most Christian Queen, that the ancient Greeks and Romans sang entire tragedies on the stage (*sulle scene*); but such a noble manner of reciting (*recitare*), has not only not been renewed, but, so far as I know, not even attempted until now by anybody, and this I thought a defect of modern music, very far

inferior to the ancient. But M.[aestro] Jacopo Peri completely took away from my mind the thought thus formed: when, having heard the intention of signor Jacopo Corsi and myself, he set to music with so much grace the story (*favola*) of Dafne (written by me, only to make a simple test—*fare una semplice prova*—of what the song of our age could do) which pleased incredibly those few who heard it.

Whence, sig. Jacopo [Corsi] having taken courage, and given better form to the same story, and performed it again in his house, it was heard and commended not only by the nobility of all this favoured country (*patria*) [Tuscany], but by the most serene Gran Duchessa and the most illustrious Cardinals Dal Monte and Montaldo. [There were indeed a number of revivals, some on the large scale.]

Peri gave a similar account in his dedication to the score of *L'Euridice* as composed by him (perf. Florence, 6 October 1600; publ. Florence, dedication dated 6 February 1600, Florentine old-style, i.e. 1601):

Although Signor Emilio del Cavalieri, first of all others, that I know, with marvellous invention caused us to hear our Music on the Stage; nevertheless it pleased Signori Jacopo Corsi, and Ottavio Rinuccini (back in the year 1594) that I employing it in another form, should set to music the story (*favola*) of Dafne, written by Signor Ottavio [Rinuccini], to make a simple test of what the Song of our age could do. Wherefore having seen, that it was a matter of Dramatic poetry, and that nevertheless one had to imitate the speaker with song (and without doubt one never spoke singing) I judged that the ancient Greeks, and Romans (who according to the opinion of many sang on the Stage entire Tragedies) used a harmoniousness (*armonia*), which going beyond that of ordinary speech, fell so much short of the melodiousness (*melodia*) of song, that it took on the form of something in the middle. . . . And because of this, laying aside every other manner of singing heard up to now, I devoted myself entirely to searching out the imitation, which is needed for these poems.

Now Rinuccini, having suggested that 'the ancient Greeks and Romans sang entire tragedies on the stage' (i.e. dialogue as well as choruses), insisted that 'such a noble manner of reciting, has not only not been renewed, but, so far as I know, not even attempted until now by anybody.' Since Rinuccini can hardly have overlooked the three Florentine pastorals of 1591 (modern-style) and of 1595, he evidently regarded them as not having served or even tried to serve that purpose, which he himself believed to be beyond the reach of 'modern music', until Peri, 'having heard the intention of signor Jacopo Corsi and myself', convinced him to the contrary by setting *Dafne*. And Rinuccini made plain that he had written the poem of *Dafne* with this express intention: i.e. 'to make a simple test of what the song of our age could do.' It would seem that when Peri responded to the challenge, Rinuccini was agreeably surprised with the results. He had not expected 'the song of our age' to be so successful as a dramatic medium.

When Peri, on the other hand, gave such generous credit to Cavalieri for having 'first of all others, that I know, with marvellous invention caused us to hear our Music on the Stage', he was surely referring to the three lost pastorals. We may therefore accept it that these, while not impressing Rinuccini as dramatic music, did impress Peri as having brought the reciting style if not into a dramatic performance, at least on to the stage. It again follows that Cavalieri's music in the three lost pastorals was incidental rather than integral to the drama, thus making out of the reciting style a musical entertainment for the stage but not an opera. For Peri continued, concerning 'our Music', that 'I employing it in another form' and in 'a matter of Dramatic poetry' encountered the necessity of 'laying aside every other manner of singing heard up to now'. But what, in such a context, could Peri have meant by 'another form'? He could have meant, and it seems most probable that he did mean, the declamatory aspect of the reciting style, which enabled him to make it not merely incidental but integral to the drama, and thereby to achieve the earliest opera—basically, in early recitative.

CAVALIERI'S CONTRIBUTION

There were certainly rival claims to having achieved the earliest opera, or to having contributed to the origins of opera that indispensable new ingredient here described as the declamatory aspect of the reciting style—i.e. early recitative. Cavalieri's claim, of which Peri's preface quoted above includes so gentlemanly a rebuttal, was set out in almost as gentlemanly a fashion for Cavalieri by his publisher Alessandro Guidotti, acting as his spokesman or his mouthpiece in the dedication and preface to the work which can on a generous interpretation be viewed (though it is not viewed by every modern authority) as the earliest surviving opera (Emilio de' Cavalieri, *Rappresentatione di anima, et di corpo*, perf. and publ. Rome, 1600). Guidotti, in language much too similar to Rinuccini's and Peri's for mere coincidence, called this work 'some singular, and novel compositions of Music, made in the likeness of that style, with which it is said, that the ancient Greeks and Romans on their stages, and in their theatres (*nelle scene, e teatri*) were accustomed to move the spectators to different emotions.' For his success in 'reviving this ancient usage' Cavalieri had been praised, i.e. for his success 'in the three Pastorals', namely *Il Satiro* and *La Disperazione* of 1590 (1591 modern-style dating) and *Il Giuoco della cieca* of 1595; while the tears drawn by Vittoria Archilei in reciting (*recitando*) the second of these, and the laughter aroused by the character of Fileno, should serve as models for the present 'recitation in music (*recitatione in musica*)'. We shall, however, see that while there is indeed some recitative in Cavalieri's *Rappresentatione di anima, et di corpo*, there is far more polyphonic madrigal, chorus and dance; and there may have been even less recitative, or more probably none, in Cavalieri's three lost pastorals.

Guidotti's dedication to Cavalieri's *Rappresentatione di anima, et di corpo* is dated 3 September 1600. Rinuccini's dedication to the text of his *L'Euridice* is dated 4 October 1600, one month later; and Peri's dedication to his score of *L'Euridice* is dated 6 February 1600 (Florentine old-style dating, i.e. 1601 modern-style dating), four months later again. The similarities between Rinuccini's wording and Peri's wording are still closer, sometimes amounting to verbal correspondence; but both are strikingly similar in certain phrases to Guidotti's on behalf of Cavalieri. It would therefore seem that Rinuccini and Peri, having recently encountered Cavalieri's claim to priority in opera, were specifically concerned to deny it, while adding, in Peri's case, the willing and honourable concession that Cavalieri did actually have the priority in the more limited respect of first introducing the reciting style into stage performances. That is almost certainly a fair statement of the matter.

PERI'S ACHIEVEMENT

The account next to be quoted is still fuller and more circumstantial, but rather pointedly contains no reference to Cavalieri, nor to Caccini either, whose own not very gentlemanly assertions will be considered shortly. This account is by Marco da Gagliano, a contemporary and a colleague of Rinuccini and of Peri, and evidently a staunch supporter of their party. After the early seventeenth century, Gagliano had himself become probably the most eminent of the Florentine composers; and he showed his practical admiration for Rinuccini by setting the same text of Rinuccini's *Dafne* in a new score of his own (perf. Mantua, 1608, publ. Florence, 1608), from his preface to which (dated 20 October 1608) the following is taken:

Having discussed little by little the manner used by the ancients in representing their tragedies, how they introduced the choruses, whether they used singing and of what kinds, and similar matters: sig. Ottavio Rinuccini devoted himself to composing [i.e. in poetry] the story of Dafne, sig. Jacopo Corsi, of honoured memory, a lover of all learning and particularly of music, in such manner that among all the musicians he came with good reason to be called Father, composed [i.e. in music] some airs on part of it, becoming enchanted with which, being resolved to see what effect it would make on the stage (*su la scena*), together with sig. Ottavio [Rinuccini] conveyed his thoughts to sig. Jacopo Peri, [a man] most expert in counterpoint and a singer of extreme refinement: who, having heard their intention and approved the part of the airs already composed, devoted himself to composing the others which pleased sig. Corsi beyond measure, and on the occasion of an evening party at the Carnival of the year 1597 [i.e. 1598 modern-style dating] caused it to be represented (*la fece rappresentare*) in the presence of the most excellent Sig. Don Giovanni Medici, and some of the principal gentlemen of our city [of Florence]. The pleasure and astonishment which this novel spectacle produced in the spirits of the audience cannot be expressed, suffice it only that on the many times that it has been recited (*recitata*), it has aroused the same admiration and the same delight. . . . [Rinuccini followed this success with his *Euridice*, where] sig. Jacopo Peri again found so artful a manner of reciting in song (*quella artifiziosa maniera di recitare cantando*), that all Italy admired it. . . . [Then came the Arianna of Rinuccini and Monteverdi. And] such was the origin of representations in music (*l'origini delle rappresentazioni in musica*).

The above statement claims firmly for Rinuccini and Peri, under the creative patronage of Corsi, the origins of opera; and for Rinuccini and Monteverdi (whose lost *Arianna* was performed at Mantua in that same year, 1608, on 28 May, between the performance of Gagliano's *Dafne* in January and its publication not before 20 October) it claims the continuation of opera.

CACCINI'S EXAGGERATED CLAIMS

Caccini, so conspicuous by his absence from Gagliano's story, made claims to priority which were not modest, and which were set out, on a number of occasions, both by himself and by others. For example, in the dedication to his own rival *Euridice* (perf. Florence, 1602, publ. Florence, February 1600, Florentine old-style, i.e. 1601, and setting the same libretto, by Rinuccini, as had just previously been set with such distinction by Peri), Caccini described his work as being in that same 'representative style (*stile rappresentativo*)' which he had already 'used on other occasions, many years ago', in a number of 'madrigals of mine of that time', composed in the manner discussed during the flourishing of Bardi's Camerata. In the preface to his *Nuove musiche* (Florence, 1602), Caccini elaborated his position, again referring to his early (solo) madrigals as 'a beginning in these songs for one voice alone', composed 'in that very style, which has since served me for the stories which were represented in song (*rappresentate cantando*) at Florence.'

Here much depends on what we take this term *stile rappresentativo* to mean in that context. Not literally theatrical, or it could not apply to Caccini's early madrigals; and not in any extended sense recitative, since that would be both longer and freer than a Caccini madrigal. But we may well describe a Caccini madrigal as being a solo song more or less in recitative style: as leaning, in short, more or less towards the declamatory aspect of the reciting style; and what this might imply can be amplified from Caccini's own notable statement in the preface to his *Euridice*: 'I have used a certain casualness (*sprezzatura*), which I think has something noble, believing that in it I have approached more nearly to natural speech.' This statement, too, was elaborated by Caccini in the preface to his *Nuove musiche*:

> I thought to introduce a sort of music, through which one could almost speak in harmony, using in it (as I have said at other times) a certain noble casualness of song, moving sometimes through some falseness [of harmonic grammar], yet holding the bass firm.

Castiglione[2] had early in the sixteenth century defined as *una certa sprezzatura* ('a certain casualness' or 'nonchalance') that kind of easy good manners which gives a man the air of fine breeding all the better for his not putting on fine airs. The 'ease and poise of the consummate dancer' have also been found by Nino Pirrotta[3] described in the sixteenth century as *sprezzatura*. And Caccini,[4] in his (second and different) *Nuove musiche* (Florence, 1614) later equated *sprezzatura* with that *leggiadria* or 'gracefulness', which: 'taking away from the song a certain limited narrowness and dryness', which it would have were it to be 'done in time (*fatto a tempo*)', thereby 'renders it pleasing, wayward and airy (*piacevole, licenzioso e arioso*).'

Clearly there is a manner of performance implied here, as well as a manner of composing; and clearly the two are intimately related. Caccini the virtuoso singer contributed much to Caccini the reformer of vocal music; and while we can hardly allow Filipo Vitali (?–1653) in his preface to his *Aretusa* (perf. and publ. Rome, 1620) to remain unchallenged in calling Caccini 'the inventor', no less, 'of the grace of singing, and of the charm of aria compositions (*musiche a aria*)', we may certainly accept it that Caccini did rare service to the vocal art. Peri the virtuoso singer likewise contributed to Peri the reformer of vocal music. But Peri, born in 1561, seems to have been substantially the younger man (the date of Caccini's birth is not exactly known); and it is therefore very credible that Caccini ('at a very young age', as Pietro de' Bardi reported) opened the way to that particular eloquence of idiom and grace of performance for which both of them soon gained such resounding reputations.

This same too-flattering compliment to Caccini, as 'inventor of the new style', recurs in a manuscript called *Prima parte de' discorsi*[5] by Severo Bonini (1582–1663), which is dated about 1650 by Gloria Rose[6] on a consideration of the composers there appearing as in course of becoming established. At the same time, Bonini borrowed much from Caccini's *Nuove musiche* without acknowledgement; possibly he felt it on his conscience that he owed him a certain unacknowledged debt; undoubtedly he was born too late to rate as an altogether contemporary witness. Bonini was, however, gracious enough, speaking as a Florentine, to concede that 'first among the foreigners was sig. Claudio Monteverdi, who enriched this style with rare ways and new thoughts in his story entitled Arianna.'

Caccini, in short, was at pains to let us know how early he embarked on that 'representative style' in which he subsequently composed his undoubted opera, *Euridice*. But this information was disingenuous, since the 'representative style' of his early madrigals (which if he really composed them while a member of Bardi's circle would date from very substantially before the *Dafne* of Rinuccini and Peri, and from somewhat before the three lost pastorals of Laura Guidiccioni and Cavalieri) was not yet by any means the early recitative which made opera a possibility.

If Galilei may have been the first in that circle to compose deliberately solo songs (and this, if anything, constitutes Galilei's small priority), then Caccini may have been the first to compose such songs with an accompaniment conceived not as parts but as chords above a bass. Both these claims, like all others of the kind, must be regarded as highly qualified and at best precarious; but there may be some such qualified truth in both of them. That does not define Caccini, still less Galilei, as the ultimate originator of opera; it merely puts Galilei a long way down and Caccini a long way up on the roster of those who contributed towards the origins of opera.

Caccini's contribution was not only his supposed claim to originality in deliberately conceiving an accompaniment as chords rather than as parts. This distinction is really too elusive in practice to comprise any one man's originality; for what are we to say of those many sixteenth-century songs which appear in versions sometimes with bass and inner parts (optionally for voices or instruments or both or for lute or keyboard intabulation) and sometimes with bass alone (for chordal improvisation not necessarily much different in execution)?

Caccini's contribution was rather his inclination in his (solo) madrigals (as opposed to some of his arias) away from the lyrical aspect and towards the declamatory aspect of the reciting style. Caccini's early (solo) madrigals, on which he himself claimed priority, are indeed songs more or less in recitative style: now rather nearer to aria for symmetry of melody and momentum of bass; now rather nearer to recitative for speech-like flexibility of melody and stability of bass; yet never in actual recitative, since they are shaped to a formal ending, whereas actual recitative is open-ended. In the closing years of the sixteenth century, songs in recitative style grew rather more frequent, and such songs were presently drawn (together with simple arias and ensemble choruses and much else besides) into the earliest operas. But not till actual, open-ended early recitative emerged out of them was the last necessary resource for opera developed. We seem to have no confirming evidence for Caccini's having had any priority in that particular development, nor for Cavalieri; but there is some confirmation for Peri. Possibly the most personal contribution of Caccini was that he brought such admirable *sprezzatura* into the reciting style; and that never deserted him.

DONI'S BALANCED SUMMARY

The account given above of priorities in the origins of opera may be amplified and supported by a careful reading of two further passages, one from a contemporary witness of the events recounted, the other from an eminent historian who was in correspondence with him. The witness was Pietro de' Bardi; the historian was Giovanni Battista Doni (1594–1647). An earlier portion of Pietro de' Bardi's famous letter to Doni on the origins of opera has already been quoted for his account of Bardi's Camerata, and the reader may wish to turn back to that (p. 85) before going on to the later portion quoted below. The letter was written in answer to a request from Doni, and is dated 16 December 1634. Pietro de' Bardi, in spite of his close family interest in the matter, told Doni a very honest and attractive story.[7] Having, in the earlier portion of his letter, given warm credit to his father Giovanni de' Bardi, and to Galilei for his early share in the activities of Giovanni de' Bardi's once influential Camerata, and having allotted due priority to Caccini but equal praise both to Caccini and to Peri for the graceful development of the reciting style, Pietro de' Bardi continued with the following cordial testimony to the priority—in staging an actual drama of words and music in the representative style—of Rinuccini and of Peri, under the inspiration, support and encouragement of Corsi. This last is especially noteworthy since Pietro de' Bardi's own father Giovanni de' Bardi and his father's social and artistic rival Corsi certainly appear not to have been always on the best of terms. Either we have now exaggerated the element of hostility expressed through their undoubted rivalry; or, more probably, Pietro de' Bardi remembered better, or better preferred to remember, the element of mutual interest and respect which must also have entered into that historic relationship. Not for the first time, we recognize the complicated connections and conflicting emotions which lie behind the Florentine origins of opera.

Pietro de' Bardi continued:

> The first poetry, which was caused to be sung on the stage in the representative style (*istile rappresentativo*), was the Story of Dafne by Signor Ottavio Rinuccini, set to music by Peri with a small number of sounds [and] with brevity of scenes for performing the scenes briefly, and recited in a small room and privately sung, and I remained stupefied with amazement.
>
> It was sung above an ensemble (*corpo*) of instruments, the which arrangement was then followed in other plays. Caccini and Peri were greatly indebted to signor Ottavio [Rinuccini]; but more to signor Jacopo Corsi, who being fired, and not content, with what was not excellent in this art, instructed these composers, with excellent thoughts and marvellous teachings, such as were fitting to so noble a matter. Such teachings were followed by Peri and Caccini in all their compositions of this kind and were composed (*composte*) by them in various manners. After Dafne, many stories were presented (*rappresentate*) by signor Ottavio himself, who, as good poet and good teacher alike, together with the most friendly Corsi, who was open-handed with his liberality, were heard with great applause; the most famous such [stories] being Euridice and Arianna, besides many little stories (*favolette*) composed by the said Giulio Caccini and Jacopo Peri. Nor were there lacking many others to imitate them, who in Florence, the first seat of this kind of music, and in other cities of Italy, but most in Rome, acquitted themselves, and acquit themselves wonderfully on the theatrical stage (*nella scena rappresentativa*); among the first of these seems to stand Monteverdi.

We may see next what good use Doni made of this and other still available information in his own very balanced, extensive and interesting comments. He made it his business to extract whatever he could from living witnesses, and in this he did later historians an invaluable service. Under the title, 'Of the origin that singing in the Theatre had in our times' (Ch. IX, p.22), Doni wrote:[8]

> In every period it has been customary to insert in dramatic Plays some kind of song, either in the form of Intermedi between one Act

and the other, or indeed within the same Act, on some occasion of the subject represented. But when they began to sing whole Plays entire (*cantare tutte le Azioni intere*), the memory of this is still fresh; since before those things that Sig. Emilio del Cavaliere a Roman Gentleman, and very knowledgeable in Music, did, I do not think anything was practised which deserves to be named. . . . It is advisable to know, however, that those melodies [composed by Cavalieri for theatrical productions before 1600] are very different from the ones of today, which are done in the style generally called Recitative; those [earlier examples] not being other than little arias with many artifices, of repetitions, echoes, and similar things, which have nothing to do with the good and true Theatrical Music, of which Sig. Emilio was unable to have knowledge in the absence of those pieces of information which are extracted from the ancient Writers. . . . [Concerning the music in theatrical productions before 1600:] This, then, can be said, that it was the first age of Theatrical Music, after so many centuries reborn in Florence, like so many other noble professions, in the manner that has been seen, although with beginnings very feeble and lowly. But notable growth was made then with the introduction of the so-called *stile recitativo*; which has been universally accepted, and practised today by many, being aware that universally it gives more pleasure than the madrigalian style, on account of the great loss which occurs there of the meaning of the words. This style began likewise in Florence, around the same time; although later it was introduced in theatres (*nelle Scene*), that is, there around 1600, the beginning of this century, and of the second age of this theatrical music.

Doni then turns back to an earlier stage (i.e. before the actual rise of opera 'around 1600'), and gives credit to Giovanni de' Bardi for his 'great love of antiquity and of music', so that his house became a flourishing centre of discussion, put into practice by Vincenzo Galilei, who 'was the first to compose melodies for one voice alone.' This was the 'passionate lament of Count Ugolini written by Dante', sung 'over an ensemble of viols'; then, on the success of this, 'in the same style he composed part of the Lamentations of Jeremiah.' Caccini, 'young in age, but a graceful and lively singer', took up 'such a kind of music, composing and singing many pieces to the sound of a single instrument', i.e. a lute, 'in imitation of Galilei, but in a more attractive and graceful style', on canzonettas and sonnets by excellent poets. Then Jacopo Peri, 'an expert composer and famous singer', began to rival Caccini 'in this *stile recitativo*', as Corsi took over from Bardi as patron and practitioner, particularly through his friendship with Rinuccini, whose combination of musical with poetical talents brought about the next stage; and 'the first action which was represented in this new style of music was Dafne.' Concerning this new style of theatrical performance, Doni wrote (p. 25)—and we may well leave him the last word on the matter:

First Peri, and Caccini. . .through the continued assistance and help which they had from sign. Jacopo [Corsi], and from sig. Ottavio [Rinuccini], arrived at that point, as is seen, which in this style can scarcely be done better; and likewise Monteverdi received very great help from Rinuccini in the Arianna. . .for with much docility and attention these three Musicians [Peri, Caccini and Monteverdi] always listened to the very useful teachings which those two Gentlemen supplied to them. . . . And thus it is known that the true architects of this Theatrical Music have properly been signori Jacopo Corsi, and Ottavio Rinuccini; and the first shapers (*formatori*) of this style the three Musicians named. . . . [Ch. X, p. 25:] How much then not only Poetry but also Music is obliged to the memory of sig. Ottavio Rinuccini can be known from what we have said. . . . [Ch. XLIV, p. 127, on why operatic progress had in Doni's opinion slowed down:] Fifth, and last, because it is not so easy to find the likes of Rinuccini. . . .

Opera Achieved

❧❧❧

THE STRUCTURE OF *DAFNE*

Dafne, which Doni and others certainly seem to have regarded as the earliest opera, exemplifies the poetic construction for which Doni gave Rinuccini the highest credit.[1] Long and medium lines of free verse are recommended by Doni (p. 17) for theatrical dialogue and action (*ragionamenti scenici*), ordinarily appearing in recitative. Short lines with systematic rhyme-schemes are recommended for reflective 'choruses', including solos or duets to passages marked *coro* in the poetry. The action of *Dafne* uses a blend of eleven-syllable and seven-syllable lines, partly unrhymed but mostly in somewhat irregular rhyme-schemes. The lyrics tend to shorter and more symmetrical lines in more intricate but also more regular structures, including strophic repetitions and refrains. This was the normal construction of the pastoral drama, though turned deliberately here towards its musical potential.

Only six short passages from the music appear to survive, one of them discovered by William Porter and discussed in a crucial article[2] as indeed a fragment of early recitative and thus of 'true theatrical music'. Though much simpler than later specimens, it sufficiently matches Peri's own description in the preface to his *Euridice*:

> I knew, equally, that in our speech some vowels (*voci*) are intoned [i.e. vocalized] in such a way, that harmony can be established there, and that in course of talking one passes through many others, which are not intoned, until one returns to another capable of moving to a new consonance. And having regard to what means, and what accents serve us in grief, in rejoicing, and in like cases, I made the bass to move in time to these, now more, now less [long on one note], according to the emotions, and I held it firm through false, and through good proportions [dissonances and consonances] until, gliding through various notes, the voice of the speaker,

arriving at what in ordinary speech is intoned, opens the way to a new chord.

Ex. 1. ?Jacopo Peri, seemingly from one of the first tentative versions of Rinuccini's Dafne *(Florence, Carnival 1597, Florentine old-style dating, i.e. 1598), messenger's description of Dafne's transformation (my transcription but based on William Porter's transcription[2]):*

The chief feature described by Peri which does not appear in this example is that bold and theoretically ungrammatical use of unrelated dissonance ('false proportions') which became so conspicuous in the declamatory uses of the reciting style. For the lyrical uses of the reciting style, which were also part of the early operatic mixture, the following brief example surviving in the Brussels MS shows charm, if not much distinction, and it may be by Corsi, or rather more probably by Peri.

Ex. 2 ?Jacopo Peri, chorus (here shown as tune and bass, but inner parts are likely) from Dafne *(Florence, 1598)—re-barred to show rhythm; my realization, but based on William Porter's transcription:*[2]

[Kindly God, who drives the burning car around heaven]

THE STORY OF *DAFNE*

The prologue to *Dafne* is sung (with that rather peculiar but unde-niable appropriateness which so often blended historical personages with mythological in Neoplatonically influenced works of art) by the Roman poet Ovid. In view of Ovid's well-known interest in matters amatory, of which he goes out of his way to remind us here, he is perhaps as suitable a personage as any to announce that he is about to demonstrate the perilous folly of those who hold cheap the power of Love. This he tells us in rhyming hendecasyllabic quartets so entirely similar to Rinuccini's prologue to his subsequent *Euridice* that we should expect to find (and to a fragmentary extent perhaps we do find) a similar musical treatment here on the part of Peri. This treatment is striking, since it has the form of a strophic aria, but the texture of a flexible recitative. It is, in fact, an aria in recitative style.

Thus William Porter may be justified in claiming that the single strophe of music, apparently for the *Dafne* prologue, which was found by Federico Ghisi at Florence, contains all that the complete prologue vocally requires. Behind this form of prologue there lie those tradi-tional formulas on the basis of which it was habitual to improvise music for *ottave rime* (eight-line stanzas commonly set to music as pairs of four-line stanzas), *terze rime* (three-line stanzas with linked rhyme-schemes) and other strophic forms of sufficient regularity and predic-tability. It is an unexpected cross between popular technique and sophisticated intention, resulting in a freely declamatory vocal line still supported on a rounded, symmetrical and indeed recurrent struc-ture; and it is in all probability at or near the very starting-point of recitative.

Now a chorus of nymphs and shepherds, and individuals drawn from them, briefly complain, to mixed poetry, of the monstrous serpent or dragon, whom Apollo with exemplary promptitude slays by an arrow from his bow. (For a probable view of the dragon, see Plate V.) Two lines of chorus here are taken from Rinuccini's previous text for the third Interlude of 1589, but the rest of the poetry seems to be new. Perhaps the dragon of 1589 (familiar to us in appearance from an original scene-design and sketch by Bernardo Buontalenti, and also an engraving by Agostino Caracci[3]) did service a second time round? Apollo, a little inflated by his victory, and thus all too vulnerable to that pride which goes before a fall, congratulates himself on the power of his bow. The chorus congratulates him on his golden mantle; on his light illuminating the heavens through the fearful, cold shadow (the familiar Neoplatonic contrast); and on his glory renewing the plants and all life across the land.

Accosted by Venus and Cupid, however, Apollo cannot resist teasing the formidable little god of love on the subject of his small bow and arrows, asking in particular whether Cupid intends to 'uncover his eyes or strike in the dark (*sbendi tu gli occhi o ferisci a l'oscura*)'. But 'if you want to know what a blind archer can do', replies Cupid pointedly enough, 'ask [Neptune] the King of the Waves, ask Jove in Heaven, ask through the deep shadows of the fearful, dark kingdom, ask Pluto, if he was safe!' And still Apollo will not be warned. The line-lengths and the rhyme-schemes vary exquisitely, but of the music we have only a strophic setting for the first half (to repeat for the second half) of an *ottava rima,* a stanza of eight hendecasyllabic lines all with one pair of alternating rhymes, sung by Cupid as a lilting aria. Dafne now appears, herself armed with bow and arrows, and hunting through the forest in a mood as chaste as Diana. But she is not Diana; and when she finds Apollo eager and flattering in pursuit of her, she tells him insistently: 'I am a mortal woman, not a goddess from heaven.' He replies: 'If such light glows in mortal beauty, heaven's no longer matters to me.' He tells her that her beautiful eyes have gained her a noble prey with no arrow shot by her, nor twang of her bow; and he would like to be her companion in archery, and hunt with her. But she wants no other company than her own bow, and dismisses him.

It is Cupid's turn to boast to his mother Venus of what his bow has done. She chides him for causing such weeping and lamentation in heaven and on earth, upon which he reminds her that he caused laughter too when she could not hide her deceit (with Mars) from the jealous smith (her husband Vulcan); and she has the grace to blush. The chorus comments very Neoplatonically that no living creature can hide from love, seeing that 'even the elements burn and love with a fine fire, and accord together.' Only silly mortals arm their hearts against love's golden arrows, but in vain; for there is no heart in human breast which does not feel love. The poetry is lyrical, symmetrical, elegant and enchanting, and most fit for music; but no music survives from this portion of the opera.

There enters a messenger with astounding news. At first with interruptions from the chorus, then in a longer speech, he narrates how Dafne spurned her celestial lover, and prayed to heaven for succour, whereupon in one moment she became immobile, her arms grew leaves, and she turned into a tree. The fragment of recitative found by William Porter[4] is to words of which the opening corresponds to the messenger's opening here, and the sequel shows enough resemblance for William Porter to accept it for an earlier version of Rinuccini's text than our oldest surviving print (Florence, 1600). From Rinuccini's preface to his *Euridice* we know that several attempts were made at the poetry and the music of *Dafne*. This appears to be one of the attempts; and we have no specimen of actual recitative which can be dated earlier.

Apollo returns to tell us that he, an immortal, languishes and dies: *ben ch'immortal, languisco e moro.* 'But always will I make your leaves and branches a garland for my golden hair', even as his noble lyre shall take up the story eternally. This, in short, shall be the transformation, not the end, of Apollo's love for Dafne. Now the poetry becomes compactly allusive. 'Let the beautiful swans of Dirce and the highest kings wear on their famed hair, as a sign of honour, garlands and adornments of her verdant branches. . .let both nymphs and goddesses draw out the happy day, sweetly singing, in the grateful shade.' Dirce, a daughter of Helios the sun, became equated with a fountain of Boetia; and Dircaeus became an epithet both for the Boetian musician of legend, Amphion, and for the actual poet, Pindar. The swan was sacred to Apollo (as well as to Venus); and swans here are poets (just as Shakespeare is the Swan of Avon). The happy singing in the shade of Dafne's laurel branches hints that we are not to take Apollo's frustration for a tragic ending so much as for a vital experience by accepting which he could move on creatively into the future. The chorus apparently takes Apollo's meaning, and applauds his attitude, while for its own part hoping to enjoy love's happiness in a manner shall we say more literal and less disembodied. We can perhaps feel some sympathy for both points of view, since human life cannot flourish on either instinct or spirit alone.

The poem of *Dafne* was set at least twice again: by Marco di Gagliano (perf. Mantua, 1608, publ. Florence, 1608), with some interesting modifications;[5] and in a German adaptation by Martin Opitz, to music by Heinrich Schütz (perf. Torgau, 1627, publ. Torgau, 1627). Caccini also claimed to have composed Rinuccini's *Dafne* 'many years before' for performance at Corsi's house; but the claim is unconfirmed and improbable. We have already seen that Corsi, Rinuccini and Peri all three of them put their work on *Dafne* through various stages and improvements; and that is probably why Peri spoke (in the preface to his *Euridice* published in 1601) of having been encouraged by Corsi and Rinuccini 'way back in 1594' (*fin l'anno 1594*) to try his hand 'in another form' (*in altra guisa*). So long a gestation and so much reconsideration suggest something of the difficulty with which the last crucial step into opera was taken, so largely on the Neoplatonic initiative of Rinuccini.

THE NEOPLATONIC IMAGES

Apollo was a favourite representative in paintings, sculptures, emblems and literature for the dynastic greatness of Florence under her Medici rulers.[6] But when we turn for more specifically Neoplatonic interpretations,[7] for example to Conti,[8] we find Apollo introduced (p. 231) as the Greek equivalent for Horus, son of Osiris, and (p. 235) as like the Sybil a prophet of Christian truth; besides which (p. 241), on the authority, though it is scarcely needed, of Cicero,[9] 'the sun is God', whom 'the Greeks call Apollo'. And 'what reveals truth more than the sun, and disperses all darkness of night from human states?' Through all the Neoplatonic poetry which we shall be discussing here, this association, by which the outer and physical factor of light also does double duty for the inner and psychological factor of illumination, runs like a groundswell. It is a metaphor; but then again it is rather more than a metaphor, since it is not only a felicitous verbal comparison but an emotional identification. We actually seem to feel the same light and the same warmth in mind and body. Hence the uncanny force of the poetical association.

For there is indeed not only the light but also (p. 242) the heat of the sun, which is the 'sole cause of the generation and corruption of things', since 'the universal life of animate beings is comprised by a balance of heat'. Thus it is that Apollo, in his symbolism as 'the universal force of the sun', may work temperately, for good; intemperately, for ill; but always with that elemental energy of life which we found Conti, in his interpretation of Circe, calling by one of our own current terms for it: libido. That life is ambivalent was taught in antiquity by Heraclitus before Plato, and became another of the Neoplatonic axioms running through the poetry here under consideration. Giordano Bruno was only repeating the ancient insight when he insisted, late in the sixteenth century, that 'all things consist in contraries.'[10]

There are seven more pages (351–8) 'Concerning the Sun'; but they add little to our purpose, except perhaps for Conti's recognition (p. 357) that 'because the sun is of such authority among all things which are seen, it was believed by the ancients to be the first God.'

This reminds me of Jung's experience among the Pueblo Indians, who still believe, not that the sun stands for God, but that the sun is God, with whose return at daybreak life itself returns; and that the source of all life is the mountain from whose awesome heights the water rushes down.[11] That might well be the kind of primeval conviction underlying the sophisticated Neoplatonism of explaining Circe's pedigree because 'from moisture and the heat of the sun all things are born.'[12] The cultural environment is enormously dissimilar; but the intuitive association may very possibly persist or recur at some enduring, because deep, level of the human imagination.

Conti derives the Python (p. 237) from a Greek root signifying putrescence, due as he suggests to an excess of moisture which only the heat of the sun can dry out. The Pythoness (p. 237) transmits Apollo's prophecies by absorbing fumes from the putrescent Python beneath her tripod. There might be some hint here of the past having to decay for the future to emerge, since these bulky dragons often seem to stand for obstructive aspects of parental authority needing to be outgrown. Apollo's big bow overcame the Python, yet failed to defend him against Cupid's little bow, for all his boasting. His education (and ours) may indeed have been advanced a stage farther as a consequence of this very natural misadventure.

Bows and arrows are suggestively phallic, whether for male sexuality or for the masculine principle more generally, so that Dafne's bow, like Diana's, may emphasize something in her symbolism to do with a woman's inner component of masculinity. There was a persistent Neoplatonic tradition[13] that the bow is for the controlled tension of purposeful endeavour, and that the arrows are for the impetuosity which flies impulsively to its target. But to what target? Of course we think it is to the immediate object of our earthly desires. But in Plato's *Symposium*[14] Socrates has a strange tale to unfold of how he was taught by one Diatoma about the Ladder of Love. First we love, or we think that we love, a beautiful body; then we pass up a step to love bodily beauty at large; next to love beautiful souls rather than beautiful bodies; next, more abstractly, good institutions, good laws, good sciences and good science; next wisdom as itself a good; and at last, beauty as the very pattern of value unattached to any images.

It was no part of this Platonic doctrine to suggest that our earthly desires (whether homosexual, as chiefly in Plato, or heterosexual, in a more general context) are in any way reprehensible, or even that they are unreal so far as they go, but merely that they are a prior stage to something much more real, much more lasting and ultimately much more desirable. It was Ficino, in his commentary on the *Symposium,* who launched the definition of these ultimately more real desires as *amore platonico,* Platonic love: a term which has remained with us for celibate relationships long after Ficino's careful explanation has been lost to sight. Ficino's explanation was that individuals sharing each a separate love of God may be united as lovers by that common factor, since what each really loves is the presence of God in the other: the result is what he called intellectual love; but he was simply using that somewhat forbidding term in its philosophical meaning as belonging to the nature of the intellect (*intelligibile*) rather than belonging to the nature of the senses (*sensibile*). And from this concept there derived a whole literary tradition: the allegorical Treatise of Love (*Trattado d'Amore*).

Ficino himself did his best to put theory into practice both at his villa outside Florence, and by widespread correspondence. His disciple Poliziano was one of the practitioners. Another disciple, Francesco di Zanobi Cattani da Diaceto, wrote[15] that 'our soul (*l'anima nostra*), since it has descended into a mortal body (*corpo mortale*), so it uses bodily beauty as an instrument of divine beauty (*se usa per istrumento la bellezza corporale alla divina bellezza*); guided by heavenly love (*amore celeste*), it recovers the lost delights of the intellectual life (*vita intelligibile*).' This eminently Platonic interpretation of love's higher flights was not confined to philosophical speculation, but inspired poetry so fine, for example, as Michelangelo's; while Pico della Mirandola wrote[16] of Benivieni's erotic poetry that we are to take as 'divine love' the hidden objective 'intended behind the enigmatic veils'. Castiglione, in course of that long and radiant panegyric on Platonic love into which Bembo enters as one of the characters, likewise wrote[17] that: 'the body where beauty shines is not the fountain where beauty is born.' Indeed it is not. The fountain is the immortal archetype of which the mortal beauty is the carrier. But, of course, it is the mortal beauty that we can embrace. The archetype shining through is for our inspiration, but not for our embracing.

And that in turn recalls another passage in the *Symposium*[18] where Plato has his Pausanias explain that Venus and Cupid have each of them a dual aspect: a theme much developed by later Neoplatonic interpreters. The Venus who is earthly has for her son the blind or blindfolded Cupid, the inciter of blindly irrational desire for mortal beauty. The Venus who is heavenly has for her son a Cupid neither blind nor blindfolded but open-eyed, the instigator of celestial longings and rational desire.

There is a wonderful painting by Titian,[19] 'Venus Blindfolding Cupid', which is thought to have been inspired by this passage in Plato. (See Plate VIII.) The painting shows Venus in the very act of blindfolding Cupid as he stands by her knee, but at the same time listening intently to Cupid's other self, whose eyes are open with mysterious vision as he whispers into her ear from behind her shoulder. On the opposite side of the picture, two female attendants appear. The one in front is shown with bared breast, probably (on Neoplatonic precedent) as a symbol for unconcealed and undeceitful truth and innocence. She is fingering a quiverful of arrows, but looking inquiringly across to the unblindfolded Cupid. The other attendant stands behind, fully clothed, holding a bow and looking down to the blindfolded Cupid. The whole painting seems like an urgent but enigmatic question on the Neoplatonic theme: which aspect of Venus, the earthly or the heavenly? And which Cupid, with eyes covered or uncovered? Or should we rather put it that the one opposite implies the other, and that both are aspects of a single whole? There is a unity about the picture which points less to the conflict of the opposites than to their complementary completeness and potential reconciliation. The whole is greater than the sum of the parts: that much seems certain from the painting itself.

Nevertheless, there is a question; and it is this question which Rinuccini causes Apollo to raise when in his pride and triumph he asks Cupid whether he intends to 'uncover his eyes or strike in the dark'. No Platonically instructed listener could have missed that deliberate reference. So Cupid warns Apollo of 'what a blind archer can do'— and shoots! Dafne, by insisting, when pursued by Apollo, that she is 'a mortal, not a goddess from heaven', tries modestly to disassociate herself from heavenly beauty, to which Apollo, smitten as he now is with earthly desire, replies that 'if such light glows in mortal beauty, heaven's no longer matters to me'; and again the reference to Plato appears to be quite deliberate. Apollo is himself not of this earth, however: Apollo is himself an archetypal image, and we mortals are not for his embracing. There are, of course, myths about gods embracing mortals; but then these mortals too appear symbolically in the myth, not literally on earth. The embrace itself is to be understood symbolically and not biologically; and when the god takes the form of a bull or a swan or a shower of gold, it is made even plainer that the intercourse is taking a symbolical form, since the biological form would not thus be possible.

Here, it seems that Dafne is standing in symbolically for a mortal woman upon whom Apollo is shown projecting, as we actual mortals so often do, the archetype of the eternal feminine glowing through her like a beacon. But we cannot embrace the archetype. We can only experience it inwardly, in so far as we can somehow withdraw it into the psyche again, where it belongs. This is perhaps what Dafne, in her mythical capacity, teaches Apollo by her transformation. He accepts his hard lesson, singing 'shall this rough bark forever close in the heavenly beauty?' The 'bark' is a Neoplatonic metaphor, which we have already encountered, for the image which half reveals in the very act of half concealing the veiled meaning. The 'heavenly beauty' is just what is accessible to Apollo, and not the 'mortal beauty' which he first hoped to embrace but then had to endure the testing frustration of not embracing. 'Eyes which saw the high beauty' (*alta*—or possibly this is to be translated as 'early' and therefore outgrown); eyes 'which were compelled to weep, look also on this foliage; here lies, and here is hidden, my good, my heart, my treasure, for whom, immortal as I am, I languish and die.'

Now it is of course true that to 'die' was then and had long been a familiar literary convention for sexual orgasm: love's physical consummation in combat with the beloved enemy, as fully detailed in Apuleius, for example; or again as implied in Petrarch's conceit of the lover begging his lady to turn on him the full light of those stars which are her eyes, though knowing (and on this metaphorical level hoping) that her glance may kill him. However, since physical consummation is just what Apollo is not achieving here, and since being an immortal he cannot die literally either, we may well wonder what is the symbolism of his startling paradox.

In 1548, Pompeo della Barba[20] informed the Florentine Academy, allegedly on both Platonic and Aristotelian grounds, that 'love is none other than death' in the somewhat involved sense that the lover dies in himself and lives only in the beloved, who lives only in him. I think we can safely dismiss Pompeo della Barba here. Giordano Bruno[21] wrote very much more in the Petrarchan vein: 'open, oh lady, the portals of thine eyes, And look on me if thou wouldst give me death'; but he then immediately interpreted himself (and perhaps, by implication, Petrarch too) as meaning the mystical death of the soul, 'which same is eternal life, which a man may anticipate in this life and enjoy in eternity'. On this side of eternity we have presumably to take that mystical death in life for some sort of transforming but nevertheless human experience, since Ficino[22] also assures us that it can be had not only in the after life but 'also in this life'.

It occurs to me that the death of the old must needs precede the birth of the new, and that there are growing pains of the psyche which recall St Paul's[23] extraordinary confession: 'I die daily.' St Paul no doubt got through an awful lot of growing up. There are even some classical and neo-classical representations of Cupid, the god of love, with his torch pointing downwards as a god of death, the still more difficult implication being that death is the goal towards which all life is turned. That, however, is certainly not the implication here.

But when we have winnowed all this potentially relevant Neoplatonic material, what remains of the true grain of Rinuccini's intention? There remains, I think, his reference to Plato's deep concern over our human ambivalence, conditioned as we are on the one side by unconscious animal instinct (as it were by Cupid blindfolded) and on the other side by the unavoidable demands and opportunities of conscious understanding (as it were by Cupid open-eyed). For all this ambivalence falls within that primal energy of life to which Sieur

Gordon, following Conti, compared his legendary Circe.[24] Barbara Hanning has made the good point that Apollo was meant to take upon himself the inner symbolism of our perceptive artistry as opposed to the crude blows of our outward sufferings.[25] Perhaps his perceptiveness here was in distinguishing with enhanced consciousness and maturity between our instinctual and our spiritual poles. He had to let the outer woman go in token of recognizing the inner muse: she whom, though 'hidden', he did well to call 'my good, my heart, my treasure', since she had become an image for his own creativity and a mythologem for his own feminine component.

Dante, who recognized our ambiguity when he wrote that 'love sows in you every virtue, and every action which merits punishment',[26] also wrote that love is 'the spiritual union of the soul and the thing loved', so that 'we can know what is in the soul by seeing those whom it loves outside.'[27] This again recalls Plato's Socrates, who thought that 'every man chooses his love from the ranks of beauty according to his own character', so that 'he sees himself in his lover as in a mirror, unawares.'[28] The Neoplatonic implication may be that what Dante saw in Beatrice as the reflection of his own soul, his *anima*, Apollo saw in Dafne, with the same healing and creative consequences. So taken, the legend is certainly instructive, on that intuitive plane where legendary insight does seem to impart itself through poetic images. It is also very beautiful.

We can if we wish seek the Neoplatonic resonance yet more esoterically with Pico della Mirandola, who reported that by some 'Cupid is said to be without eyes, because he is above intellect', as in the Orphic fragment 'cherishing in his heart eyeless swift love'; for 'as was the manner of the ancient theologians, Orpheus interwove the mysteries of his doctrines in the coverings of fable and disguised them in a poetic veil.'[29] So too in Ficino, while intellect is better than sense, there is a way 'better than intellect because it includes passion instead of rejecting it', whence Orpheus 'himself called this love blind'.[30] But blind with a difference, because accepting, what intellect rejects, that union of opposites[31] of which the practical objective, as I believe, is our very ordinary human need to achieve some measure of inward peace and reconciliation.

There is no preaching in Rinuccini's *Dafne*; simply the Neoplatonic inclination to 'disguise well the truth of things with a fabulous cloak in which they are enclosed'.[32] That was the poetical achievement of which the earliest libretto of opera seems to consist.

X
Opera comes into Fashion
❧ ❧ ❧

BORDERLINE OPERA

The earliest opera surviving in text and music, if we regard it as opera, is Cavalieri's *La rappresentatione di anima, et di corpo*, The Representation of the Soul and the Body (perf. and publ. Rome, Feb. 1600). The libretto is by P.[adre] Agostino Manni, and is on a subject not quite so sacred as most oratorios, not quite so secular as most operas, but in a word, moralistic. This is really a morality; and the only question is whether it is also, within our definition of the word, an opera. A definition can be valid without having always to be met in full. Here is a work integrally combined from words and music, sung and acted and even danced in costume, with scenery, in a stage production; here is a confrontation of forces, and a dramatic issue to be decided. But any true personification of the opposing forces is hardly attempted; the result under the ecclesiastical circumstances of the case is hardly to be doubted; and the confrontations, lacking all subtlety and complexity, may be good theatre but are by no means good drama. There is, moreover, a smaller proportion of dialogue in recitative, and a larger proportion of ensembles, choruses and dances, than makes for very active drama.

But decidedly the *Rappresentatione di anima, et di corpo* is not an oratorio: nor does the plausible circumstance of its having been performed in the Oratorio di S. Maria in Vallicella (founded by the subsequently canonized Filippo Neri) make it an oratorio; for it was intended to be staged. An opera does not have to be secular: there are a number of baroque and later operas on sacred subjects, some of them admirably dramatic.[1] Nor does a foregone conclusion preclude drama, since familiar myths do not cease to be dramatic. Yet there is the difference that a morality uses allegory more or less deliberately to point a moral, whereas a myth uses symbolism for the most part intuitively in course of telling a story. John Bunyan could do both (his Apollyon could have given points to the Python).[2] Blake, by inventing his own mythological cast in the Prophetic Books, condemned them to almost impenetrable obscurity; but the myth-like intensity is there, and there is even a considerable indebtedness to Neoplatonism. The good Padre Manni was neither Bunyan nor Blake. The choice between good and evil is always potentially dramatic; but the mere staging of such inner characteristics as several characters or choruses is only half way into drama; and Cavalieri's music, though striking, itself unfolds dramatically only in certain portions.

After an opening chorus, two young men prepare for the action by holding a spoken conversation, as young men will, on the meaning of life, and whether the pleasures of this world are as good as they seem, or whether they are best repudiated as brief, deceitful and in the long run perilous to one's future prospects in eternity. The young men then retire to make way for what they call a true representation, under the appearance of human beings, of the moral (*idea*) that 'this life, this world, this earthly greatness are truly dust, smoke and shadow', nothing being really great or stable but 'virtue, the grace of God, and the eternal kingdom of heaven'. Next, Time sings to us in free recitative that time flies; a four-part chorus takes up the point, with brief orchestral ritornelli; Intellect reminds us that 'every heart loves the good', but argues that none find it in riches and pleasure, and that his own longing is to be forever happy in heaven with God. That our only true felicity lies in heaven was, of course, perfectly orthodox and general Christian doctrine. But Intellect as an entity, cosmological and human, was a Platonic concept; and it was a Neoplatonic argument that we all long for the good, but only think that we long for such apparent goods as worldly riches and pleasure, our real longing being for the more enduring good which awaits us in heaven with God. On the other hand, it was not a very Neoplatonic method to set out the argument so plainly for general consumption in a work of art. The Neoplatonic method in a work of art, as we have seen, was by wrapping deep truths in an enchanting veil which half conceals and half reveals them. There is no concealment here, and perhaps for that very reason not much revelation.

Nor are there any of those familiar mythological personages whose mere presence draws up associations with all manner of deep and partly hidden truth. We have Intellect (*Intelletto*) holding forth very reasonably, and presently we have Counsel (*Consiglio*) and a Guardian Angel (*Angelo custode*) to back him up against Worldly Life (*Vita mondana*), Pleasure with two companions (*Piacere con doi compagni*) and the forces of seduction generally. The Soul (*Anima*) wrestles with her own team-mate the Body (*Corpo*), and they have some very shrewd and energetic exchanges of opinion, amplified by the direct testimony of contrasted ensembles: one of damned souls in hell (*Anime dannate*), to bear witness that they are indeed committed to the everlasting flames; the other of blessed souls in heaven (*Anime beate in cielo*), to bear witness that they are as everlastingly saved. Very telling effect is also made with celestial echoes: and no doubt the successive opening of hell and of heaven was very explicitly staged.

By far the most operatic passages are those in recitative, especially the passages of dialogue between the Soul and the Body. Cavalieri's recitative is both free and expressive, beautifully matched to its words, and lively and imaginative in its musical invention. Most of it flows along over a moderately active bass, so that it inclines very much towards arioso. It does not go on long enough to risk mono-tony, and it was in too new a style to have grown perfunctory. Nevertheless, it is not so much the recitative as the ensembles which remain in memory. From the charming triple-time duet in which Soul and Body celebrate their eventual unanimity, through the creamy trios of Pleasure and her two companions, up to the rousing choruses which punctuate the action at frequent intervals, there is vigour and variety, to which a small but colourful orchestra added further event-fulness. The text on which the music stands is architecturally rather more conventional and metrically rather more predictable than Rinuccini's three; but it is very arguably a libretto. The music was described as follows by Alessandro Guidotti, the publisher, who signed a preface to the score, already mentioned, which was certainly inspired and almost certainly written by Cavalieri: 'some singular and novel compositions of music, made in the likeness of that style, with which it is said that the ancient Greeks and Romans in their scenes and theatres were accustomed to move the spectators to different emotions. . .a recitation in music (*recitazione in musica*).' The work is not quite so singular or novel as this claim suggests; but it is certainly a very early specimen of the representative style. It is by no means a typical specimen, but it is of considerable stature. Subject to the reservations here expressed, we can reasonably class it as a musical morality just (though only just) over the borderline into sacred opera.

Another example, only a little more operatically developed, is Agostino Agazzari's *Eumelio*, which was published and performed at Rome in 1606. This, too, is an unmistakable morality, presenting the shepherd boy Eumelio seduced from his simple life of innocence by a chorus of predatory demons disguised as agreeable vices, but strip-ping off their disguise as soon as they have ensnared Eumelio into the infernal regions; he is however rescued by Apollo, who loves him as a son, and under the clever instigation of Mercury persuades Pluto to let him go again. The mythology here is jumbled and somewhat arbit-rary; the mixture of Christian morality with pagan deities lacks con-viction; but the roles are not out of character. Apollo is functioning traditionally, as a god of light who illuminates the error emanating from the dark underworld. Mercury, traditionally a companion of

Apollo, is functioning in one of his proper aspects, as a trickster god in some ways corresponding with the Nordic Loki. Pluto is traditionally reluctant to give anything away, and is surrounded by yet more obdurate counsellors; but in the end he is persuadable when suitably approached. However, Eumelio is let off so lightly and shows so little sign of having really learnt his salutory lesson that our sense of dramatic development is of the slightest. Worse still, the music is prevented from unfolding very effectually such drama as there is by an odd feature, to which the composer refers in his own preface: the greater part of the music, whether aria, chorus or recitative, is strophic. One verse of each poetic unit is set to music; the other verses are to be sung to the same music as the first verse. In addition, later poetry in the drama is set to music already used for earlier poetry, but with variation of the same kind which is found in strophic variation, and with each important character given his own (not very individual) thematic material for this kind of variation.

Agazzari explains in his preface that he had only a month's notice to prepare this work for the Roman Seminary, whose records ascribe it the Carnival before Lent in 1606; and he mentions that the text was by Father Torquato de Cupis and Father Tirletti, set to music by Agostino Agazzari as the *maestro di cappella*. Of this time, fifteen days went to composing and fifteen days to rehearsing the little piece; for in spite of its prologue and its three acts each with several scenes, it is very short. Agazzari accepted the invitation, he tells us, because the text pleased him 'for the beautiful and useful allegory'. And with considerable disingenuousness, he adds: 'if it seems strange to anyone that I have not diversified all the airs' (*arie*, here used quite loosely for the musical settings in general) 'of all the words, this was done both for brevity [of the time available], and for the greater convenience of whoever might wish to perform (*recitare*) it elsewhere; and also because I have not found any reason why it should always be necessary to vary the airs of one and the same character, when the rhyme-schemes (*rime*) of it do not change; excepting however the case of diversity of motives and contrary emotions, the composer then having to adjust to the emotion.'

There is more unvaried or slightly varied repetition of 'airs' than there is adjustment 'to the emotion'; and this works against a truly operatic drama. But Margaret Johnson, in a valuable article,[3] points to several ways in which the music enters at least to some extent into the drama: for example, a wider range of modulation for the infernal regions than for Arcadia, and a seductive use of triple metre (on lines of four or eight syllables, the rest of the poem being in lines of seven or eleven syllables) for the Vices in their tempting disguise but not for the Demons they presently reveal themselves to be. More of the musical texture is in recitative than in the *Rappresentatione di anima, et di corpo*;

and this recitative is in the same free and expressive idiom as is found in other very early operas. There are also choruses ranging from one part to five; and these choruses, personifying groups of shepherds, vices or demons with some suitability, make a certain contribution to the drama as well as to the artistic contrast. Thus Agazzari's *Eumelio*, like Cavalieri's *Rappresentatione*, may well be regarded as a borderline case of opera.

This class of musical morality on the borderline of opera, though never so important as fully developed opera, has had quite a distinguished history of its own. *La vita humana overa il trionfo della pietà* (Human Life or the Triumph of Piety, on a libretto thought to be by Rospigliosi) is a morality of the kind, composed by Marco Marazzoli, which was performed at Rome in 1657, though its style is earlier. There are strophic arias and strophic choruses; only the recitative shows its period in being a little quicker and drier. It is not a work of great merit dramatically or musically; but it is evidently in line from Cavalieri and Agazzari. In modern times, Stravinsky with his *Soldier's Tale* (Lausanne, 1918) and much more closely with his *Oedipus Rex* (Paris, 1927), Vaughan Williams with his *Pilgrim's Progress* (London, 1951) and certainly Britten with his Church Parables recall something of those seventeenth-century moralities which relate to opera without having quite the full dramatic impetus of opera.

THE GENRE ARRIVES

The earliest opera surviving in text and music which can be regarded as a sample of the genre is the *Euridice* of Rinuccini and Peri (perf. Florence, 6 October 1600; publ. Florence, ? February 1600, Florentine old-style dating, i.e. 1601). Rinuccini's preface to his libretto (Florence, 1600), and the libretto itself, both show him to have arrived by then at a very complete conception of what the libretto of an opera should be. The length of his *Euridice* is about half as long again as his *Dafne* (his later *Arianna* is about as much longer again). The subject is likewise mythological and pastoral; but there is one striking difference in the treatment. Whereas Rinuccini's *Dafne* moves to the traditional conclusion of the legend in an ending which, though not tragic, is certainly experienced as sad, his *Euridice* is brought to a happy ending, unlike the traditional conclusion of that myth by the dismemberment of Orpheus (it is just possible that an alternative, happy ending was known in early antiquity[4]). Rinuccini tells us in his preface why he made this change, concerning which he was obviously feeling apologetic. He explains that he thought the softened ending more proper 'to a time of so much gaiety'. The time was the wedding in Florence, by proxy, of Maria de' Medici to Henri IV, King of

France: a wedding of great dynastic importance, the outcome of long negotiation and diplomacy. It is not hard to see why the dismemberment of Orfeo should be regarded as too ill-omened a scene for this or any other wedding; and a little later on it was also avoided (though more meaningfully) in Striggio's and Monteverdi's *Orfeo*. But the central episodes of Pluto's prohibition and Orpheus' disobedience cannot really just be dropped, as Rinuccini dropped them (going farther than Calzabigi and Gluck did subsequently), without unhinging the plot in its strongest part.

A little ironically, in view of this, the prologue is sung by *La Tragedia*. The poetry is in rhyming four-line stanzas, and Peri has set it in strophic recitative (i.e. aria in recitative style), music being supplied for the first verse, and repeated unaltered for the others. Shepherds and shepherdesses, individually and to a lesser extent in chorus, exchange felicitations with Euridice and Orfeo on their newly found happiness, so much the brighter for having been preceded by Orfeo's dark torment before she accepted him. At line 53, one of the nymphs is so cultured as to quote line 9 of Petrarch's sonnet *Due rose fresche*,[5] and Peri (but not Rinuccini in his original poem) has one of the shepherds so impressed that he repeats it: 'the sun does not see a like pair of lovers (*non vede un simil par d'amanti 'l sole*).' Next, 'Euridice went out, and Dafne with other Nymphs of the Chorus.' When Dafne returns, it is with tragic news of Euridice's death through the bite of the serpent, which she can hardly bring herself to describe. But she does so, in a messenger's scene of classical intensity. Her description, and the shocked interjections of Orfeo and his companions, are in wonderfully free and declamatory recitative, until the other nymphs return and sing a substantial lyric in regular stanzas with refrains. This is treated by the composer partly as a short chorus of lamentation, partly as alternating solos for a nymph of the chorus, and at the last stanza as a three-part ensemble for two nymphs and a shepherd of the chorus: a more elaborate structure than Peri commonly employs. (But the opportunity was not taken, which Monteverdi might have taken, for the taut construction of strophic variation, with its repeating bass to varied melody.)

The scene which next follows does not advance the action, but serves to space it out by a contemplative episode which makes the next phase of action more effective when it does come. The shepherds and shepherdesses all agree that fate has been envious and indeed wicked (*invido e rio*); and Dafne (in Rinuccini's original poem, the chorus) utters the grievous phrase, 'ah bitter fate (*ahi fato acerbo*)'. Peri continues with his recitative except for an almost homophonic, five-part, lightly madrigalian chorus near the end, to strophic poetry strophically composed (i.e. only the first verse has the music notated). A shepherd of the chorus (in Rinuccini's poem, shepherds, *pastori*) sings a further eight lines in recitative, the last line being repeated (not in Rinuccini's poem) for chorus.

The score has then: 'This finished à 5, the chorus goes off, and the scene changes to Hell.' Orfeo is there seen in the company of Venus, who has led him down in search of his lost Euridice. Venus has on the face of it no other motive than the reunion of two such notable lovers; but she advises Orfeo to rely upon his still more notable musicianship, his 'noble song, to the sound of the golden wood' which is his lyre, in the well-justified hope of moving Hell (as he has evidently moved Heaven, since Venus supports him) by his sweet complaints. The poetic contrast of opposites between heaven and hell is symbolically intended, as Orfeo confirms by addressing the 'fatal slopes, shadowy fearful fields where you may never see the flashes and gleams of the stars and the sun'. For if the sun, as Ficino[6] wrote, is 'everywhere the image of the divine truth and goodness', then wherever the sun cannot reach is darkness of the mind and the spirit as well as of the eyes. We found Sieur Gordon[7] also explaining in 1582 that the sun 'signifies allegorically the clarity and light of the truth and the divine gleam which glitters in our souls.' In Rinuccini's poem, Orfeo by his sweet song and noble lyre seeks to recover from Pluto *la donna mia*, 'my woman'. In Peri's score, this has been changed (evidently by an afterthought of one of them) to *l'anima mia*, 'my soul', which brings out still better the typically Neoplatonic double meaning.

Pluto is at once enchanted, but remains reluctant until, after a brisk underworld discussion into which his own beloved Proserpina enters very tellingly on the lovers' behalf, he suddenly relents, to the obvious astonishment of a double chorus of Shades and Deities of Hell. Even this chorus, which is mainly strophic, antiphonal and homophonic, is interrupted by Peri (though not by Rinuccini) with a brief solo for Radamanto in free recitative. 'And here the scene returns as at first.' A second messenger, Aminta, is seen by the assembled nymphs and shepherds approaching 'with his face all smiling'. A few lines are given him in Peri's score which are not in Rinuccini's original poem; then, in both versions, he tells his companions to lament no more, because 'our Orfeo, our demigod (*semideo*)' is happy again, for his beautiful Euridice has been brought back to life. And as Aminta finishes his astounding story, 'Orfeo and Euridice return' to relate to us their entire adventure.

Orfeo begins in a triple-time aria with (at last) a strophic variation form, though brief and irregular, to accommodate Rinuccini's seven-line stanza in two parts: one of three lines, the other of four, each with its last line repeated in the score though not in the separately printed poem. Free recitative carries the rest of the scene until the final rejoicings. The score has: 'Ballo à 5. All the chorus together sing, and dance.' They do so in a strophic and mainly homophonic chorus, spaced out by a ritornello and alternating with a three-part ensemble; the repeats of the ritornello are 'danced by two alone from the Chorus'. This quite complex musical and choreographical structure is suited to but is not actually suggested by the poetry, which has simply six similar stanzas in very lyrical form, with diversified but regular line-lengths and rhyme-scheme. Such a lack of correspondence at times between poetic and musical structure is perhaps to be regarded as an immature feature of the very earliest operas, since it is not so often found afterwards except in specimens obviously perfunctory. In Peri's *Euridice* as a whole, however, there is more variety in the poetry than there is in the music, by far the greater part of which continues in free recitative.

So long as recitative occupied so large a proportion of the score, the relationship of poetic and musical structure was restricted by that very fact; for it is not in the nature of recitative to be highly structured in itself. Thus the very conscientiousness of the originators of opera in making their music serve the meaning of the words in detail hindered their serving so well the structure of the poetry at large. There is consequently a certain monotony and lack of expressive range; for expression is not only a matter of fine nuances in the vocal line, but also of a broad variety to match our varied moods. Much of what Rinuccini gave to the chorus (*Coro*), which could have been set by Peri as part-writing, becomes *Pastore del Coro* or *Ninfa del Coro* in recitative, although in other respects the score stays very closely with the poem. We may possibly feel that there is too much recitative, and not enough contrast either by ensemble or by solo arias. But we never feel, as we sometimes feel in later baroque opera, that the recitative is perfunctory. It is music keenly felt, from measure to measure; and what it lacks in variety and form, it makes up in verbal immediacy and spontaneous impact.

We must also take into account the virtuoso performance which this early recitative requires and received. Marco da Gagliano[8] in 1608 wrote of Jacopo Peri's own 'artful manner of reciting in song (*recitare cantando*), which all Italy admires', adding that 'one cannot entirely understand the delicacy and the force of his arias without having heard him sing them himself.' He did sing himself in the role of Orfeo, with other leading singers. And since there are so few actual arias, the term is evidently being used loosely here for his solos in general, including his extensive recitative.

A curious feature of this performance, though not an unusual feature at the time, was that portions of the music, amounting to about one-sixth part of the whole, were not by Peri but by Caccini. Peri in his preface honourably informs us that 'Giulio Caccini (called *Romano*), whose supreme worth is known to the world, composed Euridice's arias and some of the Shepherds and Nymphs of the

Ex. 3. Jacopo Peri, Euridice, Florence, 1601, (a) p. 16, Dafne's recitative in the messenger's scene, augmented triad and diminished seventh for expressive reasons (the third ♯ in the figuring of the bass seems to be a misprint for 7); (b) p. 30, Orfeo's first plea to Pluto, expressive melodic interval of the tritone C to F♯ on the word 'alas' (Ohimè); (c) p. 31, modulation similar to (a) on the words 'plaint and grief' (pianto e duolo).

Chorus, and the choruses "*Al canto, a ballo*", "*Sospirate*" and "*Poi che gli eterni imperi*"; and this because they were to be sung by persons dependent upon him, the which arias one may read in his own [*Euridice*], composed and printed indeed after this one of mine was presented to her Most Christian Majesty.' (Honourably, but also cunningly, because of course this information places Caccini in a not very favourable light, as he well deserved; and the fact remains that this is Peri's opera.) Claude Palisca, in an admirable essay,[9] has reviewed this circumstance among others; and from his patient reconstruction of the original cast, the force of Peri's statement becomes clear. Caccini's sister-in-law sang Euridice. At a performance shortly after the first, Caccini's youthful son Pompeo sang Aminta, and possibly also doubled as Tirsi. Two of the singers were described as being *del Sign. Emilio*, ([in the entourage] of Sign. Emilio [de' Cavalieri]). Peri in his preface gives further singers for the first performance, including the very distinguished tenor Francesco Rasi (who was loaned by the Duke of Mantua, and sang Aminta); as Pluto, Melchior Palantrotti, an equally distinguished bass employed at Rome by Cardinal Montalto; and as Arcetro, the tenor Antonio Brandi, who later, in 1608, achieved especial fame as the messenger in Gagliano's *Dafne*. (Peri also praises the great soprano Vittoria Archilei, but not in connection with his *Euridice*.) In publishing his score, however, Peri evidently restored his own music, since it is not the same as the corresponding passages in Caccini's *Euridice*, to the curious circumstances of which we may next turn our attention.

A FLORENTINE WEDDING

The occasion for Peri's *Euridice*, for Caccini's *Euridice*, for Caccini's *Rapimento di Cefalo* and many others notable entertainments, was the wedding of Maria de' Medici to Henry IV, King of France, which was solemnized at Florence although Henry was not present in person, but represented by proxy. Some ten days of October 1600 were given over to the celebrations. In good time, the Duke of Mantua sent his most famous singer, Francesco Rasi, on loan for the occasion; Rasi wrote to him on 14 August about the rehearsals for 'this marvellous pastoral or fable or whatever I should call it' (most probably the *Rapimento di Cefalo* discussed below). The Duke of Mantua himself followed on Monday, 2 October. We have nothing to suggest that he brought with him his still more famous resident musician, Monteverdi, and there would have been no particular motive for his doing so; but it could have happened. On Tuesday, 3 October, an ambassador arrived from Venice; on Wednesday, 4 October, the papal legate who was to conduct the wedding, Cardinal Aldobrandini, was met by the Duke of Florence some distance away, and escorted back with considerable pageantry by the large retinue with which he had come from Rome, and another large retinue brought out by the Duke. And on this same day (4 October 1600, though the figure for the date of the month was left blank in the first issue), Rinuccini's poem *L'Euridice* (the poem used both by Peri and by Caccini) was published at Florence.

On Thursday, 5 October, the wedding ceremony was duly and impressively solemnized; the evening was occupied with a ball and a banquet of ample proportions in the Palazzo Vecchio. A scenic entertainment, *The Contest of Juno and Minerva*, was devised and written for this banquet by no less a poet than Giovanni Battista Guarini, author of the famous *Pastor Fido* of 1590; the cloud-machinery in which the goddesses descended and the stage décor were by Bernardo Buontalenti, then at the very height of his reputation as a theatrical designer and engineer; the music was by Cavalieri, which was perhaps fortunate in that it seems to have contented him enough to prevent him from intruding his own music into the other composers' entertainments as he had in 1589. The goddesses merely quarrel a little as to the right of domestic virtue and martial valour both to be present at this pacific banquet, but conclude fulsomely that both qualities are to be expected where such a noble bride and bridegroom are united. No essential connection with opera is to be noticed here; but the pretence that all present were mythological personages fitted well with that background of allegorical play-acting against which opera evolved.

On Friday, 6 October, Peri's *Euridice* had its first performance, in a moderately small room (which could be looked into from another room) on an upper story of the Palazzo Pitti. There was no stage machinery, but the two scene changes and the lighting effects got enthusiastic mention in Buonarrotti's *Descrizione* (Florence, 1600).[10] The audience was very select, but also very small. Even the orchestra was distinguished, with Jacopo Corsi (as Peri informs us in his preface) playing the harpsichord, and other notables the lute, the archlute and the lyra da gamba. It was Corsi who, pleased 'with the fable and the style, arranged to have it appear on the stage at the wedding of the Most Christian Queen' (we are told by Marco da Gagliano in the preface to his *Dafne* performed at Florence in 1608). Cavalieri himself was in general charge of the direction, and took all possible credit for the fact. The immediate reaction was a little mixed, Cavalieri and Bardi both taking an unfavourable view, particularly of what they felt to be Rinuccini's too tragic poetry and Peri's too austere recitative. But both had some cause for bias, and Bardi by now was also likely to have been himself somewhat behind the times. Subsequent opinion among the best connoisseurs (Gagliano, Pietro de' Bardi, Severo Bonini, and indirectly G. B. Doni, all within the first half of the seventeenth century) was remarkably favourable; and there were further performances, including one at Bologna in 1616 (Caccini's *Euridice* got no further than its first performance).

On Saturday, 7 October, after displays of horsemanship in the afternoon, there was an evening dress rehearsal for *Il rapimento di Cefalo*, open to spectators. On Sunday, 8 October, there was a garden party, to which allegorical scenes with poetry, music, singing and dancing contributed; and in the evening, probably a pastoral tragi-comedy by Vincenzo Panciatichi. On Monday, 9 October, a theatrical work, definitely an opera, on a text by Gabriello Chiabrera, with music mainly though not entirely by Caccini, was performed before a very large audience of nearly four thousand persons, and in a very spectacular and much discussed production; this was *Il rapimento di Cefalo* (The Apotheosis of Cefalo). On Monday, 13 October, the newly wedded Queen left Florence on a leisurely journey (including nine days weather-bound in Portofino, with its tiny landlocked harbour). She was met by her husband, and began her not uneventful reign, at Lyons on 9 December 1600.

Probably in January 1600, Florentine old-style dating, i.e. 1601, and certainly very early in that year, Caccini's *Euridice* was published in Florence. Caccini's dedication is dated 20 December 1600, and the work must therefore have passed through the press with something of the same unseemly rapidity with which it was composed; for there is no doubt that it appeared in print before the publication of Peri's *Euridice*, possibly in February 1600, Florentine old-style dating, i.e. 1601 (and certainly before 25 March, when the Florentine New Year began and old-style and new-style dating reunited for the remainder of the year). Peri's dedication is dated 6 February 1600, Florentine old-style dating, i.e. 1601; and there he called his opera *Le nuove Musiche fatte da me*, 'the new works of music composed by me', over a year before Caccini used the title *Le nuove musiche* for his famous volume of Florence, 1602. On 5 December of 1602 (on either style of dating) Caccini's *Euridice* had its first and only contemporary performance. Peri was reprinted in 1608, Caccini in 1615. This sequence of events leaves Peri still ahead of Caccini in composing *Euridice*, as well as for the origins of opera generally.

Caccini's most important contribution to the celebration of 1600 was his lavishly produced opera on Chiabrera's libretto, *Il rapimento di Cefalo*. Buonarrotti (*Descrizione*, Florence, 1600) states that 'Giulio Caccini had charge of all the music, and was the composer' except for choruses by Stefan Venturi del Nibbio, Luca Bati and Piero Strozzi. The poem of the *Rapimento* was published at Florence in 1600, but not the score; and the music is lost except for a closing scene which is included in Caccini's *Nuove musiche* (Florence, 1602). Of this Caccini wrote: 'not having been able, on account of many obstacles, to have published as I desired the *Rapimento di Cefalo* composed in music by me. . .it now seems appropriate to add the final chorus of the aforesaid *Rapimento*', the solo airs incorporated in this being a demonstration of the style of ornamentation discussed in the famous preface. No mention is made of the other three composers partially involved.

Caccini describes the final scene of the *Rapimento* as having been 'concerted with voices and instruments by seventy-five persons', and as followed by 'other music and a *ballo*'. The chorus 'Ineffabile ardore' is short and almost completely homophonic. An ornamented bass air (leaning towards arioso) follows, as 'sung, with the ornamentation shown, by Melchior Palontrotti [Palantrotti]', the celebrated bass singer brought from Rome for the occasion: it is quite floridly ornamented, but only at certain points and on words of special emotional significance (*suave*, sweet; *mortale*, mortal; *ale*, wings; *risvegliarlo Amore*, awaken Love). Then comes a tenor air, similarly ornamented, but described as having been sung 'with different ornamentation, according to his own style, by Jacopo Peri'; the chorus 'Ineffabile ardore' is repeated; and next comes another tenor air 'sung with some of the ornamentation as shown and some according to his own taste, by the celebrated Francesco Rasi.' The homophonic chorus 'Quand' il bell' anno' concludes the excerpt.

The poetry on which this final scene is thus variously composed has no such variations of structure, these being imposed upon it by Caccini here in the same way as both Peri and Caccini imposed a similar variety of structure on choruses in Rinuccini's *Euridice*. The lines are of seven and eleven syllables, and the rhyme-scheme is closely knit throughout. The words are Neoplatonic of the purest vintage:

> ineffable ardour, which calls the heart back to the abodes of heaven. . .fleeting flame of charming glances gives us through death delightful assault, but true beauty reigns on high, thence (*indi*) it strings the bow (*arma l'arco*), and thence it shoots the arrows (*avventa i dardi*) which have the worth to make the wounded heart happy. Just as the sun, passing through the heavenly fields, here on earth (*quaggiù*) makes day out of the nightly darkness, so love dwells divine (*almo*) above the stars (*sulle stelle*), and spreads among us shining lights to entice others with its splendour. . . .

The 'ineffable ardour' is a more or less technical term for that indescribable but all-embracing divine love which, in this aspect of Neoplatonic doctrine, seeks us out and draws us back, if we respond, to heaven whence our souls originally descended. Mortal love can indeed give us the 'delightful' impact of sexual consummation (the familiar poetic metaphor here of 'death' standing for orgasm); but such delights are 'fleeting', and ultimately valuable rather as introductions, by way of woman's beauty, to the true or heavenly beauty shining through. For 'true beauty reigns on high', that is to say in heaven; 'thence' (i.e. from heaven) true beauty arouses that purer longing which alone can 'make the wounded heart happy' in a more than fleeting manner. (The bow as an instrument of spiritual illumination we have already encountered.) Then comes the habitual comparison between the sun, which 'here on earth makes day out of the nightly darkness', and the 'divine love' (*almo* in one of its poetic senses) which is 'above the stars' (i.e. above the seven revolving planetary spheres and the eighth revolving sphere of the fixed stars, above which is the yet more swiftly revolving ninth sphere of the *primum mobile* or crystalline heaven, topped by the tenth, stationary heaven, the Empyrean where God awaits us); but this divine love 'spreads among us shining lights' of true understanding, by which to entice others to rejoin it in that original splendour which is divine love, that is to say God. It is all quite specifically expressed; but we need the Neoplatonic clue in order to recognize what is being expressed.

For the Prologue, an immense stage mountain appears surmounted by the winged horse, Pegasus, the stroke of whose hoof causes the water (there was real water) to flow in token of inspiration from the spring Hippocrene on Mount Helicon (which we are thus supposed to recognize). There is Apollo sitting under his laurel tree, with the nine Muses and a somewhat less canonical personification of Poetry, who praises Maria de' Medici and flatters Henry IV. The mountain deflates (*sgonfiandosi* in Buonarrotti's *Descrizione*, Florence, 1600)[11] and disappears into a trap. A night scene is revealed, with forests and caverns and distant vistas dimly seen. A cloud of pink and gold and silver brings down a beautiful winged girl: Aurora, goddess of the dawn. She finds Cefalo asleep, sings of her love to him, and wakes him up for an amorous duet. They go off together, and a distraught old gentleman, Tithonus the husband of Aurora, arrives in a more complicated cloud, continually changing in size and shape. After much searching and lamenting (obviously not for the first time), he is carried off too, and the scene changes to a seascape and the beginnings of an abortive sunrise; there is a vast and animated whale on one side, and on the other, Helios in the four-horsed chariot of the sun, but he is unable to get into the sky because Aurora, the dawn, is not on duty. Cupid, blindfolded, flies around and performs an aerial dance with his companions in honour of so signal a victory of blindly impassioned love.

Another wooded scene briefly shows the lovers in transport and a further duet; but as they leave, darkness and gloom follow, with Night and her pair of small sons, Sleep and Death, a crescent moon, and a complete zodiac with celestial boys above to represent the divine power over all; and next from below, as though from beneath the earth, an Erda-like earth-mother comes up in a smaller mountain of her own. She is Berecyntia (whose mountain is Berecyntus, and who is by one account Cynthia, or under another name, Diana) come to protest because the sun cannot rise to warm her good earth. But she is routed by the return of Cupid. Now Mercury the messenger of the gods descends to rebuke Cupid, and to chase him through the air with complex motions of their cloud machinery, catching him at last and carrying him up to heaven, possibly for transformation into his other Neoplatonic role as divine love. Certainly, as the heavens open, a pantheon of twenty-five gods and goddesses is brilliantly uncovered, in full chorus. Jupiter ordains that Cupid shall unite the lovers for eternity; and they are indeed carried aloft, while Cefalo's companions down below embark on the first of Caccini's surviving choruses. In heaven, the transformation of mortal love into divine love is confirmed by the poetry already quoted; and we are to assume that Aurora, her longings thus symbolically satisfied, will be back on the job in the morning.

That earthly pleasures are also not to be despised in their proper time and place is made plain by an epilogue in which the stage changes to part of the auditorium, the goddess Fama (Fame) rises before the eyes of a heroic assembly (being a daughter of Terra, i.e. Earth, she quite properly rises therefrom), complete with trumpet, olive branch, wide wings and abundant hair streaming (like gossip) in the wind. Females representing cities subject to Florence surround her in a somewhat blatant allegory, Siena and Florence herself being conspicuously represented. The Duke having been fitly lauded in full chorus, the actors came forward to sing and dance, which might suggest that this undoubted but not entirely serious opera, with its many resemblances to the most extravagant sort of masquerade or interlude, ended (as so commonly) with general dancing, were it not that the vast size of the audience renders such a conclusion improbable. Perhaps some of the more privileged spectators did join in; a connection by means of ramps between stage and auditorium often made this possible, as may be seen, for example, in Plate IX. In any case, the proportion of allegorical spectacle and aerial capering to actual drama was very high, and this drama is itself rather implicit in the situation than explicit in the adventures of the characters. The sun not rising is a primitive enough source of apprehension.

OPERA THEREAFTER TAKEN FOR GRANTED

Caccini's *Euridice* follows Rinuccini's libretto a little more closely than does Peri's subsequently printed score; but their musical resemblance is remarkable; there are similar slight changes of casting; there is much the same division of passages, marked *Coro* by Rinuccini, into musical solos and choruses; and there is much the same equalizing of the poetic variations into almost constant recitative. However, there is a sort of singer's smoothness about Caccini's recitative which does not exactly override the verbal contours and the semantic nuances, but which does nevertheless assimilate them somewhat nonchalantly to the vocal line. The modulations and the key-relationship are more conventional and less adventurous. The balance of the phrases and the regularity of the cadences is a more musicianly balance and regularity, less disturbed by expressive deflections due to the words. On the other hand, while the syllables chosen for elaborate ornamentation are suitably and often dramatically chosen, there is more such ornamentation than Peri inserted, at least, into his notated score, and very possibly more than Peri might have thought it dramatically appropriate to sing impromptu.

Peri's recitative is the more uncompromising in his strict allegiance to the verbal contours, his firm determination to express only the semantic and emotional nuances, never to indulge in musicianly felicity for its own sake. Such single-mindedness brings its own limitations and its own rewards; for if Peri's recitative is a little austere, it is also for that very reason intensely focused. We can never doubt Peri's sincerity of purpose, even when it outstrips his inspiration. Caccini was not less sincere as a pioneer of opera; but much of his pioneering consisted in finding ways of putting at the dramatic disposal of opera some of those graceful resources of the vocal art which in themselves are not essentially dramatic. If Cavalieri was, perhaps, a poet's composer, and if Caccini was certainly a singer's composer, then Peri was more than either of them a dramatist's composer: a high priest of that consecrated union of words and music to which so much earnest thought had gone throughout the sixteenth century.[12]

And so opera reached the highest society, most of whose members hardly noticed the historic departure from the usual sort of brilliant entertainment, or if they did, grew rapidly to take it for granted. But those who did notice were above all impressed (as was Doni[13] a generation afterwards) by the novelty of *dramma tutto in musica*, of drama unfolding altogether in music; of *dramma per musica*, of drama through music; as we might say, of music drama. And this was right. The novely was indeed the unfolding of staged drama as much in the music as in the words.

'Every morning they rehearse the play which is being done in Music', announced the Resident Minister of the Estense court at Florence, Bartolomeo Malaspina, in a letter[14] of 29 August 1600; and this is shown by Claude Palisca[15] to have been *Il rapimento di Cefalo*. 'They are doing a play at the Palazzo de' Pitti in the upper salon, all in music, a work (*opera*) of Signor Jacopo Corsi and a subject (*materia*) of Signor Ottavio Rinuccini', wrote Giovanni del Maestro, majordomo at the Grand-ducal court in Florence, of the year 1600.[16] The word *opera* still has here merely its general meaning of 'work', as it also does when Buonarroti (*Descrizione*, Florence, 1600) refers to *Il rapimento di Cefalo* as *opera*, 'work'. 'Last night they presented (*rappresentò*) in the house of the Grand Duke by means of a gentleman of the city the story (*favola*) of Orfeo and Euridice in verses and always in music (*sempre in musica*), which lasted an hour and a half and was a very fine thing (*cosa bellissima*), although simple with regard to the machines', wrote the Ambassador from Parma.[17] 'There was done a pastoral (*pastorale*)

presented in music (*rappresentata in musica*)', wrote Count Giulio Thiene,[18] Estense Ambassador, to the Duke of Modena, in a letter of 7 October 1600, referring to the *Rapimento di Cefalo*. 'A play recited altogether by musicians (*una comedia recitata tutta da musici*) in the sweetest singing (*in suavissimi canti*). . .indeed made all of music (*fatte pur tutta di musica*), and with very fine interludes (*intermedii*)', wrote Nicolò da Molin,[19] the Venetian ambassador, in a letter of 7 October 1600. 'There was recited (*fu recitato*) the most noble story (*favola*) of Cefalo and his apotheosis (*composta*) by Sig. Gabriello Chiabrera and set to music (*messa in musica*) by Giulio Caccini. . .more than a hundred musicians sang in it (*cantarono*); more than a thousand other persons worked on it (*oprarono*), taking into consideration the machines of many sorts which there were and all marvellous', wrote Francesco Settimani[20] in his *Diario* for 9 October 1600. Caccini[21] himself more modestly gives 'Final Chorus of the *Rapimento di Cefalo* concerted (*consertato*) between voices and instruments by seventy-five persons'; no doubt the number grew as the story went the rounds. 'There was recited (*fu recitata*) a very fine play in the ducal palace all in music' (*tutta in musica*), wrote Francesco d'Abramo[22] of the *Rapimento di Cefalo* in his *Diario* for 9 October 1600. 'A play in Music (*commedia in Musica*)called Dafne by Ottavio Rinuccini' noticed Cesare Tinghi[23] in his *Diario* for 26 October 1604; 'a play in music was recited (*si recitò una comedia in musica*)' — and the same for 26 February 1607; 'it was arranged to recite a play (*per recitare una comedia*) called *Il Trafico* by Lattanzio Benucci, a Sienese; it was a straight play (*comedia ordinaria*), without *intermedi*'—and the same for 11 November 1612. The diarist presumably intended to inform us by 'ordinary' that this last was recited not in music but in speech.

Meanwhile, Monteverdi's *Orfeo*, though not in all respects typical, so far surpassed its predecessors, and has so much to teach us about the nature and resources of opera, that I shall take it for my central study here.

XI
Monteverdi and his Orfeo
❧❦

FROM FLORENCE TO MANTUA

The *Orfeo* of Monteverdi, on a libretto by Alessandro Striggio the younger, was first performed, with resounding success, at the Carnival at Mantua, 1607, probably on 24 Feburary. *Orfeo* was twice repeated shortly afterwards at Mantua; partially performed, also in 1607, at Cremona; probably performed at Turin, Florence and Milan around 1610. The poem was published (Mantua, 1607) at the time of the first performance. The score was published twice (Venice, 1609, repr. Venice, 1615): a most unusual tribute (shared with Peri's *Euridice* and also Caccini's) in an age when such compositions were chiefly associated with their first performances, and not regarded as legacies to posterity. At the beginning of the seventeenth century, an opera was still enough of an event to be likely to have one printing of the score—but seldom to reach two printings. Later in the century, the great majority of operas were not even printed once, but survive, if at all, in one or more manuscripts: autographs; working copies as used at original performances; copies made for collectors.

Alessandro Striggio, the librettist of *Orfeo*, was a Mantuan nobleman by birth and a court official of high rank (from 1628 he enjoyed the title of Grand Chancellor) by profession. Very little information has been established as to his other activities; but certainly he was the famous son of a more famous father, Alessandro Striggio the elder, about whom many interesting facts are known. They are interesting both in themselves, and because they help us to connect the Mantuan operas with the Florentine tradition.

Alessandro Striggio the elder was born at Mantua around 1535. He spent ten or more years, from about 1560 to about 1570 or rather later, in the service of Cosimo de' Medici at Florence. There he composed part of the music for the celebrated six interludes of Francesco d'Ambra's play *La Cofanaria* in 1565: interludes more dramatically connected with one another, and thus approximating more nearly towards the nature of opera, than Bardi's interludes of 1586 and 1589. In 1567, Florentine old-style dating, i.e. 1568, Striggio composed music for two of the pageants at the Florentine Carnival of that year; in 1569, Striggio composed music for Cini's interludes to Cini's own play, *La Vedova*. In 1574, Striggio was apparently resident and possibly in service at the court of Mantua, where the Duke released him from a troublesome law-suit in response to a letter from the Emperor Maximilian II dated 1 September 1574. In 1579, Striggio composed 'diverse works of music, with many voices and innumerable instruments'[1] for the wedding at Florence of Francesco Medici and Bianca Capello. In 1585, Florentine old-style dating, i.e. 1586, Striggio composed part of the music for Bardi's interludes for Bardi's own play, *L'Amico Fido*. Striggio was also famous as a player of the lira da gamba and of the lute, and as a composer of madrigals (for which Thomas Morley[2] cites him in his *Plaine and Easie Introduction*); he visited Ferrara as well as European courts outside Italy (Paris and London among them); he was a man noted and sought after, and as close to the developments in Florence which led up to opera as any Florentine. He probably died, in Mantua, around or a little before 1595.

Alessandro Striggio the younger (the son of the above), Monteverdi's librettist, is stated to have been born at Mantua in 1573 and to have died at Venice in 1630. That, if it is correct, makes him only sixteen (no impossibility) in 1589, when we find him mentioned in Malvezzi's contemporary description[3] as 'the said Alessandrino' (little Alexander), which was the name then used of him in distinction from his father; and as playing a *Violina* (either a treble viol, or less probably a violin), in the interludes for Girolamo Bargagli's play, *La Pelegrina*: the poetry of these interludes is in the main by Rinuccini. The reference in Malvezzi to a Sopranino di viola (a little treble viol, or violin) played by Alessandro Striggio earlier in the same interludes would also seem to describe 'the said Alessandrino' of his subsequent reference. At least it is clear that Alessandro Striggio the younger was present on this great Florentine occasion, and presumably on many others, in the company of his distinguished father.

The exchange of visits and of mutual influence between Florence and Mantua was particularly extensive through this formative period. So was the rivalry with which these two courts each sought to outshine the brilliant spectacles of the other; and their spectacles were very much in the same kind. The Duke of Mantua lent his celebrated tenor, Francesco Rasi, to the Grand Duke of Florence for the spectacles of 1600 (including both Peri's *Euridice* and Caccini's *Rapimento di Cefalo*), and was himself an honoured guest on that occasion. (The Duke of Mantua actually took a formal part at Florence in 1589, at the tourney of 11 May.) The Grand Duke of Florence in 1607 lent a tenor of his own, Giovanni Gualberto Magli,[4] to sing the title role in Monteverdi's *Orfeo*, which he did to great acclamation; the Duke of Mantua, who took a personal interest and attended many of the rehearsals, particularly approved of him.

There are small but distinct verbal and musical parallels between the *Euridice* of Rinuccini and Peri, and the *Orfeo* of Striggio and Monteverdi. And more generally, it would not have been possible for the latter to have produced a work so similar, in so novel a form, without knowledge of the former. Opera in Mantua is not different from opera in Florence; it is the same kind of opera, with the same background, and picking up only a few years afterwards. The difference between the earliest Florentine operas and the earliest Mantuan operas is not of time or place, but of individual talent.

Striggio's libretto for *Orfeo* is perhaps the equal of Rinuccini's *Euridice* in poetic imagination and verbal craftsmanship. It is certainly superior in dramatic force, because it does not evade Orfeo's second loss of Euridice. Striggio also retained Orfeo's death by dismemberment in his poem as separately printed; the version in the printed score has a different ending, but in so similar a poetic style and excellence that it seems likely to be Striggio's own work. It will be appreciated that Striggio had two out of Rinuccini's three pioneering librettos already available as models, of which *Euridice* is longer and more assured poetically (though not dramatically because of its weakened scenario) than *Dafne*. Striggio provided structures suitable for music rather more systematically than Rinuccini, and Monteverdi followed them rather more closely than Peri or Caccini. There are passages of dramatic flexibility: blank verse (*versi sciolti*) or verse rhyming unsymmetrically, with unsymmetrical line-lengths, inviting recitative and offering all the suspense of unpredictable and urgent movement. There are passages of lyrical regularity: verse rhyming schematically, with patterned though variable line-lengths and strophic repetitions, inviting aria of a more reposeful elegance. Striggio's poetry is at the service of the drama just as much as Monteverdi's music is at the service of the poetry. These are the best possible conditions for opera. But it is not only this advanced construction which puts Monteverdi's *Orfeo* ahead of the few earlier operas. Still more is it the quality of Monteverdi's genius, which towers over the opening of the baroque period very much as Bach's genius towers over the closing of it.

Claudio Monteverdi (1567–1643)[5] was born at Cremona, and trained there under Marc' Antonio Ingegneri (1545–92) as a choirboy, organist, viol-player and composer. Monteverdi was only fifteen years of age when he published his first work, a set of three-part motets (*Sacrae Cantiunculae*, Venice, 1582); but though they are good music, which was achievement enough at such an age, they are not preternaturally mature. Monteverdi was neither a child prodigy nor a performing virtuoso. He was a musician of extraordinary solidity: solidly trained; solidly mastering the techniques and idioms of his day; solidly advancing, through powerful compositions in relatively traditional styles, towards an individuality as remarkable as any which the history of music has to show. The greatest artists are not usually the greatest innovators, but those who come, as Monteverdi came, at the right time for consolidation.

There is a heightened tension of melody and line in Monteverdi's recitative, a richness of expressive detail, a flow of musicianly invention in which the rhythms and the pitches of speech are followed no less exactly than before, but more imaginatively. Recitative fluctuates with arioso and with aria no less adaptably, but the contrasting arias are more tautly constructed, and the contrasting ensembles and choruses are more powerfully composed. The musical forms are more various and more complex. The melodic arch is longer. The rhythms are more vital. The modulations of the harmony, and those sudden juxtapositions which are more startling than any modulation, are fully expressive of the words, but equally convincing and compelling as music. Time and again, the heart turns over at the force and beauty of some memorable progression or corner of melody, even as we recognize that it is exactly what the words and the drama require.

It always was Monteverdi's way to serve the words with nothing but advantage to the music. He did not fumble with the reciting style when he came to his first opera at the age of forty. He used it with greater sureness than its actual originators. For Monteverdi, his own claims notwithstanding, was not so much an originator as he was a fulfiller. Not what Haydn did for the string quartet, but what Mozart and Beethoven did, would be a fair comparison with what Monteverdi did for opera.

AN OPENING TOCCATA

Orfeo begins with an introductory fanfare, such as was habitual at theatrical and other entertainments to catch the attention of the audience with a glitter of brilliant sounds ('the accustomed signal of the sound of the trumpets', as Federico Follino[6] called it in his account of the *Arianna* of Rinuccini and Monteverdi next year, 1608, at Mantua). It was not, however, habitual to write such an introduction down. Trumpeters, with their attendant kettle-drummers, did most of their work half improvised and half by memorized tradition. In later Italian operas of the seventeenth century, similar introductions, overtures or curtain tunes are sometimes written (completely or incompletely) into the score, and where missing or incomplete have probably to be supplied or completed. Here, Monteverdi has written out a brief but brilliant specimen, which he used again, as a background to vocal parts, for his own *Vespers* at Mantua in 1610.

Monteverdi's instructions for this introduction read: 'Toccata which they play before the raising of the curtain three times with all the instruments, and they make it a tone higher wishing to play the trumpets with mutes.' The trumpets were long (8-foot C) narrow-bore instruments without valves: capable of notes close enough together for melody only in their high register; but in that register delicately colourful in the hands of those specialists, known as clarino players, who spent their lives among these high harmonics and could manage them with virtuoso brilliance. The mutes used on baroque trumpets raise the pitch by one tone: hence the introduction, though notated in C major, is intended 'a tone higher' (i.e. it is written C major for concert D major); and we have to make the necessary transposition. Then it leads smoothly to the ensuing Prologue in D minor, as it is meant to lead.

The term 'Toccata' as used here is borrowed from the vocabulary of the early baroque trumpeters and writers on the trumpet. So used, it strictly meant the flourish which was commonly attached to the basic cavalry calls when the occasion was not merely military but ceremonial. The calls were action signals which it was vital to recognize immediately, and each call consisted in a short, repeated figure, commonly on the second and third harmonics, a fifth apart, of which the second, i.e. the lowest note, was sounded first. But for ceremonial occasions, a flourish in freer rhythm and reaching a little higher in pitch was often added before and after the signal call. It is this flourish, in fanfare patterns using mainly the notes from the third to the sixth harmonics and repeating three or four times with variations, which was strictly called 'Toccata'. But more elaborate pieces were also performed incorporating such material, and these too might be called Toccata. Still longer pieces, carried up to the eighth harmonic, were called Sonata, and in spite of their limitations in the matter of harmony, were composed and notated in large numbers.

Monteverdi's Toccata here at the opening of *Orfeo* is an elaborated but not an extended example of the method.[7] The foundation is a double drone on the second and third harmonics, played by the *Basso* and the *Volgano* trumpeters, and giving the tonic and the fifth above. Next higher sounds the *Alto e basso*, which consists of an actual Toccata in the strict sense, taken in an abbreviated form from existing versions. The next higher part again is called *Quinta*, and is also an abbreviation of an existing version. The top part, called *Clarino*, is the only part freely composed by Monteverdi, and the only part to have a melodic line.

Drums are not specified; but they habitually came with the trumpets borrowed from the ducal retinue for performances of this kind. In later baroque opera scores, we sometimes find parts written out for drums (Lully included written drum parts in his *Amadis*; and Handel's *Semele* gives them an unaccompanied solo as well); but drummers expected to improvise their own parts traditionally. The *alto e basso* part in the Toccata to *Orfeo* includes patterns of repeated sixteenth-notes (semiquavers) and eighth-notes (quavers) which could suitably have been picked up by the drummer as the rhythmic basis of his part. His pitches would be at the tonic and dominant: here, therefore, concert D and A.

And what, apart from the trumpets and drums, were 'all the instruments' as here prescribed? Most unusually for the seventeenth century, we have a moderately complete indication of them, in a list at the beginning which, though it does not include all the instruments later indicated at different points in the score, includes most of them. This list shows a typical mixed orchestra such as late renaissance entertainments (especially interludes) are known from many descriptions to have employed.[8] The Florentine interludes of 1589, for example, employed as we saw lutes of various sizes including the big *chitaroni* or arch-lutes; liras [*da braccio*] and a lira da gamba (*arciviolata lira*); harps, guitars, psalteries, a cittern and a mandola; violins and viols (sopranino, tenor, bass and double-bass, as well as a viola bastarda and a bass viola bastarda—possibly meaning viols with sympathetic strings); flute, cornettos, trombones (including bass trombones); three chamber organs and a regal, and a 'little cembalo (*cembalino*) adorned with silver bells'.[9] In the same year as *Orfeo*, we find in Thomas Campion's *Description of a Maske. . .in honour of the Lord Hayes*, London, 1607, violins, lutes, bandora, harpsichord, cornettos, voices ('sixe Cornets, and sixe Chapell voices'), sackbut (trombone) and solo singers, to a total number of nearly forty musicians, as well as the dancers.

The list of instruments at the beginning of *Orfeo* names two harpsichords; two double-bass viols; ten ordinary members of the violin family; a double harp (of great depth and compass, as its written-out part in one passage shows); two tiny violins (dancing-masters' kits, playing an octave above their written parts); two archlutes (but three are indicated in the score); two little chamber organs (with wooden flue pipes); three bass viols (gambas); four trombones (but five seem to be required in the score); a regal (miniature organ with beating reeds, diminutive pipes, and unexpectedly powerful and snarling tone); two cornettos (short wooden horns of narrow conical bore, capable of extreme virtuosity and a silvery brilliance of tone); one sopranino flute (probably a recorder, and sounding two octaves above its written part); one clarino (long trumpet played very high) and three other trumpets (the same instrument, but played lower, and here specified as muted). Over forty instruments in all are concerned: a sizeable and varied orchestra. On the other hand, the passages where the full orchestra is meant to be playing at once seem to be quite few; and this was undoubtedly standard practice for the seventeenth century. The accompaniment of early recitative and aria was not yet reduced to the continuo of harpsichord and cello so usual in late baroque opera; but it was invariably in chamber style. The full orchestra was used only for brilliant but occasional contrast.

The 'Toccata' which forms the introduction (played by 'all the instruments') to Monteverdi's *Orfeo* is no more than sixteen half-notes (semibreves) in length. It stands throughout on a tonic pedal (in notation, C, in performance, D). There is no modulation; there is not even a chord change, not so much as an alternation of dominant and tonic harmony. In tonic D major the little piece begins; in tonic D major it remains. Not only is the harmonic material of the simplest possible; so also is the melodic material which Monteverdi composed for it in the *Clarino* part. This is virtually confined to portions of the diatonic scale, ascending and descending, in a slight though sufficient variety of rhythms. Yet there is something about this slight and simple musical gesture (it is hardly long enough to be called a move-ment) which is arresting and memorable. Scales and variants of scales are as common and as ordinary as musical material can well be; and never more so than in the early seventeenth century. Yet because material is ordinary, it does not follow that it is insignificant.

Ex. 4. Monteverdi, Orfeo *(Mantua, 1607), scale passages in opening Toccata used subsequently as thematic material:*

A NEOPLATONIC PERSONIFICATION

After the introductory Toccata in (concert) D major, we change to D minor with a Prologue for (of all appropriate personifications) the allegorical figure *La Musica*: she who is herself the moving music to which the protagonists are about to sing their moving words. 'I am Music,' she sings to us, 'who with sweet accents can make each troubled heart tranquil, and now with noble anger, and now with love can inflame the coldest minds. Singing to my golden lyre [*cetera*, kithara] I am accustomed at times to caress the mortal ear, and in this manner I draw souls more to the sonorous harmony of the lyre [*lira*, lyra] of heaven.' This is the text as set; as separately published by Striggio (Mantua, 1607), the text reads: 'and in such manner I draw souls more by the sonorous harmony of the lyre [*rote, rota*] of heaven.'

We notice that La Musica starts off by claiming, like the good humanist she evidently is, the ancient classical power over specific emotions, now noble anger, now the flame of love. Next she informs us that her lyre is 'golden', a purely allegorical advantage, since a wooden one would be literally, I suppose, a good deal more 'sonorous'. But Pindar[10] mentions 'Orpheus of the golden lyre', and the epithet partly implies supremely valuable (as in *aurea aetas*, the golden age); partly it is connected with Apollo, whose emblems, as befits a god of the sun and the light, are consistently golden. Music which can not only 'caress the mortal ear' but 'draw souls more to' (or 'by') 'the sonorous harmony of the lyre of heaven' recalls, as Giordano Bruno put it, that 'since (as the chief Platonists were not unaware) continual migration occurs from light to darkness. . .nothing hinders lower things from being gradually recalled to higher, under the sound of Apollo's universal lyre': Bruno, to whom the sun as a Neoplatonic symbol for God was so necessarily the centre of the universe that he patronized Copernicus rather slightingly for needing to demonstrate mathematically anything so patently evident.[11] The lyre to which Ficino himself used to sing Orphic hymns was painted with a portrait of Orpheus,[12] whose dark origins and nocturnal rituals recall a profound saying of Heraclitus, reflected in Neoplatonic doctrine, that 'God is day and night.'[13] Orfeo will have to visit the dark underworld before being drawn to heaven in just the manner intended by La Musica here; and 'therefore', she goes on now, 'a desire spurs me to speak to you of Orfeo, of Orfeo who drew the wild beasts to his singing and made Hell the servant of his entreaties.' Her music, as commonly in the Prologue to the earliest operas, can be called a strophic aria in recitative style.

We have here a poetic form which is strict and regular, set to music of which the form is also strict, but not quite regular. The poetic form is a conventional *canzonetta*. This term was applied historically to a strophic poem, in which the strophes may be of any number, comprising any number of lines, of any number of syllables and with any rhyme scheme, provided that each strophe is the same in all these respects. This example has five strophes, each of four eleven-syllable (hendecasyllabic) lines, with the rhyme-scheme *abba*. It is a most craftsmanlike and delightful short piece of lyric poetry, of which the delight comes in fact very largely from the inconspicuous strictness of the craftsmanship and the graceful regularity of the form. It is all done with easy mastery, but is also done with exact precision.

The musical form, at the same time strict in construction and flexible in texture, is that known now (though it was not known historically) as rondo strophic variation. This one is strophic in setting each strophe of the poem to a melody substantially unchanged, on a bass and harmony hardly changed at all; and rondo-like in having an instrumental ritornello as prelude, interludes and postlude which are unchanged except by shortening the interluding repetitions. The vocal melody, however, has enough variation to fit the words of each strophe with equal exactness. So might an eloquent actor have declaimed these verses; and so might his declamation have been heightened into song.

And here we may notice a small feature which in course of the opera becomes cumulatively evident. Both the ascending scale of the opening Toccata, and the descending scale which is its mirror opposite, are present here, in the original tonality of D (i.e. the concert pitch of the Toccata owing to the transposing mutes on the trumpets, which bring it a tone higher than its notated pitch of C; but in the major there and in the minor here). That is not at first a very striking resemblance (especially with the change of mode). It seems more a coincidental effect of idiom than a deliberate stroke of craftsmanship; and so indeed it may in some degree have been. But as the opera proceeds, we find very numerous appearances of these mirrored scales; many of them are in D minor, and repeat the same or virtually the same notes as this present instance; and there can be no doubt that such frequent and close reiterations contribute greatly to that overall impression of unity which is so marked a characteristic of this first of Monteverdi's operatic masterpieces. Peri and Caccini also use similar passages, but without achieving either Monteverdi's intensity or his unity.

The Toccata itself cannot have been very specifically associated by Monteverdi with the texture of the opera, since he used it again in his *Vespers* of 1610, to support an independent structure for the voices; and in any case, the traditional ingredients drawn from normal trumpeters' conventions far exceed the small addition of these scales in the *Clarino* part. But once the scales get into the vocal texture of the opera itself, they do have a unifying effect beyond the reach of mere coincidence. It may be doubted whether there are any mere coincidences in a work of art: perhaps there are only correspondences planned sometimes more and sometimes less deliberately. The following examples from the Prologue and Act I are representative of similar passages throughout the opera where these expressive portions of the descending and ascending scales often in D minor (and sometimes the same actual notes in related tonalities) recur.

*Ex. 5. Monteverdi, Orfeo (Mantua, 1607), Prologue, (a) the Ritornello
leading to (b) the start of the first strophe—both descending D minor—and (c)
fragment notable for the unresolved seventh; Act I, (d) the opening recitative,
descending D minor—this looks like a deliberate recall of (b) with a different
continuation; (e) succeeding chorus with the same descending notes, but in G
minor through D minor to F major—certainly appearing to be a deliberate
recall of (d); (f) ensuing recitative, ascending G minor; (g) ascending
chorus; (h) irregularly descending scale notable for the chromatically prepared
seventh (if it can be called prepared) and two further sevenths, the first unresolved leading to the second unprepared; (i) and (j) from Orfeo's first entry,
descending G minor, then descending and ascending G minor to A minor;
(k) from Euridice's reply, descending A minor—compare the ascending and
descending scales in D minor (concert pitch) at Ex. 4 above (realizations
are mine):*

e) Choro (chorus)

Vie – ni I – meneo_____ deh vie – ni

[Come Hymen, ah come]

f) Ninfa (nymph)

Mu – se, ho –nor di Par–na – – so a –mor del cie – lo

[Muses honour of Parnassus, love of heaven]

g) Choro (chorus)

La – scia-te i mon–ti la-scia–te i fon – – – – – – ti Nin [fe]

S.
S.

La – – scia-te i mon– – ti la-scia–te fon [ti]

[Leave the mountains, leave the fountains, nymphs]

h) Pastore (shepherd) [=♮]

[fe]-sti la -gri-mar que – – – – – ste cam- pa – – gne

[made these fields to mourn]

i) Orfeo

Ro – sa del ciel vi – – ta del mon – – do

[Rose of heaven, life of the world]

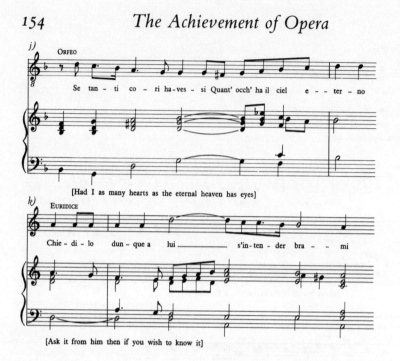

j) ORFEO

Se tan - ti co - ri ha-ves - si Quant' occh' ha il ciel e - - ter - no

[Had I as many hearts as the eternal heaven has eyes]

k) EURIDICE

Chie - di - lo dun - que a lui _____ s'in - ten - der bra - - mi

[Ask it from him then if you wish to know it]

ACT I: A PASTORAL IDYLL

Act I opens in a familiar pastoral setting: the glades of Thrace. It is familiar not as it is on the map of Greece, but rather as it may be somewhere on the map of the psyche, where our poignant fantasies of Arcadia or Eden or Circe's enchanted island linger. For those earning a hard living in the fields, perhaps the townsfolk hold the secret of happiness in their rich cities? For those enduring the noisy bustle of the cities, perhaps the country-folk have it in their peaceful cottages? But no, it must have vanished with the Golden Age. It is the old nostalgic dream of a stage of life before care and consciousness and adult human responsibility; but it carries one overriding disadvantage. There is no growing up in Arcadia.

Orfeo, we learn, has just come from such lover's despair into such bliss at being accepted by Euridice that we cannot miss the dramatic irony, based as it is on the classical theme that extremes are dangerous, which indeed they are in so far as they go with inflated states of mind. Moderation in all things is the classic moral. But for the moment these sober thoughts are dismissed, as a shepherd (recalling the previous music in a descending D minor scale—for which see Ex. 5d above) urges his companions to sing worthily of Orfeo (he calls him *il nostro semideo*, our demigod—which is what Rinuccini's Aminta also called him): Orfeo who has this day won his Euridice after her long scorn of him. The poetry again lays out, and the music takes up, a characteristic blend of formality and liberty. There are three hendecasyllabic (eleven-syllable) lines without rhyme; six heptasyllabic (seven-syllable) lines in *rime baciate* (rhyming couplets); a hendecasyllabic (eleven-syllable) rhyming couplet; and back (with the first words changed) to the opening five lines. Monteverdi's music makes of this a strophic variation after a contrasting middle, i.e. a miniature da capo aria, but in the texture of recitative. Sometimes we notice Monteverdi making Striggio's rhythms flex themselves a little beyond their natural declamation in speech: for example, adjacent syllables may be elided (run together as one syllable) by the scansion of the poetry but given separate notes in the music; or conversely, compact elisions may be set to one short note requiring extreme compression to get them in. But this does not go beyond what the great flexibility of the Italian language itself can tolerate.

The chorus now reiterates (but in regular outline) the same descending scale-passage (see Ex. 5e above) to invoke Hymen as divinity of marriage: 'and may your burning (*ardente*) torch be like a rising sun to bring tranquil days to these lovers', keeping from them 'the shadows of suffering and grief'. The poetry is very similar to what it was in the preceding recitative: a quatrain of three heptasyllabic lines and one hendecasyllabic line, rhyming *abba*; and a couplet of one heptasyllabic line and one hendecasyllabic line, rhyming *cc*. But the music moves in mainly homophonic symmetry, with five voice-parts of frottola-like simplicity. The couplet at the end is reiterated by Monteverdi: first, in C major; second, in A minor returning to G major to match the G minor opening. Thus again the musical form, while using the poetic form well, adds something to it independently.

The 'burning torch' of Hymen is a phallic symbol, both for the flesh and for the masculine principle which is 'like a rising sun' of the spirit. Hymen himself, like Orfeo, was the son—by one of the Muses—of Apollo, and is thus suitably invoked against 'the shadows of suffering and grief'. Ficino [14] called the sun an 'Orphic mystery'; and 'if we do not want to claim this Orphic mystery as true, we may at least imagine it as being true, so that, looking thus at the celestial sun, we may see in it, as in a mirror, that supercelestial One who has pitched his tent in the sun'—just as Plato's Socrates 'took refuge in moral philosophy so that with its help the mind, dispelling the bodily clouds, may become more tranquil and at once receive the light of the divine sun that shines at all times and everywhere.'

And now one of the nymphs takes up the Neoplatonic metaphor, asking the Muses to sound their lyres and 'tear away the dark veil of every cloud'. She sings this, once more, in mingled hendecasyllabic (eleven-syllable) and heptasyllabic (seven-syllable) lines (rhyming *abbaccdd*), to recitative in which the ascending scale (see Ex. 5f above) is cheerfully prominent at the start and towards the end. The five-part chorus imitates this more melismatically and tunefully, almost floridly, in the lightest of madrigal-like counterpoint (see Ex. 5g above). They dance as they sing, very agreeably, in G major, 'to the sound of five violins' (in various sizes), 'three archlutes, two harpsichords, a double harp, a double bass viol and a little flute at the second octave' (a silvery edging, perhaps, to the top line of the chorus). With a musical ambivalence matching the poetical ambivalence, however, the chorus, half way through, darkens into C minor while at the same time brightening into brisk triple rhythm. It is no longer contrapuntal, but chordal, and with a nicely ambiguous cross-relation between E flat and E natural to sophisticate the harmony.

Ex. 6. Monteverdi, Orfeo, *Act I, Chorus showing cross-relation:*

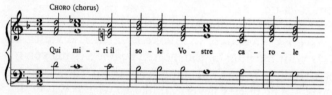

[Here let the sun look upon your dances]

The words, in lines of five to seven syllables with irregular rhymes, are still full of charming conceits. 'Let the sun see your dancing, prettier than that of the stars to the moon at dark night.' Natale Conti[15] has this to say: 'do you not see, that the Sun is God, and the moon [is God], of whom the Greeks called the one Apollo, and the other Diana'—and we may once more remember the Orphic doctrine 'that God is day and night'.[16] For the moment, it is the light side which is uppermost; for 'out of the torment of their desires they rejoice blissful at last.' Torment yesterday: bliss today; but tomorrow? For the moment, a shepherd is singing in carefree recitative, set to four unrhymed hendecasyllables and a rhymed couplet of pentasyllables, as he contrasts Orfeo's past tears (to a chromatic darkening of the descending scale) with the present happiness which he asks him (brightly diatonic) to celebrate with his famous lyre.

Orfeo, hitherto silent amidst all this rejoicing in his honour, responds by praying to the sun, which is 'the life of the world', and which 'sees all things'. These timeless sentiments, occupying two symmetrically rhyming couplets (three hendecasyllables and one heptasyllable) have in spite of their poetic regularity been set by Monteverdi in appropriately free and timeless recitative, above a tonic pedal in G minor, as the melody sketches in the descending and ascending scales (see Ex. 5i and Ex. 5j above). The poem next breaks away from rhyme, mingling unrhymed heptasyllables and hendecasyllables, with the shorter lines predominating. The words here

(Ex. 5i) recall, by what must surely be a deliberate reminiscence, the same line from Petrarch which Rinuccini quoted; and at once it imparts a less timeless and more personal reference (though the Neoplatonic double-take would again not have altogether escaped notice at the period): 'Rose of heaven, life of the world, and worthy offspring of him who bridles the universe, the sun which circles all things and looks at all things from the star-strewn circuits, say, have you seen a more happy and fortunate lover?'[17] The music, too, moves more into time, as the tonality begins to modulate; as the melody becomes more tuneful; as the bass becomes more active; in short as recitative verges towards arioso. Orfeo turns his thoughts yet more warmly to Euridice herself; and with this the form approaches that of a little aria, with the last phrase but one of the melody repeating, though the words do not, and though the melody itself hovers between the freedom of recitative and the symmetry of aria. The elements are felicitously mixed, and arioso is probably the best description for the mixture.

A DRAMATIC IRONY

Donald Grout well pointed out, in a perceptive essay,[18] the formal symmetry of this entire act, in which Orfeo's warm words to Euridice, and the radiant answer which she at once makes to him, provide a central pivot, balanced on either side by choruses to repeated words and music. The impersonal choruses are like a contemplative framework, and the personal encounter of the two lovers is like the picture framed. The entire act is a lyrical preparation for the harsher events to come; but it has its high point of intensity here, where the lovers sing to one another. And so Euridice makes her radiant answer, in two elegant rhymed couplets (each of one heptasyllabic and one hendecasyllabic line), and another couplet (of two hendecasyllabic lines). But even as she answers (see Ex. 5k for the usual scale), Monteverdi makes one of those unexpected comments which it is the uncanny prerogative of music to pass upon words. The music does not openly contradict the words; but it points behind the words to something very different which is latent in the future, and still unknown to the characters (yet hardly unknown to the audience, since this was and is one of the most familiar of classical Greek legends).

The musical interval outlined by Euridice in her first notes, to her first words of rejoicing and of the joy she is bringing to Orfeo, is a tritone, begun on D natural and landing on the G sharp a diminished fifth beneath (see Ex. 7a below). Now the tritone is that strange musical interval (little enough favoured in Monteverdi's period) which divides the octave ambiguously in the middle, leaning neither to the one tonal direction nor to the other. Ambivalence cannot be more unmistakably suggested in music than by a prominent emphasis on the tritone interval. And where, in this opera, do we next prominently encounter the tritone interval? We encounter it (between the same notes D and G sharp) in the messenger's account of Euridice's death (Ex. 7b below). Whether deliberately or intuitively (and deliberately seems probable), this is a most poignant touch of dramatic and musical irony. Euridice's first words of happiness (hesitant words, it is true, when we read them carefully) are sung to the music of her subsequent tragedy.

The opening chorus of this scene, shortened, and after that the opening chorus of this first act itself, are both brought back to round off the scene with an effective verbal and musical recapitulation, which is at the same time a dramatic line of division; for after this comes a new mood, new poetic treatment and new musical material. A shepherd rather pointedly proposes, in unrhymed hendecasyllables and heptasyllables set to a brief and simple recitative, first, that since good fortune comes from heaven, thanks should be sent up for present blessings; second, that since you never can tell, prayers should also be sent up against future misfortunes. A closing passage of ritornello, ensemble and chorus, in rondo-like alternation, continues the un-rhymed hendecasyllables and heptasyllables (the longer lines now preponderating) to the end of the act; while Monteverdi's musical treatment brings brief repetition of words much more frequently, with much greater over-lapping contrapuntally, and altogether with much more obscuring of the words by the music, than at any previous point in the opera. It is as if we were being prepared by both poet and musician for that troubling of the opening mood of happiness which the plot next holds in store.

The poet, too, has now begun more explicitly to draw, and the composer to reinforce, the classical moral. Never fall into extremes. Never despair when things look bad; for 'as after the guilty (*rio*) pregnant (*gravido*) cloud, the womb (*seno*) of the tempest, has horrified the world, the sun displays more brightly its shining rays, and after the harsh frost of naked winter, spring clothes the fields with flowers, see Orfeo, for whom just before sighs were his food and laments his drink. Now he is so happy that there is nothing further which he can desire.'

Nothing, indeed; yet we continue to detect, under this cheerful felicitation, the same hint of unspoken irony. For if bliss can succeed to misery, then misery can succeed to bliss; and with our presumed foreknowledge of the plot, we in the audience are likely to have this somewhere in the back of our minds. In fact, Striggio in his printed poem concluded this Act with some lines which Monteverdi did not set, perhaps as being too moralistic for so fashionable an occasion; for they explicitly account the suffering of misery as a moral merit, and the enjoyment of happiness as a moral danger. That is more austere

Ex. 7. *Monteverdi,* Orfeo, *(a) Act I, prophetic tritone; (b), (c) and (d)*
Act II, the prophecy fulfilled (my realizations):

than the most usual Neoplatonic attitude, and Striggio himself may
either have made or approved of the change; for since he and Monteverdi were in Mantua together, they are likely to have discussed
personally the progress of the opera, and no letters passed which
might decide the point for us. The text as set is certainly better theatre
and perhaps better poetry than the text as separately printed.

These concluding lines, occurring in the printed poem but not in the
opera, are still in unrhymed hendecasyllables and heptasyllables except for one beautifully pointed internal rhyme (*gioire* at the end of one
line, *morire* in the middle of the next), and one rhyming couplet (of one
hendecasyllabic line and one heptasyllabic line) coming very artistically at the end. They read: 'But why so much rejoicing (*gioire*) after so

much dying (*morire*)? Eternal Divinities, mortal eye does not see your lofty works because a shining (*splendente*) mist overshadows them (*adombra*)'—the paradox is of course typically Neoplatonic and intentional—'yet, if it is permitted to unfold an inner thought only to change it where error reveals itself, we shall say that in this manner, while heaven favours Orfeo's prayers, it wishes to make a more certain proof of his virtue: for suffering miseries is small merit (*pregio*), but the gracious turning of propitious fate is wont to mislead souls from the straight path. Gold is thus more prized for [having passed through] the fire; hard-won merit will thus enjoy a more exalted honour.'

Even in the less patently moralistic lines which Monteverdi did choose to set, we must marvel at the highly condensed suggestiveness with which the poetry hints at ominous potentialities beneath the propitious surface. A cloud 'guilty' (*rio*), 'pregnant' (*gravido*) as the 'womb (*seno*) of the tempest'? Clouds cannot literally be accounted guilty, nor are they pregnant wombs except in metaphor; but we can indeed project on to them our own guilty feelings, followed by our relief 'as the sun displays more brightly its shining rays'. It can hardly be pointed out too emphatically that human happiness is not really guilty. But it may seem so to a moralist who envies it, or to a hedonist who seeks it as obsessively as his own guilty apprehensions for ever debar him from attaining it. Indeed I think we carry as a species an unavoidable burden of uneasiness, half pulled back as we are to that Arcadian fantasy of animal or at least childhood irresponsibility, and half drawn on whether we wish it or not towards the actual responsibilities and cares of human consciousness. We may project part of this ambivalence against other people as if they were our persecutors, and part of it against ourselves as if we were born wicked; but it is still a self-imposed torment. If the gods seem jealous of an inflated happiness, it is the inflation and not the happiness which is the real danger: what the Greeks called hubris; and it has a terrible way of bringing its own revenge, since we are never more vulnerable than when we feel invulnerable. The 'guilty' cloud might picture some such uneasiness, and it might be 'pregnant' of some growth of character, since Striggio added that 'gold is thus more prized for the fire; hard-won merit will thus enjoy a more exalted honour.' A very worthy and Neoplatonic sentiment, though we may well feel that Monteverdi was very wise not to set the last few moralizing lines of it.

ACT II: SUDDEN CATASTROPHE

The second act of *Orfeo* has a different structure from the first act, because it has a different purpose. The purpose of the first act was to draw us into the enchanting though deceptive world of the pastoral fantasy; to build up the atmosphere of its poetical convention, at once so unreal outwardly and so real inwardly, so impossible historically and so convincing emotionally; to show us the nymphs and shepherds rejoicing, and at the mid-point of their rejoicing, to introduce us to the pair whose touching fortunes we are to follow. But the purpose of the second act is to intensify the idyll, only to break it at its most joyful point. Thus this act, also, is divided in the middle; but this time with violence and a complete change of tone.

The change of tone in the middle of this second act is produced by a change of style, both in the poetry and in the music. The early part of the act delights us with a flow of regularly rhyming quatrains: in octosyllabic (eight-syllable) lines for Orfeo, and in heptasyllabic (seven-syllable) lines for individual shepherds and chorus; but the rhyme-scheme in all quatrains is a simple *abba*, and we are in effect close to that most conventional of metres for musical setting, the *ottava rima* (eight-line rhyming stanzas of varying line-lengths). The elegant and symmetrical poetry is matched by Monteverdi, not literally, but with a device of musical form which catches just the same touch of elegant artfulness: when Orfeo sings, the first two lines of each quatrain are repeated after the second two lines, to make of it a tiny da capo aria. In this and other ways, Orfeo stands out in his music just a little above his companions: he is one of them; but he is the most famous singer of them all, and his music, with its added touch of subtle craftsmanship, tells us so. In the second part of this act, after the catastrophe has broken, we shall not hear much of Orfeo's celebrated songster's art; he is himself too broken for the moment, and he is given, with great dramatic appropriateness, only broken phrases to sing until he gather his forces for his courageous resolution to go after his Euridice down to hell itself.

The sinfonia which introduces Act II is new music and nowhere repeated, but it uses the ascending and descending scales; and so does the shapely little aria (in miniature da capo form) with which Orfeo at once greets 'the dear woods and beloved slopes made happy by the sun through which my nights have day'. A shepherd replies in a brief rondo-strophic variation, of two strophes only, and with a new ritornello; but the descending scale is conspicuous in the arioso-like melody; and the poetical symmetry is beautifully rounded off in its musical setting. And so the taut construction and the limpid inspiration unfold together. The next ritornello (descending scale) alternates with a duet for two shepherds; the ritornello after that (ascending scale plain, descending scale ornamented, and two little flutes to give a pastoral sonority) alternates first with a further duet for which it provides substantially the same bass; and then with a choral re-working of that duet in solider rhythm. Do we notice all these meticulous connections, and their poetical foundation, when we hear the music? Only as an overall impression of unity, perhaps; but that is sufficient. The art is to conceal the art.

Orfeo's response is the weightiest passage so far in Act II: an aria in strophic rondo form, but virtually without variation. The ritornello is scored in five string parts for the violin family, with a double bass viol (violone) in support, and with two harpsichords and three lutes for crispness and sparkle (the scoring of such ritornellos may often be continued wholly or partly through the strophes too, though in that case we shall usually have to provide the instrumental parts for ourselves); the strophes are each in miniature da capo form. This gives a cyclic pattern within a cyclic pattern. And within this again, there is that delicious superimposition of two concurrent rhythms (simple triple and compound triple) which makes the hemiolia.

Ex. 8. Monteverdi, Orfeo, *Act II, simple with compound triple (re-barred to show the rhythm — my realization):*

[Do you recall, O shady forests]

A more brilliantly craftsmanlike and radiant scene could not have been composed. But into the very middle of it there falls catastrophe. In true classical manner, this catastrophe happens off-stage, and is narrated to us by a messenger. That in no way diminishes its impact. On the contrary, the intensity of the effect produced is equalled only by the simplicity of the means. If we can see just what is being contrived here, and with what consummate artistic certainty and ease, we shall have gone a long way towards understanding the greatness of early opera. The primary contrivance comes in the poetry, to which the music adds its further intensification. The poetic contrivance (but it is a stroke of genius) was to take out on the instant every trace of graceful elegance and charm, replacing these with a mere two lines of ponderous, unrhymed hendecasyllables, a mere weighty intimation of grief unspecified, from Silvia, the messenger of ill tiding, as she arrives distraught upon the happy scene. From here to the end of the act, these two lines, this couplet not even graced by the customary couplet rhyme, will be heard at repeated and shortening intervals, as a grievous refrain of woe. They make a strong link formally, and a cumulative menace emotionally. Their menace and their weight are built into their verbal structure. We could not find a better illustration of that high poetic art of making sonority meaningful, and meaning sonorous, which particularly since Bembo's celebrated treatise of 1525 had so influenced the advanced schools of humanist poetry. Here is Striggio's couplet, and its literal translation:

> Ahi caso acerbo! ahi fato empio e crudele!
> ahi stelle ingiuriose, ahi cielo avaro!

> Ah bitter chance! Ah pitiless and cruel fate!
> Ah wrongful stars! Ah covetous heaven!

The very load of syllables weights down the lines and plants in them a grievous meaning. Eleven scanning syllables make up the measure of each line; but how many more have to be pressed in by violent elision? There are eighteen syllables in the first and sixteen in the second of these two hendecasyllabic (eleven-syllable) lines. Elided syllables are not supposed to be counted in; but they have to be got into the declamation somehow just the same. The very effort of compressing so many of them in a line adds to its weight. These are ponderous sonorities for a ponderous state of feeling, over and above their semantic meaning and their musical setting; and all the more so through the abruptness of their sudden contrast with the light and elegant versification immediately preceding.

As to the semantic meaning, we may first notice further some verbal similarities with Rinuccini, who for example has *Fato invido e rio* ('envious and wicked fate') and *ahi fato acerbo* ('ah bitter fate'), as well as an overall similarity which was only to be expected. Next, both authors bring out that rather frightening idea of a covetous heaven, an envious fate, already foreshadowed. For the gods to be jealous of human happiness is a projection of our inner unease, but none the less unsettling on that account. We have already been prepared with cunning dramatic irony for this sudden reversal of fortune, and it hits us the harder because it comes like the confirmation of our worst forebodings.

On the same instant, the music leaves off all its previous elegance. We have been softened up by lyrical verses and shapely airs. The sudden and perfectly deliberate change to plain simplicity conveys better than any elaboration the dazed shock of tragedy. We are by now quite off our guard, as we enjoy one of those fairy-tale shepherds inciting Orfeo to further song. The verse is a rhyming quatrain; the key is untroubled C major; the metre is a lilting triple-time; the words are 'go on with your golden plectrum to sweeten the air' (in two senses) 'on so happy a day'. Then the bass note C is wrenched

ominously to C sharp, for a six-three chord of A major: later in
history, an overworked commonplace of recitative; but here as fresh
and poignant a twist to the music as the twist to the poetry which it
accompanies. 'Ah bitter chance! ah pitiless and cruel fate!' As the
messenger enters on this change of chord, and more exactly when she
sings 'to thee I come, Orfeo, unhappy messenger', that sinister tritone
(as D to G sharp) is outlined to which we heard Euridice's own first
hesitant words of happiness back among the carefree rejoicings of Act
I (see Ex. 7 above). Thus in the music, as in the poetry, the irony so
cunningly prepared is sprung. Out go the surging strings, the harpsichords, the double-bass, and all but one of the three lutes. One
remaining lute gives sharpness to the flue tones of a wooden chamber
organ. Their sound together is very clear, but very quiet. Here are no
histrionics of grief; here is an intimate disclosure from the heart, such
as the early reciting style excelled at expressing. The sudden stillness is
more arresting than any clamour.

Ex. 9. Monteverdi, Orfeo, *Act II, the turn of fortune and of harmony (my
realization):*

Throughout this tragic scene, the same uneasy interval of the tritone (mostly between D and G sharp) becomes increasingly prominent. The hard and bitter interval of the minor seventh further exacer-
bates the vocal line. There are, however, several interruptions to the
message of grief. The first two are from one of the shepherds, as
Striggio's printed poem indicates although Monteverdi's score does

not. The shepherd returns each time to C major, as if not quite taking
in the bad news; but he has already been shaken out of his rhyming.
We are wrenched back again to E major or A major by the messenger
as before; then at last Orfeo breaks in, at first uncomprehendingly,
soon with agonizing comprehension. The progressions between his
music and the messenger's are scarcely rational: E major to G minor; E
flat major to E major — harsh juxtapositions rather than modulations.
It is bewildering music for a bewildering situation.

And so Orfeo learns that his beloved Euridice is dead. The messenger (the nymph Silvia, one of Euridice's companions) now describes
the catastrophe in a long and eloquent recitative. As Euridice was
gathering flowers, 'a treacherous snake hidden in the grass stung her
foot with his poisoned tooth, and at once her lovely face grew pale and
the light faded from her eyes with which she put the sun to shame';
neither 'fresh water' nor 'powerful incantations' could revive her;
calling (sudden E major) 'Orfeo, Orfeo', she breathed (abrupt G
minor) 'a heavy sigh' and died. Thereupon, a shepherd repeats, as a
kind of grievous refrain, the messenger's heavy opening phrase, both
words and music. Another shepherd (distinguished as *secondo* in
Striggio's separately printed poem, though not at all in Monteverdi's
score) adds a new phrase of pity on the descending scale; the first
shepherd (*primo* in Striggio, no indication of any change in Monteverdi, but it should be made on the words *Ahi ben havrebbe un cor di
Tigre o d'Orsa*) adds another, modulating as he does so; but both are
heavy with tritone leanings. Orfeo responds by singing a longer
lament in impassioned recitative, at the peak of which (and at the top
of the ascending scale) he determines (down goes the scale) 'if verses
have any power, to go unharmed to the deepest abysses and having
softened the heart of the king of the shadows', to bring her back, or if
that fails, to stay with her in death. 'Farewell earth, farewell sky and
sun, farewell!'

The act is concluded by a sad finale, to balance in structure the
happy opening. The chorus picks up the words of the refrain which is
the messenger's first phrase, but to new music (though the scales
ascend and descend as usual). The messenger in her grief proposes to
hide herself from the light of the sun (yet again the sun); but we can
only hope that her melancholy fit will soon leave her; for she, of
course, is in no way to blame for the sad news she brings. Now two
duetting shepherds draw explicitly the bitter contrast between the
morning's joy and the ensuing sorrow, their music still restless with
tritones. A sad sinfonia on the descending scale leads the chorus back
with the prevous refrain, and also the duetting shepherds with their
tritones and some further chromatic shiftings (they have an arioso,
almost a recitative, in two parts at once, which is decidedly unusual).
The chorus sings again; but as in the previous act, it is not given

Ex. 10. Monteverdi, Orfeo, Act II, the crazed progressions of the messenger's scene (my realization):

Striggio's last lines to sing. There are seventeen more of these than Monteverdi set, the last pair being the couplet refrain, which also concludes the two sections of chorus set by Monteverdi. The unset lines ask what funeral rites, with what funeral lamp, can be worthy of Euridice. At the very end of the act, Monterverdi has a surprise of his own contriving in store for us. He brings in, most unexpectedly, the original ritornello with which (after the toccata or opening flourish) the whole opera began. Is it the quietest of hints that the beginning is not to be lost in the end, but that it may still come round full cycle? We cannot know as yet, but there is a sense of hidden potentialities in this formal recollection. Ambiguity is most strangely represented in the music here.

THE MYTHOLOGY OF SNAKES

The snake which bit Euridice calls up mythological associations of a typically archetypal ambiguity. In many religious rituals, including the Orphic rituals, snakes are prominent, as they are on the caduceus carried by Apollo's traditional companion, Mercury; by the Egyptian Thoth whom some Neoplatonists associated with Mercury; by Aesculapius, the son of Apollo, who used snakes for healing like those American-Indian shamans and others well known to cultivate inner power through their fearless handling of the dangerous reptiles. The snake holds power through its venom, which can both kill and cure; the snake is elusive and mysterious; the snake is a common ritual image for the soul. The snake in Eden tempted Eve, and she tempted Adam, to taste of the fruit of the tree of knowledge, thereby bringing that awareness of good and evil, of responsibility and mortality, which in retrospect feels like being ejected from a paradise on earth (but was it anywhere on earth?) as a punishment. But there are theological references to the Fall itself as a fortunate crime (*felix culpa*); and there can be little doubt that the knowledge thus prohibited, and gained by disobeying the prohibition, was in essence the self-knowledge which brought us out of animal irresponsibility into the beginnings of human awareness. The Fall on this level was the gradual start of consciousness, focused for dramatic effect into a sudden mythological crisis; and the snake was the initiator, cast as so often into the villain's role. The snake is an archetypal image, as the devil is. And the devil is certainly in the dark, where all manner of good and bad potentialities for our future development lie ambiguously concealed.

There was, again, that extremely potent snake-dragon, the Python, overcome by Apollo so that its decaying fumes might inspire his priestess the Pytheness to prophesy; and we have asked already whether this might have been in token of letting an outgrown stage of development give rise to a future stage. The snake-dragon killed by Siegfried in Norse mythology was another of them: obstructive beasts while they are still uncontested, but guardians of great treasures when the contest has with danger been won over them. Part of their symbolism concerns the risks of retrograde dependence on unconscious fantasies of being perpetually mothered, for which reason it perhaps was that the snake-dragon was a female monster in one Homeric Hymn;[19] and that in *Beowulf* the most dangerous monster was not Grendel but Grendel's mother. The danger is the fascination of getting back to the mothered state, and indeed of possessing in fantasy that most desired of inner images which stands for mother, so that our normal on-going process of growing into adult independence gets held up. Thus the complement of the obstructive Python is the seductive Circe, who may arrest our growth by seducing us just as surely as the Python may by devouring us. Those who overcome their dragon and gain a treasure have by that token gained some inner value; those who rescue a princess have gained some image of inner femininity which is not a mother-image but has been got away from mother; those who like Ulysses get away from Circe with their integrity intact may emerge the wiser for that potentially revealing experience. It all depends on how we manage in our unconscious fantasies to confront the adventure, of which in consciousness we may have no awareness.

In Virgil's[20] account of this present legend, which was followed by Poliziano though not by Rinuccini or by Striggio, Euridice was stung or bitten by the snake while being pursued among the flowers by one Aristaeus, who was another son of Apollo and thus half-brother to Orpheus, as well as being a fellow pupil with Aesculapius (yet another half-brother) of the Centaur Chiron in the art of healing. How these mythological figures do cross and connect together, and how ambivalently! That is perhaps one reason for their boundless suggestiveness. For here is Aristaeus, a legendary healer, attempting a rape and precipitating a death, all of it leading to a loss of Arcadia through the sting of a snake, which can also be taken symbolically as an access of awareness. If the flowers hint at Euridice's maidenhead, and the sting at phallic penetration, we can still ask whether what really hurt was not the sting of new self-knowledge. The sequel looks so very like a typical mythological quest, potentially for growth of character. The sequel is that Orfeo seeks his lost bride in the dark and dangerous caverns of the underworld.

ACT III: THE DESCENT

To announce Orfeo's arrival in the underworld at the start of Act III, 'here enter the trombones, cornettos and regals; and the viols of the arm' (violin family) 'and the organs of wood and harpsichords are silent, and the scene changes.' The trombones (sackbuts) were already traditional for scenes of the underworld, and remained so well into the nineteenth century; the cornettos, though wooden, are lip instruments which belong structurally and acoustically with the brass; the snarling regals, like other reed instruments, had also traditional associations with the powers of darkness. Altogether a darkly colourful sonority, very apt to our impressive descent; and the change of scenery is likely to have been impressive too. The music, of seven real parts, is in a steady pavan rhythm, and is new, but full of the familiar ascending and descending scales.

Ex. 11. *Monteverdi,* Orfeo, *Act III, opening Sinfonia; scales resembling* Toccata *as at Ex. 4 above:*

Orfeo arrives in the company of the allegorical figure of Hope, whom he thanks for guiding him 'to this sad and dark kingdom where the rays of the sun never reached'; and he asks her to help him 'to see again those happy lights' (*beate luci*: Euridice's eyes) 'which alone bring day to my eyes.' The poetry is in relaxed *versi sciolti* (blank verse); the music is in very free recitative; the images of light suggest that search for illumination represented by so many lost or chained or imprisoned heroines of mythology, for whose sake so many monsters or ogres or other champions of brute unconsciousness must be over-come and such grim forests or murky depths penetrated at such risk to life or sanity. Hope herself has done as much mediating for Orfeo as she can, and she points to the famous words from Dante,[21] inscribed in letters of iron on the stone gateway to the lowest regions: *Lasciate ogni speranza voi ch' entrate,* 'Abandon hope all ye who enter here.' It is like the very depth of a depression, potentially healing if we can hang on as Orfeo now does against the grim person of old Caronte (Charon) the ferryman of the underground River Styx, which has next to be crossed.

Caronte's is the first bass part to be heard in the opera, and a very low one at that, capable of taking us to the bottom of the world by the mere sound of it. Orfeo confronts him with the utmost of his own legendary musicianship; for at least La Musica, as she promised at the start of the opera, has not abandoned him. The scene now reached is the central point of the middle act; and it is worthy of its pivotal position. Caronte begins it with a short but magnificent arioso in tripartite strophic variation (three repetitions of a short bass un-changed except in rhythm, and one striking modification at the end; the melody not much more changed, but moulded to every rhythmic inflection of hendecasyllabic lines rhyming *abba*). Next there sounds a Sinfonia even darker than the one which introduced the Act, and best kept in the same brassy scoring (though none is indicated); it is in five parts, uses the descending scale, and lies uncommonly low. Then comes Orfeo's reply, in the most famous and elaborate aria in all this famous opera: *Possente spirto,* 'Powerful spirit and terrible divinity without whom no passage is made to the other shore'. To persuade that spirit no resource of the singer's art can be too much; it is dramatically appropriate for Orfeo to show the utmost of his virtuos-ity, and so he does.

The poetic metre, with a singular if somewhat unexpected appropriateness, is that *terza rima* of three-line stanzas (rhyming progressively *aba, bcb, cdc* etc., always with a final quatrain *yzyz*) with which Dante worked so extended a miracle in the *Divina commedia*. There are six long verses mainly of rondo strophic variation. The refrain is a ritornello of which the bass is in each case substantially the same (with the usual slight changes—but only of rhythm this time). This ritornello follows each of the first three verses, but thereafter drops out; it is melodically quite different at each appearance, and scored for different instruments, the first time for a pair of violins, the second for a pair of cornettos, the third for a double harp. In each case, the previous verse has already used the same instruments for obbligato accompaniment. Both obbligato and ritornello parts are fully written out, and are of a brilliance and virtuosity comparable to that of the vocal writing; they give us a remarkable insight into what might otherwise have been improvised (and in like situations may habitually have been improvised) to meet the musical challenge of so dramatic a scene. The fourth verse has obbligato interjections for two violins and cello. The fifth verse (of which the bass is different) has no obbligato accompaniment written out. The sixth verse (back to the strophic bass) has a simple four-part accompaniment written out, with the instruction: 'the other parts' (other than the voice part and the bass part) 'were played on three violins' (*viole da braccio*, probably two violins and a viola), 'and let a double-bass viol play very softly' (*tocchi pian piano*). In addition, there is a basic accompaniment throughout of chamber organ and lute.

For the first four verses, two versions are given of the vocal part, with the instruction that Orfeo 'sings one only of the two parts'. One of these two versions is relatively plain; the other is exceedingly ornamental. At the first performance, the role of Orfeo was taken by the tenor Giovanni Gualberto Magli,[22] lent for the occasion by the Grand Duke of Florence, and praised for his extraordinary vocal accomplishment by those most closely concerned. It seems possible that the ornamental version sets down an approximation to what Magli sang at the first performance, whether written out for him by Monteverdi, or (more likely) more or less improvised by Magli for the occasion and subsequently written out. The plain version may have been Monteverdi's notation as a basis for such improvisation; for it cannot have been meant to be sung as plainly as it is written. We have a parallel in Bartolomeo Barbarino's second book of solo *Motetti* (Venice, 1614), also with plain and ornamental versions, of which the Preface explains that those who wish to ornament for themselves can do so on the basis of the plain version, while those who cannot or will not ornament for themselves can use the ornamental version provided.

Thus the choice here in 'Possente spirto' is not between the plain version and the ornamental version: the choice is between ornamenting the plain version for ourselves, on the one hand, and using the ornamental version as provided for us in Monteverdi's score, on the other (or a little of each). Both voice and instruments are notated in this scene with written-out parts of exceptional elaboration. But it may not be the fact of their being elaborate which was exceptional, so much as the fact of their being notated. Having dazzled Caronte and us by his display of virtuosity, however, Orfeo passes to simplicity with a still more moving appeal, from the heart to the heart, in the last two verses, neither of which has an ornamental version written out; and surely it is good drama and good musicianship to refrain from adding any elaborate ornamentation beyond the little which is given in the (single) notated version here.

The hidden cunning of the composing is again worth noticing. The same sequence of bass notes supports (though with different durations) the first four verses (with two interpolations of three extra notes each in the fourth stanza while the voice is momentarily resting but the strings are playing). For the fifth verse, the bass is free, with some grievously chromatic inflections towards the end. For the sixth verse, the original bass strictly returns, save for the one interpolated B flat leading to a repetition of its last six notes as the support for a little coda. Meanwhile the refrain has been reiterating its own strict but different bass: a lesser strophic variation within a greater strophic variation. The seemingly uncalculated spontaneity of Monteverdi's inspiration is no illusion. The only illusion is in its seeming to be uncalculated. The entire scene should be looked up in the score, since it is of too broad a scope to be shown by a brief example here. Ex. 12 is from the written-out harp part.

Caronte admits to his delight and ravishment in a somewhat varied repetition of the music of his first sonorous arioso, the bass being substantially the same. He adds that pity would little become his own true worth (*valor*); but even while Orfeo renews his appeal in a recitative full of lamentable suspensions, and merging into arioso as the tension grows and the bass line presses into more urgent movement, Caronte is beginning to nod; and during a 'very soft' (*pian piano*) repetition of the low-lying Sinfonia (now 'with violins, one organ, and one double-bass viol') he falls asleep. Another short recitative for Orfeo, but leading to the same arioso, on the same bass (now realized by chamber organ 'alone'), and he has jumped into Caronte's boat and pushed out manfully for the further shore. There are times when the best thing that can happen to the stern censor who stands guard at the threshold of the unconscious, repressing its contents and debarring our potentially healing contact with them, is that he should fall asleep.

The opening Sinfonia of this third act returns to introduce a 'Chorus of spirits, to the sound of a regal, five trombones' (*tromb.*—but probably not, for the underworld, including trumpets, *trombe*), 'two gambas and double bass'. Their music is new, in five parts more polyphonically developed, and at greater length, than previous choruses. Being spirits, they are perhaps speaking for our own intuitions when they tell us, in a stanza of ten rhyming lines of mixed lengths ending with a rhymed couplet, that Orfeo has 'ploughed the wavy fields of the unstable plain, and sowed the seeds of his labours, whence he reaped golden harvest', crossing the water in his 'fragile boat'. There are in Striggio's separately printed poem two more stanzas, not set by Monteverdi, in which Orfeo's boldness is compared favourably with that of Daedalus. The 'golden harvest' links up with Apollo 'rich in gold', as Conti[23] recalls from Callimachus (*fl.* Alexandria, *c.*250 B.C.); and gold links up with light as well as with value in much

Ex. 12. *Monteverdi, Orfeo, Act III, ritornello for 'Arpa dopia':*

1) to 2) following Malipiero's emendation: original a note higher. Most editorial accidentals are also in agreement with Malipiero. The augmented second appears, clearly printed, elsewhere in the opera (e.g. early in Act V: see Ex. 16a. Nevertheless, they *may* be erroneous here.)

traditional mythology (gold 'gave forth light beneath the waters', for example, in the Prose Edda).[24] Light and value are I think both being sought on this symbolic journey.

ACT IV: THE UNDERWORLD

As if to emphasize the dramatic continuity, the same majestic sinfonia which opened Act III, and which returned just before its concluding chorus, comes now at the beginning of Act IV. We are in the underworld palace of Pluto (Hades); and his queen Proserpina (Persephone) is already pleading with him, by his own once impetuous love for her, to restore Euridice to the lamenting Orfeo. We twice hear a lamentable tritone in the melody, as if to recall the tragedy which gave rise to the laments; and there is a particularly clear entry of the descending scale, at its original pitch. 'If ever you drew amorous sweetness from these eyes' (but Proserpina too uses the poetic word *luci*, 'lights'), 'if the smoothness of this forehead ever pleased you, which you call your heaven, so that you swear to me that you do not envy Jove his destiny [i.e. as ruler of heaven], I pray you, I pray you by that fire with which once love lighted your great soul, let Euridice return, to rejoice in those days which she used to draw out, living, in feast and song; and do thou console the weeping of the wretched Orfeo.'

So for Pluto, king of the underworld, there is 'light' and 'heaven' too, in the person of his beloved Proserpina; and she it is who mediates for Orfeo. Pluto consents, subjecting Orfeo to the famous condition: 'but before he draws his feet from this abyss, let him never turn to her his eager eyes' (*lumi*, another poetic use of 'lights' for 'eyes'), 'for a single look shall be the certain cause of her eternal loss'. And to a particularly haunting turn of melody: 'let Orfeo understand it, and let Euridice understand it, nor let any other one hope to be allowed to change it.' (See Ex. 13 below.)

'Lights' for 'eyes' is just the kind of poetic licence, the pretty juggling with words, that we are so apt to take for granted: but the sense behind the licence is that we see light through our eyes; so, poetically, our eyes are the light. This is a typical poetic identification of the subject with the object. We project something which is in ourselves out on to something associated with it or resembling it outside ourselves. And what in ourselves have we to project on to the light outside? We have consciousness, which is to the psyche what light is to the universe. For even in the underworld, it appears that the sun may hint poetically at the masculine component. Proserpina, in thanking Pluto, sings, to the descending scale in almost exactly the slight variation used by La Musica at her very first entry (but here in B flat to D minor): 'Blessed be the day when first I pleased you, blessed

Ex. 13. Monteverdi, Orfeo, Act III, Pluto's condition:

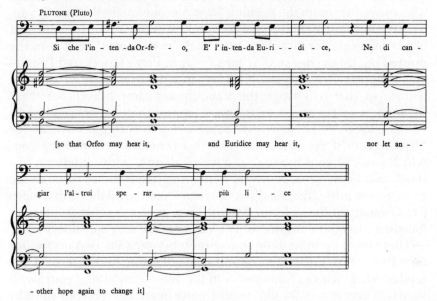

be the rape and the sweet deceit, whereby through my fortune I made conquest of you, capturing sun (*prendendo sole*).' And that, in these underworld circumstances, is a remarkable image, even for a Neoplatonist.

Ex. 14. Monteverdi, Orfeo, Act IV, Proserpina's reply, varied descending scale to D minor, recalling Ex. 5b above:

Proserpina's mediation here is brought out by Poliziano, Rinuccini and Striggio alike; it seems clear once more that each later poet was aware of his predecessor's work. The first version of Poliziano's *Orfeo* has Orfeo reminding Pluto of his 'celebrated ancient love' for Proserpina; the second version has both Proserpina and Orfeo doing so.[25] 'But,' sings Orfeo almost identically in both these versions, 'if any memory remains of your ancient and celebrated love, if you have the old abduction in your mind, give back to me my dear Euridice.' In

Rinuccini's *Euridice*, Orfeo pleads with Pluto, 'if the beautiful goddess who moved through the burning (*acceso*) mountain to flee you in vain retreat and avoidance always shows and turns to you the tranquil rays of her heavenly forehead', to give back 'my woman' (*donna*, in the printed poem) or 'my soul' (*l'anima mia*, in Peri's score); and Proserpina supports Orfeo's plea, 'O King, in whose semblance I am contented, so that to change the tranquil and clear heaven for these shadows is sweet and dear to me. . .appease the lamentation of so noble a lover.'[26] These words come close to Striggio's words for Monteverdi: 'if the smoothness of this forehead ever pleased you, which you call your heaven'; and we recall now with something of a shock that Proserpina, too, was wandering like Euridice through the grass, innocently gathering flowers, when Pluto caused the earth to open (traditionally at the volcanic Mount Etna, which is what Rinuccini's 'burning mountain' means) and raped her away into the underworld.

There must be something in common between the two myths; for now Pluto shows that he too is still afraid of losing his Proserpina. He replies to her, with a reminiscence of the descending scale, 'your sweet words of love renew the old wound in my heart. Let not your spirit be any longer so desirous of heavenly delight that you desert your marriage bed.' If ever Proserpina were to desert her marriage bed, if ever she were to betray the legendary bargain by which she spends part of her year on earth, and part in the underworld, she could no longer fulfil her mediatory function. Kerényi[27] has well suggested that by part of her year, we are being told in mythological imagery: part of her function. No adventurer has yet found the throne of the queen of the underworld empty; it is unthinkable. She is there and she is elsewhere; she is below and she is above; she is a mediating influence. It was with the connivance of her father Zeus that she was raped away, not only from the light of day, but from what was perhaps too immature an identification with her mother Demeter—as if in token of our need to draw our unconscious image of femininity away from too much identification with the mother. The bargain by which she could then partake of both the upper and the lower spheres was a notable reconciliation of which the significance was not lost upon the Neoplatonic mythographers. But Hades must keep his side of the bargain, too, or Persephone would be a prisoner, not a mediator. As on conditions he then agreed to let her go free, so now on conditions he, at her instance, lets Euridice go free.

THE PROHIBITION DISOBEYED

The chorus praises the triumph of 'love and compassion'. Orfeo rejoices with an aria in rondo strophic variation, the ritornello for

which has two violins in thirds, charmingly inverted to sixths for the
repeat. But then in sudden doubt he slips from G major to G minor,
and from impetuous aria to agitated recitative. 'Alas', he sings to that
anguished tritone so directly associated with earlier disaster (at first, C
down to F sharp; then actually D down to G sharp, as orginally at
Euridice's first entry so many dramatic scenes earlier, and again at the
messenger's announcement of Euridice's death). 'That which Pluto
forbids, Love commands! It is the stronger power, who conquers men
and gods, that I must surely obey!'

It must be admitted that the music sounds less like love than like
compulsion. At least there is a 'noise behind the curtain', or what
Orfeo's imagination persuades him is a noise, and he gets more
frightened than ever. He turns round, and there she stands. And
thence, even as he sees her, she vanishes away. He enjoys for a
moment the sweet light of her eyes (*dolcissimi lumi*); 'but alas what
eclipse darkens you?' The music too is darkened with the same ominous tritone, to which her answer gives a still crueller wrench by
jerking it through C minor and E flat major violently into E major.
'Ah sight too sweet and too bitter!', she sings. 'By too much love have
you lost me? And I, wretched one, have lost the power to enjoy light
and sight, and lose with it what is more dear, my husband'—for that,
she leaps the tritone D to G sharp directly, landing on an augmented
second to the bass note F natural, which only then drops to the
anticipated E natural. It is a progression very similar to Dido's lamenting 'Remember me' in Purcell's *Dido*, three-quarters of a century
later, also a moving death scene with symbolical potentialities.

For, of course, there is no literal sense to be made out of Euridice
having to die a second time. There can only be a symbolical sense.
When Rinuccini's Apollo sang 'immortal as I am, I languish and die',
Dafne's transformation had probably something to do with Apollo's
growth of character. I think Striggio here may be showing us something to do with Orfeo's growth of character.

Plato[28] blamed Orpheus for being unwilling really to die for Euridice like Alcestis for Admetus. Poliziano[29] enlarged on this by stating
his opinion that Ficino, at any rate, had 'brought back with his lyre the
true Euridice, that is, by the fullest judgement, Platonic wisdom'.
When Ficino[30] saw himself as 'born' of the distinguished physician
who was his father, but 'reborn' of Cosimo de' Medici who was his
patron, friend and counsellor, he was presumably referring to John
3:3—'Except a man be born again, he cannot see the Kingdom of
God'; for 'that which is born of the flesh is flesh, and that which is born
of the Spirit is spirit.' We might almost get the feeling here in this
portion of the myth, at least as it is treated in Striggio's poem, that
Euridice has to die again in order for Orpheus to be born again. And
once more we can, if we so wish, pursue the Neoplatonic associations.

Ex. 15. Monteverdi, Orfeo, Act IV, (a) Orfeo's tritone of grief on losing Euridice for the second time; (b) Euridice's answering tritones, first with descending scale and chromatic sideslip, then direct but with chromatic delay in bass; (c) Purcell, Dido and Aeneas, comparable progression in Dido's final lament; (d) Monteverdi, Orfeo, Act IV, further tritones in the melody and as harmonic progression (realizations mine):

Euridice calls that forbidden yet somehow pre-ordained sight of Orfeo which causes her to die again: 'sight too sweet, and too bitter (*troppo dolce, e troppo amaro*)'. Ficino[31] wrote that 'Love is called bitter (*amaro*) by Plato because whoever loves, dies; and Orpheus also called love γλυκύπικρον, that is bitter-sweet (*dulce amarum*), because love is a voluntary dying'. Sappho[32] had called love 'a bitter-sweet, irresistible snake (γλυκύπικρον ἀμάκατον ὄρπετον)', thus confirming the erotic associations of that snake whose sting first caused Euridice to die. In Poliziano's *Orfeo*, we read[33] that 'too much love has undone them both'; here Euridice asks 'by too much love have you lost me?' Boccaccio[34] put it that natural desire (*concupiscentia*) tends towards lower things (*ad inferos*) but can be led back to higher things (*ad superiora*), that is to say virtuous (*virtuosa*), as Euridice would have been led back if Orpheus had not unfortunately been overtaken by too much concupiscence on the way.

Conti,[35] reverting to Poliziano's metaphor from wisdom, has it that Orpheus in his role of poet and musician, having reconciled 'the lower powers (*inferis*), that is to say, disturbers of the spirit', tried to lead back to the light of day his Euridice, 'who as her name implies is no other than justice and fairness' (compare Remigio:[36] 'Euridice is said to be the wife of Orpheus because judgement ought to be the companion of eloquence'). Euridice, continues Conti, 'was drawn back to the lower regions (*ad inferos*) through too much love of Orpheus'; for even justice should not be 'too desirious (*cupidum*)', in that 'disturbances of the spirit (*animi*) are to be reconciled by reason; and if anyone should be more negligent in this or more desirious, he will be thrust back as if by some external force, and slide back to the same place'—in which account we may notice how tacitly it is assumed that he and she are both parts of one another's inner experience. Then more explicitly: 'others however explain this story of Euridice in such a way, that they say she is that soul (*anima*) which is married to Orpheus or the body (*corpori*), and Aristaeus is seized by love of her, which is properly to be understood as the good.'

It seems to me that if Orfeo had not looked round while still within those twilight borders of the underworld, he would have lost his chance of seeing that, to use Conti's word for it, he had been putting on to Euridice the image of his own soul. He has just been singing longingly of her 'white breast' (*candida seno*, also meaning 'womb'), that aspect of a woman's beauty which most invites a man's fantasies of his mother-image; and there may be something immature in him here which he does need to lose. There is a comparable Japanese myth about a certain husband who was permitted to recover his lost wife from the land of the shadows on this same condition of not looking on her face during the journey up. When he nevertheless disobeyed by taking a lighted torch to her (in which he resembled Psyche taking her forbidden torch to Cupid), he saw his wife indeed, but as a vampire who chased him to the very exit, and would have fastened upon him to his destruction if she could. But he had the cunning to delay her by dropping fruits along her path (and in that he resembled Hippomanes who escaped death by dropping three golden apples along the path of Atalanta in his fateful race with her). He was thereby just in time to block the exit against her with great rocks; but if he had not looked, he would have lost his chance of learning how an outgrown image of femininity, contaminated as this one evidently was with internalized elements of the 'terrible mother', may endanger a man's virility if not his life by sucking his vital energies away.

There are several North American Indian stories stressing sometimes the positive and sometimes the negative potentialities of the search (and sometimes the other way round with the wife in search of the lost husband), but commonly depending for a variety of outcomes on this very issue of looking round or not looking round. Stories told in so many variations are likely to be on themes of urgent interest. One of the oddest in this area is the story of Lot's wife, who was turned into a pillar of salt for looking round at the doomed Cities of the Plain; but since salt is a near-Eastern symbol for fidelity and hospitality (and esoterically for wisdom dancing before the Lord), there was perhaps a certain encouragement in salt having been the substance of the unfortunate lady's petrifaction.

Prometheus; Pandora; Psyche; Bluebeard's wife; even (on one theological view) our first parents, Adam and Eve: all these are legendary instances of prohibitions which at first it appeared disastrous but later salutary to have disobeyed, since any further growth depended on doing so. Surely Orfeo was meant to look back. But he was not meant to slither back. In his inevitable shock and dismay, he now sings a brief recitative full of unprepared sevenths, and recapitulating the grim scale just sung by Euridice. Grinding down from D, through the tensely diminished third B flat to G sharp, and there completing the anguished tritone as before, the music well illuminates Orfeo's wish to share that downward path which she must tread and he must not. 'But who denies me now?' sings our outraged hero. 'What hidden power', he impotently complains, 'draws me against my will to the hateful light?'

The hidden power which may draw us towards increased consciousness and maturity even against our will has surely to do with that latent self which may know better than we can yet see how to carry forward our lives. With an irony which this time is on the happy side, the music concerns itself, not with Orfeo's very real surface agitation, but with the underlying serenity which may be waiting for him if only he can accept his own unwilled development. For here, where on the surface we might most have expected them, we find none of the previous harsh juxtapositions of unrelated or scarcely related tonalities. The orchestra, taking up a fine new Sinfonia in seven parts, glides from chords of A major and D minor to G major and C major, on to F major, back smoothly through A minor, and, touching the dominant E major, to A major: nothing arresting or remote; but these are genuine, progressive modulations, not the shocks and sideslips of the previous turmoil. An equally fine five-part chorus of spirits, some of it quite closely contrapuntal, assures us in familiar Neoplatonic language that 'virtue, a ray of celestial beauty, merit of the soul from which the sun itself finds value (*s'apprezza*)' alone is lasting; but that Orfeo, who conquered hell itself, was conquered by his own feeling; whereas only the man who can conquer himself is really worthy of fame. We shall have to wait for Act V to see how far Orfeo, with the timely assistance of his father Apollo, is now capable of such conquest of himself, in the paradoxical but desirable sense of accepting defeat by his own deeper self.

ACT V: IMMORTALITY

Act V delights us at once by an artistic recapitulation as effective as it is unexpected. In place, though not in time, we find ourselves back again in the radiant glades of Thrace where we began; and we also find ourselves listening to that memorable first ritornello with which (after the fanfare toccata) the opera opened. 'The cornettos, trombones and regals are silent', we read (and only thereby learn that they must have been playing in the sinfonia before and after the concluding chorus of Act IV, and perhaps accompanying that chorus as well); 'and there came in to play the present Ritornello, the violins, organs, harpsichords, and harps and lutes and citterns, and the scene changes.' But though we are being taken back, it does not follow that we are being taken full circle. Let us say that we are being taken back full spiral. Human development may often return to the same recurrent problems, yet if we are fortunate, on a higher level of consciousness and maturity than the last time round. Not only was this present music heard when first we encountered Orfeo in Act I, just after he had swung from misery into happiness. We also heard it at the end of Act II, just afer he had swung from happiness into misery, and was leaving the radiant glades for the shadowy underworld. Now we hear it again just after he has swung from his recovered happiness once more back into misery; but it may well be back with a difference, as this fifth and last Act is going to decide.

Next 'two [chamber] organs of wood, and two arch-lutes accompany this song playing the one in the left corner of the stage, the other in the right.' On the one side, Orfeo, in mixed hendecasyllabic (eleven-syllable) and heptasyllabic (seven-syllable) lines with irregular rhymes, fit to his still disordered emotions, seeks solace in these lovely pastures where unlovely grief first smote him; from the other side, Echo consolingly answers him with a reflected word or two each time he stops. Such solace from mother nature is itself a kind of mothering, and many of us have turned to it gratefully at one time or another. But it does not solve anything, and it may quite easily serve, not just for solace, but for escape. It is no real solution when a man finds that he can love all nature except for human nature.

The music meanwhile adds its usual informed commentary on the situation. So far from hearing comfort in the music, we find that we have slipped back into the poignant intervals and harshly juxtaposed harmonies previously associated with Orfeo's grief and Euridice's. We hear an ascending scale which spans a minor ninth; we hear one peculiar wriggle from E major through D major to E flat major; we hear many of the familiar, painful tritones. We hear the original notes of the descending scale; but also we hear a chromatic twist to this descending scale, as Orfeo sings of his tears, with (a rare interval then but here plainly marked) an augmented second, from C sharp to B flat. All this is dramatically convincing: it is right and necessary to Orfeo to experience the full bitterness of his grief, and we with him. But we can only hope that he will not get too unprofitably caught up in it. (See Ex. 16 below.)

When Echo answers with repetitions of his own words, he thanks her courteously; but getting tired, to our relief, of hearing nothing but echoes, he turns away from mother nature to address the shade of his own Euridice. Striggio comes into the open here, almost as if he too had just been reading Conti (and perhaps he had). Orfeo addresses Euridice as 'my soul (*anima mea*)' and sings: 'To you I dedicate my lyre and my song, as before I offered my burning spirit on the altar of my heart.' This closely recalls Rinuccini (whom Striggio must indeed have been reading) where Apollo offered to Dafne his 'noble lyre' and his 'heavenly singing'. It is not as a mortal woman but as a carrier for the immortal archetype that a man may thus put his beloved into the role of muse.

Ex. 16. Monteverdi, Orfeo, *Act V, Orfeo's complaint, (a) unresolved seventh, and descending scale with augmented second, (b) harmonic sideslips, then descending scale in plain G minor (realizations mine):*

The most celebrated instance of this is Dante, who told us at the end of his *Vita Nuova* (well called 'New Life') about his vision of his lost Beatrice which determined him 'that my spirit should go hence to behold the glory of my lady', as he did eventually behold her at the climax of his *Paradiso*. It was this search, through his poetry, for his own feminine inspiration and his own inner meaning, rather than any further erotic expectations from the actual woman of whom death had deprived him, which Dante was describing when he explained in his *Purgatorio*[37] that: 'I am one, who when Love inspires me (*Amor mi spira*), takes note, and in that manner which speaks within, I set out to reveal.' And so again it was when Petrarch related his vision of his dead beloved, Laura, in the Second Canto of his *Trionfo della morte*. In the same way, Boccaccio's Fiammetta served him best for inspiration after her living original, Maria d'Aquino, had ceased to be his mistress. For Spenser, the carrier of his projected femininity went for poetical purposes by the name of Rosalind. Sidney had his Stella; Tyard his Pasithée; Ronsard his Cassandre, his Hélène, and others, since it is not every soul-image that requires constancy to her mortal embodiment, so long as the inner dedication remains with her own archetypal essence. And if we want a picture of the sort of woman who most readily invites the projection, we might think of Leonardo's Mona Lisa with the famous smile, so much more mysterious than directly sexual; or that model whose elusive fascination so caught Botticelli's imagination in the wonderful *Primavera* (after Poliziano's *Giostra*)[38] and other masterpieces both sacred and secular.

It is more likely to be the actual woman who feels obscurely but uncomfortably jealous of the inner muse, so demanding of an artist's vital attention. And not only an artist, since all men have their feminine component and all women their masculine component, and our growth and our well-being depend very largely on our coming to terms more or less intuitively with our own contrasexed component. Poised as Orfeo now stands between unprofitable despair and creative acceptance, his character is in a very Neoplatonic manner being put to the test. And it is, interestingly enough, at this very moment of crisis that the poem as separately printed by Striggio and the libretto as composed by Monteverdi, and shown in the score, part company in apparently the most decisive manner possible. But since the altered ending shows no falling-off in poetic quality, nor indeed any change in poetic style, the probability is that, whether at Monteverdi's suggestion or on his own initiative, Striggio accepted the desirability of this notable alteration for so festive and popular an occasion, and did the re-working himself, while leaving it for his own readers to accept the harsher symbolism of the unaltered ending as separately published.

Like Poliziano in his *Orfeo*, but unlike Rinuccini in his *Euridice*, Striggio gave to his poem as separately published the classical ending in tragedy. Orfeo breaks off his lamenting for the very good reason that the Maenads come after him with invocations of their 'drunken god' Dionysus, and threats of the extremest violence against 'our impious enemy, the Thracian Orpheus, despiser of our lofty merits'. No stage directions are given, and it is unlikely at this period that the tragedy would have been represented visibly, but we are not left in any doubt that the traditional dismembering of Orpheus is imminent, and that we are to make what we can of the implied symbolism of this. It is apparently far otherwise in the ending of the poem as composed by Monteverdi. As if to hint that Orfeo has now sunk so deeply into his depression that any turning can only be for the better, that low-pitched sinfonia which in Act III introduced Caronte (Charon) deep in his murky underworld glows out at us again; and movingly, healingly, the heights answer to the depths. 'Apollo descends in a cloud singing.'

And Apollo, of course, is father to Orfeo. Caronte and Pluto both carried stern suggestions of the father's authority, though perhaps Pluto, in setting up (like Wotan for Siegfried) a prohibition which it was seemingly part of Orfeo's education to have the experience of defying, was stern only to be kind. Apollo, himself the wiser for his humbling experience over Dafne, comes quite into the open here as the kindly and helpful aspect of the father's authority. And by now Orfeo has sunk so low that he has no false hopes left, and is ready to let true hopes come to him. The poetry, mainly in mixed hendecasyllabic and heptasyllabic lines, is once more full of rhymes, and has a verbal lightness of sound, except where actually looking back to Orfeo's recent tragedy. Losing no time in coming to the point, Apollo asks: 'why, son, do you give yourself as victim to your anger and sorrow? It is not the counsel of a noble heart to be the servant of its own emotion.' Apollo (on the ascending scale) then makes offer of fresh life to Orfeo, who (leaping straight out of G minor into E major) admits that excess of anger and love has brought him to the verge of a desperate ending, but that he is ready now for a promising continuation of his life's development.

Apollo (calmly back in G minor) draws the classic moral: 'too much you rejoiced in your happy fortune; now too much you lament your bitter and hard destiny' (notice here the heavy syllables, *Tua sorte acerba e dura*). 'Do you still not know that no joy down here endures? Therefore if you wish to enjoy immortal life, come with me to heaven which invites you.' But, asks Orfeo (G major, E major) 'shall I never again see the sweet radiance of my loved Euridice?' And Apollo answers: 'you will look with love upon her fair semblance in the sun and the stars (*nel sole e nelle stelle vagheggerai le sue sembianze belle*).'

'No joy down here endures': that is the saddest of mortal realities. We have twice shared Orfeo's grief in painful words and music, and but for the ameliorating conventions of pastoral drama, we might have expected his grief to be more harshly protracted here. That might have been dramatically more powerful. But the remedy itself is not falsified. The only remedy for grief is by living it through and looking inwardly for an answering strength and wholeness. In the broadly Neoplatonic imagery which Christendom adopted, the centre at which all our inner striving aims is God in his uppermost heaven above the sun and the stars. We might put it, a little differently, that our potential wholeness (rather than our insistent wilfulness) is our real centre: the latent self rather than the deceptive ego. But there was nothing in the essence of Neoplatonic doctrine to imply that our joy and our pain down here are not real and meaningful. When Plotinus[39] called our human love a 'courting of shadows which pass away', he was simply comparing it unfavourably with his expectation of a heavenly contentment which he nevertheless insisted he had on several occasions already experienced in this earthly life. Ficino[40] likewise thought it 'right for the lover to delight and rejoice in the loved one', if only as a natural anticipation of the heavenly love which alone endures, though that comes later. There is no sermon here in other-worldly austerity. The mortal beloved is really loved, and the lost partner is really grieved for. But in that grief there still remains a choice (assuming that it is not just evaded by distractions and self-deceptions) between unprofitable despair and creative acceptance. Orfeo, like Apollo before him (and we might add, like Dante, too), chooses acceptance; and he chooses well.

Ex. 17. Monteverdi's Orfeo, *Act V, the cheerful duet of Apollo and Orfeo (my realization):*

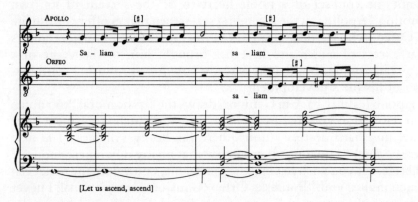

[Let us ascend, ascend]

And so Euridice goes back to hell, but her 'fair semblance' is taken up to heaven; while Orfeo, having been through hell, goes to heaven too, as the chorus (framed in ritornello, singing two lightly octosyllabic stanzas of six lines each to the same strophic music, and playing light-heartedly with the usual scales) comments, perceptively as ever, that 'he who has sown in pain shall reap the fruits of all grace.' A danced Moresca (Moorish or Morris dance) lets us down gently with the gayest of G major versions of the original scale, and the happiest of landings on the opening D major tonality (concert pitch) of the opera, into the outer world again, like the relaxing comedy after the tragic classical trilogy, or the improvised jig after an Elizabethan tragedy; and with that, this early masterpiece of opera is finished.

THE NEOPLATONIC ENDING

We need not be affronted by the apparently conventional and in this case quite literal reliance upon the *deus ex machina*, the god from the machine, to resolve the dramatic situation; for the preparations towards this resolution were already well in progress, and it is not really so sudden as it seems. However, it is conspicuously bloodless, which was not at all traditionally the case. There may just possibly have been a very early version of the legend in which, as in some parallel stories in other parts of the world, the return from the underworld is accomplished successfully and uneventfully, with neither the hero nor the heroine suffering any tragedy or acquiring any illumination;[41] and if so, that might have given Rinuccini a slightly better excuse than he was aware of for doing the same, in his version of *Euridice*, against all true classical precedents. For the truly classical versions of the legend all insist upon the tragedy and invite our enquiry into the illumination, although the commentators offer us a considerable option among their interpretations, and it was evidently found rather a hard matter to understand. Plato,[42] as we saw, merely thought—but it is an interesting thought—that Orpheus was 'justly doomed to meet his death at the hands of women,' because he was 'lacking the courage to die as Alcestis died for love, and choosing rather to scheme his way, living, into Hades': in other words, to evade the real challenge to his responsibility. Conti,[43] however, summarized for us a very wide range of alternative explanations, propounded at different times but available for choice and consideration in Striggio's own time.

One of these alternatives, taken from Pausanias,[44] was that Orpheus was torn to pieces by women insanely jealous because he preferred to console himself with their husbands instead. But while Orpheus, like both Dionysus and Apollo, was commonly depicted with soft glances and flowing locks, this was probably not so much for overt homosexuality as for strong inner femininity, appropriate to their symbolic roles. However, that in itself might be enough to make some women feel obscurely jealous and revengeful. Or (following Apollodorus Gelous[45]) it was because Venus incited the women to avenge her for a judgement by his mother, the muse Calliope, that Adonis should be shared by Venus and Proserpina; as a variation on this, Venus made all the women love Orpheus, and he got torn to pieces in the mad scramble. Or again (following Agatharchides[46]) Orpheus killed himself after believing in vain that Euridice could be restored by magic; while 'others think that Orpheus was killed by a thunderbolt because he divulged the secrets of the mysteries to the uninitiated and ignorant'—presumably the mysteries of Dionysus.[47] But the first century historian Conon[48] has it, on the contrary, that Orpheus infuriated the women by not admitting them to his own Orphic mysteries, which honoured Dionysus but with a novel refinement. Against that, there are scholiasts' references to the lost *Bassarids* of Aeschylus[49] where Dionysus is said to have incited his own unrefined worshippers to dismember Orpheus—together, it seems, with the sacrificial kid eaten raw in the usual course of their robust ceremonies. But since these ceremonies were ritual re-enactments of that part of the myth of Dionysus in which he had himself been dismembered, this points, as does much other evidence, to a remarkable measure of assimilation between Orpheus and Dionysus.[50]

And here we do indeed touch upon one of the most significant themes in all mythology: the ubiquitous species of gods or god-like heroes whose destiny it is to die in order to be born again. The event itself is commonly relegated to the remote past, but may be repeated every year in ritual form. Thus there is an evident connection with the annual solar cycle which causes the seasons, and with the decline and renewal of the earth's vegetation on which human life physically depends. But as usual with mythological imagery, there are the answering echoes from within the psyche. There are regressions of the spirit and there are ensuing transformations of the spirit, and these too can be known intuitively and expressed symbolically. There are common features from Tammuz or Gilgamesh, Osiris or Dionysus, Attis or Adonis, Baldur or Odin all the way through to Christ himself. For Dionysus, too, was a sacrificial god, a twice-born deity: the son of Zeus and Demeter (or Persephone), torn to pieces by the Titans on Hera's jealous instigation, but recreated by Zeus and Athena from his still living heart; or else Dionysus was the son of Zeus and Semele, from whose dying womb Zeus rescued him after being tricked by Hera into blasting her to ashes with the full presence of his undisguised form, whereupon he hid Dionysus in his own thigh to be born again in due time and season.

It was Nietzsche[51] who so interestingly contrasted Apollo, for his tendency towards order and distinction, with Dionysus, for his tendency towards feeling and connection. Orpheus, that son of Apollo[52] who refined the worship of Dionysus, emerged in Greek mythology like some reconciling middle; or if, as others relate, Orpheus was the son of Oiagros,[53] then it was Dionysus who taught his sacred rites to the father of Oiagros, who passed them down to Orpheus, who refined them. Diadorus[54] explained that Orpheus journeyed to hell 'like another Dionysus; for the myth says that Dionysus raised his mother Semele from hell and gave her a share in immortality.' Again, Dionysus is crowned with ivy and laurel, and Orpheus too wears a laurel wreath, the gift of Apollo (who likewise wears it) to poets and musicians in memory of his lost beloved and transcendent inspiration, Dafne. The music of Orpheus does not (like the pipes of Pan, or of Marsyas the Pan-like follower of Dionysus) incite to fury or madness—or to panic. The music of Orpheus (like the music of Amphion) moved sticks and stones to fall of their own accord into order and structure; it organizes; it soothes; it charms; it persuades wild beasts to listen amicably side by side; it drowned out the seductive singing of the Sirens so that the Argonauts were not lured to their destruction. Apollo was also credited with drawing wild beasts to him and taming them with his song; but when Marsyas with his earthy reed-pipe was rash enough to challenge Apollo with his heavenly lyre, Marsyas was judged the loser by the Muses, whereupon Apollo hung him on a tree and flayed him alive.

Marsyas was flayed. Dionysus and Orpheus were dismembered.

Odin wounded himself with his own spear and hung himself for nine days and nights on the Tree of Life, in order to gain inner wisdom. Christ, in order to redeem mankind, was crucified on a cross which became the Tree of Life as a theological symbol, and on the third day he rose from the dead. The harshness of these related images is extreme; but it did not deter Dante[55] when he called upon Apollo to 'enter my breast, and breath you as when you drew Marsyas from the sheath of his limbs': that is to say, Neoplatonically understood, at once in painful purification and in poetic seizure. For Plato himself made it clear that he valued both the ordered spirit and the divine frenzy.[56] He saw the same unknown power as visionary when coming from Apollo, initiatory when coming from Dionysus, poetical when coming from the Muses, and impassioned when coming from Venus or Cupid. It was characteristically Neoplatonic, however, to insist so emphatically that, since our life is in any case an unavoidable tension of opposites, we had better do what we can through healing symbols to reconcile these opposites. In the myth of Orpheus, many influential Neoplatonists sought such symbols of reconciliation; and it must be admitted that the legendary material, as they understood it, can be seen that way.

The dismembered remains of Orpheus were buried excepting for his head, which floated down the Hebros and could not be recovered —a little like the missing phallus of Osiris in one late version of that partly parallel legend. The head presently drifted out to sea, singing sweetly as it went, and with it the lyre (but on another version this was taken up to heaven to become the constellation Lyra). Head and lyre having been washed up on Lesbos, that island of lyric poetry (and Lesbian femininity), the lyre was preserved in the temple of Apollo; and perhaps the head too, though according to Lucian,[57] the head was buried beneath the temple of Dionysus. There are classical depictions[58] of the head lying on the ground with parted lips; for (as with the Celtic Bran or the Norse Mimir or the Arthurian Green Knight or Grimm's[59] wise horse Fallada) this was a talking head though severed from the body, until Apollo (according to the late story of Philostratos[60] in the third century A.D.) got so jealous that he commanded it to fall silent.

But here, too, the mythological threads link up. Apollo had his most famous oracle at Delphi; and there, at the foot of the tripod where his priestess absorbed the decaying Python's fumes and prophesied (but according to Plutarch,[61] only at night), Dionysus had his tomb, or so Delphic legend insisted. There is actually one extraordinary Orphic identification of 'Lord Bacchus lover of the laurel, Paian Apollo skilled on the lyre'[62]—Bacchus being one name of Dionysus, whence his worshippers the Maenads are also called Bacchantes. Still more remarkably, there is a fragment of Heraclitus[63] recalled by Hippolytus[64] in the third century A.D.: 'Hades is the same as

Dionysus'—Hades, who is Pluto (from πλοῦτος, 'wealth', as in our 'plutocratic', perhaps because of his buried potential for good as well as for ill). Delphi was thus the scene of a certain reconciliation between the Apollonian and the Dionysiac; and there in the temple could be read the two famous mottoes which expressed so much of the fullest Greek spirit: 'nothing too much (μηδὲν ἄγαν)'; and 'know thyself (γνῶθι σεαυτόν)'.

Just as Diadorus[65] compared Orpheus with Dionysus who brought Semele from hell and 'gave her a share in immortality', so now Apollo promises Orfeo that he shall recover not the mortal Euridice but 'her fair semblance in the sun and the stars': not the woman on to whom (like Rinuccini's Apollo on to Dafne) Orfeo has been projecting an archetypal image, but that image itself. For on the Neoplatonic interpretation of the legend which the commentators discussed and the libretto suggests, the real issue is growth of character, and the softened ending takes care of it without the necessity of dwelling on the gruesome details. The truth thus softened was no doubt as much as that fashionable audience could have been expected to accept. But it was not a little.

XII
Consolidation

❦✣❦

THE HUMAN TOUCH

After the fashionable success and the artistic triumph of *Orfeo*, consolidation quickly followed.

In the early years of the seventeenth century, the most eminent Florentine composer was Marco da Gagliano (*c*.1575–1642), born at Gagliano outside Florence (whence his father took this name on moving into Florence), and with a distinguished career which included his appointment before 1611 as *maestro di cappella* at Florence to the Grand Duke of Tuscany. Gagliano did not eclipse the reputation either of Caccini or of Peri; and with Peri he presently collaborated to the extent of introducing some music by him into his own operas, *Il Medoro* (perf. Florence, 25 Sept. 1619) and *La Flora* (perf. Florence, 11 Oct. 1628, publ. Florence, 1628). But of these three great musicians, Gagliano was the most solidly trained and the most broadly accomplished; he was a leader of his profession in a much more general sense than the other two.

Gagliano's first opera was his setting of a slightly changed and expanded version of that same earliest libretto by Rinuccini, the *Dafne*, which in Peri's setting (perf. Florence, 1598 modern-style dating) was indeed the earliest opera. Gagliano's *Dafne* (perf. Mantua, in or after January of 1608, publ. Florence later in 1608) is a somewhat richer and more varied example of this by now established pattern of opera. The *Prologo Ovidio* (prologue for Ovid) took the common form of strophic aria with the texture of recitative. There is next a succession of textures: solo recitative for *Pastore del Coro* (shepherd of the chorus), and *Altro Pastore* (another shepherd); a five-part chorus in madrigalian light polyphony; a duet *Coro* (two from the chorus), after which the chorus 'is repeated'; a further duet; a repeat of the chorus; recitative for the first shepherd; repeat of the chorus; recitative for the second shepherd, the first shepherd, the second shepherd, the first shepherd, and the second shepherd again.

As the pattern thus proceeds with little break, there is continuous drama unfolding in music which varies in texture, but remains otherwise very consistently within a single style. The choruses might almost as well be madrigals from a Florentine interlude; the recitative is very near to arioso; the duets are a sort of arioso in two parts. The structure is at once fluid and balanced: more elaborate than Peri; less tautly organized than Monteverdi. There is some ornamental passagework reminiscent of Caccini; but as Gagliano himself instructs us in his important preface, while such ornamental passages may enhance 'the exquisiteness of the song' in the proper places, nevertheless 'where the story does not look for them (*dove la favola non lo ricerca*), we are to leave off from every kind of ornament.' One passage notated as highly ornamented (but only on certain expressive words) is Apollo's lament, a most impassioned recitative, followed by a brief *Coro* and *Ballo*, in five parts, and a strophic *Coro* in three parts.

We are again reminded of the close links between Florence and Mantua in the very early history of opera. The Florentines Rinuccini and Gagliano were both well at home in Mantua, where their *Dafne* became part of the particularly extensive spectacles there for the year 1608, the wedding year of Francesco Gonzaga, the hereditary Prince of the ruling house of Mantua, with Margherita di Savoia. But *Dafne* came earlier in the year, seemingly at the Carnival; while the wedding took place, at Mantua, in late May of 1608, and was marked by entertainments designed to score a new triumph in the long rivalry between these two cities for prestigious spectacle. The main events were, indeed, divided between Florentine talent and Mantuan; and once again we are obviously dealing with one and the same tradition of stage performance, including although not confined to opera.

We shall find the Florentine poet Rinuccini collaborating with the Mantuan resident court composer Monteverdi; we shall find Chiabrera, for some time a resident in Florence, writing interludes for Guarini's prose comedy *L'Idropica*, the music being composed, among others, by both the Monteverdi brothers, Claudio and Giulio Cesare. There was a recently completed wooden theatre outside the walls of which the capacity was estimated by contemporaries variously between 4,000 and 6,000 spectators;[1] foreign visitors were deliberately given precedence over local inhabitants, and even then the crowd became almost out of control. The size of the audience is relevant to our understanding of the works performed, since an opera given to an audience of several thousand spectators is no chamber opera, and cannot be performed adequately in mere chamber style, nor with an orchestra of chamber size. The main events celebrating the wedding were the opera *Arianna* by Rinuccini and Monteverdi (28 May); an aquatic tourney and fireworks (31 May); Guarini's *L'Idropica*, with the interludes by Chiabrera including music of little importance by Claudio Monteverdi, Salomoni Rossi, Gastoldi (a very distinguished musician at the Mantuan court), Giulio Cesare Monteverdi and others (2 June); and the dramatic ballet, *Il ballo delle ingrate* by Rinuccini and (Claudio) Monteverdi.

The *Arianna* of Rinuccini and Monteverdi (perf. Mantua, 28 May 1608) is not the last opera to have been composed on a libretto with deliberately Neoplatonic implications; but it is already moving a little away from them. Nearly all the music has been lost; and there is no loss in the history of opera which we more regret. The portion which survives is the celebrated 'Lamento d'Arianna', the lament of Ariadne after being deserted by Theseus. This is so magnificent a specimen of expressive early recitative that we may well suppose the rest of the opera to have been as good as many contemporary references to it suggest. It had a resounding success, and a revival which probably occurred during the Carnival at Florence in 1614, Florentine old-style dating, i.e. 1615, modern-style dating; and more remarkably (since few early operas remained so long in memory) a further revival probably in 1640.

We have, besides Rinuccini's poem, a vivid description of *Arianna* by Federico Follino.[2] There was a rocky sea-girt reef, and to very sweet instrumental music, a cloud 'full of the most brilliant light' came slowly down, bearing Apollo, but vanishing 'in a moment' as he stepped to earth. Next, the Prologue was sung by Apollo to regular quatrains of hendecasyllabic lines, in the rhyme-scheme *abba*, such as are most likely to have been set by Monteverdi in rondo strophic variation. Venus and Cupid were next seen taking counsel on a situation only the immediate aspect of which is discussed, since the events preceding it are assumed to be familiar to the audience. They are briefly that Theseus, Prince of Athens, has journeyed voluntarily to Crete among the seven youths and seven maidens due each year to be sacrificed to the bull-man monster, the Minotaur, as tribute to Minos, King of Crete. This Minos had for a wife Pasiphae, a daughter of Helios, the sun; and the Minotaur was the offspring of Pasiphae and a bull, so that the Minotaur, an ambiguous progeny if ever there was one, seems to stand for some sort of mixture of the darkest instinct with the brightest spirit. He was difficult of access, living as he did at the centre of a maze constructed for him by Daedalus; and he was hatefully notorious for this annual destruction of twice seven of the noblest young humans from subject Athens.

But Minos also had some notable daughters by Pasiphae, among them Ariadne, half-sister to the Minotaur, whose bright complement she may in a manner represent, being very beautiful and herself a granddaughter of the sun. At all events, she fell in love with Theseus, provided him with a sword with which to kill the Minotaur instead of being killed by him, and equally important, with a thread to trail behind him into the maze, so that he was able to find his way out again by tracing it back. She then accompanied Theseus and his companions in flight from Crete, with the justifiable expectation of becoming wife of Theseus and in due course Queen of Athens. But Theseus deserted her on the rocky island of Naxos; and it is this regrettable situation, now in course of occurring, to which Venus and Cupid are giving their shocked consideration. Venus proposes a remedy, and Cupid agrees to implement it, as the remainder of the opera will unfold for us.

Both Theseus and Ariadne were mortals, but both stand close to the gods. Theseus is a son of Poseidon, Neptune, in Bacchylides;[3] and Ariadne is only one generation further from her grandfather the sun, Helios, whose legends are closely collateral to those of the god of the sun, Apollo. The legends of Theseus[4] are extensive and in part primitive; but this is not the feature on which Rinuccini lays stress. On the contrary, the human side of Theseus is brought out. He becomes a man in conflict, no longer at all anxious to meet his promise by bringing Ariadne, the hostile tyrant's daughter, to Athens, yet understandably shrinking from the actual moment of telling her so, or even of admitting to himself that he is already tired of her.

In the scene next following, Theseus is if anything overly courteous to Ariadne, on whose face he is nevertheless perceptive enough to notice signs of apprehension; and the more he protests his undying gratitude and affection, the more she seems to intuit his change of heart, and to recall with grief her own abandoned parents and country. She retires; and Theseus embarks upon a remarkably unheroic conversation with a character called Consigliero, counsellor, who gives him some very worldly-wise advice. Theseus comes further into the open with some confused but proper sentiments about the shamefulness of betraying the woman who is the very 'cause of my glory and of my life'; but his counsellor assures him of the much greater propriety of not being bound by vows given in the heat of passion and incautious love, from which honour really requires him to disengage himself, and virtue also. The wind now proving favourable, they decide to set sail furtively.

There is no scene quite like this in Rinuccini's two earlier librettos. Apollo and Dafne, Orfeo and Euridice: these are all images radiant with archetypal glory and timeless significance. Perfidious Theseus and his shady counsellor likewise stand, no doubt, for age-old types of human behaviour; but their presentation here is decidedly reduced in stature. We cannot help wondering whether the disgraceful scene was not meant to be played for laughs. The purely personal side, the human quality in its individual rather than its archetypal aspect, was always important to Monteverdi. His music catches the archetypal quality, none better; but he had to see this quality in personal projection, with a sort of creative innocence. There is a famous passage in one of Monteverdi's letters,[5] about 'the little libretto (*librettino*) for the maritime tale of the marriage of Thetis', in which 'the winds have to sing'. Monteverdi asked: 'how shall I be able to imitate the speech of winds, if they do not speak! And how by their means shall I be able to move the feelings! Ariadne moved [the feelings] through being a woman, and Orfeo likewise moved [the feelings] through being a man and not a wind.' For 'Ariadne leads me to a just lament; and Orfeo to a just prayer, but this to I know not what conclusion.' The 'little libretto' was not in the end composed by Monteverdi.

These are questions of degree and approach. No character in opera, and perhaps no real character in art, altogether lacks the archetypal dimension. But some characters are given a more particular personality, less numinous but more approachable. A few seem, like Falstaff, to get the best of both worlds. It is in cultivating this more human touch that Rinuccini's libretto for *Arianna* is in transition from the elevated Neoplatonism of his first two librettos towards the more mixed and popular styles of libretto next developing.

Arianna and her attendant Dorilla now exchange fears which the reports of a chorus of fishermen do nothing to allay, and which a messenger soon confirms. Ariadne has indeed been abandoned by her Theseus; and so she begins that 'Lamento d'Arianna', that Lament of Ariadne, the recitative of which survives to sharpen our regret for the lost remainder (apart from a few insignificant fragments quoted by Doni) of this most celebrated of very early operas. The verse is in a diversity of forms, line-lengths and rhyme-schemes, and is interrupted at intervals by terzets for the chorus, the regularity of which serves to set off the freedom of the lament, but for which the music is not preserved. The intensity of the recitative is of astonishing inspiration and unflagging power. This is certainly an outstanding scene, even on Monteverdi's high standard for such affecting episodes; and it is no way surprising that it became famous at once and long remained so. (See Ex. 18 below.)

It is of the melodies in Monteverdi's *Arianna* that Marco da Gagliano, in the preface to his own *Dafne*, wrote that 'they renewed the excellence of the ancient music, in that they visibly moved the whole theatre to tears.' Federico Follino[6] recorded the same tribute of tears freely flowing at this performance, and also at Monteverdi's *Il ballo delle ingrate* performed during the same wedding festivities at Mantua in 1608; so did the Resident Minister from the Estense Court,[7] the day after the performance; so did Coppini,[8] adding that 'whoever heard it afterwards' likewise shed 'thousands and thousands of compassionate tears'; so did the enthusiastic Doni,[9] mentioning particularly 'the lament of the same Arianna, which is perhaps the most beautiful composition which has been done in our times in this kind.'

Ex. 18. Monteverdi, Arianna, *Mantua, 1608, the opening section of the famous Lament (realization mine):*

Sir J. A. Westrup[10] noticed that of the only two complete surviving copies of the Lament, one is in the handwriting of Luigi Rossi. Among the second generation of Italian opera composers, Luigi Rossi, though he seems to have produced only two operas, was of importance not only for the eminence in his own country of his chamber cantatas, but also from having his *Orfeo* (1647) produced in Paris, with a strong effect on the subsequent origins of French opera. Monteverdi[11] himself recomposed and published most of the 'Lamento d'Arianna' as four madrigals in five parts, sacrificing the rhythmic flexibility of the recitative for a decidedly polyphonic regularity and complexity. He also made a sacred parody late in life.[12] Around 1650, we learn from Severo Bonini[13] that 'there was not a house which, possessing harpsichords or Theorbos, did not have the lament' of Ariadne—some forty years after its performance, and nearly a decade after the death of Monteverdi.

Ariadne's Lament brings us back again to another emotional level: less individual, and more archetypal. There is a certain air of finality, as of a life-story broken in the middle and a past gone beyond recall; it is like some timeless image of universal grief. But now, beyond expectation, there comes a new stirring. Even as Ariadne insists that the moment has come for her to die, sounds of trumpets, drums and horns are heard. 'To the shore, to the shore', cries Dorilla; 'see Theseus, who returns'; but it is not Theseus, nor would Ariadne trust him again if it were. To that past, she is dead indeed; and now from another messenger we learn what has really happened. It is Bacchus who has crossed the sea and, as the wonderful remedy planned by Venus and Cupid, has fallen instantly in love with Ariadne.

All past suffering is redeemed in a concluding ballet, during which Cupid calls on heavenly beings and mortals to 'admire the lofty glory of love'; Ariadne sings that 'happy above all human desire is the heart which has for comfort a god'; Venus ('rising from the sea') and Jove ('the heavens opening') add their blessing and encouragement; and Bacchus, inviting his bride 'to the eternal sky', promises that 'the brightest stars will make of your beautiful hair a garland of gold, glorious reward of a soul which despises, for the sake of heavenly desire, mortal beauty (*alma che sprezza, per celeste desio, mortale bellezza*).' And so Ariadne becomes for Rinuccini and Monteverdi as Euridice became for Striggio and Monteverdi, a 'fair semblance in the sun and the stars'. We recognize, with some astonishment, the same deliberately Neoplatonic resolution to the human drama. Not mortal beauty, but celestial beauty, is the ultimate reward. The mythological image of the 'sacred marriage', with its implications of inner as well as outer union, may be part of the veiled associations here: a possible implication of such exalted scenes in early opera to which we shall have further occasion to return.

NEOPLATONIC OPERA IN DECLINE

The Neoplatonic inspiration had less to do with opera soon after its earliest beginnings. It is true that many Neoplatonic images persisted, and that while they persisted, their inherent suggestiveness and force to some extent remained, since our deeper intuitions in such matters do not substantially alter. Indeed, for the majority of the audience the appeal of the Neoplatonic images had always been intuitive. It made less difference than might be thought, therefore, when the artist himself became less aware of the truths which his creative vision was encompassing; but, of course, it did make some difference, since an artist who does not know what his own insistent images really mean lacks the power to focus them intellectually—which may not be altogether disadvantageous, but is certainly no help when inspiration wavers. The Neoplatonic librettos of the earliest operas are immensely strong and purposeful. Neither for poetic inspiration nor for intellectual concentration can most librettos of the ensuing generation compare with them.

We have also to bear in mind that the mixed dramatic and musical spectacles, the interludes and the masquerades, which had previously served opera for a nursery, did not go out of existence now that opera had come of age. That celebrated dramatic ballet by Rinuccini and Monteverdi, *Il ballo delle ingrate*, the ballet of the ungrateful ones, at which Follino[14] noted the audience's tribute of tears during the performance at Mantua in 1608, is a good example. And there we meet with a renewal of that same French influence which had already entered into the origins of opera through the admiration of Rinuccini and Chiabrera for the Neoplatonic poetry of Ronsard. For Rinuccini, just after the new French Queen, Marie de' Medici, reached Paris, spent some time at her court between 1600 and 1604, when he returned finally to Florence. His object was not, gossip suggested, exclusively artistic, since he was popularly supposed to be her lover; but so impressed was he with the French *ballet de cour* as he found it at Paris that, on the evidence of his son, G. P. Rinuccini,[15] he took the first opportunity, around 1605, of introducing it into Italy.

The *Ballo delle ingrate* is an example of this enthusiasm. None of the basic ingredients of the *ballet de cour*, it is true, can have been unfamiliar in Italy, many of them having come from there to France at least a century before. But there was at Paris evidently something especially impressive about the ingenuity with which successive entries of dance and song were strung together in a loose but effective theatrical sequence: not exactly a drama, but at least a dramatic entertainment. In a very impressive article, Iain Fenlon has argued that it was the extraordinary choreographic elaboration, and the dramatic and symbolic power of the danced entries (far beyond the familiar steps and figures of the normal court and ballroom), which linked up with the most advanced Italian interludes and ballets, especially at Ferrara and at Mantua.[16]

Rinuccini's text here is an elegant and amusing little morality in reverse. By the special intervention of Cupid at the request of Venus,

Pluto is persuaded to release on a brief visit to the upper world a small bevy or chorus of women damned to hell, on the doubtless sufficient if not altogether conventional grounds of having been wickedly scornful of love, and shamefully ungrateful to their suitors, by *not* acceding to their carnal desires. These are the Ungrateful Women whose Ballet it is. They repent bitterly but unavailingly now of their lost opportunities and hardness of heart; they are held up in solemn warning to the noble ladies of Mantua to take the more rewarding path of enjoying love and sharing it; and after a full measure of singing and dancing, they are returned firmly to their eternal punishment. While it would be quite possible for a determined Neoplatonist to allegorize this away as eternal damnation for rejecting the divine love of God, somehow the impression prevails that Rinuccini was perfectly capable of writing poetry with his Neoplatonic tongue in his court entertainer's cheek, and that he and his audience thoroughly enjoyed his doing so on this occasion. Monteverdi's music for the scintillating text is altogether beautiful: some of it has a French grace and charm of melody; some of it is nearer to his own advanced reciting style, and quite in the operatic manner. This is not opera, of course, nor is it on an operatic scale, but it is very closely related to opera.

A much more original and powerful work of Monteverdi's later years, at Venice, which is also close to opera without being opera, may be mentioned here. This is the celebrated *Combattimento di Tancredi e Clorinda* (perf. Venice, 1624), on verses from Tasso's *Gerusalemme liberata*: an experimental and very remarkable dramatic scene, with a narrator (*Testo*) who describes the action in recitative much of which is of an unusually assertive and rhythmic kind, the accompaniment being written out for strings and continuo (an early example of fully accompanied recitative). But there are also the two combatants, costumed in armour, and miming their parts in stylized dance and gesture, while exchanging insults in freer recitative. There is a deliberate contrast of two styles, *concitati e molli*, agitated and soft. In the *stile concitato*, the agitated style, rhythms in quickly repeated notes of obsessive regularity represent the agitation in an idiom of which Monteverdi considered himself to be, and perhaps in some degree was, the originator in this actual work. As we saw, we may take the agitated style, the *stile concitato*, as a sub-division of the emulating style, the *stile concertato*, which was itself a division of the modern style, the *stile moderno*. But for the miming, it might be possible to describe this extremely powerful and unusual work as a secular oratorio. But for the narrator, it might be possible to describe it as a miniature opera. It is in fact neither, but just one particularly impressive example of early baroque fluidity and inventiveness, related to without being opera.

At Florence in this same year, 1624, a work was produced under circumstances which were not altogether typical for opera; but it was an opera. During the regency at Florence between 1621 and 1628, an unusually religious disposition was maintained at court; and it was under these circumstances that, in 1624, Gagliano's sacred opera, *La regina Sant' Orsola*, was performed there. The music is lost. The libretto is by Andrea Salvadori (Florence, 1625, on the title-page; but the dedication is dated Florence, 29 January 1625, which being Florentine old-style dating, makes it on modern dating 1626). The libretto states explicitly that the play 'can be recited without music', although on the occasion described 'the music was by Sig. Marco da Gagliano, the scenery and the machines by Sig. Giulio Parigi, the combat and the dance by Signor Agnolo Ricci.' There is also an *Argomento* (Florence, 1624) claiming that 'our souls receive far more pleasure and astonishment from the true and glorious Christian deeds than from the empty tales of the pagans.' This seems like a deliberate reaction against the pagan and Neoplatonic tendencies hitherto prevailing. But the prologue is still for pagan nymphs and the local river god, Father Arno; and the scene changes to hell and back, with the heavens opening at the end, in quite the usual spectacular way. The work may have been a normal opera of the early variety, on a sacred subject; there is nothing in the libretto which precludes it, and so far from there being any deficiency in dramatic development, both the situations and the characters are, in a crude way, changing all the time. We cannot withhold the title of opera merely on the ground of crude melodrama, or we should be in trouble with *Norma* and still worse with *Robert le diable*, both of which splendid operas bear some unintentional resemblance to this early specimen. A repeat performance was given on 28 January 1625, Florentine old-style dating, i.e. 1626, in the same year as the following.

We do not necessarily refuse the title of opera to a work with horses (though Brünnhilde's Grane used to be a great nuisance in old-fashioned performances of *Götterdämmerung*). We can also stretch a point in the matter of ballet. But horse-ballet? Francesca Caccini's *Liberazione di Ruggiero* (perf. Florence, 2 Feb. 1625, Florentine old-style, i.e. 1626), on a libretto by Ferdinando Saracinelli, after Ariosto's *Orlando furioso*, is in part a normal opera. The drama is short (a prologue for Neptune and three scenes on the enchanted island of Alcina), and more or less in the style of mingled recitative and ensembles soon to be typical for Roman operas. There were stage settings and machines by Giulio Parigi or his son Alfonso Parigi; there were expensive transformations, including a sea which turned into fire; the scenario, though not (after the prologue) either pagan or mythological, does not lack for magic and witchcraft, both white and black.

The music, by this distinguished daughter of Giulio Caccini, is not outstanding, but it is entirely adequate. There are three isolated indications for instruments: p.38 has 'Ritornello; Played by 4 Viols, 4 Trombones, an Organ of wood [chamber organ] and a [plucked] keyboard Instrument'; p. 40 has 'Ritornello; Played by the same instruments, as were named above'; then comes a recitative; then a 5-part 'chorus of the enchanted trees [discarded lovers of Alcina], concerted with the same Instruments above named'. The rest of the scoring is left to our initiative; but the instruments named were certainly not silent for the remainder of the evening. On p.67 we read: 'here comes the dance (*ballo*) of Eight Ladies of the Most Serene Archduchess with Eight chief Knights, and they did a most noble dance.' No music being given, we are left to supply our own. On p. 70 occurs a 6-part 'Chorus of liberated Knights which comes to be sung so soon as the ballet of the Ladies and the Knights has been finished.' On p. 71 we read: 'the dance on horseback being finished they sang the following [8-part] madrigal to finish the whole festivity.' On the title-page of the printed libretto (Florence, 1625, Florentine old-style dating, i.e. 1626), the work is called 'Ballet represented in music (*Balletto Rapp[resenta]to in Musica*)'; and on the title-page of the printed score (also Florence, 1625, Florentine old-style dating, i.e. 1626) it is called 'Ballet Composed in Music (*Balletto Composto in Musica*)'. In spite of its operatic opening, we might do best to follow these titles and call the work a ballet with operatic features. In short, a horse-ballet; and they were, in fact, not uncommon.

Marco da Gagliano's *Flora* (perf. Florence, 14 October 1628, publ. Florence, 1628) is again on a libretto by Andrea Salvadori, in a prologue and five acts; the stage settings were by Alfonso Parigi (son of Giulio). The scenario employs some familiar characters of classical Greek mythology, but their adventures are seemingly contrived for the occasion and not particularly traditional at that. The poetry shows great charm and the plot has skill, but we miss the conviction and authority which genuinely mythological material brings. To invent new adventures for mythological characters had long been a common recourse in masquerades and ballets and interludes and all manner of slighter occasions requiring a pretext for play-acting or entertainment; it could be a graceful formula, or it could be considerably more than that; but in itself it is no guarantee of dramatic force.

The printed *Argomento della Favola*, argument of the story, explains that Jove wishes earth to have, like heaven, its own stars, in the shape of flowers to be born from 'the loves of Zephyr, and Cloris, the one a Wind of Spring, the other a Nymph of the Tuscan countryside; now Cupid being angry with his Mother Venus, refuses to make Cloris fall in love with Zephyr: Venus at this, with the aid of Mercury, steals the weapons of her son, wounds the Nymph with the Arrow of gold, whence she suddenly responds to the love of Zephyr. Cupid 'digs out

Jealousy from Hell (*cava dall' Inferno la Gelosia*)', which upsets not only the love-affair but the weather, leading to a 'chorus of the tempest', until Cupid's weapons are restored, the lovers reconciled, and flowers spring up, watered from the Muses' fountain of Pegasus by Apollo in person, and more 'particularly the Lilies Insignia of Florence, and of Parma', united by this marriage now being celebrated between Odoardo Farnese Duke of Parma with Margherita of Tuscany. There are interesting touches, as when (p. 68) Jealousy is said to 'make Hell not the Styx or Avernus, but the lover's heart'; there are amusingly mock-Neoplatonic touches, as when (p. 76) a Triton insists that 'Woman is the most beautiful gift of the stars, she is a ray of the sun, and I see in a beautiful face all that is beautiful in the world, and all that is good', but Pan on the contrary will have it that 'Woman is wicked poison, and an inner serpent, who eats away the heart, she is a Monster, rebel in heaven, the plague of souls, and a hell for the living'; and there are traditional touches, as when (p. 69) Cupid appeals to Pluto to place Jealousy at his disposal by reminding him of his burning love for Proserpina. But there are no real touches either of timeless myth or of Neoplatonic earnestness.

Whereas Francesca Caccini's music for her court ballet *La Liberazione di Ruggiero*, in its operatic aspects, looks forward to one of the two ensuing schools of opera (the Roman, as opposed to the Venetian), the score of *Flora* has already an old-fashioned look. Most of it is by Gagliano; but the entire role of the heroine, Cloris, is by Jacopo Peri, and is distinguished in the score by his initials, I. P., printed carefully against each of her entries. Neither composer has changed his style since last we met his work. There is the same rather austere concentration upon dramatic essentials; the same reluctance to indulge very much in purely musical felicities; and the same focused intensity of melody and harmony as a reward for this close devotion to the original ideals of opera.

The prologue is in rondo strophic variation form—the bass remaining virtually unchanged under the slightly varied melody; and the rondo element being provided by the instrumental ritornello, of which the bass but not the upper parts are given in the score. Monteverdi would have done it no otherwise in his earliest style; and as the drama unfolds, nearly all of it in recitative of the earliest operatic quality, there is much the same proportion of contrasting ensembles and choruses (with dancing) as we find in Monteverdi's *Orfeo*. Nothing in the arias, however, approaches the musical elaboration and inspiration of, for example, the compound strophic variations of 'Possente spirto' in Monteverdi's *Orfeo*. In that respect, Gagliano's score, with Peri's insertions, is not more advanced but more conservative. Nevertheless, it is a genuine opera, and would be a good one but for its libretto. This is not exactly undramatic; but it is dramatically weak. It lacks both the archetypal conviction of a real myth and the sympathetic interest of a good human story. We begin to see better what Doni meant when in about 1635 he wrote of a decline in opera 'because it is not so easy to find the likes of Rinuccini'.

INITIATIVES OUTSIDE ITALY

There was only one initiative outside Italy which, if the circumstances had been more propitious, might have led at this early date to a rival tradition, of another nationality, in true opera; and this, curiously enough, bears out Doni's opinion,[17] since it actually depended on Rinuccini's poetry. Martin Opitz (1597–1639), a German poet of high reputation and a pioneer in the literary purification of the German language, made an adaptation of Rinuccini's famous first libretto, his *Dafne*, which Peri and Gagliano had both already used to such good effect. This German adaptation, or free translation, was composed to music by Heinrich Schütz (1585–1672), who of all his generation of German musicians was the greatest genius and the warmest admirer of the new Italian idioms. From 1609 to 1612, Schütz studied in Venice with Giovanni Gabrieli (1557–1612). In 1628, Schütz returned to Venice; and though he cannot actually be shown to have made contact with Monteverdi, then the most famous of all Venetian musicians, he is hardly likely to have missed the opportunity, which may well have been the purpose of his visit.

Schütz's own music is the best evidence for his admiration: particularly the *Symphoniae sacrae* of 1629, followed by a second part in 1647 and a third in 1650. These he described[18] as in 'the modern Italian manner' under Monteverdi's influence; and though his opera preceded his second visit, he could have studied at least the printed *Orfeo*. There survives one partbook for the *Testo* (narrator) of Monteverdi's famous *Combattimento*, with the original music slightly adapted to a German text which Osthoff, in a most interesting article,[19] suggests was the work of Schütz or someone in his circle. Most unfortunately, Schütz's score for *Dafne* (performed at Torgau in 1627) does not itself survive; we should certainly expect it to have been in some variety or modification of the reciting style. But in 1631, the Thirty Years War (waged from 1618 to 1648) struck Saxony in force, and disrupted the musical establishment at which Schütz served. The devastating effects across most of Germany precluded any direct continuation of this potential start to a national German opera; and although, at Hamburg later in the century, some German opera was achieved, it was in a different idiom, under French as well as Italian (but later Italian) influence, and indeed it presently succumbed to the all-fashionable Italian style of the day.

In other German-speaking regions, particularly at Vienna as the imperial capital, Italian opera was both imported and imitated, but without any essential development of a native style; we merely notice that in Vienna, great displays of chorus and ballet could be afforded in which only Rome (and subsequently Paris) elsewhere indulged. In France opera took no hold whatsoever until much later in the seventeenth century, though the Italian reciting style as an idiom of solo song was familiar from early in that century, and was up to a point influential upon the French solo song which remained an important (never a predominant) feature in many elaborately staged and moderately dramatic varieties of court masque and ballet. In England Nicholas Lanier (1588–1666) was a real pioneer of the reciting style, of whom Ben Jonson, the poet of the 'Masque presented at the House of Lord Hayes' at London in 1617, *Lovers made men*, wrote that: 'The whole Masque was sung after the Italian manner, stylo [*sic*] recitativo, by Master Nicholas Lanier, who ordered and made both the scene and the music' (he had already a small share in *The Squires' Masque* of 1613). The artistic importance of Ben Jonson's masques was outstanding, especially since his choice of subjects and his poetic treatment were conspicuously Neoplatonic. In *The Masque of Blackness*, performed at London in 1605, the 'daughters of Niger' can be seen as suitably black representatives of our dark and shadowy underside brought by the power of the 'temperate' sun (imaged as James I) to regain whiteness, in token of a reconciliation of that darkness with our bright reason; the material here is drawn from Conti.[20] Of *The Masque of Beauty*, performed at London in 1608, and using material drawn from Conti, Giraldi and Cartari,[21] Ben Jonson himself commented with remarkably Neoplatonic conviction:

> Had those, that dwell in error foule,
> And hold that women have no soule,
> But seen these move; they would have, then,
> Said, *Women were the soules of men*,
>   So do they move each heart, and eye
>   With the *worlds soule*, true *harmony*.

In 1613, the costume for Capriccio in George Chapman's *The Memorable Masque*, staged by Inigo Jones at London in February of that year, was taken from Cesare Ripa's illustrated Neoplatonic *Iconologia*; while James I is again Neoplatonically addressed as the sun, 'the true Phoebus' (Apollo). And not only was *Circe*, the French *Ballet comique de la royne*, a persistent influence for Jonson's masques; that influential ballet itself was given in quite a close English adaptation as Aurelian Townsend's *Tempe Restored*, which was performed at London in 1632, and published with an English translation by Inigo Jones (the great architect and stage producer of many masques) of the

Neoplatonic explanation included in its original publication of 1582. Next year, Thomas Carew's *Coelum Britannicum*, performed at London in 1633, included verbal recollections of Giordano Bruno's rather oddly Neoplatonic allegory, *Spaccio della bestia trionfante* (Expulsion of the Triumphant Beast), a fruit of Bruno's stay in England from 1583 for some two years—in which his acquaintance with Sir Philip Sidney and others may have left some further traces on English literature. Spenser's youthful translations of du Bellay and his early *Shepherd's Calendar* based on Marot's anticipations of the French Pleiad were other channels of continental influence, while his *Faerie Queene* recalls, not only Ariosto and Tasso, but Dante by the dark wood of the spirit in which its allegory unfolds. There were other links: for example, Bruno's influence on Shakespeare's *Love's Labour's Lost* is thought to have been directly significant; and this is a play probably reflecting an actual occurrence at the Italianate French court of Catherine de' Medici. But neither the plays of Shakespeare nor the masques of Jonson led on into opera, full of incidentally dramatic music as they were; and when native opera did make a serious start with Blow and Purcell in Restoration England, it was rather under the later French influence of Lully than of the contemporary Italians.[22] Moreover, it soon enough declined before the fashion for Italian opera and above all for the Italianate Handel.

XIII
Rome and Venice

❦❦

ROME AND VENICE COMPARED

What Florence and Mantua were for the very beginnings of opera, Rome and Venice became for its early continuation. There were other active centres, for the most part in close touch with one another's work and idioms; but first the Roman output passed into the lead, and second the Venetian output—based as it was on Roman models—took over a prominence which it maintained for the rest of the seventeenth century.

The great princes of the church were as dominant in the cultural life of Rome as the ducal families were in so many secular principalities of Italy, as the Emperor was in Austria, and as kings were in other parts of Europe. The families from whose almost closed ranks cardinals and popes habitually came were in part the same as the ducal families, in part distinct and even hostile. Allegiances changed, alliances came and went, but the ecclesiastical leaders did not stand aside from the incessant conflict and intrigue of politics, nor were they very different as poets and as patrons, except perhaps that where the dukes of Florence or Mantua were arbitrary but persistent in their conspicuous expenditure on opera, and the oligarchs at Venice between them quite remarkably sustained, the Roman princes of the church were intermittent, depending in part upon how permissive or restrictive an attitude the ruling pope was maintaining towards theatre in general, and opera in particular; in part on the current financial situation of the papacy, which became inconveniently critical during much of the seventeenth century.

These two leading schools, the Roman and the Venetian, had almost everything in common except for the use of large ensembles and choruses, often up to eight parts, occasionally twelve. These were for long fashionable in Roman opera, in that showy kind of multi-voiced polyphony stemming from Venice and the Gabrieli family, which later culminated in the 'colossal baroque' style of seventeenth-century church music. In the theatre, it was never colossal, but it might certainly be showy. Venetian audiences never acquired much taste for it. Even at Rome, we find the following rather pointedly dry comment after the table of airs and choruses at the end of Domenico Mazzocchi's *La Catena d'Adone* (perf. and publ. Rome, 1626): 'There are many other half-airs (*mezz' Arie*) through the opera which break the tedium of the recitative (*il tedio de recitativo*).'[1] That was certainly a change of taste, since opera virtually began as recitative.

In a musically less important respect, we notice that some Roman operas achieved a printing, but very few Venetian operas. Indeed, had it not been for the collecting instincts of that great seventeenth-century patron and connoisseur of opera, Marco Contarini, whose manuscripts now rest in the Marciana library at Venice, there might be very little we could do about Venetian òpera of that century. This is the more strange in that Venice was then a leading centre for Italian music-publishing; and we commonly find Roman operas printed in Venice, but not Venetian operas printed in Rome. The reason is probably that any seventeenth-century opera in Rome was an event still private and still prestigious, requiring to be celebrated by an edition in commemoration of the patron, rather than in consideration of posterity. But in Venice opera houses became public though not altogether self-supporting concerns, and there was no comparable incentive of prestige to set up the working manuscript in print.

ROMAN SPECTACLE

An early example of the Roman style, although it is not actually known to have been performed at Rome and very possibly was not, is *La morte d'Orfeo* (The Death of Orpheus, performed in 1619 and published in the same year at Venice). The libretto is now thought possibly to be by Francesco Pona; the composer was Stefano Landi.[2] The libretto does not appear to have been published separately. The sub-title to the print of 1619 is *Tragicommedia pastorale*, meaning in this case not merely a tragedy in pastoral style with happy ending, but actually a tragi-comedy, in which the comic relief (familiar enough from masques and interludes) really gets the upper hand. The stage machinery and the changes of scene contributed a predominant share to the success of the entertainment: but strange as we might consider the whole confused affair, it is undoubtedly an opera.

There is an *Argomento* appended to the score, which tells us that Orfeo, when celebrating his birthday with a grand banquet of the gods, made the social blunder of deliberately excluding Bacchus from the invitations. In revenge, Bacchus ordered his formidable female Maenads to kill Orfeo, after which Jove translated Orfeo to the heavens. Act I celebrates the birthday. As with so many prologues to very early operas, there is an opening recitative in rondo strophic variation form. There are trios and duets, separated by rather than separating the quite brief passages of recitative—and we notice an independent instrumental bass to three voices all in the soprano clef; there is a strophic *Coro de Pastori A 8* (chorus of shepherds in eight parts), a duet for two basses and a repeat of the eight-part chorus. Act II shows Orfeo inviting gods and shepherds to his banquet; he sings a solo aria in rondo strophic variations, the ritornello being in three parts; he shares a recitative with his father, Apollo; there are duets for two pairs of satyrs, and a *Coro di Satiri A 8* (chorus of satyrs in eight parts), returning where 'one repeats the chorus a 8'. Apollo advises his son Orfeo to keep away from women, and come to heaven in cheerful mood. The satyrs, at least, make merry.

Act III shows Bacchus enraged at being slighted, and Nisa trying unsuccessfully to calm him down; they end, however, by working up their grievance together, and plot with Furore (fury impersonated, but not, unfortunately, much brought to life) the traditional dismemberment of Orfeo by the Maenads. There is a four-part strophic *Coro de Menadi*, chorus of Maenads (three soprano parts and one alto); and a strophic *Coro di Pastori A 5*, a five-part chorus of shepherds, who lament but do nothing whatsoever to prevent Orfeo's impending doom. Act IV shows Mercury, a *Coro di dei* (chorus of gods), and Orfeo haunted by fears and premonitions as he feels the shade of his lost Euridice calling to him. In a second scene, there is a *Coro delle Menadi infuriate* (chorus of infuriated Maenads) with solo interjections from individual Maenads, encouraged by Furore. Scene iii has 'Calliope Sola' (the mother of Orfeo); in Scene iv she is joined by *Fileno Nuntio* (Fileno a messenger), actually one of the shepherds returning to announce the expected bad news in a simple strophic recitative of five verses, in which 'at the end of each stanza there is rendered the present Ritornello adagio'; then comes more dialogue in which the messenger fills in the details of Orfeo's dismemberment; and a *Coro de Pastori A 6*, a six-part chorus of shepherds, once more lamenting.

Act V shows Orfeo, now himself a shade, pleading with Caronte in the underworld to be let across, which should not have presented any technical difficulties this time, now that Orfeo is no longer living. But next Mercury asks Orfeo to leave the realm of the dead and go instead to heaven, where he is invited. Upon Orfeo replying that he would rather suffer with Euridice in hell than go to heaven without her, Mercury assures him that Euridice will not love him or even know him down here. And to prove it, Orfeo is taken across after all by Caronte; whereupon Euridice denies recognizing or ever having seen Orfeo, and turns away; Orfeo cries after her in vain. Mercury tells

Orfeo not to be afraid, but just to get drinking; and Caronte, to show the good fellow he is at heart, at once breaks into a drinking song. Mercury bids Orfeo fly after him to Heaven; Caronte tells Orfeo to go away and not bother him again.

There is a grand and spectacular choral finale. On the earth, a four-part *Coro de Pastori* (chorus of shepherds) rejoices that Orfeo is not really dead, but lives in heaven, where Jove now welcomes him visibly and in person. A four-part *Coro de Dei* (chorus of Gods) confirms that Orfeo is not dead but lives in Heaven as a celestial Demigod. The two choruses unite. Orfeo has evidently made the same choice, though under more pretentious circumstances, as he made at the end of Striggio's and Monteverdi's *Orfeo*; and while no further attention appears to be paid here to Euridice, Orfeo himself is asked to dwell where the 'beautiful stars' and the 'bright sun' will serve to adorn his 'blond tresses and golden locks'.

This reads like a parodied or distorted recollection of Striggio's 'look with love upon her fair semblance in the sun and the stars' at the end of *Orfeo*. But of course the whole Neoplatonic point in Striggio is that Orfeo, in losing the woman who carried the projection of his inner femininity, has at least gained the advantage of withdrawing that projection, and of being in better possession of his own feminine component: a very significant advance in consciousness and maturity. And since Orpheus is a myth and not only a man, his achievement stands for all of us: it is the archetypal image of femininity, the fair semblance, upon which Striggio's Orfeo will look. But for the librettist of Landi's *Morte d'Orfeo*, Euridice just is dead, a mere mindless shade who cannot even recognize her Orfeo when he goes down into hell to search for her, which, if it suggests anything psychologically, suggests a state of schizoid alienation. There she stays; and there her image rests. There is no answering image to recall the archetypal femininity which Striggio and his Orfeo saw glowing through her like a distant beacon, and transferred to orbit timelessly in the sun and the stars.

That is the measure of the decline in Neoplatonic insight. Mythological characters are still abundantly in evidence. Fragments of archetypal imagery make their own way in, and something of their inherent power comes with them; but unless the poet has perceived by intuition the connections which Neoplatonism expressed deliberately, neither the mythological characters nor the archetypal fragments can tell their story properly. That is at bottom, I think, very often what we really mean when we say that an opera has a bad libretto: it is such a jumble of intrinsically potent fragments. This libretto is a bad libretto, and there have been many such, though of course there have also been a great many good librettos owing nothing to Neoplatonism or to deliberate symbolism of any kind.

The first certainly Roman opera in both style and place is *L'Aretusa*, performed and published at Rome in 1620, at the house of Ottaviano Corsini, who was the librettist. The composer was Filippo Vitali, the opera is called *Favola in Musica*, and the preface informs us that text and music were prepared, rehearsed and performed within forty-four days. The Prologue is in strophic recitative form, with music notated only to the first of five verses, and no ritornellos are supplied though these are probably needed. At no point is any sinfonia or prelude notated, but it is most unlikely that none were performed, perhaps by orchestral improvisation as described by the Romans Agazzari, Pietro della Valle and Doni.[3] There are extensive recitatives, some duets, and a number of ensembles or choruses marked *Coro*. Each act ends with such a chorus; the last act includes the instruction *Ballo* for a long scene with solo interjections by various main characters and a *Pastore del Choro*, a shepherd of the chorus, working up to a big choral ending on the typical Roman scale. The plot presents Aretusa as a nymph of the chaste goddess Diana. Aretusa is eagerly pursued by the huntsman Alfeo, who loves her dearly. He is about to seize and possess her; but like Dafne in her similar predicament with Apollo, she prays for rescue. Thereupon, Diana transforms her into a stream. In Greek mythology, Alpheius pursued her further as the Peloponnesian river of that name, in which form she plunged intact under the sea to rise again in her fountain on the island of Ortygia. But whatever the symbolical potential of the myth, it goes for very little in this somewhat undistinguished opera, of which the chief interest lies in its historical position.

NEOPLATONISM AGAIN

An early Roman opera of much more philosophical and musical consequence, in an intermittently serious vein, is *La Catena d'Adone*, the Chain of Adonis (perf. Rome, 1626, publ. Venice, 1626; libretto publ. Rome, 1626, as *Favola boschereccia*, rustic tale); the librettist was Ottavio Tronsarelli, after Giovanni Battista Marino's *Adone* (Paris, 1623); the composer was Domenico Mazzocchi (1592–1665). There is a main *argomento* printed at the beginning, and a brief separate *argomento* before each scene. Although in the score there is no overture notated, we need to supply one, if only as a formal flourish of trumpets and drums. There is a prologue of recitative in rondo strophic variation form, with six verses separated by ritornello; then a sensitively madrigalian *Choro di Ciclopi A 3* (a three-part chorus of Cyclops) with a partly independent instrumental bass, and a second verse to the same music (which is not repeated in the score).

Act I has some free recitative for two characters, with echo effects (common enough by now); then a passage in rondo strophic variation with ritornello in three or four parts; more recitative for two characters; a six-part *Choro di Ninfe, e Pastori* (chorus of nymphs and shepherds), again in madrigal style, but a full chorus rather than a solo ensemble is again the probable intention (the difference would not be crucial in performance); a *Ballo A 3* (a sung dance in three parts) with an independent instrumental bass; the six-part chorus 'as above'; a 'solo' apparently by one of the chorus, on a basso continuo which is the same as the bass of the chorus, for a second verse; the chorus 'as above'; the third verse, to the music (not repeated in the score) of the second; the chorus again, the fourth verse to the same music (not repeated in the score); the chorus again to end the Act.

This is a careful and quite complicated structure, with something of the tautness of Monteverdi. As a composer, Domenico Mazzocchi stands out for the small quantity but excellent quality of his output, setting his own creative talent the same exacting standard as we know, from the important preface to his *Madrigali* (Rome, 1638), that he desired of his performers. The polyphony of Domenico Mazzocchi's choruses and ensembles here is light and open, as befits the idiom; but they are remarkably well composed. The reciting style, both lyrical and declamatory, is also employed with boldness, variety and feeling beyond the ordinary.

The third scene of Act II is more or less of a divertissement. There is more chorus and ensemble than there is recitative; but there are links throughout. A sinfonia and a brief recitative lead to a *Choro di Ninfe A 3* (three sopranos with instrumental bass) and a *Choro di Pastori A 3* (alto, tenor and bass, with instrumental bass); another sinfonia, another brief recitative, another *Choro di Ninfe A 3* and another *Choro di Pastori A 3*, but through all these choruses the bass is the same and the other parts use the same material in much the same way. The same material, though not the same bass, sustains a duet (soprano and alto) for Idonia and Oraspe, and a *Choro di Ninfe, e di Pastori A 6*, to end the Act.

The scenario thus agreeably unfolded takes the hero Adone through adventures not unlike those of *Circe* in 1581. He is enticed into an enchanted captivity by a seductress, Falsirena, who (taking a palpable hint from Plato's spiritual or celestial Venus), has disguised herself as the true Venus, and in that disguise pretends to malign her actual self. Adone is largely but not altogether deceived. Presently Falsirena is confronted by the true Venus, thus momentarily disconcerting not only Adone, but Amor (Cupid), who sees himself possessed of two mothers identical in appearance. Need it be added, however, that the true Venus releases Adone from his enchantment, so that he recognizes and returns to her, while Falsirena is duly discomfited?

This victory is celebrated by a trio for Venus and Amor (sopranos) and Adone (tenor), with instrumental bass, and a ritornello; a strophic *Aria A 3* for the same voices; ritornello; recitative; *A 3 Primo Choro* (soprano, tenor, bass with instrumental bass); *A 3 Secondo Choro* (same voice-ranges and instrumental bass, in similar music); *Tutto il Choro*, combining 'all the chorus' with new music in eight parts, very cheerful and at considerable length. The Roman predilection for ensembles and choruses is thus well indulged throughout; and both in this, and in the prominence of dancing and ballet, we may see an influence from the French *ballet de cour*. The line between dramatized ballet and opera containing much ballet and divertissement is never a very firm one. But there is enough purely musical development in this attractive work to keep it well on the side of opera. The *Allegoria della favola*, the allegory of the fable, printed at the end, spells out the Neoplatonic moral:

> Falsirena counselled by Arsete to the good; but persuaded by Idonia to the bad, is Soul counselled by Reason; but persuaded by Concupiscence. And how Falsirena yields easily to Idonia, shows thus, that every Feeling is easily overcome by Sense. And if the wicked Falsirena is eventually tied to hard Rock, one must likewise understand, that Punishment in the end is follower of Guilt.
>
> Adonis then, who far from the Deity of Venus goes through encounters of various labours, is the Man, who far from God makes many mistakes. But how Venus, returning to him, frees him from every trouble, and brings to him every happiness, thus God, after he returns to us with his efficacious help, makes it [the soul] advance over worldly harms, and renders it participant of celestial pleasures.

ROMAN OPERA FALLS BACK

In 1632, the rich and influential Barberini family had a newly prepared theatre ready to be inaugurated in their great Palazzo Barberini by the Quattro Fontane at Rome. The work chosen was Stefano Landi's[4] improving though not exactly sacred opera, *Il S.[ant'] Alessio* (perf. Rome, 1632, revived Rome, 1674, publ. Rome, 1634), on a libretto by Giulio Rospigliosi, the powerful aristocrat who became cardinal and, in 1677, pope, as Clement IX. It was entirely in the Roman tradition that this wealthy ecclesiastic should take a broad interest in literature and a special interest in opera; and that the ecclesiastically still more notable Barberini family should support opera to the utmost of their not inconsiderable bent (Maffeo Barberini became Pope Urban VIII in 1623). Their theatre seems to have been no more than the enormous main hall, in which stage, stage machinery and tiers of risers for seats could be built in as required; but it was certainly the scene of some memorable performances.

Sant' Alessio, or Saint Alexis, was a legendary worthy whose edifying story provides the main plot; but he is surrounded by a number of earthy characters, who enliven the proceedings with scenes some of which are serious in a human way, and others comical. The usual provision is made for spectacular scene-changes and machinery; and the music is not less varied. There are substantial overtures written out before each Act. There are a few suggestive hints for orchestration, though no consistent instructions. There is expressive recitative and lyrical arioso, with some more formalized aria. The ensembles and choruses have the customary Roman prominence.

Giulio Rospigliosi was also the librettist for a complete comic opera, not the earliest (since Monteverdi's lost comic opera *La finta pazza Licori*, perf. Mantua, 1627, preceded it), but possibly the earliest to have survived: *Chi soffre, speri,* He who suffers, Let him Hope (perf. Rome, 1637, 2nd version, Rome, 1639, not published except for an *Argomento at allegoria della comedia musicale intitolata Chi soffre speri*, Rome, 1639). The joint composers were Vergilio (brother of Domenico) Mazzocchi (1597–1646) and Marco Marazzoli (c.1619–62). Both known performances were at the Palazzo Barberini. At the performance of 1639, not only was Mazarin, the future cardinal and virtual ruler of France, present (he had been in the employment of Cardinal Antonio Barberini from 1632), but also the English poet Milton.[5] The characters of the opera include earthy human types as in Rospigliosi's *Sant' Alessio*, and conventional figures related to the familiar *commedia dell' arte*. The comic dialogue moves in brisk recitative; but the music is not as a whole much different from usual.

The quarter of a century, from 1632 on, during which the Barberini theatre was the mainstay of opera in Rome, saw ever more flamboyant scene changes and machinery, ever more perfunctory scenarios, ever more disconnected scores. Already in 1637, the architect Giutti de Ferrare took obvious precedent over the poet (again Rospigliosi) and the composer (Michelangelo Rossi) in the vaguely moralizing opera *Erminia sul Giordano*, entitled *Dramma Musicale* (perf. Rome, 1633, publ. Rome, 1637). The libretto is based on parts of Tasso's *Gerusaleme liberata*; it has very slight dramatic development. The music is chiefly notable for its many rather blatant choruses and ensembles; there are several interesting indications for instrumentation, with some high scoring for four independent violins above a normal bass.

A welcome exception to this general decline is the beautiful late example of true pastoral opera, *La Galatea* (perf. Rome, 1639, publ. Rome, 1639), of which the libretto and music were both by the celebrated castrato, Loreto Vittori. This work was dedicated to Cardinal Antonio Barberini, and produced at the Palazzo Barberini. There is much excellent recitative, with some ensembles and choruses skilfully interspersed. The opera builds up to a grand finale with strophic aria set between repetitions of a big eight-part chorus, and a charming trio for Acis, Galatea and Proteus (soprano, alto and tenor over an instrumental bass). There is real poetic and musical continuity, and the whole work stands as a refreshing contrast to the general decline.

But the decline was not arrested. We see its effects in an intermittently attractive but uneven opera, *Il palazzo d'Atlante incantato*, or *Il palazzo incantato* or *Il palazzo d'Atlante*, etc., the Enchanted Palace (of Atlante), on yet another libretto by Rospigliosi, set to music by Luigi Rossi (perf. Rome, 1642); and again produced at the Palazzo Barberini. The scenario, drawn from Ariosto, is one more of those theatrically effective rather than dramatically developing stories of enchantment by witchcraft and eventual release from imprisonment of which the original mythological potency is no longer much in evidence. Its highly potent original was the seduction of Odysseus by Circe on her enchanted island, and his escape from her dangerous charms with the aid of Athene and Hermes, as told in Book X of Homer's *Odyssey*. Scene follows scene here with the obvious intention of affording the stage manager and the stage machinist the utmost scope for their extravagant inventions. The extravagance, the production and the singing earned much praise; but the effect as a whole was reported by a French observer in a letter to Mazarin of 27 February 1642, as being 'extremely boring'.[6] The music is actually full of quiet beauty, and at least Rospigliosi gave Rossi better opportunities than Buti in their perfectly dizzy *Orfeo* designed five years later for the Parisian audience. Yet the weakness of both these unsatisfactory librettos lies in the same excessive indulgence of the stage machinery and spectacles, with too little genuinely dramatic unfolding of words and music.

The five manuscripts in which the *Palazzo incantato* (which was not published) survive show some variants, and one has pages pasted over or added as corrections—a glimpse into the composer's workshop if as is plausibly supposed this is his autograph.[7] There are considerable portions of the opera which in some of the manuscripts have instrumental parts (up to seven) fully notated, whereas in others of the manuscripts these are only sketched in (e.g. as treble and bass) or merely requested by the words: 'the usual accompaniment (*il solito accompagnamento*)'. Some choruses are notated in their full parts (up to twelve) in some manuscripts, but shown only by their two outer parts in other manuscripts. Trumpets and drums are sometimes indicated, and there are several indications for 'all the instruments (*tutti li stromenti*)'.[8] Some ritornellos are notated in full, others by their treble and bass lines only, others not at all. It is, as usual, for us to supply any missing material required.

There are in this Roman opera many long scenes of recitative and arioso for one or two characters, as well as arias; and almost as many

duets, trios and choruses as in the subsequent French-flavoured *Orfeo*,
Luigi Rossi's only other opera. The *Palazzo incantato* ends with a
Madrigale. a. 10., a ten-part madrigal, with instruments. Luigi Rossi is
known to us as a superb and prolific composer of chamber cantatas;
his operas are unfortunately not equal to the best of him, coming, as
they do, somewhat at a point of decline in Roman opera. The causes of
this decline were doubtless many, but among them, so extreme a
passion for eventful stage spectacle did probably take a share. (See
Plates X and XI for a back view of stage machinery.)

VENETIAN OPERA TAKES UP

Dramatic works anticipating opera had been a tradition at Venice
annually since 1571;[9] and actual operas included Monteverdi's almost
entirely lost *Proserpina rapita* (Proserpina Ravished), on a libretto by
Giulio Strozzi, at the wedding of Lorenzo Giustiniani and Giustiniana
Mocenzio (perf. and publ. Venice, 1630), with ballets and stage
machinery.[10] There were theatres specially built by Venetian aristo-
crats for spoken plays with much incidental music, run by professional companies and admitting members of the public on pay-
ment of an entrance price, it also being possible for other gentry to
rent boxes on indefinite lease.

One such notable theatre, belonging to the wealthy family Tron,
the Teatro Tron di San Cassiano, had eventually been rebuilt after a
disastrous fire in 1629. To celebrate its reopening, this theatre was put
at the disposal, not of a local company of actors, but of two experienced Romans, Francesco Manelli, a composer, and Benedetto
Ferrari, a poet and a man of business, of whom the second took the
main initiative. An opera set by Manelli on a text by Ferrari was
mounted: *L'Andromeda* (perf. Venice, 1637, libretto publ. Venice,
1637). The production was intended to be economical, though the
stage machinery was certainly elaborate, as the description in the
libretto relates at some length. The music has not survived. But the
success of this production was such as to encourage other theatres
devoted to opera in rapid succession.

Another lost opera by Manelli on a libretto by Ferrari, *La Maga
fulminata* (perf. Venice, 1638), followed up their first success, at the
Teatro San Cassiano; there was a revival at Bologna in 1641. In 1638, a
particularly large and well-equipped theatre was prepared for opera by
the wealthy Grimani family, who not only lavished a considerable
outlay of money upon it, but took an active share and interest in its
productions: the Teatro Grimani dei Santi Giovanni e Paolo. The
opening opera was *La Delia o sia La sera sposa del sole*, Delia or Evening
Bride of the Sun (perf. Venice, 1639, libretto publ. Venice, 1639), on a

libretto by Giulio Strozzi, set to music (lost) which the libretto makes clear was by Francesco Manelli; there was a later performance at Bologna in 1640. (This opera is discussed in Ch. XIV below.) Manelli was in charge of the opening production; he and Ferrari may already have terminated their connection with the San Cassiano.

It was at the San Cassiano that a star of much greater magnitude now rose: that of Pier Francesco Cavalli (1602–1676). His first opera, the *Nozze di Teti e di Peleo* (perf. Venice, 1639), was given at that theatre, as were many of his later operas. The librettist was Orazio Persiani; and the music (unlike that of the earlier Venetian operas) has most fortunately survived. Cavalli was the greatest opera composer of the generation which succeeded to Monteverdi; we meet him here at the beginning of his career, which just overlapped with the ending of Monteverdi's career, his direct model if not his actual teacher; and we shall be coming back to him.

Meanwhile we find Benedetto Ferrari (1597–1681) in the role of composer as well as librettist: his lost opera *L'Armida* (perf. Venice, 1639), based on Tasso, was produced in the splendid Teatro Grimani a S.S. Giovanni e Paolo. There, too, was produced Manelli's (lost) *Adone* (perf. Venice, 1640), on a libretto by Paolo Vendramin after the poem by Giovanni Battista Marino. In 1640, the Teatro San Moisè (successively owned by the Giustiniani family, the Zane family, and the Giustiniani family again) may have (on the insecure evidence of Ivanovich) opened with a revival of Monteverdi's *Arianna*; holding only about 800 persons, it was considered very small. In 1641, the Teatro Novissimo opened with *La finta pazza* (The Feigned Madwoman) by Sacrati on a text by G. Strozzi; this theatre ceased to function in 1645, but was famous for the décor of the great stage architect and engineer, Torelli. And so the remarkable list proceeds: almost a dozen theatres intermittently functioning in the seventeenth century, upwards of four functioning simultaneously for most of the time, and over 350 productions of opera at Venice in the course of that century.[11] It was a genuine popularization, reflected to some extent in the quality and character of the works produced.

POPULAR OPERA AT VENICE

Roman opera arrived at Venice fundamentally unchanged. The almost ritual intensity of the very earliest operas had already given place to a more relaxed entertainment, in which spectacular décor and breath-taking machinery were almost as significant as virtuoso singing, and considerably more significant than either the subtlety of the poetry or the fine details of the music. The librettos blend suspense and sentiment with comic relief, for most part with little deliberate symbolism. The scores flow freely in flexible declamation, plentifully varied with arias and duets and occasional trios; but choruses declined as they did not decline at Rome.[12] This, of course, saved some money;[13] nevertheless, Monteverdi used choruses freely in his *Ulisse* at Venice in 1641 and not in his *Poppea* there in 1642, though had he wished for them he would hardly have been refused them at this stage of his career and reputation. Several of Cavalli's first operas use choruses. Large ensembles of soloists already in the cast cost nothing extra; actual choruses, nothing excessive. Both alike went out of Venetian fashion, after which the rare choruses are usually confined to cries of *viva, viva,* or *vittoria, vittoria,* or other such simple ejaculations, which could have been and probably were managed by the considerable retinues of otherwise mute attendants already on stage to lend dignity to the principal characters.

We have the interesting testimony of the English visitor John Evelyn[14] in his famous diary concerning his attendance in June 1645, at the Teatro Novissimo for a performance of *Ercole in Lidia:*[15] 'this night, having with my Lord Bruce taken [i.e. secured] our places before, we went to the Opera, which are Comedies and other plays represented in Recitative Music by the most excellent Musitians vocal and Instrumental, together with a variety of Sceanes painted and contrived with no lesse art of Perspective, and Machines, for flying in the aire, and other wonderful motions.' To this Evelyn added his dry comment: 'So taken together it is doubtless one of the most magnificent and expensfull diversions the Wit of Man can invent.' This tallies with much evidence for habitual extravagance, and though complaints of rising costs are found, good resolutions to counter them by economy are not apparent.

Venice at the time was full of professional wind-players and others seeking a precarious living from weddings and funerals, festivities and entertainments, certainly including plays and possibly including operas. We have always to remember that showy entertainments in the tradition of the sixteenth-century masques and interludes did not abate in the seventeenth century. The Florentine interludes of 1589, for which some music survives in notation, do not record in that notation the orchestration, rich and varied as we know it to have been from the contemporary descriptions. Similarly, it is only from the full *Description of a Masque. . .by Thomas Campion* (London, 1607) that we learn of its thirty or so instrumentalists in addition to the singers. The French *Balet comique de la royne* of 1581 is a little more specific (ed. Paris, 1582), and Monteverdi's *Orfeo* of 1607 much more specific; but it was in being specific, rather than in being richly and variously orchestrated, that *Orfeo* was at that time exceptional.

We have evidence enough that rich and varied orchestration continued in masques and interludes. James Shirley's masque, *The Triumph of Peace* (perf. London, 1633),[16] had 'Fourty Lutes at one time, besides other instruments and Voices of the most excellent Musicians in Consort', with a continuo group ('Symphony') of twelve selected instrumentalists, and a full orchestra including at least fifteen strings, twelve winds, and in addition eleven trumpeters (borrowed with their accompanying kettle-drummers from noble establishments). This may have been decidedly above average, but it was not otherwise untypical. It does not, however, follow that opera after *Orfeo* had necessarily the same advantages; and the most likely conclusion is that through the middle of the seventeenth century in most circumstances it did not.

There is a scruffy and in parts almost illegible passage (but Thomas Walker read it all) in some accounts at Venice which records for 1658 (Venetian old-style for 1659) enormous sums paid to virtuoso singers, very large sums paid for scenery and effects, but seemingly trivial sums paid to eight string and lute players and one tuner—so trivial that Denis Arnold very reasonably questioned whether other payments to further musicians are somehow concealed elsewhere in the accounts; but it does not appear that they are.[17] For 1664 (old style for 1665) there are likewise listed three keyboard players, one person unspecified, four strings and two lutes. These forces are much too small artistically for the size of pit and auditorium found in the larger Venetian theatres, and I see no reason for not enlarging them within the historical possibilities now.

Fifteen years later we read, in the fashionable Parisian journal generally known as the *Mercure galant*,[18] of a performance in the Venetian theatre of S. Giovanni Crisostomo of Pallavicino's *Nerone* in 1679, that 'forty instruments, of the best that could be found, played the *Simphonie*': a French term commonly used (as its English equivalent was in the description of Shirley's masque previously cited) for the small continuo group who accompanied most solo passages, but here apparently indicating the full orchestra, where 'a quantity of all sorts of instruments was present: recorders, trumpets, drums, viols and violins'. Again this occasion may have made exceptional demands, including instruments on stage for special effect; but there are scattered mentions of all these instruments, and also of flutes, bassoons, harpsichord and organ, in the crucial Contarini manuscripts of seventeenth-century Venetian operas, as Taddeo Wiel,[19] who discovered them in the Marciana Library in Venice, already noticed in 1888; while manuscripts of Venetian operas surviving in the Nationalbibliothek at Vienna add horns, cornettos, trombones and theorboes to the list of instruments named in one such source or another. When the score of Cavalli's *La Didone* (on a libretto by G. F. Busenello, perf. Venice, 1641)[20] indicates, after four measures of a chorus, that 'all the instruments come in', though parts for these are not in the notation, and when it later has 'aria with all the instruments', we can perhaps infer a somewhat larger and more varied group than a mere handful of bowed and plucked strings. How large and varied that might have been, we have no direct evidence to show. But it is, as always, important to realize that the instruments which might come in with a big chorus, or for sinfonias and ritornellos or for the overtures to Acts or to accompany a ballet, would in any case be more numerous though not necessarily more various than those which might support passages for solo voice—the vocal melody being, after all, the main purpose of these Venetian operas, and still accounting for much the larger portion of the score.

If, as now seems probable, the opera orchestra did significantly decline in the middle years of the seventeenth century at Venice, it recovered in the later years; but the continuo group, at all events, remained small, as it needed to be in order not to impede the solo voices. A year after the *Mercure galant* report on the forty instruments for Pallavicino's *Nerone*, Alexandre Toussaint de Limojon, Sieur de Saint Disdier, published his intelligent travel book,[21] where, speaking as a Frenchman of the Venetian opera, he wrote that: 'The Symphonie' (and here the meaning seems to be the common French meaning, i.e. the small continuo group within the full orchestra, not that full orchestra itself) 'is not much, inspiring melancholy rather than gaiety: it is composed of Lutes, theorboes and harpsichords, which accompany the voice with an admirable exactness.' At this period in France, the continuo group normally included a gamba, with one or two flutes or violins, as well as the plucked instruments.[22] On the other hand, 'this great Choir of Music which so often fills the whole French Theatre, and of which it is hardly possible at all to distinguish the words, displeases the Italians, who say that it is more suited to the Church than to the Opera; the great quantity of Violins, which obliterate, while they play, all the other Instruments of the Symphony' (but here the meaning has apparently shifted to the full orchestra) 'can only, they say, please the Frenchmen, except when they play by themselves in other passages.' This not very well expressed description at least conveys that the Italians within de Limojon's experience did not like rich and varied continuo accompaniments to their solo singing, and did not like choruses at all, or a quantity of strings obliterating the other instruments, but that they made an exception in favour of certain passages, purely instrumental or purely strings alone (it can be taken either way).

François Maximilien Misson,[23] at the end of the seventeenth century, criticized the costumes, the lack of dances and, commonly, of 'fine Machines' or 'Illuminations', the long vocal figurations and the castrato heroes of Venetian opera, which indeed was perhaps well past its best by then; he only admitted that 'they have most excellent

Ayres', which would have been approaching by then close to the style of number opera; he added that 'The Symphony is much smaller than at *Paris*', which at that time may certainly have been true, since large forces were becoming the fashion at the French opera. An opera orchestra of about forty would have been average elsewhere in the early days of number opera, and for some time afterwards; but the French average at Paris appears to have reached nearer to fifty. We are in a different world there from the Italian opera of the middle of the seventeenth century, in this as in so many other particulars.[24]

Perhaps the mere extent of opera during the seventeenth century in Venice was its most distinctive feature. The brilliance and costliness of Venetian opera were by no means unique; but they were for most of the seventeenth century perhaps uniquely famous. One reason both for the quantity of Venetian opera and for its international reputation was simply the number of visitors from all over Europe who came to Venice, particularly during the carnival, for pleasure and relaxation and a taste of foreign life. It was a high point in that Grand Tour which young people of good education were habitually encouraged to take. It was a continued attraction for those in a position to travel, with a particular fascination, it seems, for rich visitors from more Northern climes. The free and easy ways, the liberties allowable when masked, the picturesque setting, the variety of dazzling entertainments all contributed to the legend; and opera was among the dazzling entertainments. (See Plate XII for a dazzling spectacle.)

XIV
Monteverdi at Venice
❧❧❧

MONTEVERDI'S LATER OUTPUT

Monteverdi, and his brother Giulio Cesare who had been assisting him, were dismissed, or dismissed themselves, from the Mantuan court, where they had long had cause for dissatisfaction, in July of 1612, five months after the death of the duke, Vincenzo Gonzaga I, and the succession of his son Francesco I. In August of 1613 Monteverdi was appointed to the eminent post of musical director at St Mark's, Venice, where he was responsible for much church music, but found time and energy for great secular activity in addition, responding to good treatment and high appreciation with splendid productivity for the remainder of his long life.

The operas of Monteverdi's Venetian period are lost except for the last two. This is all the more to be regretted because concerning *La finta pazza Licori* (libretto by Giulio Strozzi, perf. Mantua, 1627), we read in a letter[1] from Monteverdi, probably written to Striggio on 1 May 1627, of its 'thousand ridiculous little inventions'; and this is a very early date for a comic opera. Moreover, we know that Monteverdi conceived it as that best kind of comedy which leaves us not quite sure whether to laugh or to cry; for he spoke (letter of 7 May 1627) of wanting to move the audience 'to laughter and compassion', and of the hard work it would take him to put into it 'my inner feeling (*interno affetto*)'.

Thus our first surviving Venetian opera by Monteverdi is *Il ritorno d'Ulisse in patria* (The Return of Ulysses—i.e. Odysseus—to his Native Country), to a libretto by Giacomo Badoaro. The first performance is now known to have been at Venice for the carnival in 1640. A second performance at Bologna in 1640 is attested, and a third is known at Venice in 1641 (previously thought to have been the first). The opera survives in a MS score in Vienna[2] anonymously; one MS libretto (out of seven versions known to survive) attributes the music to Monteverdi, but differs from the libretto in the score, especially in being divided into five Acts, whereas the score is divided into three Acts.

The attribution to Monteverdi has been questioned[3] on these grounds, but without good reason, since it is common to find librettos of baroque operas with substantial variants. Moreover, in the score itself a contemporary hand, possibly the same hand, has made subsequent corrections in a different ink which include indications of the division into five Acts: e.g. on [p. 162], at the end of Act II, Scene x, the second ink shows '*Fine de L'atto 3°*' and (but crossed out) '*Atto quarto*'. Eitner gave *Ulisse* as a lost opera: Kiesewetter identified this unascribed manuscript as Monteverdi's *Ulisse*; Ambros accepted the attribution; Mantuani, author of the catalogue of the *Musiksammlung*, also accepted it; Emil Vogel questioned it, but in a very scholarly and provisional manner; Goldschmidt nevertheless accepted it; Robert Haas accepted the attribution and published the opera in the Denkmäler der Tonkunst in Österreich with a careful *Revisionsbericht* noticing the different inks, and he also published an excellent commentary. Some rather unscholarly arguments followed in the 1940s, mainly from Italian writers, suggesting quite incorrectly that the music is altogether poor and unworthy of Monteverdi, that the manuscript is of eighteenth-century date, and other inept conclusions. But Wolfgang Osthoff brilliantly restored the position taken two generations earlier by Robert Haas, thus justifying, as quite often happens, one of the great pioneers of modern musicology against his lesser critics.

Osthoff confirms that the surviving Vienna manuscript of *Ulisse* is an ordinary professional scribe's copy of about 1640. It was in the Library of that very musicianly and enterprising Emperor Leopold I (who composed considerably, and on whom the article in MGG is most informative), as the binding shows (Haas had already stated that the Emperor's likeness is stamped on the front cover, and the likeness does indeed resemble other portraits of Leopold I). The same binding, and the same likeness, are found on cantata manuscripts, including a small one of two Carissimi cantatas, which enabled Gloria Rose[4] to add this very distinguished crowned head of the Hapsburg line to others at the French and English courts (Charles II at Whitehall in particular) aware of Carissimi's greatness in his own lifetime. No reputable musicologist seems to doubt now that *Ulisse* really was composed by Monteverdi.

The libretto of *Ulisse* is dramatically a little discontinuous and awkward, so that the opera does not flow quite so easily, nor is the music quite so consistently inspired, as in the astonishing *Poppea* which followed. But the overall effect in a good performance is very wonderful: not only is this Monteverdi, but vintage Monteverdi. The second performance at Bologna in 1640 shows how close were the artistic links between various centres of Italian opera, and how early. An opera, *Andromeda*, by Girolamo Giacobbi, on a libretto by Ridolfo Campeggi, was performed at Bologna in 1610; the libretto (publ. 1610) states that it was 'recited in music of the representative style (*fatta recitare in musica di stile rappresentativo*). . .with magnificent machinery (*con apparato magnifico*).' In 1616, Peri's *Euridice* was performed at Bologna. Manelli's *La Delia o sia La sera sposa del sole*, on a libretto by Giulio Strozzi (perf. Venice, 1639), was performed at Bologna in 1640, the date 1630 being a modern mistake, and the attribution to Sacrati by Ivanovich an old one. Manelli's second opera, *La maga fulminata* (perf. Venice, 1638) was performed at Bologna in 1641, and so in the same year was Ferrari's *Il Pastor regio* (perf. Venice 1640). Domenico Mazzocchi's *Catena d'Adone* (perf. Rome, 1626), was performed at Bologna in 1648. Cavalli's *Egisto* (perf. Venice, 1643) was performed at Bologna in 1647, and his *Giasone* (perf. Venice, 1649) in 1651. Though not a leading centre of opera in the first half of the seventeenth century, Bologna was an important subsidiary centre.

There can be no doubt that this Bologna performance of *Ulisse* did take place. In a collection of congratulatory poems, *Le glorie della musica celebrate dalla sorella poesia*— The Glories of Music celebrated by her Sister, Poetry (Bologna, 1640: not 1630, as in Leo Schrade,[5] following Guetano Giordani)—we read 'there having been produced (*rappresentandosi*) in Bologna the *Delia* and the *Ulysse* at the theatre of the most illustrious [family] Guastavillani'. Poems are included addressed to Sig. Filippo Guastavillani, 'for the Ulysses, opera of Sig. Claudio Monteverdi' (p. 6); 'for the Ulysses, Drama of the most illustrious Sig. Giacomo Badoaro, and Music of Sign. Claudio Monteverdi' (p. 7); 'for the Delia, Drama of Sig. Giulio Strozzi, and Music of Sig. Francesco Manelli' (p. 8: notice the definite attribution to Manelli, confirmed by the scenario of 1638); and for the singers in these two operas, which must therefore both have been 1640, especially as (p. 21) mention is made of 'Sig. Benedetto Ferrari' who 'played the Theorbo in Delia' (for Manelli and Ferrari came North from Rome in 1637, but presumably not by 1630). A performance of *Ulisse* at some time in Vienna might account for the presence of the manuscript there in the Emperor's library; but no evidence has been found confirming it.

GODS AND MEN

The ultimate source of this powerfully theatrical libretto is Homer's *Odyssey*,[6] to which, although condensed, it adheres quite closely. In Homer, the action is divided between the divine and the human characters. We are never quite sure whose willpower is being most effectually displayed by the course of events; but in some measure it is always both, and ultimately it is always the gods who prevail. The gods and the goddesses in Homer are not intellectual abstractions, and they are not literary devices. They are the living personifications of archetypal human impulses, projected upon their still numinous though no longer primordial images. Depicting as they do the inner causation of which the human actions show the outer consequences, they are necessary to the story, and can never be dismissed merely as perfunctory or irrelevant.

When it subsequently came to an altogether more deliberate use of mythological symbols in Neoplatonic artistry, the projection of inner experiences on to outer images became more sophisticated, though it may in its different context be scarcely less numinous; and Striggio's libretto for Monteverdi's *Orfeo* is an excellent example. Rinuccini's *Arianna* mingles the human with the archetypal, and Badoaro's *Ulisse* carries this transition to a further degree. Homer, too, has many human touches. The difference is that in Homer, the presence of the archetypal forces is never far from our awareness, but on the contrary is felt, even when unseen, as a sort of conditioning pressure upon everything that happens; whereas in Badoaro, we are apt to forget all about the gods and goddesses when they are not on stage. This was by no means the end of the genuinely mythological libretto; but it was perhaps a pointer towards much perfunctory mythologizing to come.

The Prologue introduces Human Fragility (soprano), Time (bass), Fortune (soprano) and Love (soprano) as if to remind us that there is an archetypal undercurrent to our human affairs; but only the last of them (Amor, Cupid) is an established deity; the other three are the merest puppets; and their discussions on the subject of destiny are not of the keenest interest. Monteverdi does his best for them with his usual cunning in rounding off a taut and balanced musical construction. Thus Human Fragility provides a refrain by returning with strophic variations on a repeated bass: at first, with repeated words; then again, with new words. The opening sinfonia also serves as ritornello; and there is a good ensemble for climax.

The first Act is connected with the Prologue by using as ritornello this same opening sinfonia. Thereupon we are confronted in the score with two measures of a simple bass note C, and the instruction: 'this sinfonia', i.e. the sinfonia which it is the intention that we should now construct in sufficient quality and quantity on our own initiative, 'to be repeated as many times [as needed] until Penelope arrives on the stage'. This she does in a formal (and probably a danced) entry. She is accompanied by her faithful nurse; and they outline for us the familiar, haunting situation. The interminable absence of Ulysses, the inexhaustible fidelity of Penelope: Badoaro and Monteverdi show obvious sympathy for the personal overtones; but now that we are into Homer's own material, the archetypal ground-swell carries us along as the ancient tale unfolds and the glorious music rings in our ears. There is a rondo strophic form to give tautness to the structure; there is an intensity of declamation to give focus to the melody. The refrain as Penelope sings 'return, return, return, oh return, Ulisse' turns our hearts over in Monteverdi's warmest vein.

And as if in answer, there follows a scene in which Ulysses returns indeed. An interesting change of design may have happened here, somewhere between Badoaro and Monteverdi, or between one performing version of the opera and another. For Scene iii, described by a different ink in the score as 'Maritima', and comprising a short chorus of Nereids and Sirens, has no music, unless we supply our own for a danced entry with choral singing, using the text of the libretto. But perhaps the impact of what now follows comes more powerfully in immediate succession to Penelope's lament. In the libretto, Scene iv 'is a dumb-show (*e muta*)', but with instructions which (as they appear in the score) read: 'here comes out the boat of the Pheacians, who carry Ulysses, who is asleep, and so as not to wake him, the following Sinfonia is played (*toccata*) softly always on one chord'. And again the only music supplied in notation is a bass note C (with a flat marked on the space above to indicate E flat, so that C minor and not C major is the tonality intended). We may recall that the opening toccata of Monteverdi's *Orfeo* is likewise on the bass note C (written C major for concert D major in that case); that it is all on one chord (the tonic); and that it is nevertheless a lively, interesting and indeed rather beautiful little piece, introducing some thematic material which is subsequently developed throughout the opera. We might well use it for our model when composing the necessary music here.

The boat of the Pheacians was undoubtedly brought on stage, and probably rocked realistically on a series of cams and rollers to represent the motion of the waves. Machinery for these purposes was habitual, and extravagant Venice would hardly have missed the opportunity. But the most remarkable features here are the silence of the Pheacians, and the sleep of Ulysses. His homecoming is presented like a dream. And in his dream, or in his waking vision, there is his divine helper of old, Minerva (Athene), an unchallengeably archetypal image of inner femininity. Born as she was fully armed from the head of her father Zeus, Athene is every bit an Olympian and a stalwart of the prevailing patriarchal order: quite the opposite of Aphrodite (Venus) whose birth was from the sea and whose nature retains all the instinctual attributes of matriarchal impulse. But in so far as the deeper theme of the *Odyssey* is the growth of the character of Odysseus (Ulysses), Athene (Minerva) stands for that aspect of the eternal feminine which can most help and least hinder him. On his side,

Ulysses in this scene appears like a man who needs to wake, and is in course of waking, to his own true self.

Scene ix of Act I has for stage direction (in the later ink) a 'Chorus of Naiads, Minerva, Ulisse': but the chorus is left to be supplied by us in our capacity as performers. The same necessity arises in Act II, Scene vi, where the stage direction (in the original ink) reads: 'here 8 Moors come out who do a Greek dance, sung to the following verses', for which music is again left to be supplied. In Scene xii (the last) of Act II, we see *Sinfonia da Guerra*, sinfonia of war, with the further instruction: 'here comes a flourish (*tocco*) of war from all the instruments.' This is the first and only indication in the score that an orchestra large and varied enough to be called 'all the instruments' is meant to be present. But present it was, and we have to decide what instruments it is to include and what they are to play, supplying for ourselves, where necessary, orchestral parts for them to play, both by themselves and as accompaniment. Wolfgang Osthoff[7] makes the admirable suggestion that we should follow the advice given by Monteverdi himself in his letter from Venice of 9 December 1616, to Alessandro Striggio: for a maritime scene, 'wind instruments' such as 'trombones and cornettos' (rather than 'string instruments') and 'citterns or harpsichords and harps'. Surely not just strings alone, or just continuo alone. We do find in the score, however, what was still rare at the time, a few notated expression marks: e.g. [p. 38] '*presto. . .tardo*'; [pp. 103–4] '*pian. . .forte. . .piu forte*'; [p. 198] '*adagio*'; and (end of Prologue) 'the present sinfonia being finished *in tempo allegro*'.

Scene ii of Act III is next accounted for by the rubric: 'Left out, because it is melancholy.' Act III (the last) ends, in the score, with the duet of Penelope and Ulysses. In the libretto, a 'Chorus of Ithicans' concludes the opera; but in performance it was evidently preferred to end with the duet. We shall surely wish to follow the score rather than the libretto here. Nevertheless it is the incompleteness of the score which may possibly mislead us into exaggerating the difference in orchestral colouring between *Ulisse* and *Orfeo*. In the voices, we see once more the same intensely eloquent recitative and arioso, the same strength given by concealed structural tautness and coherence, the same intermittent ornamentation with virtuoso embellishment and the same possibility of adding some, but not too much further ornamentation on our own responsibility. We also see, however, the tendency already beginning to use more small ensembles (especially duets, and to a certain extent trios), likewise with some similar but judiciously added embellishments. We see, too, the tendency to use fewer choruses and dances, though some are present, and others not written out are left to be supplied. But the beginnings of the subsequent almost total disappearance of choruses from Venetian operas is still a few years away, with Monteverdi's own *Poppea* (perf. Venice,

1642), or Cavalli's *Egisto* (perf. Venice, 1643). We may conclude that *Ulisse* is not yet, whereas *Poppea* is, altogether an opera in the mid-seventeenth-century Venetian idiom.

THE FAMILIAR HOMERIC SCENARIO UNFOLDS

Ulisse unfolds at leisure, but on the whole with inspiration. In Act I, Ulysses may be on the verge of recovering his true identity; but he is not yet in a position to let the world recognize him for what he really is. He is therefore brought by the goddess into the guise (not just the clothing) of a decrepit old beggar: the weak shadow (which indeed it may be quite valuable for him to experience) of his own strong and royal self. There may also be some glancing reference to the familiar fairy-tale test of our ability to see worth (our own included) beneath an unprepossessing exterior. Penelope herself is going to find it hard to recognize her husband; but this difficulty is evidently part of the test, and contributes to the genuine resolution of the drama.

In Act II, the three wicked suitors on the stage, and their toady Iro, certainly cannot see the true worth of the seeming old beggar who will presently undo them all; but we can in the audience, and we enjoy the dramatic irony. The suspense begins to rise in both words and music as (in Scene v) the suitors yet again lay siege to Penelope's long-tried fidelity. There is a complex structure, as a distinctive solo virtuosity for each several suitor alternates with a common refrain in the trio 'Ama dunque' ('love then'); and with another refrain for Penelope in eloquent arioso: 'Non voglio amar' ('I do not wish to love'). Then as their renewed confidence brushes their present frustration aside, the suitors break out in a united trio again: 'All' allegrezze, dunque al ballo' ('with cheerfulness then to the dance'). It is here (Scene vi) that the Greek dance 'by the 8 Moors' is stipulated; and for a short while the tense scene is broken up with pure *divertissement*. The suitors themselves, though serious in their involvement and tragic in their ending, are also exploited for their comic possibilities, with a mixture of pretentious bragging and unheroic slyness which yields rich dividends in this direction. Iro, a straight comic, but a stutterer, enacts a caricature of Monteverdi's own virtuoso vocalizing. He now thinks he can win easy glory by wrestling with the old beggar who is Ulysses in disguise; his discomfiture has the other characters surprised and laughing, and us laughing but not surprised.

The excitement increases as the suitors try their fortunes again, each with a rich present to win Penelope's favour; and now indeed she consents to love, on a condition which we know, and she surely hopes, will prove insuperable, but which they take to be quite a practical proposition. She will marry that suitor who can bend, and string, and shoot straight the great bow of Ulysses. Had this bow been merely and literally a weapon, it would be a little difficult to understand why Ulysses left it behind when he went off to fight in the Trojan war. But now Badoaro has Penelope call it 'the bow of Ulysses, or rather the bow of Love which must pierce my heart'. The suitors try to bend the bow, each in turn, and each is unable in his turn. A certain repetitiveness in their endeavours is underlined musically by repetitions of the same introductory sinfonia, and by their praying enthusiastically for success (the first to Love; the second to Mars; the third to the very person of Penelope) in symmetrical recitative. But they have none of them the quality of independent manhood, it seems, which that strong bow implies. A *Sinfonia da Guerra*, a sinfonia of war, now preludes the success, not easy but very assured, of Ulysses, whereupon he shoots the presumptuous suitors down.

Act III takes its time in arriving at the final resolution. We are regaled by a comic scene for Iro, the stuttering failure, which may not strike us as quite so comic if we have much compassion for stutterers and failures. There is a long council of the gods, in which Minerva (Athene) pleads eloquently with Juno (Hera), Juno with Jove (Zeus) and Jove with Neptune (Poseidon) in a crescendo of prayer on behalf of Ulysses, against that divine but partisan anger which is supposed to have kept him wandering for all these years. No doubt these Homeric divinities stand for inner forces of the human psyche; no doubt Badoaro was in a measure aware of it; but we might not be very tolerant of the dramatic hold-up were it not that Monteverdi has given them (especially Neptune with his characteristically low bass) such splendid music. And when we come to Penelope, she is very properly suspicious (as Homer made her), and needs to be helped by Ulysses' old herdsman Eumetus and by her own faithful nurse. Penelope's acceptance of Ulysses is certainly the more real for not being too readily accorded. Then as she consents to recognize him beneath his fast vanishing disguise and all the deeper estrangement of his twenty years away from her, and as he returns to her and to his own true self at one and the same time, they reward us with a closing duet of the same kind, and almost the same quality, as the famous ending of *Poppea*, discussed below.

MONTEVERDI'S LAST OPERA

Monteverdi's last opera, *L'Incoronazione di Poppea* (The Coronation of Poppea), to a splendid libretto by Giovanni Busenello (perf. Venice, 1642), survives in two manuscript scores, both unfortunately dating from so late as around 1650. One[8] is in Venice, with alterations and additions once thought but now known not to be in Monteverdi's hand (there are however some in Cavalli's hand). The other[9] is in Naples, where it seems likely though not certain to have been used for a performance there in 1651.

Like Verdi, Monteverdi ended a long life with a fine late flowering: he was seventy-five when this brilliant opera (his fourth within three years) was produced. It has, in its different way, something of that intoxicating lightness, that artistic sureness, that warmth, vitality and serenity which made Verdi's *Falstaff* the miraculous consummation of his eighty years. In Monteverdi's *Poppea*, there is likewise a sunset glow of genius and of compassion. Yet the libretto thus compassionately composed is not on the surface of it compassionate. On the contrary, it is hard and wordly, not to say cynical.

There are operas which need explaining because their ostensible content is absurd, or incoherent or sentimental; this opera needs explaining because its ostensible content is shocking. It is not the love-affair which is shocking, but the crimes committed for the sake of the love-affair. As events in the outer world, they would almost certainly have shocked Busenello, and quite certainly Monteverdi; for while Monteverdi's letters reveal a man of some considerable impatience and irascibility, they also reveal a sense of human values which would not be compatible with condoning murder. This is supposed to be a historical libretto. History is supposed to be fact, not allegory. And this particular slice of history is very nasty fact indeed, as may best be appreciated by summarizing in brief outline the accounts of it presented by Tacitus and Suetonius.[10]

The historical Nero reached the throne in A.D. 54. His mother Agrippina had seduced the previous emperor Claudius; got him to marry her; then to adopt Nero in place of the rightful heir Britannicus; next to marry Nero to his daughter Ottavia—after which it was a simple matter for Agrippina to expedite the succession by having poor old Claudius poisoned. Like mother, like son. For some years, however, Nero's previous tutor and current adviser, Seneca, kept him reasonably popular by encouraging him in a liberal policy, taking the real responsibilities of power off his hands, and indulging his vanity and his sensuousness alike as a deliberate distraction from politics. Part of the distraction was the beautiful freedwoman Acte; but Agrippina, always a problem with her intermittent intrigues, got so violently jealous over Acte that she took up Britannicus in retaliation. Nero disposed of Britannicus by poison, and of Agrippina for the time being by what Tacitus[11] ironically called honourable captivity.

In A.D. 58, Poppea Sabina, a woman after Agrippina's own stamp, captivated Nero, and quite obviously because she *was* a woman after Agrippina's own stamp. No woman can have such hidden power over a man, whether for good or bad, as a woman who matches that part of his inner femininity which he has built up unconsciously on the mother-image. How can he help responding to that dangerous fascination? How can he help reflecting in his own character for good and bad the woman he necessarily clung to in his own helpless and impressionable infancy? Even with good mothering, the mother-image remains to some extent thus ambivalently influential into adult life; with bad mothering, it may remain irresistible, since the grown man may then seek blindly to find, projected on to other women, the good mother he did not find at the proper stages of his own childhood. Suetonius[12] actually reports to us in his gossipy way that Nero was with difficulty prevented from consummating a physical passion for his mother Agrippina, which her jealousy over Acte suggests that she returned or more truly instigated. The psychological relationship between mother and son must have been almost unmitigatedly Oedipal and incestuous.

Poppea set out to become Nero's wife, as Agrippina had set out to become Claudius' wife, and with the same nefarious but ultimately unreal success. Her first move was to turn Nero against Agrippina, whose death he then obliquely arranged. His agent Anicetus first, we are told by Suetonius, brought her on board a ship designed to fall apart. It did so; but she could swim. Soldiers led by Anicetus later cut her to pieces, which frightened Nero until he found public sympathy, after all, inclining to his side. Poppea became Nero's wife and empress. Several potential enemies were removed by poison; Nero's previously ruling empress Ottavia was divorced, banished and murdered in quick succession; Seneca merely retired in comfort, on his possibly quite ill-gotten gains at court. But Nero's luck had turned against him, in a crescendo of calamities and unpopularity: even the severe damage to Pompeii by the earthquake of A.D. 63 (the volcanic eruption was in A.D. 79), and still more the destruction of much of Rome by the great fire of A.D. 64, were counted against him. So, more reasonably, was the heavy taxation extorted to rebuild the city of Rome on more resplendent lines. Conspiracy grew; murder mounted; Seneca, now seemingly implicated in a plot to murder Nero, was himself among the victims in A.D. 65. Revolts in Germany and Spain were followed, in A.D. 68, by the defection of the palace guards. Nero fled. Galba was proclaimed emperor, and Nero was sentenced to death. He took courage just in time and killed himself, unlamented, at the ripe old age of thirty-one.

Here, then, is a historical tale which could be told censoriously; or it could be told compassionately. Busenello did not really tell it at all; he merely borrowed some of its salient events, and the glamour not so much of its debased historical characters as of their romanticized legend. For just as many myths may have had some forgotten episode of history embedded in their origins, without in the least diminishing their symbolical validity when subsequently developed by the poetic imagination, so too may historical figures serve subsequently as myths. The historical Macbeth and the legendary Lear serve Shakespeare equally well when, as Dr Johnson perceptively expressed it, he 'holds up to his readers a faithful mirrour' for the very reason that 'his characters are not modified by the customs of particular places', but 'act and speak by the influence of those general passions and principles by which all minds are agitated.'[13] Archetypal characters and situations, historical or otherwise, abound in Shakespeare.

As in the case of Shakespeare with Anthony and Cleopatra, then, so in the case of Busenello with Nero and Poppea: history yields gracefully to romance. When in Grimm's fairy-tale[14] the two children must be killed without any ostensible foreknowledge that this will bring both them and Faithful John back to life again, our moral sense is not outraged because our intuitions pick up something of the veiled growth of character which the fairy-tale implies. Our moral scruples in *Poppea* are taken care of by our feeling ourselves so very much less in historical Rome than in timeless fairyland, where the only morality required is the courage and integrity to go through with the adventure.

WHAT HAPPENS TO THE HISTORY

The Prologue encourages this fairy-tale impression by bringing in Fortune, Virtue and Love (Cupid or Amor): familiar personifications, all three, but not exactly historical. As they debate their relative importance in the affairs of men, Love gets the better of the argument, and confirms it later by intervening successfully in the action. Nevertheless, these allegorical representatives are not the main carriers of archetypal symbolism in this opera. The human characters carry their own archetypal traits, as is usual in a fairy-tale.

Act I gives Poppea a husband, Ottone, who returns just in time to find (tragically) Nero's soldiers on guard (comically) outside his house, and to watch Nero, on his way out, sing (romantically) a duet with Poppea. Further light relief comes later on with the charming exchanges of two young servants in love. This was later a regular operatic convention; and so also was the old nurse (Arnalta), and so was the lullaby or 'sleep-music' (sung by her to Poppea in the second act). The music for these contrasted developments is inexhaustibly melodious and brilliantly constructed: the art which conceals art, always a remarkable characteristic of Monterverdi's operas, was never displayed to better advantage than in this magnificent score.

We now watch two murder-plots unfolding: Poppea's against Seneca and Ottavia; Ottone's and Ottavia's against Poppea. When Nero is cajoled by Poppea into ordering Seneca to kill himself, the fine old man (as he is in the opera) greets death as a not unwelcome friend; while his loyal retinue try to dissuade him, in a scene of alternating solo and ensemble outstanding both for dramatic and for musical inspiration.

Ex. 19. Monteverdi, Poppea, *Venice, 1642, the quiet opening bars by Seneca's retinue on p. 125 in Raymond Leppard's ed.:*

[Do not die, do not die, Seneca]

When Ottone, in turn, tries to kill Poppea, aided by Drusilla (a young lady in Poppea's entourage but in love with Ottone), Love foils the attempt in person: but Ottone and Drusilla are magnanimously spared by Nero, and banished congenially enough in one another's company. Such magnanimity by the injured victor also became an operatic convention. Ottavia is put out to sea in an unseaworthy vessel. This recalls Agrippina's history; but it is also curiously reminiscent of those leaky ships, stone troughs, open coffins and other improbable vessels of mythology which may nevertheless complete a miraculous sea-journey, perhaps in token of some precarious transition across the uncharted waters which so often stand in myths or in dreams for the deep unconscious. The purely human pathos, on the other hand, of Ottavia's banishment to exile or worse is caught beautifully in her farewell lament. (See Ex. 20 below.)

THE FAIRY-TALE BENEATH THE HISTORY

The musical climax of the opera, as it survives today, coincides with the dramatic climax: the radiant duet sung by Nero and Poppea to

Ex. 20. *Monteverdi*, Poppea, *Venice, 1642. Ottavia's Lament (p. 200 in Raymond Leppard's ed.), opening, showing tritone interval for grief as so often in* Orfeo *(realization mine):*

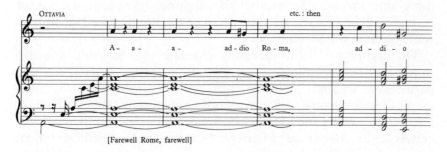

[Farewell Rome, farewell]

celebrate their official union, in royal splendour and personal delight. They are, on the face of it, simply happy to be together, all obstacles overcome. The poetry itself is of the simplest: a mere reiteration of their brief words of mutual pleasure. The music is simple also, but with a limpid ecstasy which goes straight to the heart. Some considerable doubt has arisen as to whether it is actually by Monteverdi.[15] The closing duet of *Ulisse* was apparently an afterthought; this duet which closes *Poppea* may not only be an afterthought but actually by another hand, though we have to take into consideration that at all events it is in the best of Monteverdi's own style and quality.

The situation at the end of *Poppea* is on the surface of it an erotically satisfactory but not otherwise particularly inspiring situation. We do not, as we did with Rinuccini and Striggio, find evidence in the text of *Poppea* that Busenello could not have written his poetry without some measure of deliberately Neoplatonic hindsight. True, Busenello presumably knew his Tacitus and his Suetonius well enough to be aware of treating them, shall we say, with a certain artistic licence; but it does not follow that he did so with deliberately symbolical intentions. We have every appearance of simply enjoying here a vicarious gratification which in the ordinary world outside would probably feel (and under these murderous circumstances would rightly feel) too guilt-ridden to be enjoyed at all.

Yet it is not only that we have a perfectly untroubled conscience in thus identifying in the theatre with characters who in history were human monsters, and who even in this frankly romanticized scenario are not exactly scrupulous in their pursuit of pleasure. It is still more that we experience a radiance of the spirit beyond what any gratification of the senses can evoke, unless linked with a much more deeply committed state of the emotions than we are being shown here on the surface level. On the fairy-tale level, we may be picking up very much what we might expect from a young couple in search symbolically for hidden treasure or wisdom or reconciliation, with Seneca and Ottavia

opposing them as Wotan opposes Siegfried to give him the experience
of achieving his own adult independence: a familiar scenario in archetypal imagery. It all feels so right and proper in the theatre. We take
the young lovers' side without the slightest hesitation. We are, of
course, touched by the cruel fortunes of the losing side. But still we
want Nero and Poppea to win.

The archetypal theme looming through the historical scenario
might be that mythological ἱερὸς γάμος or sacred marriage whose
partners are set apart by being royal, priestly, orphaned, incestuous,
divine or in some such way not just ordinary mortals. Michael Tippett,
inspired in part by the *Magic Flute*, renewed the ancient theme deliberately in his *Midsummer Marriage*. Nearer to my present argument
(and in fact performed at Venice in 1639, only three years before
Poppea) we might compare a consciously Neoplatonic example, *La
Delia o sia La sera sposa de sole* (Delia or Evening Bride of the Sun).
Francesco Manelli's music is lost; Giulio Strozzi's libretto was already
in preparation around 1630 (and shows some signs of it) for Florence,[16]
but was published at Venice, also in 1639. We read in the *Allegoria*
(p. 10):

> Delia, that is to say knowledge, who shines with doubtful light,
> and under the name of Evening: after the fact that our knowing
> never arrives at complete awareness (*intera cognitione*). She comes
> courted by Mercury, the God of clever persuasiveness, but she falls
> in love with the Sun, that is to say with truth, with which true
> Knowledge is joined in marriage.

Delia is one name given to Artemis (Diana) in her aspect as twin-
sister to Apollo, god of the sun, their mother being Leto and their
father Zeus; for they were born on the island thereafter known as
Delos. Delia was in this aspect a goddess of the moon, later equated
with Selene, the moon, sister of Helios, the sun; and we have already
learnt from Conti[17] that 'the sun is God, and the Moon [is God] of
whom the Greeks called the one Apollo, the other Diana'. A marriage
of the sun and the moon is therefore a brother-sister marriage like the
marriage of the Pharaohs in ancient Egypt, itself both royal and
sacred, and reproducing symbolically the incestuous mating (even, as
we are told, in their mother's womb) of the twin deities Osiris and
Isis. In one strange vision produced by late renaissance alchemy, the
sun (Sol) and the moon (Luna) first incestuously embrace and then
fuse into a hermaphrodite, whose dying soul returns reborn as a spirit
child.[18] These are esoteric representations; but our longing to be born
again is a common theme of art and fantasy. Literally, it cannot be;
symbolically, we can go some distance in our search for inner wholeness, and to attempt that through a multiplicity of images seems to be

almost as innate a human disposition as our urge to survive and to propagate the species.

Busenello had, I think, no such esoteric intentions. Yet perhaps our intuitive longing for wholeness is being stirred by the mere image of the royal union, so that we feel more warmly in response to it than its cynical surface enchantment altogether explains. We are perhaps enjoying that enchantment as freely as we do just because this old and honourable theme is also glowing through.

Ex. 21. Monteverdi, Poppea, Venice, 1642, the closing duet (p. 216 in Raymond Leppard's ed.), in the best style but not now thought to be at all certainly from the hand of Monteverdi (realization mine):

PART THREE

The Broadening of Opera

XV
The Venetian Succession

❧❧

THE END OF THE BEGINNING

By the death of Monteverdi in 1643, the rise of opera was an accomplished fact of history. Florence achieved it; Mantua confirmed it; Rome and Venice modified without essentially altering it; other centres in Italy and outside Italy promoted it. But all of this was Italian opera, recognizably if not always very closely within the original intention of the form.

The original intention was drama unfolding continuously and flexibly in words and music: at first, with priority given to the words over the music, as the pristine theory demanded; but already in Monteverdi's *Orfeo*, with equal inspiration lavished on both words and music, as the ideal practice demands without very often being able to achieve it. Indeed, the highest standards were in course of relaxing from the very beginning, after the normal fashion of human endeavour, so that there was already an element of popular appeal and compromise at the production of the *Rapimento di Cefalo* in 1600 which was evidently absent from the production of *Dafne* in 1598. We have no cause to regret this quite natural widening of the artistic base. It is a very limited and sterile art which cannot speak at least to a fair proportion of the recipient public, and by the death of Monteverdi in 1643, this had been proved abundantly feasible for opera.

We might put it that by the middle of the seventeenth century, opera had arrived at a very practical working compromise. On occasion, it is true, its librettos were of an exalted seriousness; more often, they struck a balance between good poetry and good theatre, artistic integrity and box-office attraction, dramatic significance and popular entertainment. Provided that each scene offered scope either for powerful emotion and expressive music, or for comic or sentimental relief and vivacious music, the connection between the scenes might be somewhat inconsequential, and the motives or even the identity of the characters obscure, until the required happy ending tied the loose ends up to everyone's satisfaction in the last few minutes of the opera. Pathos, suspense, contrast enhanced by striking scene-changes and glorified by ambitious stage-machinery: these were more fashionable ingredients than the growth and interplay of personalities or the subtle inevitabilities of plot evolving out of them. It is the situation of the moment rather than the logical impetus of the drama which is most likely to be exploited, by every felicity of poetry and music, every resource of production, every nuance of the singer's virtuosity and the actor's skill. There is no wonder that the subsequent development of these tendencies was number opera. Meanwhile, there was continuity enough of a kind, but perhaps rather of the kind which John Masefield as English Poet Laureate must have had in mind when he called that lively piece of his (1926): *One Damn Thing After Another*, or *Odtaa* for short.

Among other contributory elements, there were the comic and sentimental stereotypes of the Italian *Commedia dell' arte*,[1] in which the art consisted in improvising swift and topical dialogue around certain conventional scenarios: a tradition stemming from classical originals, but gaining fresh impetus around the period of the rise of opera. The types are earthy, and brought a welcome contrast to the superhuman nobility and subhuman villainy of so much contemporary tragedy; but they are nevertheless types rather than personalities. Another contribution to early opera came from the popular enthusiasm, especially in Rome, for the eventful comedies and tragedies of the contemporary Spanish theatre of Lope and Calderon, with their picaresque characters and bizarre situations: three, for example, of Rospigliosi's Roman librettos (*Dal male il bene*, 1654; *L'armi e gli amore*, 1654; *La comica del cielo*, 1668) are adapted and in part translated from identified Spanish comedies.[2]

Altogether rather lurid and melodramatic; but at least a mixture of types comes nearer to a human picture in the round than does too much unalloyed virtue and vice. It was a feature of the subsequent reforms of Zeno and Metastasio that comic types were seldom allowed to intrude upon serious librettos, with much obvious gain in dignity and consistency, but some loss in raw vitality; one side-result was an unprecedented increase in the output of wholly comic operas. At their worst, the Italian librettos of the seventeenth century fell into a confusion to which those reforms administered stern correction. At best, they approach on their lesser level an almost Shakespearian richness and diversity, proliferating with a lively humanity which the reformers rejected as incompatible with their own more austere and classic aims. The change of intention and of idiom between early and late baroque Italian opera became indeed very conspicuous.

CAVALLI AS SUCCESSOR

The most direct successor to Monteverdi, and a composer very worthy to fulfil this role, was Pier Francesco Cavalli (1602–76).[3] His family name was Caletti-Bruni, and his father was an experienced though not a very prosperous professional musician, for many years the master of the cathedral choir and eventually organist at Crema, a town lying just within Venetian territory on the Milanese boundary. Francesco, at first taught by his father, sang in the choir so admirably that he attracted the attention of the mayor, a Venetian nobleman called Federico Cavalli, who at the end of his term of office brought Francesco to Venice, at the age of fourteen, and undertook his education there. Next year, in 1617, Francesco was admitted to the Chapel of San Marco, where he certainly came under the influence and perhaps under the tuition of Monteverdi. By 1639, his first opera, *Le nozze di Teti e di Peleo* (The Marriage of Thetis and Peleus), on a libretto (entitled, perhaps for the first time in this sense, *opera scenica*) by Orazio Persiani, was produced successfully at the Teatro San Cassiano, under the name of Francesco Cavalli which at some time previously he had assumed in tribute to his patron, after a not uncommon fashion; and as Cavalli he was appointed in 1640 to be second organist at San Marco, against strong competition. By 1665, he was certainly first organist. Eventually, in 1668, he succeeded (though not directly) to Monteverdi's own prestigious position as Master of the Chapel.

Twenty-seven operas credibly attributable to Cavalli survive in score, out of thirty-three of which librettos are known.[4] Both for good and for bad, these operas between them are remarkably representative of their period. Already in 1639, *Le nozze di Teti e di Peleo* confirms a further dissipation of true mythological intensity into looser spectacle and entertainment: that is to say, it is nearer to the ever-popular tradition of the interludes and masquerades than to the original aspirations of opera. The libretto, by Orazio Persiani, reproduces in rather a garbled version certain of the themes but scarcely the profounder implications of Jupiter's legendary struggle to espouse Thetis with Peleus against the jealous opposition of Juno, whose agent Discord is thwarted here only by the superior power of Love. The main distinction of the drama consisted in its many and ingenious changes of scene (including a sea-shore, Hell, the Elysian Fields, Mount Pelion and the Groves of Ida) and in several episodes of more or less incidental ballet; but there is in the music much melodious recitative, brought into contrast with some extensive and ambitious choruses.

Gli amori d'Apollo e di Dafne (The Loves of Apollo and Dafne, produced at Venice in 1640) and *Didone* (Dido, produced at Venice in

1641) both had the advantage of librettos by a much better poet and dramatist, that same Giovanni Francesco Busenello who gave Monteverdi the ostensibly historical text for his *Poppea* of 1642. *Didone* is ostensibly epic, and builds up splendidly towards its traditional climax as Dido, deserted by Aeneas, prepares the funeral pyre for her self-imposed immolation; but at the last possible moment, this climax, with its veiled suggestion of inner transformation, is averted by her old suitor Iarbas, who persuades her not to kill herself but to marry him instead. That gives another sort of climax, with perhaps some hint of reconciliation comparable to the ending of *Poppea*, and likewise expressed by a love duet ('one hope, one life' in the poem, becoming 'one hope, one soul, one life' in the score); but it remains a decidedly weak evasion of what is after all the culminating symbol of the story as related in antiquity, both before and after Virgil remodelled it for his *Aeneid*. Originally, Dido's motive was to escape Iarbas out of fidelity to the memory of her first husband. Virgil, ignoring a discrepancy of some hundreds of years between the dates traditionally ascribed to the sack of Troy (1184 B.C.) and the foundation of Carthage (853 B.C.), brought Aeneas along to win her love but then desert her in order to found Rome, in despair at which she killed herself—but likewise impressively on a funeral pyre.

Cavalli's *Statira principessa di Persia* (Statira Princess of Persia, produced at Venice in 1655) had another fine libretto by Busenello, but in the chivalric vein so usual in the second half of the seventeenth century, of which the leading features are amorous intrigues and misunderstandings complicated by baffling disguises. It is not only the characters on the stage, however, who are so baffled; for what with heroes disguised as women and heroines disguised as men, and what with castratos or even feminine sopranos singing the parts of heroes in the female register, we may hardly feel sure ourselves quite who is who, and who is seeking to do what, and with whom; but everything works out smoothly in the end, and no true lovers are finally disappointed or villains triumphant; or if tyrants do triumph, it is only to show their better side by turning generous and forgiving in the final scene.

On the face of it, there could hardly be a more improbable variety of libretto. And yet in actual performance, experience has shown that it can result in wonderfully enjoyable and even moving opera. There is evidently that within us which responds with sympathy and not with ridicule. Perhaps the confusion on the stage lies closer than we suppose to some of our own unavowed inner conflicts; perhaps the finally relenting and forgiving tyrant appeals to our own need to accept and forgive ourselves, since no outsider can do us that healing service if we will not. Perhaps there is more logic of the heart than of the reason in these extraordinary librettos; and certainly they make for very good theatre, to the glamour and excitement of which Cavalli contributed music of outstanding individuality. While big choruses and ensembles were still acceptable at Venice, Cavalli composed them just as brilliantly as the Romans. When duets led the fashion, Cavalli's were as creamy as the best. When recitative began to set towards less tuneful declamation and arias towards more formal pattern, Cavalli kept up with all his old mastery. But through every modification, his supreme talent was for melody. No composer of his generation enjoyed a wider or more prolonged reputation, nor wielded more influence upon that broadly international style of Italianate opera which linked so many active centres through the middle and later years of the seventeenth century.

A PIONEERING OPERA OF INTRIGUE

A fairly early and very good example of the new tendencies in text and music may be seen in Cavalli's *L'Ormindo*,[5] produced at Venice in 1644. The librettist was Giovanni Faustini, a poet and dramatist who owed his eminence as a librettist to his highly successful collaboration with Cavalli, between *La virtù de strali d'amore* (The Power of the Arrows of Love, produced at Venice in 1642) and *Eritrea* (produced at Venice in the Carnival of 1652, a few days after Faustini's death; he was also drawn upon much later by Pietro Andrea Ziani and by Carlo Pallavicino). There is a sinfonia (in G minor concluding with the major triad) of the usual brevity and simplicity, and displaying the scale passages (here in contrary motion) customary with these introductory gestures (for they are hardly more), derived as they are from the trumpet fanfares, of which we noticed a fine example in the 'toccata' for 'all the instruments' (brass included) of Monteverdi's *Orfeo* in 1607. Brief though it is, this present sinfonia is begun and interspersed with pairs of prolonged chords which may have been elaborated as trumpet fanfares, as traditionally improvised; for certainly these traditions were not yet in abeyance. The clefs are treble, treble, alto, tenor, bass; no instruments appear by name in this score, but we have seen that the actual instrumentation may not necessarily have been confined to strings alone, though recent scholars have certainly been inclining to that opinion.

The Prologue is in the soprano clef for L'Armonia (Harmony personified), whose concise but eloquent recitative is interrupted by condensed repetitions of the bass, and nearly of the melody, of the opening sinfonia, taken from the closing bars: D minor, ending major, at first; but returning to G minor, ending major. Meanwhile, the recitative grows rather more florid, and turns presently into arioso, soon becoming yet more florid; and a longer passage of recitative, much of it very florid indeed, moves into B flat major and back to G minor.

The sinfonia which next follows is new, and though it precedes the written title *Atto Primo Scena i* (First Act, Scene i), it is structurally the introduction to this Act—a peculiarity of notation not uncommon in early prints and manuscripts, which can be misleading to a modern editor unless he is aware of it. The Act itself begins with the sinfonia; but the first 'scene' begins, in the usual terminology of the time, with the entry of the characters concerned in it, and changes to the next 'scene' so soon as there is any change in the characters on stage. The Prologue is a completed entity in itself; but while it is smoothly composed, it is neither so taut in construction nor so restrained in manner as the earliest operatic Prologues. The relaxing of the idiom is already evident; and the rest of the opera confirms it. The scenes (in our sense) are built up over longer stretches, especially towards the ending of the Acts; they give wider opportunities for vocal showmanship; but they are not so closely dovetailed. There are, for example, musical refrains in the repeats of the sinfonia throughout the Prologue, but not unifying reiterations of a strophic bass as so often heretofore. And while the musical material of the opera is sufficiently consistent, it does not show so much of the direct thematic connection which we were able to trace out through *Orfeo*. We do not particularly miss it; yet there is no doubt that both in the poetry and in the music, a certain quality of refined craftsmanship has been allowed to disappear for speed and ease of working. There has been some slackening in the workmanship as the commodity became more popular.

Prince Ormindo sings in mellifluous arioso of his good fortune in having, while in the midst of warfare, fallen victim himself to a radiant vision, a woman whose identity is not yet revealed to us. His first six measures stand on the same bass as the preceding sinfonia; the rhythm notated undotted there is notated dotted here, but the performance should probably all be dotted in accordance with convention. A 'ritornello' in flowing $\frac{3}{2}$ time leads to an 'aria' in the same; and again, the first six measures of the aria have the bass of the ritornello, but then become free. What might well have been a taut construction, had it continued as it began, is quite felicitously hinted at but not sustained. The concluding 'Ritor:' repeats the last eleven measures of the previous 'Ritornello' with a few small discrepancies. We become aware both of the kind of formal symmetries in which Monteverdi had so often worked, and of the casualness with which Cavalli and his contemporaries may refer to them without really carrying them through. For when we look into the spontaneous effect of Monteverdi's structures, we usually find close connections and we often find strict forms. When we look into Cavalli, we still appreciate the spontaneity, but we seldom find the taut construction.

Now Prince Amida enters in a like elation, and from a like cause. But when the two friends agree to exchange a sight of the portraits of their respective divinities, consternation follows; for she is one and the same. Since comedy and not tragedy is for the moment at issue, they at once agree that it will not be necessary to fight the matter out at the point of the sword; it will be sufficient for their heroine to choose, and that seems to each hero tantamount to victory. Her name, it seems, is Queen Erisbe; and they lose no time in going off to look for her, leaving Amida's impertinent little page-boy Nerillo to comment on the situation with a cynical wit beyond his tender years. The whole swift flow of arioso, recitative and duetting, with no very obviously formal architecture, has an unfailing appropriateness of style to matter. There is plenty of vocal brilliance, and a considerable stir and excitement in the orchestral interludes, brief as they are. There is also a delightfully ironical and very funny stage situation; and, of course, the fun is only just beginning.

It does not occur to either of our young heroes that there might be any further complication due to the fact that Erisbe is already married; but she is—to old King Ariadeno, at first a mere caricature of stiff and unsympathetic ineptitude, but later proved capable of both passion and compassion; for this is a drama which, beginning in heartless though very amusing comedy, reveals greater depths of feeling the more it advances to its resolution. In short, Ariadeno is a tyrant characteristic of his operatic kind: more dangerous than he looks at the start; but also more firmly destined by convention to generosity in the final stretch. In this case, there is all the warmth and character of Cavalli's music to ease us over from heartless comedy to heartfelt sympathy; and as in the gradual deepening within Mozart's *Marriage of Figaro*, part of the cunning is that it does not happen too soon. The confusion and the conflict on the way intensify the recognition and the reconciliation when they come.

Meanwhile, here is Erisbe perfectly happy to take on both young men in turns; or when they unmask her blatant duplicity, both at once. It is a frivolous situation; but the plot darkens with the arrival of a second and more tragic heroine. This is Princess Sicle, who has with her a waiting-woman, Melida, by turns cynical and sentimental; and an old nurse, Erice, equally ready to croak comically against the male sex and to make it obvious that she would like nothing better than to resume relations with any male available. These three are in disguise as Egyptians, but in the folk sense of Gipsies with all their eerie powers of witchcraft and divination. Sicle has arrived because she is in pursuit of Amida, once her lover (as we now learn) but at present (as we have already seen) otherwise occupied. Sad as this story may be, they have us laughing as they rehearse some sinister play-acting in which to trap the faithless Amida. The sadness in Sicle's heart, however, shows darkly through against the comic brilliance as she questions that impertinent young Nerillo for the latest news of his master's entanglement. There is a sort of residual flicker here from the old Neoplatonic contrast of light and dark when Ormindo tells Erisbe that he is 'wounded by your eyes (*lampi*)' and that he has 'fallen burnt up like Phaeton'. The poetry is not much less classically loaded than before; what has declined is the symbolical intensity and the dramatic compactness. The dialogue is swift enough, often in that rapid exchange of single lines, that stichomythia, taken over with so much else from classical Greek drama. Scene by scene, it is all remarkably cogent in both text and music. We find scenes of increasing complexity and length, in recitative or overlapping dialogue in the style of recitative, sometimes as melodious as Monteverdi's, sometimes tending towards the later dryness. An Act may start with any texture that best suits the story: there are no rigid patterns yet. But on balance, melodious recitative still predominates.

Like mistress, like maid; and soon we see the lighthearted Erisbe with her equally lighthearted waiting-woman, Miranda, who consoles her in her annoyance at having an old husband by pointing out that at least she has now two young lovers in addition. Both lovers opportunely enter; and by hiding in turns, each is able to hear her pouring out fond feelings for the other. On this tense scene her old husband appears with a pompous sentimentality which does nothing to commend him as yet to our sympathies. She welcomes him hypocritically, and disposes of him rapidly. But next she overhears Sicle and her attendants cunningly bringing Amida into the open by another mock-solemn ritual of divination, in which he is revealed as Sicle's former lover, without yet discovering that this 'gipsy' in front of him is Sicle disguised. Nor does Erisbe yet learn this interesting fact; but she knows now that he has been a faithless lover, and something in her feelings for him begins to change for the worse. Or more truly, perhaps, we should say that her unfeeling flirtations are not any longer quite satisfying her heart, which is beginning to show her that she is capable of real feeling after all. And it is not for Amida that this new susceptibility is breaking through. When Ormindo returns with the bad news that he has been peremptorily ordered abroad by Ariadeno (evidently not such a fool as he has so far seemed), Erisbe finds the true warmth and direction of her feeling; and the young pair resolve to elope together, confirming their resolution in an exultant love duet. The comedy is taking a more sentimental and even serious turn.

RELAXING THE CRAFTSMANSHIP

We may pause for a moment here to compare the relaxed methods of Cavalli and his generation with the higher standard of craftsmanship of which we took Monteverdi's *Orfeo* as our main working sample. A typical passage from *L'Ormindo* is Act II, Scenes iii onwards. Amida, Sicle, Erisbe and Melida have shared two long and complete scenes in free recitative and recitative-like dialogue, some of it melodious, some of it brisk. In Scene v Melida, alone, sings to us very cheerfully about the unjust power and caprice of Amor, God of Love. As a mere servant, Melida was allowed a more lyrical and less heroic disposition than the nobly-born characters. Of her four stanzas of strophic aria, the first has three lines of seven syllables, one of eleven, one of seven and one of eleven, with the rhyme-scheme *ababcc*. The second, the third and the fourth have four lines of eight syllables followed by two of seven, with the rhyme-scheme *abbacc*. There is also a loose suggestion of near-rhymes picking up from one another in a manner resembling the dazzling symmetry of that difficult *terza rima* (*aba, bcb. . .yzyz*) to which Dante lent such prestige and brilliance. But the scheme here is no more than irregularly maintained. Each of the last three stanzas has the refrain 'Tuo poter non temo nò / Credi à me mè non amerò' (Your power I do not fear, no, believe me I shall not love).

The music for the first stanza consists of fifteen measures of common-time arioso in F major, D minor and F major again. A five-part 'Sinfonia' or ritornello uses similar but not identical material for twelve measures in F major, C major and F major. At the end of the recto folio the instruction *'segue aria'* (the aria follows) appears. Then on the verso the second stanza (that is to say the first of what is called the 'aria') takes six staves, with the clefs: treble, treble, alto, tenor (for instruments), soprano (for the voice) and bass (for the bass instrument or instruments). The signature is C_2^3, in effect a lively three-time varied with hemiolias (notated, though not consistently, with tail-less black minims); there are forty-three measures of dotted-semibreve duration, not quite regular in barring. The parts for the upper instruments enter two measures after the voice (rests are not shown), in free imitation, and are kept going with the voice except that in measures 11–12, the first treble and the tenor parts are left blank (but this appears to be by inadvertence). Nine measures from the end, all the instruments (but not the voice) proceed in a very light and fluid imitation based on previous phrases in the voice, but not in any fugal manner contrapuntal.

This concludes the first four lines of the stanza, in F major, C major and F major again. The last two lines, which constitute the refrain, have (l. 1) three measures of common-time arioso in F major with no upper instrumental parts shown or required; leading (l.2) to thirty-five measures of dotted-semibreve duration, not quite regular in barring, on six staves as before. Here the signature is $\frac{3}{2}$, in effect once more a lively three-time, but with no hemiolias or black minims (hence the difference in the signature); there are similar touches of free imitation. Then a 'Rit.' carries on the instruments for seventeen more measures, using a figure taken from seven measures previously. The remaining two stanzas repeat the same music with insignificant variations of notation and of harmony. The effect of the entire scene is rich, diverse, and sufficiently unified for its own light-hearted purposes. It is not particularly impressive musical architecture; but it serves extremely well in the theatre, and is quite typical of the method in scenes of more or less lyrical disposition.

Scene vi, for the page-boy Nerillo, likewise a servant and very sharp and amusing, is somewhat similarly though less elaborately constructed. But Scene vii takes a more serious turn. The libretto has (but the score has not, as in a number of other places) the ambitious stage-direction: '*Si cangia il Cortile in una dilettevolle riviera dell' Oceano, situata fuori della mare d'Ansa*' (The courtyard changes into a pleasing coast of the ocean, situated beyond the sea of Ansa); if music was required, it was no doubt supplied, but none is shown in the score (we noticed similar cases in *Ulisse* where we know that it was required). Erisbe has seven measures of recitative leading to nine measures of $\frac{3}{2}$, in aria style; a gap follows where two and a half lines of the libretto show no music, if ever they had it. The 'Ritor:' adds four measures of the same for treble, treble, alto, tenor and bass. Miranda has nine measures of recitative to different music and ten measures of $\frac{3}{2}$ in aria style to the same music as Erisbe; and the same 'Ritor:' repeats. Erisbe has thirteen measures of different recitative and nineteen measures of $\frac{3}{2}$ in aria style, beginning as before but at measure 10 becoming a duet with Miranda; the concluding ritornello is the same again.

The arrival of Ormindo brings, as usual, a new scene heading (viii) although the other two characters remain; the scene is all in recitative (leaving out another line and a half of the libretto) until a rhyming hendecasyllabic couplet (another half line of the libretto being omitted) concludes it with a duet for Erisbe and Ormindo. Scene viii with 'Miranda solo' has only the bass part written in for the ritornelli, but with clefs for the other (uncompleted) staves as before; and the same occurs in Scene x, where 'Sin.ᶠᵃ' is the heading for what becomes called ritornello at the last of its three appearances. This is sung by Fortuna, an allegorical character who is made more impressive by being given her recitative in a conspicuously florid style. After the Sinfonia (ritornello), her recitative is renewed ('2ᵃ') above a bass of which the intervals are the same as before, but very freely disposed for rhythm; the Sinfonia repeats; the recitative proceeds ('3ᵃ') more briefly, but on a shortened version of the same intervals in the bass; the ritornello ends the scene. This is an evident gesture towards rondo strophic variation form, but with a casual freedom unknown to Monteverdi.

The last scene ('Scena Ultima') of Act II is notable for a four-part 'Choro' in C_2^3 with two soprano and two bass clefs, and with changes of signature to $\frac{3}{2}$ for ten measures, and to C for three measures, before returning to C_2^3 for six measures identical with the opening six, and already anticipated by a solo personification called 'Vento' (Wind). And in the libretto, although not in the score, this is allotted to a Chorus of Winds (*Choro di Venti*), which at least strongly suggests that it was intended as a chorus in the full modern sense and not merely an ensemble of soloists already on the stage (as opposed to the *Choro di Soldati taciti*, the chorus of silent soldiers, which the libretto though not the score mentions as following Ormindo and Erisbe on stage in Act III, Sc. xi). But it may not have been sung that way, since there are many small discrepancies between the libretto and the score. They include lines not set, though occasionally the character is mentioned in the score, with clefs written in but the stave left blank, as if music were intended to be added but never was—or not in writing. So free and easy were the composing methods of seventeenth-century opera, and so open is our responsibility in completing it for performance.

COMEDY AND PATHOS

The winds are in the picture because a mighty storm has to take part in the plot by driving the escaping lovers back into the harbour, where they are taken prisoner. The other couple have been more fortunate. In a scene mingled most brilliantly from comedy and sentiment, Amida has been persuaded by a hilarious parody of witchcraft and conjuration to take Sicle for her own ghost, raised from the dead to accuse him of his own cruel infidelity to her. He seems genuinely regretful, as well as not a little frightened; upon which, she forgives him handsomely, says she still loves him, and with some difficulty persuades him that she is after all a creature of flesh and blood, no ghost but a woman to embrace and cherish; and this he is now most eager to do. Thus the secondary couple, after their due measure of misunderstanding and mental suffering, are reunited as the plot requires, happy in their reconciliation and their felicity.

Not so the primary couple. We have been given the stirring spectacle of Ariadeno in real anger at his wife's elopement with Ormindo, and singing one of those powerful and widely ranging bass recitatives verging on arioso which Monteverdi already knew so well how to exploit for the great bass singers of the day. He sends his captain Osmano to chase them down at sea; but the storm has already hounded them home, and Osmano is at once ordered by Ariadeno to bring them poison. On his way, Osmano falls in with Miranda, for whom he yearns; but she in a cynically witty dialogue rebuffs him while he tries to get it to her that his present distress is not for her, but for the imprisoned couple he is about to dispatch. When he determines after all to rescue them, she approves of that brave resolution and at once promises him her person in reward. We cannot help smiling: indeed, we are meant to smile; but it is oddly touching too, like a children's story which holds more truth of the heart than many a sophisticated narrative.

We are not meant to smile now at Ormindo and Erisbe, but to feel deeply with them. A long and eloquent prison scene (used also in *Erismena*[6]) is built up (Sc. xi). The frame of it is a short C$\frac{3}{2}$ ritornello five times repeated, on a bass the opening of which, though not the continuation, agrees with the bass of the loosely strophic variations in $\frac{3}{2}$ contained within it. Ormindo and Erisbe sing this by turns; after the last entry of the ritornello, the recitative for Ormindo becomes a duet with Erisbe. At Scene xii, Osmano enters, whose purpose is at once plain to the courageous couple. He is their friend, but he comes as the messenger of death, serving them at the king's command with what he calls a 'poisonous drink', and dropping no hint in front of the silent soldiers (the *Choro di Soldati taciti*) that its effects may be any less permanent than they suppose. Erisbe snatches it first, and against Ormindo's wishes, drinks, hoping to die before him: he drinks too; and she enters upon a splendid $\frac{3}{2}$ aria of love and resignation, the musical material of which is related to the previous ritornello.

The bass is a short ostinato figure, five measures in length, the first two measures being left blank for instruments with two treble clefs above the bass before the voice comes in at measure three. This is a lament in the familiar form so common in seventeenth-century opera, including the late but famous example in Purcell's *Dido and Aeneas*. It is the very closeness of the form which in such a case as this confirms the stern grip and inevitablity of the tragedy; and Cavalli knew well how to resort to such closeness when the situation really demanded it. There was no obligation, however, to maintain the ostinato unbroken throughout; and this fine example has Ormindo breaking in very tellingly with recitative, from which Erisbe's lament takes up again as before. They bid each other farewell in recitative and dialogue, and as she sinks, he grieves for her as his 'bright sun eclipsed' (with a confused rather than symbolical recollection of the old Neoplatonic image), and sings his own, briefer $\frac{3}{2}$ aria of lamenting, on a similar but not the same ostinato bass.

The climax follows when Ariadeno arrives to gloat over the corpses of his hated victims, only to learn by a characteristic reversal of the situation that Ormindo is his very own son, of whose whereabouts and even existence he was in ignorance. On a surface level, this reversal holds neither probability nor conviction; but for our deeper intuitions it feels extraordinarily apt. For on a deeper level, the inner merit of these outwardly fantastic librettos is that they may genuinely reflect intuitions of which neither the authors nor the composers nor the audiences need to have much if any ostensible awareness. It all seems such arbitrary fantasy; but if it were, it would not work. Poets would not have the conviction to versify it, and composers would not have the inspiration to set it; while audiences would scarcely tolerate the implied insult to their integrity. Instead, there is enchantment, and satisfaction, and no insult at all except perhaps to the intellectual snob in us. Opera is drama, and bad drama redeemed by good music would not be good opera; it would be very nearly a contradiction in terms. There must be something good about a drama which can elicit good music in an operatic function, so that an audience knows that it is experiencing a total work of art and not just a vocal recital in stage costumes. It is, I think, the archetypal levels of our imaginations which are filling in the picture.

When the surface of the drama is not convincing, then the conviction is surely coming from somewhere deeper down. It is not superficially convincing for Ormindo to turn out to be Ariadeno's long-lost son. But it works dramatically, I think because it brings to a focus our subliminal awareness that all these fanciful characters take their conviction from reflecting characteristics which are not fanciful, but which hold, each of them, something native to our human character. They are all parts of one another, and they are all parts of us.

And so it is that Ariadeno, too, carries to us a sort of inward conviction in his operatically conventional role as the relenting tyrant. For 'I am human, after all', he discovers; and this poignant admission makes his refrain for a brief arioso confession of remorseful compassion. His joy when Osmano owns up to having given the young couple not a lethal drink but a mere sleeping potion, and his delight when they make a timely recovery before our eyes, complete the dramatic reversal; and he approaches the traditional role named by students of mythology the 'wise old man', when he knows (like Wotan) that it is time to withdraw from outward activity, and passes both his wife and his kingdom over to the youthful energies of his new-found son and appropriate successor, Ormindo. This transaction has a fairy-tale rightness and a poetic validity which leave all present, including the audience, contented as the curtain falls on one of those enchanting love-duets with which so many of the best operas of the mid seventeenth century conclude. It is a fine specimen of the kind.

SYMPTOMS OF TRANSITION

La Calisto (performed at Venice in 1651)[7] has an openly mythological libretto, also by Faustini; it is another of Cavalli's quite enchanting scores. Two myths are in fact rather uncomfortably combined: that of Phaeton, the son of Apollo, driving the flaming chariot of the sun too close to the earth, to which he set fire while plunging to his own death; and that of Calisto, the nymph of Diana, loved by Jupiter and turned into a forest bear by jealous Juno, but set in the heavens by Jupiter as a new constellation. This apotheosis seems to be a Neoplatonic recollection, and there is another when Diana is equated with the moon; but this is not a Neoplatonic opera, and it is only a mythological opera in the sense of adapting mythological characters and situations (drawn mainly from Ovid) to good theatrical entertainment, complete with ballets for which no music survives although the stage directions do. And, of course, in the more general sense that mythological implications will break in, especially when images once richly mythological are exploited for however frankly theatrical an entertainment.

The music throughout is superbly felicitous. The score itself is an interesting manuscript. The copyist is apparently one whose hand is also found predominantly in the Venetian manuscript of *Poppea*; though he made neat work of it, there are many omissions and some additions, clear but smaller and less neat, in another hand which may be that of Cavalli himself. Numerous transpositions of pitch are detailed, probably decided upon in rehearsal; and there are a number of cuts not quite precisely indicated in brown crayon. The text as set departs in many small and some larger particulars from the libretto; and there are a few alterations written into the score. The final chorus is not set at all, whether because singers proved unavailable or because Cavalli on this occasion decided otherwise. A number of ritornelli lack upper parts though blank staves with treble clefs are left open for them; and sometimes even the basses are crowded in as if by afterthought. We are brought in these ways very close to the actual conditions of rehearsal at which Cavalli could be present to take decisions, supply additional material, and generally help sort out problems as they arose.

For us, not having that help, the situation calls for a blend of tact and boldness, of knowledge and inventiveness, of authenticity and inspiration by no means easy to achieve. But we cannot evade this responsibility, since merely to reproduce the contents of the manuscripts falls far short of authenticity and good sense alike. What is missing must needs be replaced. This is well understood for the necessary realization of the continuo bass and the desirable adding of ornamental embellishment, in both of which cases too much is worse than too little, but nevertheless a ready imagination is of the utmost value. For the adding of missing overtures, ritornelli, dance music and the like, the need is similar but the solutions are more difficult. Some may think it wisest to borrow suitable passages from elsewhere in the composer's works; others may venture upon what that composer's contemporaries and immediate successors would have done, and compose new passages fitted to the purpose, which is perfectly legitimate and very enjoyable if you have the flair. At all events, it will be necessary to compose the upper parts for which blank staves are left above a given bass, and to supply further material, including accompanying parts for instruments where the want of them is felt on the analogy of passages fully surviving elsewhere. The manuscripts are nearly always sufficient in the main melodies and basses, while nevertheless leaving considerable subsidiary matter to be worked out in their instrumental environment.[8]

Performances of Venetian operas by Cavalli and others were carried to Genoa, Milan, Naples and elsewhere, in his lifetime and after, very largely by travelling companies whose resources were more restricted than their resourcefulness. Italian cantata manuscripts always circulated very widely; opera scores far less so, yet we cannot doubt the close contacts between composers of opera at different European centres. We do not find local styles so much as current styles, with no one centre much in advance of others. Not until the rise of French opera did nationality become a distinguishing factor. We shall come presently to the influence of Cavalli in France, and to the opera, *Ercole amante*, which he composed for Paris, and which with Luigi Rossi's *Orfeo* and a very small number of other Italian works gave French opera its point of departure. But meanwhile, Italian opera, even in Cavalli's lifetime, was anticipating some of those modifications which subsequently carried it away both from its own origins, and from its French collaterals. We can assess this situation most clearly if we now take a sampling from the development of Italian opera during the second half of the seventeenth century, before turning to the native background and the Italian importations which set French opera on its separate course during the last third of that century.

XVI
The Italian Sequel
❧❀❧

ITALIAN OPERA ON THE CHANGE

Of the younger contemporaries and successors of Cavalli, probably
the most noted internationally was (as he always signed himself)
Antonio Cesti (1623–1669).[1] The name Marc' Antonio apparently
attached itself to him, after his lifetime, by a confusion with Fratre
Antonio, under which style he was received into the order of the
Minorite Friars in 1637. His baptismal name was Pietro. It now
appears less probable than it used to be thought that he had a Roman
training, and certainly the suggestion that he studied with Abbatini
and Carissimi cannot be documented.

Cesti's career was brilliant but erratic, and he alternated variously
between Venice, Rome, Innsbruck, Florence and Vienna, dying at
Florence at the height of his musical and at the bottom of his social
reputation. His private life was adventurous and partly responsible for
keeping him on the move. His years in Vienna from 1666 to 1669 were
especially productive and prestigious; but from the first he never
lacked for opportunity. According to the unreliable Ivanovich, the
first of Cesti's output of about a dozen operas was *Orontea*, but the
music of this particular performance is now thought by Thomas
Walker[2] to have been a lost score by Francesco Lucio; Cesti's came
later. The librettist was a famous playwright very much in the
fashionable Spanish idiom, Giacinto Andrea Cicognini, who presently turned to opera. He was a Tuscan, but spent many years of his
working life in Venice. This libretto, it is now suggested, was composed by Cesti for Innsbruck in 1656.

In the best traditions of Rinuccini and Striggio, Cicognini provided
an arrangement of poetic forms deliberately planned for an operatic
lay-out: mainly long lines and open forms inviting the composer to set
them as recitative; mainly short lines and lyric forms inviting the
composer to set them as aria. There is a certain bravura in the poetry
and melodrama in the plot which show the influence of Spanish

comedy and tragedy, especially from Lope de Vega. Disguises, misunderstandings, intrigues and final reconciliations form the substance
of this eventful species of libretto; improbabilities abound, but not
supernatural interventions or ostensibly mythological ingredients.

We have here the full development of the species previously anticipated by Faustini in *L'Ormindo*, and subsequently imitated and
exaggerated by many other librettists of variable and often inferior
ability. The entire species was severely and somewhat unfairly criticized by Crescimbeni and others towards the end of the seventeenth
century, and replaced by the stricter patterns of Zeno and his generation, followed by those of Metastasio and his; but both Faustini and
Cicognini were in fact masters of their craft, and *Orontea*, though even
more extreme in its melodrama than *L'Ormindo*, is just as good
theatre, and for much the same reasons. Almost every scene offers
strong drama or strong humour, with plenty of excitement, and the
liveliest blend of very funny comedy and very romantic entanglements—some cynical, some heartfelt, but all obviously destined to
work out happily in the end.

Here in *Orontea* the ostensible conflict is that the personable young
hero with whom the Queen falls somewhat spasmodically in love
seems of too lowly a birth to share her throne, where she at first
resolves and then declines to place him. Though a little bewildered by
her unqueenly vacillation, he makes no difficulty over accepting
alternative consolations, until in the final scenes he is proved to have
had a royal father after all, and with no further hesitation is fitted into
his proper place as spouse and consort, while the remaining lovers
likewise pair off in their appropriate combinations. The theme of a
royal infant brought up as a commoner, but in due course revealed in
his true worth as the rightful successor or consort, may be thought to
hint with the usual fairy-tale suggestiveness at some hidden value
which we shall not find within ourselves until our growth through
sufficient adventures has made us ready for it; and I think that it is
probably this almost autonomous fairy-tale logic which carries us
unprotestingly through such bizarre episodes to the final recognition.

The charm, the scintillation and the abounding intelligence of
Cesti's music, so felicitously allied to the easy elegance of Cicognini's
poetry, raise no problems and bring their own rewards. There are
transitional touches to the music as well as to the poetry, but they are
far from radical. We find in *Orontea*, for example, an occasional
advanced-looking bass-line, striding along in steady quavers as in a
typical Corelli allegro somewhat afterwards. But the ritornelli are
often canzona-like rather than in the more advanced trio-sonata
texture.

A dozen years on from *Orontea*, in the very celebrated *La Dori,
ovvero La schiava fedele* (Dori, or The Faithful Slave-girl, performed at

Innsbruck in 1657 and taken as a present to Florence in 1661),[3] the Overture is notated in three parts, but with a stave bearing a tenor clef and left consistently blank, as it is elsewhere in this and other similar scores: either because the composer meant to add a fourth part, or to allow for a subsequent enrichment of the texture in that way, but in either case very suggestive of the haste with which the scores were made and the freedom with which they were liable to be modified at different performances (and indeed this is born out by innumerable discrepancies both small and large between surviving scores and librettos of the same operas). There is a brief but stately introductory section in C time, amounting to ten measures if reckoned as four crotchets to the measure; the texture approaches quite markedly to that of an instrumental canzona. A lightly fugal passage follows, still in C time; this leads to a distinct passage of two sections, each with repeat marks, in $\frac{3}{2}$ time; then C time again, but with different material, and a coda still in C but with a slower rate of harmonic motion. The whole movement is quite short, but it is certainly looking forward to the substantial overtures found later in some Italian and all French opera. The Prologue ensues, and then Act I with no further overture. But again we may notice some decidedly canzona-like ritornelli, with the aria imitating the opening material (and in one case, the entire material) of its ritornello framework. We notice, too, a duet partly though not wholly on the same bass as its ritornello framework. We notice how readily points of thematic imitation and strophic variation are made, and how loosely they are then let go rather than being pressed through to their formal conclusion.

Act II has a new ritornello in three parts (but copied, as usual, before the title *Atto Secondo*); then a bass (with blank staves above) of three measures, two of which repeat to support the entry of the voice, going on freely, but ending, after the voice has stopped, with the first three measures again needing to be completed instrumentally as before. Presently there comes a ritornello in three notated parts with a fourth stave left blank; a brief aria starts with the same bass and top melody, but soon proceeds freely; then we read 'Ritor? ut sup?' (i.e. *supra*, 'ritornello as above'—it does not appear elsewhere). There is next some recitative, an 'aria', and a 'Ritorn?' of which the last few bars recall the last few measures of both the bass and the vocal melody of the aria just heard. Scene xiv has recitative in C; 'Ritorn?' unsigned but in $\frac{3}{4}$; arioso $\frac{3}{4}$; 'Ritor?' $\frac{3}{4}$ starting on the same bass and with a vague similarity in the upper parts; more arioso $\frac{3}{4}$, almost the same as before; and 'Ritornello' using the bass of the opening recitative of this scene with some differences towards the end.

There seems to be no clear system for such loosely connected scenes, of which there are a great many; and no two of them are quite alike. We merely get the broad impression of an on-going develop-

IX. The easy interchange of actors and audience: this engraving by Jacques Callot, after Giulio Parigi, of the Teatro Uffizi, Florence, in 1617, shows the ramps between stage and auditorium which continued to allow general dancing at the end of a fully staged performance in courtly circumstances.

X. The indispensable stage machinery: cloud apparatus at the Teatro Farnese, Parma. Torelli was especially noted for his originality in using counterweights to increase the mobility of his appliances; specimens of such counterweights may be seen here, marked with the letter C. The stair-like platforms could be folded or extended in various directions, and would accommodate a fair number of persons. All the machinery was concealed from the audience by cloth or other material, which itself could be moved to hide or reveal the passengers while remaining in full view of the spectators. We can see how by such means effects could be produced approximating to those shown here in Plates II, III, XIII and XV. Compare Plate XI.

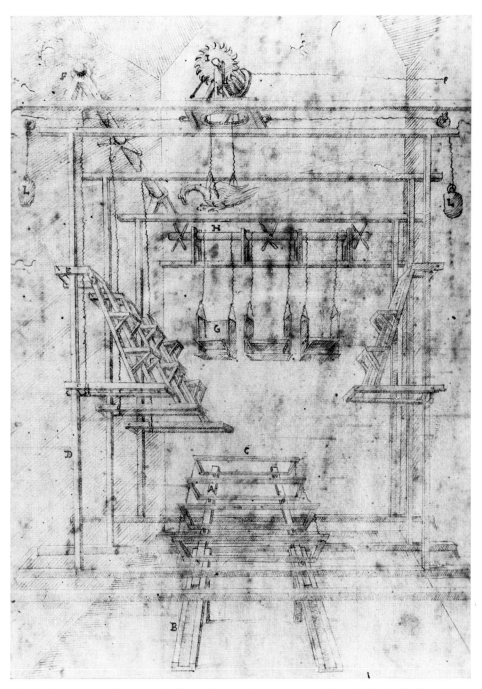

XI. *Further stage machinery at the Teatro Farnese, Parma: compare Plate X. Notice the big windlass, top centre. The platforms to the sides and below were collapsible, extensible and movable in various directions. It will not escape attention that* Parsifal, Act I *would have presented no problems with regard to the swan at this well-equipped theatre; and indeed our productions of Wagner generally might benefit from a study of baroque techniques.*

XII. *Stage spectacle, (?) at Venice in the first half of the seventeenth century: Apollo kills the dragon (but in an elaborately Neoplatonic imagery which stresses the complementariness of the opposites — since each appears to emit fiery rays at the other — but perhaps rather more symbolically than artistically); the signature is Lo: Burnacinius, i.e. Lodovico Burnaccini.*

XIII. Il pomo d'oro, *Vienna, 1667: the heavens open. Engraved by Matthaeus Küsel after Lodovico Burnaccini.*

XIV. The famous Jacomo Torelli: one of his sets for the Paris production in 1647 of Luigi Rossi's Orfeo. *Orfeo plays for the dancing Scythians.*

XV. The ageing Gasparo Vigarani: one of his sets for the ill-fated Paris performance of Cavalli's Ercole amante *in 1662.*

XVI. Lully's Amadis, *Paris, 1684. Prologue: 'the theatre represents an enchanted place' as the benevolent enchanters Alquif and Urgande with their companions wake from sleep. From the illustrated (not the first) edition designed by C. Gillot and engraved by Scotin l'aîné.*

XVII. Amadis, *Act II: 'the theatre represents a forest' in which Amadis confronts the malevolent enchanter Arcaläus and his demons, here shown in dragon shape.*

XVIII. Amadis, *Act III*: 'the theatre represents an old ruined palace: and we see the tomb of Ardan Camile'. The malevolent enchantress Arcabonne stands to our left; the tomb is centre; Florestan and Corisande look balefully across at Arcabonne; Amadis, in chains, crouches to our extreme right.

XIX. Amadis, *Act IV*: 'the theatre represents an agreeable island'. To our right stand the malevolent enchanters: Arcaläus is directing his magic wand against the prostrate figures, centre, of Amadis and Oriane. But to our left, Urgande the benevolent enchantress is stepping out of that remarkable dragon-boat, and in turn pointing her wand at the bewitched hero and heroine. The moment of revival and of reconciliation is at hand.

ment with some slight but sufficient thematic or harmonic unification. In some ways, the style looks forward, and in other ways, back. Thus Act III, Sc. iii has a big accompanied aria in which voice and instruments mainly alternate, in the later manner; Sc. iv has another such aria, but with the voice continuing through the instrumental accompaniment in the earlier manner; and Sc. viii has another with the alternation of voice and instruments in the later manner. The opera ends with a scene which points still farther ahead, not so much to the Italianate sequel as to the French, so that we see here something of what was diverted into that direction when in due course the parting of the ways occurred. Quite a substantial ensemble works up, starting with one voice and its bass, upon which other voices enter. As these fall silent, three instrumental parts take over (i.e. two parts above the continuing bass), followed by voices duetting over the bass; another duet for different voices; then full chorus (or possibly solo ensemble) with instruments, in nine parts (reminding us of those famous Roman 'choruses'); back to a solo voice and bass, but with other voices entering and dropping out; finally six voice parts (likely to have been instrumentally doubled) and two further parts for instruments in addition.

MID-BAROQUE OPERA

We are reminded by this construction how adaptable the Italian opera still remained in the second half of the seventeenth century. That famous festival opera (*festa teatrale*) by Cesti, the partially surviving *Il pomo d' oro* (The Golden Apple, performed at Vienna in 1667),[4] is a further indication to the same effect. (See Plate XIII.) The libretto is by Francesco Sbarra, who allied himself with the advance party when he wrote: 'this species of poetry today has no other end than to please, whence it is fitting to adapt ourselves to the usage of the time; if the reciting style [here meaning the recitative] did not come intermingled with the like jests [scherzi: i.e. the *ariette* or little arias whose introduction for dignified personages Sbarra is defending], there might be more repugnance than pleasure.' The scenario here is not merely ostensibly but ostentatiously mythological; yet there is perhaps more of the costuming than of the true flavouring of myth.

The orchestra was as colourful as the cast and the scenery: strings in all sizes, both of the violin and the viol families; flutes; trumpets and the implied kettledrums; cornettos; trombones; bassoon; harpsichord; regals; *graviorgano* (most probably a normal chamber organ of wood). Both in its size and its constitution this orchestra resembles that used by Monteverdi for his *Orfeo* sixty years before. Moreover, the selection of instruments indicated for various scenes is made on similar principles. First the flutes and then the viols with the wooden organ set a pastoral atmosphere for Act I, Scene iv; the trumpets support a chorus of celebration in the Prologue, and ring out for warfare and victory in II, xiv and IV, xii. In Act I, Scene i, the scene is set in the underworld, and the scoring is for two cornetti, two trombones and a continuo group of trombone, bassoon and regals. This is quite close to the 'Regal Organ, Organ of wood, five Trombones, two Bass viols, and one Double Bass Viol' in Act III of *Orfeo*; and still closer to the preceding scoring of which we learn indirectly from the subsequent instruction at the end of Act IV of *Orfeo*: 'The Cornetti, Trombones and Regals become silent.' Viols and the wooden organ play Ennone to sleep in *Pomo d'oro*, IV, i; 'violins, an Organ of wood, and a Double Bass Viol' play Caronte to sleep in *Orfeo*, Act III. The association of the glowing trombones and the snarling regals with the depths of the underworld is particularly interesting, since it can be found in the sixteenth-century interludes, and persisted at least in the trombones through to Mozart's *Don Giovanni* (for the Commendatore) and Weber's *Der Freischütz* (both for the devilish Samiel and for the saintly hermit, perhaps as opposite aspects of the otherworldly). The association no doubt comes partly from inherent suitability, but partly also from unbroken tradition. Hence the question arises once more as to how representative the scoring of Cesti's *Pomo d'oro* may be for Italian opera of the mid-seventeenth century.

It can be argued that so close a resemblance between the scoring of Monteverdi's *Orfeo* in 1607 and Cesti's *Il pomo d'oro* in 1667 suggests some unbroken tradition in between: but not, of course, necessarily in opera. Festivities at Vienna, while not always on an ostentatious scale, were more apt than in most localities to be lavish. From the performance at Vienna of Cavalli's *Egisto* in 1643 onwards, Venetian opera became prominent there, possibly though not necessarily in unusually lavish productions. We are not actually told that the scoring of *Il pomo d'oro* was a conspicuous exception, any more than we are actually told that the 'forty instruments' including 'recorders, trumpets, drums, viols and violins' observed by the *Mercure galant*[5] at Venice for Pallavicino's *Nerone* in 1679 were regarded by that observer as either novel or exceptional. But *Nerone* at any rate certainly looks to have been exceptional, and a pointer towards that fuller scoring which we take to have been returning around the borders of the seventeenth and eighteenth centuries; that is to say, around the borders of the first great period of opera and the second great period.

CHAMBER CANTATA IN ADVANCE OF OPERA

In considering the operas of Cesti as contributing some early pointers towards that gradual transition whose outcome eventually was number opera, we must not overlook the fact that he was as much a composer of chamber cantatas as he was of operas. On the standards of his time, he was not overly prolific in the field: some fifty-five chamber cantatas are ascribed to him with fair reliability. Cavalli composed only a few cantatas and many operas. Luigi Rossi composed nearly three hundred cantatas and only two operas; he worked mainly in Rome, and Cavalli mainly in Venice, but the crucial difference was probably one of temperament. For in the chamber cantata, the composer could work to please himself and a small audience of knowledgeable connoisseurs, with no need or opportunity to bid for a wider popularity. The limpid perfection of melody and the balanced symmetry of form achieved by the best of the Italian cantata composers was generally a step ahead of opera, both in manner and in quality.

Giacomo Carissimi (1605–1674) seems to have taken some hand with opera in addition to his one hundred and fifty cantatas and his fifteen oratorios properly so called; for Père Duneau, in a letter from Rome in 1660, referred to a certain 'composer of plays and ballets, in which he is not second to Carissimi'; and Giuseppe Ottavio Pitoni later mentioned 'compositions' by Carissimi 'for the theatre, as in his plays which are kept at the [German] College' at Rome.[6] There is preserved in Bologna a libretto having the title *L'Amorose Passioni di Fileno. Poste in Musica dal* [set in music by] *Sig. Giacomo Carissimi. Academia fatta in Casa delli* [in the house of] *Sig. Casali in Bologna*, and dated Bologna, 1647; but there is no record of a public performance, and the music of which this is the only known documentation has not been traced. Cesti, however, achieved an equal distinction in both fields; and the lilting melodies in easy triple metre, the long, sustained melismatic lines and the wide vocal ranges found in his cantatas also appear in his operas, only a little modified to suit their more popular audiences. In both styles, we find Cesti's arias on the whole surpassing his recitative, and in this feature he was certainly pointing towards the future. It is interesting that as late as 1688, the cantata composer Giacomo Antonio Perti wrote of 'the three greatest luminaries of our profession, [Luigi] Rossi, Carissimi and Cesti'.[7]

There was a mutual influence between opera and cantata, particularly in the construction of extended dramatic scenes. The famous 'Lament of Ariadne' by Monteverdi is an early instance of an impassioned scene from opera (his *Arianna*, performed at Mantua in 1608) which remained in use exactly as if it were a chamber cantata for at least a generation subsequently, so that as we saw, Severo Bonini observed of it in about 1650 that there was 'not a house which, possessing harpsichords or theorboes, did not have the [Ariadne] lament'.[8] But by the middle of the century, the cantata was conspicuously leading in the development of those great structures of alternating recitative and aria which gradually enlarged the changing forms of opera. Some of these cantatas are sacred, but most are secular. As with opera, the words are in the vernacular Italian, since cantata-like works with Latin words, however similar in their music, were habitually distinguished as solo motets and not as cantatas.

No other form in Italian music of the seventeenth century was so enormously prolific as the chamber cantata, nor on the whole of so consistently high a quality. The cantata spread later across Europe with little change, except that in Lutheran Germany it developed a liturgical function and a public aspect, with chorus and orchestra in addition to the usual operatic idiom of vocal melody for the solo singers. Both oratorio and church cantata (church concertos was Bach's preferred description) extended something of the public character of opera to contexts away from the theatre; chamber cantata, on the other hand, was like a private microcosm to the operatic macrocosm. And when, in the mid eighteenth century, the production of chamber cantatas at last died down, the wheel came round full circle, and complete scenes from operas were brought back into the drawing-room to serve in just the function of chamber cantatas.

As a composer of chamber cantatas, Carissimi had an especially high reputation for shaping his music in the very image of his words. This, in theory, was the same aim which had inspired the originators of the reciting style; but in practice, we notice a considerable difference. The concern for the words shown by Carissimi and Luigi Rossi in the generation of Cavalli, and by Cesti as the next generation began to take over, was no doubt very genuine and at best very sensitive and musicianly. But we may feel that Carissimi's concern and skill were rather for the long arch of his superb melodic line than for the details of his verbal nuance. His own delicate ear and practised craftsmanship almost always took good care of the detail; but his loving attention was less for the individual words than for the shapely whole. And this tendency, which undoubtedly increased in the younger men, was one of the most important aspects in which what was pioneered in cantata soon showed up in opera. The overall melodiousness of the reciting style, and its easy gradations from recitative to arioso and from arioso to aria: these are the most notable features of the mid seventeenth century.

By 1681, Angelo Berardi could write of the *stile rappresentativo* that it 'consists in this alone, that singing one speaks, and speaking one sings';[9] but that evidently refers to a slightly further step onwards in the gradual transition from continuous opera towards number opera: the step by which recitative began finally to lose its arioso-like melodiousness and to become sharply distinct from aria. And then indeed the fine balance of words and music was disturbed. At one extreme, recitative allowed the words such supremacy over the music that melodiousness almost vanished and declamatoriness counted for almost the entire effect. At the other extreme, aria allowed the music such supremacy over the words that sentences were fragmented and even single syllables protracted over lengthy figurations and sequences of the melody, displaying the expressive virtuosity of the singer in all possible contrasts of style. And at the same time, overtures and ritornelli and instrumental interludes and accompaniments of various kinds grew to be so elaborate, and often so independent, that we find certain features of the concerto grosso and of the trio-sonata actually developing previously within opera. All these were changes of which the beginnings can already be detected in the operas (and especially in the later operas) of Cesti, but of which the full growth arrived not until around the turn of the seventeenth and eighteenth centuries.

TRANSITION ACCELERATES

The generation which pressed forward only just after Cesti with the transition from the flexibly unfolding and relatively continuous operas of the first great period towards the sectionally constructed and relatively discontinuous number operas of the second great period included Giovanni Legrenzi (1626–90), Carlo Pallavicino (c. 1630–1690), Antonio Draghi (1635–1700), Bernardo Pasquini (1637–1710) and Alessandro Stradella (1644–82).[10]

Legrenzi's once famous *Totila* (performed at Venice in 1677),[11] on a stirring libretto by Matteo Noris, is a splendid example of this transition. The form, the texture, the overall idiom are unmistakably different; yet the differences are no more than tendencies so far, and appear in alternation with much that is little changed. Thus the recitative stands farther apart from the arias, while remaining very flexible and prone to arioso interludes. The arias are often powerful, supported by active basses which are often imitated by the vocal entry, and sometimes exchange further imitations with the voice; that subsequently fashionable device by which the voice, having entered briefly but pregnantly, drops out and starts again after a few more instrumental measures (the 'motto beginning'), is already in evidence; and altogether the supremacy of the aria in general, and of the *da capo* aria in particular, has gone some way towards being established. The instrumental passages are strongly elaborated and prolonged, and include trumpet parts in the notation. The planning is laid out in units of considerable scale, and gives the impression of following not so much dramatic as musical considerations. The only chorus consists of five measures of 'Viva la pace, viva Roma' ('Long live peace, long live Rome') at the end of the opera, almost certainly sung by soldiers and other attendants already on the stage as inexpensive extras who could manage that much singing without the cost of paying a full professional chorus.

We have the same impression of musical excitement taking precedence over dramatic immediacy in Pasquini's *La caduta del regno delle Amazzoni*[12] (performed at Rome in 1690, the librettist being G. D. de Totis), which starts with a short 'Sinf?' in quite an old style; it then goes at once into a big strophic aria on a vigorous ground-bass, with a recurrent 'Ritorn?' of which the bass is free. The ensuing recitative leads into another big aria, accompanied, with a motto beginning, and repeating entire, but with only a hint of a middle section, so that we are into the mood but not quite the form of the *da capo* principle. But the recitatives stand well apart; and altogether we are more than half way into the emerging idiom.

The generation which completed the transition into number opera was the generation of Agostino Steffani (1654–1728), of Johann Josef Fux (1660–1741) and of Alessandro Scarlatti (1660–1725). Steffani did most to plant Italian idioms in Germany, crossing them most interestingly with French features and some native German qualities (especially of harmony). Fux was amazingly prolific in the Italian style at Vienna. But Scarlatti was the greatest of all the composers of Italian opera (and of over 800 chamber cantatas) immediately before the culminating generation of Handel (1685–1759), of Nicola Antonio Porpora (1686–1766) and at the end of the line before opera took on yet other forms in its third great period (the classical period), of Johann Adolf Hasse (1699–1783).

Even as late as 1708, when Scarlatti's *Il figlio delle selve,*[13] on a libretto by Carlo Sigismondo Capace, was performed at Rome, we find a mixture of older and newer idioms. A French-style *ouvertura* passes into a transitional-style recitative. There are short *da capo* duets as well as arias. There is a short ensemble for three voices in Act III, Scene ix, and another short ensemble for five voices early in the last scene, which ends with 'balletti' and 'choro' in four parts, having six solo characters (two doubling) named to sing it; there is a separate ground bass for the continuo instruments in support. But ten years later, when *Il Telemaco*, also on a libretto by Capace, was performed at Rome in 1718, Scarlatti shows in full development that conventionalized but exceedingly powerful species of *opera seria* to which the description Neapolitan has so often been attached. It is a misleading title, because no serious opera evolved at Naples which did not evolve at least as early and significantly in other centres as well. Scarlatti himself was born at Palermo, and opened his operatic career in Rome; he spent some twenty years at Naples, but taught little there, and left in 1702 because he found the prevailing taste in opera at Naples uncongenial; much of his best work was done for Rome (where in 1706 he was elected to the Arcadian Academy at the same time as

Corelli and Pasquini), for Florence, and for Venice (where he super-
vised his unsuccessful *Mitridate Eupatore*, on a libretto by Girolamo
Frigimelica Roberti, in 1707); he returned to Naples in 1709 or perhaps
in 1713, and there he died. But in so far as he was the leading figure in
the growth of serious Italian number opera, he was not so much a
Neapolitan as an international leader.

In *Il Telemaco*,[14] we are already in the same world as Handel. There
is any amount of brilliantly exciting instrumental passage-work, in
that energetic, assertive style to which Scarlatti also contributed so
greatly in his *concerti grossi*. The very first aria of *Il Telemaco* is an
accompanied *da capo* aria on the massive scale, with a substantial
middle section—and the *da capo* repeat again written out in full as if to
prevent any possibility of neglecting it; then a very symphonically
developed scene of solo and duetting. Duets are not infrequent
throughout, but the only larger ensemble comes at the end. It is called
'coro' and is once more in four parts, but for six named soloists of
whom two are doubling on each of the middle lines. Only in admitting some comic scenes does Scarlatti show any feature here which by
this date might have been regarded as a little behind the times.

Here is an idiom very greatly transformed from early opera; but it is
also a fine idiom in its different way. In certain respects, it may seem
constructed to be more convincing musically than dramatically; but
before we turn back to the rise of French opera, where dramatic
eloquence took admitted precedence over musical brilliance, it would
perhaps be fitting to give to Scarlatti the last word on how this
question of dramatic feeling in opera looked to him. In a letter to
Prince Ferdinando de' Medici at Florence, dated 29 May 1706,
Scarlatti wrote of the first Act of Antonio Salvi's *Il gran Tamerlano*
(Tamburlaine the Great, composed by Scarlatti, and performed at
Pratolino in September 1706): 'This is truly, of the things for drama
which I have had through my hands, if not the best, at least among the
most choice and sure of good results, because it has a strong plot,
handled with all the art possible for drama, and in such a way that it is
almost impossible, at the mere reading of it, not to feel the movements
of the different passions which it contains. I confess my weakness: in
some episodes, when I was fitting the notes to it, I wept.' And on 18
June 1706: 'in the course of all this beautiful work, I know the plot to
be so strong, pleasing, new and ingenious, that the strength and the
merit which the recitative contains, in itself (in which the dramatic
actions are presented) will not make the arias to be longed for, as
usually happens.'

PART FOUR

The Dividing of Opera

XVII
The Approach to French Opera

❦

FRENCH COURT BALLET

To discuss the rise of French opera, we need to turn in retrospect to that strange *Balet comique de la royne*, the *Circe* of 1581, from which a direct path into opera might so readily have opened up in France if the artistic and political circumstances of the case had been a little different.[1] The artistic circumstances were the rather artificial pre-occupation of the Pleiad and their associates with classical scansion by quantity, and the attempt to find a strict match to this poetic scansion in musical rhythms. The political circumstances were a succession of external and internal wars and dissensions of quite extraordinary persistence and ferocity, and a consequent shortage of money, leisure and enterprise for entertainments on the scale of *Circe*, though masquerades of a less ambitious character were often mounted.

The Italian reciting style became known in France at the beginning of the seventeenth century. Rinuccini, the first librettist of opera, and himself so significantly under the French influence of Ronsard, spent some considerable time as a visitor to Paris. He first arrived there in 1600, shortly after the new Queen of France, Marie de' Medici, whom he had known well enough in Florence for gossip, as we have seen, to take him for her lover. In 1604, the year in which Rinuccini finally returned to Florence, he introduced Caccini, his family and a boy pupil to the French court; they did not leave until 1605. They were altogether a noted family of singers; and Caccini's famous daughter Francesca (known as La Cecchina, and in due course, as we have seen, a composer as well as a singer) so particularly pleased Henry IV that he pressed her to extend her visit beyond the others, which she may have done. Caccini sang Italian music of his own, in the reciting style; he sang French airs; he was a fashionable success in both. Caccini himself may have learnt something from the French songs, and he certainly imparted an enthusiasm for his own manner of singing. As to his manner of composing, the lyrical aspects of it seem to have had more effect on the taste of the French musicians who heard him than the declamatory aspects; and indeed the French airs so prominent in the ballets of the early seventeenth century remained very much more symmetrical and restrained than their Italian counterparts.

For a short period after the death of Henry IV in 1610, there seems to have been a fashion again for more highly dramatized ballets (for example, the *Ballet d'Alcina* in 1610, or the *Ballet des Argonautes* in 1614), in which there is some tentative approach to declamatory recitative in place of the usual spoken dialogue. The main instigator of these dramatic ballets was de Luynes, in his capacity as official organizer of the King's entertainments, his preference being divided between heroic and mythological subjects. Much the most fertile and accomplished composer of the music for them was Pierre Guédron (1565–1621), whose talent was vigorous and imaginative. When in 1621 both de Luynes and Guédron died, the dramatic impetus was not so well maintained. The place of de Luynes was taken by the Duc de Nemours, a much less enterprising and more economical organizer; the place of Guédron was chiefly taken by Antoine Boesset (c. 1586–1643), who was perhaps as gifted musically, but not theatrically. The result was a return to more conventional ballets and masquerades.

A further influential contact between Italian and French music resulted from the arrival at Rome in 1633 of Pierre de Nyert (c. 1597–1682), as assistant to the Maréchal de Crequey on his diplomatic mission to the Holy See. De Nyert not only made the acquaintance of some prominent Roman musicians, but took part in operatic performances mounted by the Barberini family. He was a gentlemen of sufficiently professional accomplishment as a singer, and at least of respectable attainment as a lutanist and a composer of fashionable *airs de cour*. So impressed was he with the fire and the expressiveness of the Italian reciting style, and with the impassioned manner in which it was performed, that he resolved to introduce something of it into the French art of song. On his return to Paris in or before 1638, de Nyert made a point of collaborating with two younger musicians in particular, both of them marked out for successful careers as teachers of singing. One was Bénigny de Bacilly (c. 1625–1692), a beneficed priest and in due course the author of an extensive and valuable treatise on the art of fine singing: *Sur l'art de bien chanter*, a literal translation of the Italian term *bel canto*. The other was Michel Lambert (c. 1610–1696), fifteen years older but active over a longer life-time, and highly significant in due course for his part in coaching Lully's singers. He cemented the professional relationship by becoming the father-in-law of that famous founder of French opera, who rated him a valued colleague and respected him throughout some sharp differences of opinion.[2]

The state of French singing at the time of de Nyert's return to Paris may be gathered from a discussion in 1636 by Mersenne, where he suggests that the Italians 'represent as much as they can the passions and the feelings of the soul and the spirit; for example, anger, fury, spleen, rage, faintheartedness, and many other passions, with a violence so strange, that one judges them as if they were touched with the same feelings as they represent in singing; in place of which our Frenchmen are content to caress the ear, and use nothing but a perpetual sweetness in their songs; which hinders their energy.' Mersenne's explanation is that 'our musicians, it seems, are too timid to introduce this manner of recitation (*de récyt*) in France, although they are as capable of it as the Italians.' On the other hand, 'the Italians, who make a special profession of Music and of recitations (*de recits*), avow that the French make passages' (i.e. of more or less improvised ornamental figuration) 'the best.'[3]

These suggestions are confirmed by a letter of 1639 from Rome in which the celebrated French viola da gambist André Maugars called the Italian singing 'more animated than ours; they have certain inflections of the voice which we do not have at all; it is true that they make their [improvised] passages with more crudity (*rudesse*) than ours, but nowadays they are beginning to correct that.' Maugars then added a tribute to 'a French gentleman', not named but presumably de Nyert, 'who has well reconciled the Italian method with the French', and instanced 'the great Monteverde', whom he described as having 'found a very admirable new manner of composing', and as 'one of the foremost composers in the world'.[4]

Though Italian opera was not yet known in Paris as early as Mersenne's book, the Italian reciting style on which it stands was familiar, not only through the visits of individuals, but through manuscript copies of vocal chamber music, which were freely in circulation from early in the seventeenth century and afterwards. It is remarkable how little effect, on the whole, this had on French vocal idioms, though French voice production was considerably influenced. Another field in which Italian influence became significant was the invention or improvement of elaborate scenery and stage machinery, especially in spectacular changes of scene with ample provision for monsters and for aerial manoeuvring. In the course of the seventeenth century, such famous Italian stage architects and engineers as Francini, Torelli and the Vigarani dynasty all helped to instruct the French taste for these fashionable extravagances.[5] Yet a divertissement composed of poetry and music, dancing and stage spectacle, however extravagant, is not an opera, even when all its words are sung, until a genuine drama of character and of situation is being unfolded by this rich combination of the arts. That was no more the case in French entertainments during the first half of the seventeenth century than it had been in Italian entertainments during the second half of the sixteenth century. In both, the necessary resource awaited was the same: a style of open-ended melody flexible enough to carry the impassioned declamation which is the central problem and essential substance of opera. In short, a reciting style.

It may be just because the French were so very ingenious in their moderately dramatic court ballets, and so very pleased with them, that they were slow to follow the Italians into opera. There were nearly always balls and masquerades in progress of which the context was more social than theatrical. The décor of these might range from very simple to very ambitious; but there was sure to be above all a party atmosphere, and general dancing either all through, or at the evening's end. In England, this social function remained fairly constant; but in France, there was an increasing discrepancy between entertainments in which the guests were the chief participants, and spectacles at which they were in the role of audience to a strongly professional cast, though very distinguished performers indeed might also be displaying themselves among the participants. The distinction between these two categories was never absolute; but it did grow wider as the scenery and the machinery tended to become too elaborate to set up anywhere but in a properly equipped theatre, with a regular stage taking the place of a ballroom floor as the primary ground of operations.

There were, of course, always many more or less formal balls in which social dancing and not costumed play-acting was the object of the gathering; but the court ballet itself generally tended to be something of a disguising, in which high society indulged in the childlike but very natural passion for amateur theatricals. The need for professional support in the more ambitious of these divertissements was recognized; but we have also to remember how assiduously the art of dancing, and to some extent the arts of singing and instrumental performance, were cultivated in the ordinary education of persons of quality. Not merely social dancing but dancing for theatrical display could be and was undertaken by lords and ladies, including the highest in the land. Most of the accompaniment, however, was in professional hands, such as could normally be supplied by regular members of the royal establishment.

The ballets were contrived, written and choreographed by both amateurs and professionals, but composed mainly by professionals. The steps, and to some extent the figures, were drawn from the familiar court dances, which were similar though not identical in all European centres of polite society: pavans, galliards, tourdions, voltas, sarabands, courantes, minuets and others in a swift succession of fashions.[6] In the more active of these dances, such as galliards and voltas, steps were required or might be introduced needing the virtuosity of a highly trained and skilful dancer. Thus the four-time pavan in a social ball brought on with suitable decorum all present; but the galliard, though its tempo and often its thematic material is the same in three-time, allowed very intricate steps, within the steady beat, in which the younger people could display both their precision and their agility. Even in the ballroom, there was scope for such display, and still more so on the stage; but there, a judicious mixture of professional stiffening with prestigious amateur talent no doubt ensured the standards necessary for public success.

In those ballets which most resembled masquerades, the masks and the dressing-up and the spontaneous pretence were really more important than the literary excuses for them, so that the plot might be not much more than the slender pretext for the evening's activities. In ballets of a more ambitious variety, each of a substantial series of 'entries' might be introduced by a briefly sung or spoken recitation, and consist of a more or less sensational group of dancers or singers or both, in character of any kind, whether serious or sentimental or comical or grotesque, so long as it was sure of catching the attention. The final entry and climax was the 'grand ballet' coming at the end, in which character and plot frankly yielded to the intricate patterns of the dance itself. The earlier entries, and especially the grotesque or comic entries, were entrusted increasingly to professionals; the *grand ballet* was more especially kept for the nobility, led perhaps by the king or the queen in person, but not, according to the prevailing court etiquette, for both sexes together.

When eventually French opera evolved, the tradition of the *grand ballet* passed strongly into it, leading to big final scenes in which dances of great complexity and extent provided the main substance. French opera cannot be understood without taking into account the large native element of divertissement which it derived from the *ballet de cour*,[7] and which it retained undiminished throughout the classical and romantic periods. But what caused it to be opera did not come from native French so much as from imported Italian resources.

THE ITALIAN INFLUENCE

The year of Boesset's death in 1643 was also the year in which Louis XIII died. During the ensuing court mourning, there could be no public entertainments; when these resumed, the political circumstances had taken yet another turning, due to the power of Cardinal Mazarin. Jules Mazarin (Giulio Mazarini, 1602–1661) received an excellent Jesuit education (which included a musical education) at Rome. There he entered the service of that prominent Cardinal Antonio Barberini, whose musical inclinations he shared to such an extent that he seems to have taken some part at an early stage in his operatic enterprises: especially the first in the new Barberini theatre (the *Sant' Alessio* performed at Rome in 1632, by Stefano Landi on a libretto by Giulio Rospigliosi). Before he was thirty, Mazarin had displayed his diplomatic abilities and usefulness to Pope Urban VIII; and not much later, in 1634, Mazarin was established in France by Cardinal Richelieu, whom he assisted so valuably that, having previously been naturalized, he was made cardinal in 1641, and on Richelieu's death in 1642, succeeded him as chief minister to Louis XIII.

When Louis XIII died in 1643, Mazarin had already won the confidence of the queen, Anne of Austria, who became regent to young Louis XIV. He weathered the wars and disturbances of the Fronde, returning from temporary retirement to help build up the royalist party which presently, in the general revulsion against the quarrelling nobles, was able to secure the absolute monarchy of Louis XIV. And Louis XIV, in turn, asserted his personal authority after Mazarin's death, by disgracing, in 1661, the ambitious Fouquet, who thought too confidently to find himself Mazarin's successor.

Each of these twists and turns of political fortune was reflected in the fortunes of Italian opera at Paris. The ascendancy in French politics of the Italian Mazarin might itself seem strange enough; but it can be seen as a lingering consequence of that unifying medieval conception of Christendom which retained for Rome, even after the Byzantine secession, a certain imperial as well as spiritual prestige. There had, moreover, been the two Medici Queens of France: Catherine (1519–1589) and Marie (1573–1642). The Italian presence was long established; but it was not undisputed. Marie de' Medici was mainly in exile from 1617. Marazin's career was not by any means unopposed. The clash of nationalities was as if betokened in the clash of cultures. The contrast noticed by Mersenne in 1636 between French and Italian music remained one of the most persistent distinctions of the entire baroque era; it was a strange and revealing antagonism, breaking out intermittently into a wordy warfare of pamphlets, and still confirmed in 1752 when Quantz[8] reported that 'other nations are ruled in their taste by these two'.

Already from 1643, Mazarin was resolutely assembling Italian singers at Paris. In 1645, when public entertainments were resumed at court, Mazarin presented an Italian opera in conjunction with a French ballet, for the first official rejoicings under young Louis XIV. The *Gazette de France* of 4 March 1645 reported for 28 February 'an Italian play in the Great Hall and a ballet danced by several noblemen of the Court'. It was a small but select occasion. Being neither the first nor the last Italian entertainment at court with plenty of music and with dancing to follow, it attracted no particular attention. But it was certainly an opera, though we are not sure which opera. That brilliant young castrato Atto Melani wrote on 10 March 1645 to his regular employer, Prince Mathias,[9] that 'we have at last recited the opera which was very fine, and Her Majesty wants to hear it over again, next Sunday. Everyone played his part very well; as for me, to do honour to Your Highness, I endeavoured not to be the last and, thank God, I succeeded beyond my wishes. Signora Checca acquitted herself as well as it was in her power to do'—and no doubt better than this slightly catty comment was intended to suggest, since she was in fact a very noted operatic soprano. And that seems to be as much as we have been told about this historic though little noticed occasion; except that it was indeed noticed by a troop of Italian actors, the Fideli, who had been brought to Paris in 1613 by Marie de' Medici, and who had since been intermittently in residence there under the leadership of Giambattista Andreini. So jealous of the imported singers were these resident Italian actors that they planned a retaliation in kind. At their urgent request, the Queen—not Mazarin—invited from Italy a further reinforcement of singers for them. To these her agent, for good measure, added the famous Jacomo Torelli, whose stage machinery, with a system of counterweights said to be of his own designing, was then the wonder of the Venetian spectacles and the talk of Italy. (See Plates X, XI and XIV.)

The choreographer employed was Giovanni Battista Balbi, who wrote on 2 October 1645, to the secretary of the Duke of Parma, that 'the work (*opera*) will be done with scenery and machines not seen before in French countries.'[10] At this date, the term *opera* was still used more commonly for 'play' than for 'opera'. The 'play' on this occasion was the *Finta pazza* (The Feigned Madwoman) by Giulio Strozzi. As an opera composed by Francesco Sacrati (1605–50), it had opened the Teatro Novissimo at Venice in 1641, causing amazement by Torelli's staging. The music is lost; the text is comically mythological, exploiting the farcical potentialities of Achilles disguised in woman's dress with the vain hope of keeping him safe from the Trojan war, and of his trying to avoid marriage with Deidamia, by whom legend relates that he fathered two children. There were performances throughout Italy in changing versions. The Paris version which opened on 14 December 1645 had extensive ballets in animal costume for the especial pleasure of young Louis XIV, then seven years of age. It is possible though not certain that some of Sacrati's music may have been used; but while rich in song and dance and stage spectacle, the play was not on this occasion given as an opera.

The distinction is more important to us historically than it was to contemporary audiences and commentators, who merely looked for an eventful entertainment well spiced with poetry and music; brought up as they were on the lively *ballets de cour*, it was all one to them whether the recitations were spoken or sung or some of each. When real Italian operas began to attract attention, the French journalists still referred to them as *ballets royaux*. On this occasion, the *Gazette de France*[11] wrote of 'the entire audience being not less delighted by the recitations of poetry and of music, than it was by the decoration of the theatre, the contrivance of its machines and its wonderful changes of scenery, hitherto unknown in France'—though this last-mentioned novelty can only have been a matter of degree.

Meanwhile, Mazarin's Italian singers had arrived in force. Their first identifiable opera was in mid-February of 1646: a scenically modest performance, though to a brilliant audience, of Cavalli's *Egisto*, on a libretto by Giovanni Faustini, and first performed at Venice in 1643. There is a pastoral story of tangled love and prolonged suspense leading predictably to a happy ending. The music, in Cavalli's customary blend of recitative and arioso, aria and occasional ensemble, is expressive; it is lyrical; it is even a little inclined towards a pathetic sadness. There is a 'sleep-scene' such as had grown to be almost indispensable since Monteverdi's *Poppea*; there is an excellent example of the still more obligatory lament—the 'Lamento di Climene', on a chromatically descending ground bass identical with Purcell's in *Dido and Aeneas* except for being shorter by one measure at the end. The Queen, Atto Melani reported, took particular pleasure in such songs of sadness; and other lovers of Italian music were no doubt gratified. But the impression made generally was quite unremarkable.

The impression made by Mazarin's next move was by no means unremarkable. With characteristic cunning, he took Torelli over from the Italian actors, and gave him a free hand, regardless of expense, to mount a performance of an opera boldly commissioned from Luigi Rossi, *Orfeo*,[12] and given at Paris in 1647. Torelli had already become involved in preparations for a different entertainment, which was being much talked about as the *Ballet du duc d'Enghien*. Mazarin seems in fact to have been talked out of this by Francesco Buti, secretary to Cardinal Antonio Barberini, with whom he had just arrived in Paris because the newly elected Pope Innocent X, a member of the Pamphili family, was then an enemy of the Barberini family—until in 1553 the feud was mended and Antonio Barberini resumed his habits of prosperous patronage at Rome. Buti meanwhile had so won the confidence of Mazarin as to be made his director of Italian entertainments at Paris. He persuaded his new master to divert the intended ballet into a fresh opera with himself as librettist; and it was to compose this libretto that Luigi Rossi, a trusted Barberini associate, was brought to Paris in June of 1646, and at once began to send for yet further Italian singers.

But the expensive machinery on which Torelli was already far advanced? That need not be wasted: a little adjustment to the story of *Orfeo*, perhaps? Certain small additions and improvements to the legend? Buti was perfectly agreeable. His taste in any case ran to the extraordinary, and he saw no objection to working in the necessary opportunities for using the existing machinery to good effect. Success was ensured by exploiting every excuse which the legend affords (and a good many which it does not) for marvellous occurrences. The artistic weakness of this method is not that it is spectacular, but that it is arbitrary. The attention is scattered from the true images of the myth by diluting them with others introduced for their own effect. It is a temptation to which modern producers of opera are also liable.

Buti's libretto for Luigi Rossi's *Orfeo* (perf. Paris, Palais-Royal, 1647) makes just such a scattered impression. But wherever a scene occurs which gives even a passing pretext for emotion, Luigi Rossi's music makes the most of it. The score, as a score, is uncommonly fine. Being composed in Paris and for Parisians, it includes still more choruses than most Roman operas; and very skilful they are, in a lightly polyphonic idiom. More generally, the style is that of Luigi Rossi's other opera, *Il palazzo d'Atlante incantato* (performed at Rome in 1642). Lully, who reached France in March of 1646, was certainly around and perhaps involved as a minor dancer and participant. And there for all to see and hear were those features around which Lully later moulded French opera—the patriotic prologue; the interplay of love and glory; the misfortunes heroically endured and happily reversed; the opportunities for resplendent entries and extended ballets; the scenery and the stage machinery; the touching sentiments and the harrowing situations, not pressed to uncomfortable extremes; the whole enhanced by a musical imagination of splendid integrity and warmth of feeling, sufficiently varied between the declamatory, the eloquent, the brilliant and the lyrical, yet flexible and continuous enough to remain well within the expressive tradition of the reciting style. This was not the last presentation at Paris of Italian opera in its mid-seventeenth-century condition; but it may well have been the most impressive and was certainly the most successful. As a model for French opera, Luigi Rossi's musicianly eloquence was of the utmost significance, confirmed as it shortly was by Cavalli's still more excellent though less appreciated example.

The delays were protracted, the postponements seemed interminable, and the impatience at court was only a little assuaged by concerts from Rossi and his singers of his own and other Italian and French music. Rossi went out of his way to admire his French colleagues, and no doubt did much to recommend his own native Italian cause; but Mazarin's enemies were already taking the opportunity to protest at the mounting expense. Curiosity increased; Mazarin himself could hardly drag himself away from the numerous rehearsals; rumours and reports multiplied. Bagni wrote to the Pope's secretary on 1 March 1647, that 'the story of Orfeo with machines, which will be recited (*recitata*) by the Italian Musicians in the Palais Royal, is greatly praised by those who have seen the rehearsal';[13] while a few days earlier, on 22 February, Venanzio Leopardi reported to the Duke of Modena that *Orfeo* 'will be a work (*opera*), for the richness of the costumes, of the music and machines, the most beautiful which has been seen in France, and, what delights more, there are eight ballets of every kind composed by an Italian Dancing Master and danced by twelve principal masters of Paris.'[14] One takes the very French implication. Costumes, music, machines, all very fine. But for real delight, the ballets and the dancing. (See Plate XIV.)

Under ultimatum from the Queen, the first performance was at last achieved on 2 March 1647. The crowd was immense. The start was delayed by the confusion. The machinery did not work so smoothly as on subsequent occasions. But the success was unmistakable. Since the Italian poetry was incomprehensible to most of the audience, booklets explaining the argument scene by scene had been thoughtfully distributed. The *Gazette de France*[15] commented on 8 March 1647: 'It was not the least marvel of this piece that all of it being recited in song (*récité en chantant*), which is the ordinary sign of cheerfulness, the music of it was so well fitted to the subjects, that it expressed no less than the poetry all the emotions of those who recited them.'

Except during Lent, performances continued till 8 May 1647. The opponents of Mazarin tried to pretend that the audiences were bored. The audiences were not bored: they fought for entry. Their attention may have been mainly for the ballets, the scenery, the machinery and the general splendour; but there was also warm applause for Luigi Rossi and his music and his musicians. He left for Rome, but for reasons unknown was brought back again, only to run into the full hostility of the Fronde, that outbreak of anti-royalist and anti-Mazarin resentment which sent the court into flight and Mazarin into discreet retirement between 1648 and 1653. Rossi shared first the alleged discomforts of the court, and then the exile of Antonio Barberini, with whom he returned to Rome after the reconciliation of the Barberini and Pamphili families in 1653. But in that same year, Luigi Rossi died, having left a stronger influence upon the still latent future of French opera than he could have possibly suspected.

THE ANTI-ITALIAN REACTION

In February of 1653, after the collapse of the Fronde, Mazarin went back to Paris completely the master of the political situation, but not at all the master of his own compulsive extravagance or of his own imperious taste for everything that was most expensive in Italian opera. The carnival season that year was particularly costly. Torelli's machinery came into full operation for the brilliant *Ballet de la Nuit*.

There was an openly patriotic swing in favour of French ballet and against imported opera. Nevertheless, Buti was sent off to Rome for more Italian singers. He returned in addition with a new libretto and a composer, Carlo Caproli, to set it, nominally as a *ballet de cour*, but actually as a blend of ballet and opera of which the eventual consequences for French opera were considerable. This was *Le nozze di Peleo e di Theti* (The Marriage of Peleus and Thetis), a work dramatic enough in words and music to rate on balance as opera, but also diversified enough with dance and mime to please the courtiers. The young King himself danced one brilliant role in it; the young Lully danced another. The singers were divided tactfully between Italian and French professionals. The production was in April of 1654, and aroused the greatest enthusiasm. Every courtier of importance was either pleased with it, or found it politic to be thought to be pleased.

Mazarin now decided to save the expense of bringing Italian singers specially to Paris by the still more expensive economy of having them in residence. Buti was installed as regular master of ceremonies; Atto Melani was installed to superintend the vocal forces, and took the opportunity, as his rash habit was, of indulging in a little secret diplomacy on the side. By 1659, Mazarin was persuading Buti, with no great difficulty, to undertake another libretto, and also getting his envoys to persuade, with very great difficulty, the famous and by now somewhat elderly Cavalli to come to Paris to compose it and rehearse it. This new opera was *L'Ercole amante* (Hercules in Love).[16] Singers came from Rome, Turin, Florence, Venice, Vienna. It seems that Torelli had got himself on to bad terms with Buti and also with Colbert. Gasparo Vigarani, very celebrated but now seventy-one years of age, was commissioned to prepare not only new machines but a new theatre. He proved himself to be another troublesome intriguer, and a great muddler into the bargain.

The preparations were supposed to be for the marriage of Louis XIV to the Infanta of Spain, a dynastic alliance the parties to which were less enthusiastic than the politicians arranging it. The marriage was actually celebrated on 9 June 1660, a month before Cavalli's arrival in July; but the festivities were continuing. The new theatre was obviously not going to be ready for some time, even if the new opera was. Mazarin took Cavalli off *L'Ercole amante* to rehearse instead a revival of his *Xerse*, first performed very successfully at Venice in 1654 and subsequently at Florence, Bologna and elsewhere. Quite characteristically for the times, Lully (that remarkable young Florentine cuckoo in the Parisian nest, to whom we shall return) was commissioned to compose an overture, and six *entrées de ballet* as *intermèdes* between acts, in which he also danced the leading parts.

To accommodate the interludes, the original three acts were divided into five, and the original choruses reduced. Nevertheless, the total length was regarded as excessive. Both heroes and heroines were sung confusingly by castratos, one of whom, Filippo Melani, a man of sorts, was singing the part of a woman disguised as a man. For most of the audience there was also the language difficulty. The performances at the Louvre from 22 November to 5 December 1660 attracted no great attention, not having the benefit of spectacular machinery; only Lully's share of the music was much admired. But Mazarin insisted on a revival in January of 1661. He was exhausted already, and exhausted himself further in the effort; two months later, on 9 March 1661, he died. The Italian singers lost their protector. But Lully, Italian as he was, stood associated with the French cause, and prospered.

In February of 1661, as another substitute for *Ercole amante,* the brilliant *Ballet de l'impatience* by Buti and Benserade was performed, to music which was probably for the most part by Lully: it combines symmetrical French airs with some passably flexible Italian recitative. On 2 July 1661 Lully's *Ballet des saisons* (Ballet of the Seasons) was produced. It is remarkable for including none of the recently fashionable Italian airs or recitative. Such recitative as appears is to French words and in a French manner, more flexible than it could have been but for Lully's own experience in Italian recitative, more symmetrical than the truly French recitative which Lully developed subsequently for his operas: a transitional compromise which was successful both diplomatically and artistically.

And meanwhile, the preparations for *L'Ercole amante* ground slowly along. The self-destructive ambitiousness of Fouquet, who saw himself quite mistakenly in the role of successor to Mazarin, not only brought him down, but others including the disliked Italians, Torelli and Atto Melani. Buti had already fallen out with Atto Melani, and in any case had put out of his mind any important castrato roles, on the sensible grounds that the Parisian audiences really disliked them very much. New Italian singers had to be invited, and when they came were no less unpopular. But the king insisted; the royal pressure was unremitting; and at last, on 7 February 1662 Buti's and Cavalli's *Ercole amante* took the boards in the pretentious new theatre (Paris, Tuileries) set up for it. (See Plate XV.)

The pretentious new theatre turned out to be an acoustic disaster. Big enough to seat 7,000 spectators, and to carry through the air by stage machinery 100 performers at a time, its resonance was so intolerable that it was almost unusable for its intended purposes, for which indeed it was very little used. Under such unfavourable conditions, Cavalli's excellent music would not have had the best chances of success even if the feeling against everything Italian had not been so strong and general. The very considerable concessions made by Cavalli to the Parisian desire for spectacle, dancing and choruses put

L'Ercole amante almost in succession to *Le Nozze di Peleo e di Theti* a few years before. It was certainly an opera, but it incorporated also the main features of an elaborate *ballet de cour*, brought more integrally into the dramatic structure. And for opera to succeed in France, these features were no doubt indispensable.

The Prologue to *L'Ercole amante* is characteristically French both for the length to which it extends and for the blatancy with which it praises the French nation and the French king, while congratulating both France and Spain on the dynastic union. There is a Sinfonia in three sections, the third of which brings in trumpets, and by implication drums. There is an eight-part 'Chorus of the Rivers', with alternating recitative; there are arias, duets, trios and even a quartet of soloists. There is (f. 15v.) an instruction 'here comes the Royal Ballet' —royal because both the king and the queen had parts—'and then when finished follow on' to the next chorus; but the music for the ballet is not shown in our surviving manuscript, for the excellent reason that Lully and not Cavalli composed the ballets for *L'Ercole amante*. And it did nothing to soothe the ailing old gentleman's feelings that such applause as this unfortunate production occasioned went far more to Lully's music than to Cavalli's.

Each of the ensuing five acts takes more or less a similar form. The Sinfonias at the start of them tend towards the form subsequently standardized as the French Overture, though the models for it had been common in Italian opera during much of the seventeenth century. Act I, for example, has for Sinfonia a slow section with four minims to the measure, and a quick section with three crotchets to the measure. Act II has a slow section with four minims, a quick section with six crotchets (and a scribbled note in French, 'another time Gentlemen'), then a coda in the first tempo. At or near the end of each act, there is some pretext for ballet. There is a magnificent 'sleep scene' in Act II, Scene vi: a combination of smooth airs with a languid chorus, divided by a ritornello, which would not seem out of place in a Lully opera. Throughout, the only passages quite different from Lully are the relatively few actual recitatives with or without orchestral accompaniment, and the comic episodes.

The opera climaxes with a long and elaborate scene including an eight-part chorus, which separates into two four-part choruses and unites again; it is supported by 'all the instruments', two of which superimpose added upper parts. Dancing was certainly prominent in this scene, after which the manuscript has 'End of the Opera'. This manuscript, the only surviving source, must be the working copy, showing as it does many additions and alterations and crayon markings, with scribbled comments or instructions in both French and Italian. It is indeed a historic document, a tangible point of confluence between French ballet and Italian opera, whence French opera soon flowed. For Cavalli was, as even Luigi Rossi was not, a living link between Monteverdi and Lully, knowing them both in person and standing somewhere between them in mood and idiom as well as in chronology. So closely was the rise of French opera dependent upon the rise of Italian opera, in spite of the long generation and more which divided them.

XVIII
The Rise of French Opera

TWO FAILED ATTEMPTS

The first alleged attempt to compose an opera in French[1] was by
Michel de la Guerre (c. 1605–79), organist of the Sainte-Chapelle at
Paris from 1633, who set in music throughout a one-act pastoral
drama by the court poet Charles de Beys. The music being lost, there
is no means of testing the worth of this allegation. A public rehearsal
of some kind was given in 1654, a court performance without staging
at Paris in 1655, and with staging in 1657. The little drama is entitled
Le Triomphe de l'Amour sur des bergers et bergères (The Triumph of Love
over some Shepherds and Shepherdesses), and survives in two editions. The first was published at Paris in 1654; the second bears no
date, but seems to have been brought out in order to dispute a rival
claim made by Perrin in 1659 and again in 1661, on behalf of his own
pastorale of 1659. *Le Triomphe de l'Amour* is called a *comédie des chansons*,
a play of songs, and there is nothing in the text to suggest that it
differed materially from the many other little scenes in dialogue and
lyrics so familiar at the time, or that it contained any music declamatory enough to rate as recitative.

The claim by the poet Pierre Perrin on behalf of himself and his
musical collaborator, Robert Cambert (c. 1628–77), can be tested
against some surviving material. There can be no doubt that the
unlucky pair were afforded an ample opportunity for originating
French opera, and that their own deficiencies of talent and of personality prevented them. Their pastoral without a title, but first performed
at Issy in 1659 (and therefore known commonly as the pastoral of Issy)
was heard at Vincennes a month afterwards at the king's request.
Rather unexpectedly, Mazarin had already, in spite of his Italian
predilections, bestowed his approval on de la Guerre, and he renewed
it for this further French initiative; but his death in March of 1661
removed that powerful encouragement. Perrin himself, having hopefully resolved his own financial embarrassments by marrying for

money an elderly wife, found himself entangled after her death in an interminable process of law with her relatives that left him considerably more impoverished than before. Chronically in debt and frequently in prison, he nevertheless suffered from strange delusions of grandeur about his poetical abilities in general and his influence on the French drama, with its evident operatic potential, in particular.

Perrin may have succeeded in enlisting the powerful interest of Colbert, whose undoubted preference for French musicians over Italian was perhaps decisive in the matter; for Perrin received in 1669 the royal privilege to create for France one or more Academies 'for presenting and singing in public Operas and Representations in music and in French verse, comparable and similar to those of Italy'.[2] The privilege makes no mention of Cambert, but he shared fully in the preparations, especially in assembling a suitable company. Two further persons of somewhat sinister aspect became associated with the financial and administrative requirements of the venture, to its subsequent disadvantage (they were the Marquis de Sourdéac and the Sieur Champeron); intrigue and incompetence marked it from the start, compounded by a very considerable element of dishonest dealing, to the wretched Perrin's further undoing. But a five-act opera, *Arianna*, was at least taken far enough to be partially rehearsed and performed in private before being abandoned in favour of the pastoral drama *Pomone*, also in five acts, but evidently of a less exacting character, having been written in haste by Perrin and composed in less than three months by Cambert.

This work, performed in an improvised theatre at the Salle du Jeu de Paume de la Bouteille on 3 March 1671, inaugurated the newly-formed Académie des Opéras, as it was first called in 1671, or Académie Royale de Musique, as it became called from 1672 (i.e. the Paris Opéra). The libretto was published at Paris in 1671, with its disingenuous preface claiming priority in French opera. Of the music, only the Prologue, the first act and fragments of the second act survive. The text is laboured and devoid of dramatic impact. The music confirms this fundamental weakness, lacking as it does any recitative of sufficiently declamatory freedom or expressive impact. A mere staged pastoral so devoid of unfolding situation and character is only to be accepted as in form rather than as in substance an opera; and it is not on such weak foundations as these that French opera arose. As with de Beys and de la Guerre over a dozen years before, there was certainly an attempt here at French opera; but for lack of adequate recitative, it was a failed attempt, amounting in effect to no more than continuously but not dramatically sung *ballet de cour*.

LULLY SUCCESSFUL

Meanwhile the composer was around, namely Lully, who could show a mastery of declamatory recitative, setting French words to French music with all the suppleness and exactness combined which he had learned in part from Italian operatic recitative by Luigi Rossi or Caproli or Cavalli as he had heard it sung in Paris, besides composing some of it himself; and in part from French spoken declamation, as he had deliberately and intelligently absorbed it at the spoken theatre. In addition, Lully had long commanded those graceful French equivalents to Italian aria and arioso which comprised so much of the normal repertory of Boesset or Lambert, distinct as they still were from the related idioms of Luigi Rossi, of Cavalli, or of that much favoured composer of chamber cantatas, Carissimi—all well known at the French court by now. Lully's hand was just as skilled in massive choruses, on the one hand, and in lively dances of numerous varieties, on the other hand: both of them likewise strong recommendations to the Parisian tastes.

Yet Lully, who could weigh up a situation in politics just as adroitly as he could in music, was slow to convince himself that the French public, having so pointedly repudiated Mazarin's best efforts to acclimatize Italian opera at Paris, could be induced to accept anything of the same ambitious order in French. When the favourable response aroused by Perrin and Cambert did to his surprise convince him, he lost very little time in accomplishing with success the rise of French opera. He was successful precisely because the form in which he accomplished it, derived as it directly was from the currently available Italian models, nevertheless struck out so boldly for a variant genuinely French. The most remarkable feature of Lully's achievement was not his intelligent use of Italian precedent. The most remarkable feature was the still greater intelligence with which he taught his Italianate melodiousness to sing in French.

Jean-Baptiste Lully[3] was the son of probably quite humble Florentine parentage, his name being originally Giovanni Battista Lulli. He was brought to France in 1646, at the age of nearly fourteen, as a promising young page-boy who could give practice in the Italian language and generally make himself agreeable to Mademoiselle de Montpensier (La Grande Mademoiselle, Mlle. d'Orléans, a cousin of Louis XIV), to whose private orchestra he was appointed as a violinist so soon as his early talent for that instrument came to notice. Mademoiselle was a great presenter of ballets, masquerades, chamber concerts and other entertainments, in which young Lully sometimes played, sometimes danced with conspicuous agility and grace. He also began to compose music for such occasions.

During the ten years from 1653 to 1663, Lully composed the whole or parts of well over a dozen ballets of which the words were by the prestigious Isaac de Benserade. Many ballet scenes by Lully, from the audacious *Amor malato* (Love Unwell) of 1657 onwards, resemble and anticipate opera; and opera, as understood in France, from the start virtually incorporated ballet. In 1661 (the year of Mazarin's death) Lully was granted French nationality, dropping his Italian spelling as Lulli. The Superintendent of the King's Music, Mazarin's supporter Jean de Cambefort, having died, Lully was given 'charge of composing the music of the chamber of the king', to which was added in 1662 the title of 'master of music of the royal family'; whereupon (in the same month of July) Lully allied himself to the 'master of the music of the court', Michel Lambert himself, by marrying his daughter. In 1663, Lully began his still more distinguished partnership with Molière,[4] which he continued for almost a further ten years, though without ceasing to collaborate in more ballets with Benserade and perhaps other poets as well.

Lully's collaborations with Molière at this period were not just ballets with dramatic interludes, but stage plays which included ballet; some were called *comédie*, others were called *comédie-ballet*, but all brought a considerable proportion of dancing and divertissement into a story, complete in itself, which was at least ingenious and often touchingly sentimental. The best and most famous is the last, *Le Bourgeois gentilhomme* (performed at Chambord in 1670 and again at Paris later in the same year), a *comédie-ballet* of fine satirical wit and excellent good humour which remains in the repertoire of the famous Comédie Française—the company formed in 1680 from the fusion of Molière's old company with the only rival company then active. So traditional are their performances that we may really catch still some echo of the stylized declamation and theatrical virtuosity which enchanted Lully and inspired his moulding of French operatic recitative.

For it has again to be remembered that the basis of French recitative is twofold. On the one hand, there was the Italian recitative as it had developed by the middle of the seventeenth century, and as Lully not only heard it in Italian opera and chamber cantata, but also imitated it in his long experience with court ballets having Italian words and music (in whole at first, and in part for some time afterwards). And on the other hand, there was the spoken declamation brought to extreme virtuosity in the stylized conventions of the classical French theatre as it was developed by Hardy, Corneille, Molière, Quinault and Racine, all of which was of close interest to Lully[5] and some of which involved him professionally through his association with Molière, and after Molière, with Quinault.

Lully's earliest collaboration with Quinault had already occurred in 1668, with that splendid entertainment, called an 'Eclogue', *La Grotte* (the Grotto) *de Versailles*, especially notable for its fine and abundant choruses. *Les Amants magnifiques* (The Magnificent Lovers) in 1670, a *Comédie* by Molière and Benserade in co-operation, is a particularly graceful example of pastoral simplicity and sentiment; but its interest for us here is that it was composed by Lully to music of quite remarkably operatic breadth and eloquence, the long final scene being particularly impressive. Above all do we find here a most ample deployment of Lully's own special idiom of flexible, melodious, expressive French recitative. Thus it was that he developed it so extensively in his actual operas to follow; and thus with very little essential modification was it inherited through to the generation of Rameau and beyond. French recitative was Lully's monumental contribution. He could not have evolved it merely on his own, of course; but he shaped it to his own personality, and it bore his stamp for so long as it remained a recognizable species.

Psyché, in 1671, had the unusual title of *Tragédie-ballet*. The poetical drama, by Molière, Pierre Corneille and Quinault, is of a still more solid and imposing substance; and so also is Lully's music, except for the important difference of dispensing here with that operatic recitative which had made of *Les Amants magnifiques* so striking an anticipation. In 1678, a re-worked version of *Psyché* was actually prepared, in which Thomas Corneille reduced to lighter and more varied verse some of his brother Pierre Corneille's heavy alexandrines, and Lully composed them as recitative, thus revealing the splendid work as the effective French opera it always had been in potentiality. Lully by 1671 was certainly equipped to embark on opera; and so astonished and impressed was he by the popular success accorded, two months after *Psyché*, to *Pomone*, for all its poetic and musical deficiencies, that he took prompt steps to enter directly now into a field which only his fears of an unpopular reception had so far made unattractive to him.

In 1672, the last of Cambert's attempts at French opera, entitled *Opéra, pastorale heroique des Peines et des Plaisures de l'Amour, en vers lyrique . . . représentée dans musique* (Heroic Pastoral of the Pains and Pleasures of Love, in Lyric Verse . . . Represented in Music), on a text by G. Gilbert (perhaps because Perrin was in prison again), was performed at Paris; the prologue and first act, which alone have their music surviving, show no advance on *Pomone*. By that year, moreover, the affairs of Perrin's enterprise had become so confused, his entanglements with his business associates had grown so vitriolic, his own prospects under an intolerable burden of debt and litigation were so evidently desperate, that he responded as it seems very readily to an offer made by Lully to purchase for hard cash the whole troublesome privilege. The sum paid by Lully is not known, but it was enough to get Perrin finally out of prison. It was a shrewd but not dishonourable transaction, which the king not only approved but enlarged upon by conferring on Lully, then as usual high in his royal favour, still more exclusive and lucrative rights over all performances of opera than he had previously conferred on Perrin. The ground was taken from beneath Cambert by the same transaction; but Cambert, at his own wish, had by that time withdrawn from whatever formal share in the enterprise he ever held; and in any case, there was no redress. He turned up in London not long afterwards, and contributed, without lasting consequences, to the abortive initiative there towards a Restoration opera.

LULLY AND QUINAULT

Whereas Perrin's privilege in 1659 only mentioned opera in the French language, Lully's in 1672 gave him similar rights over opera (and any other stage representations involving substantial elements of music) 'composed as much in French verse as in other, foreign tongues, comparable and similar to the Academies of Italy'. The inaugural performance at what was now officially the Paris Opéra took place in the Salle du Jeu de Paume de Bel-Air on 15 November 1672; but this consisted merely of a pastoral entertainment put together in the form of a pasticcio of scenes composed earlier. The real initiation came in August of 1673, when the first *tragédie-lyrique*, by Quinault and Lully, was produced in the same building (but transferred to the subsequent site of the Opéra at the Palais-Royal in 1674): the start of a long line which ended only the year before Lully's death in 1687.[6]

Philippe Quinault (1635–88) was already celebrated for his spoken dramas, and although by no means a poet in the class of Pierre Corneille or Racine, he was of considerable stature, with a classic sense of form and a fine sense of language, all of which he was content to place intelligently at Lully's disposal. History shows no more sustained and successful partnership of librettist and composer. Both men shared the same ambition to present a form of opera fitted not only to the French genius, but also to the French court, with all its pretensions to heroic glory and social brilliance. Flattery was an essential ingredient; grandeur was a necessary condition; passion might take either base or lofty directions, so long as the scale was epic; love and hatred, duty and inclination, nobility and villainy might contest for supremacy, but always in language of impressive rhetoric and actions of heroic urgency.

It is in the nature of any opera to present characters and situations of more than ordinary life-size. It was in the nature of baroque opera to inflate them beyond all credible outer experience; but whereas the leading characters of serious Italian opera in the middle of the seventeenth century tended to be decidedly exaggerated and their deeds altogether confusing and bizarre, those of French baroque opera inherited a certain restraint and dignity from their predecessors in the French classical theatre. It is not that the plots and the personages are less improbably romantic, but rather that they are more lucid and comprehensible. What Buti had presented chaotically in his libretto for Luigi Rossi's *Orfeo* or Cavalli's *Ercole amante*, Quinault presented coherently in his librettos for Lully. His poetry, too, is not only smoother and more technically accomplished; it is also on a much higher level of verbal felicity and symbolic imagery. Lully was both wise and fortunate in his choice of partner.

There can be no doubt that such lucidity and felicity were among the assets of the classical French theatre, nor that they presently became an inspiration to that noted Arcadian Academy at Rome where the reforms of the Italian libretto culminating in Zeno and Metastasio first took their origins. Much stress was laid on the three dramatic unities of action, time and place by then so confidently attributed to Aristotle, though the celebrated passage in his *Poetics* on which this attribution rested is not nearly so specific as was commonly thought, merely insisting that the plot shall have sufficient unity to be comprehended as a single experience, whence tragedy generally tries 'to keep within one revolution of the sun' or not much more.[7] But as a precept in favour of dramatic simplicity, the 'three unities' worked to the advantage of the classical French theatre. In Quinault's librettos, their application is by no means strict; but enough of the dramatic simplicity remains to give an admirable directness to the unfolding of events, no matter how far these events may be from the course of ordinary experience in the outside world. It is not only that mythological divinities or chivalric magicians do not intervene in the outside world; heroes and villains of such consistent quality do not occur. To personify a single quality of good or evil in one character, without allowing him the usual human mixture, is no falsification provided that other qualities are represented in other characters, and provided that their interractions are taken, at least on the intuitive level, as the inner workings of a total personality. That was the secret of the French classical theatre; and while Quinault's leading characters do not carry nearly so much of that classic force and quintessential truthfulness, they are in the same tradition.

The form of Quinault's librettos was adopted almost unchanged from Buti's formula. The prologue is indispensable because it is here that under the thinnest of disguises the ruling monarch, the Sun King Louis XIV, is held up for admiration and congratulation. The pretext for the prologue is sometimes connected with the ensuing plot, sometimes unconnected; it commonly gives an opportunity for slighter elements than the main plot itself, which is taken very seriously and hardly ever indulges in comic scenes or characters, nor even very often in purely pastoral elements. The main plot then unfolds in five yet more extensive acts, each introducing at least some further opportunity for ballet, and in the case of the last act, a fully developed divertissement of dances and chorus. It was customary to include, at or near the end of the last act, a very long and complex danced Chaconne or Passacaille. The proportion of dancing in the earlier acts was variable; but at least it is generally given to priests and priestesses or nymphs and shepherds or demons or soldiers or other attendants whose presence on the stage is sufficiently apposite for their breaking into song and dance to cause no gross interruption. It may even help to carry forward the action by some appropriate ritual or contest or social celebration.

From 1673 to 1677, Quinault and Lully produced operas on this heroic scale at a steady and almost unbroken rate of one a year. In 1678, the respectable Quinault was in disgrace, under suspicion of having deliberately slighted Madame de Montespan, the king's mistress, in the libretto of his *Isis* of 1677 where Juno attacks the nymph Io—a most improbable charge; but nevertheless the opera that year was the re-working by Thomas Corneille and Bernard de Fontanelle of *Psyché* with Lully's added recitative. In 1679, Thomas Corneille, perhaps with the help of de Fontanelle and of Nicolas Boileau, provided the libretto for *Bellérophon*, in the course of which Lully 'drove him at every moment to despair'.[8] In 1680, Quinault, having been banished from the court for two years, made his return as the librettist of *Proserpine*. The year 1681 saw, by way of exception, not an opera but the ambitious ballet (it has twenty entries) *Le Triomphe d'Amour* (The Triumph of Love), on a text by Quinault and Benserade; from 1682 to 1686 there was again a full opera each year on Quinault's librettos, as well as a *Divertissement* on a text by Racine and a ballet on a text by Quinault, both in 1685; and in 1686, a *Pastorale héroïque*, on the favoured subject of Acis and Galatea, with a text by Jean Galbert de Campistron, who also (perhaps because of the devout scruples which overtook Quinault in the closing years of his life) provided the libretto in 1687 for an opera, *Achille et Polyxene*, of which Lully had concluded the first act at the time of his death; it was completed by Colasse.

THE FRENCH ACADEMY

We have some interesting information about the working methods used by Quinault and Lully in the course of their collaboration. Thus Le Cerf de la Viéville[9] wrote that:

> Lully did not associate with, [rather] he attached Quinault to himself: this was his Poet. Quinault sought out and drew up several

subjects for operas. He took them to the King, who chose one of them. Then Quinault wrote a plan of the design and sequence. He gave a copy of this plan to Lully, and Lully seeing what was in question in each Act, what was the purpose of it, prepared in his imagination the divertissements, the dances and the little songs (*chansonettes*) of Shepherds, of Boatmen, etc. Quinault wrote up (*composoit*) his Scenes: so soon as he had finished some of them, he showed them to the French Academy (*Académie Française*), to which as you know he belonged: after having gathered and put to profit the opinions of the Academy, he took the Scenes to Lully . . . You imagine that Lully received the Scenes from Quinault without considering them after such skilful revisers; not he. He did not rely at all on their authority. He examined word by word this Poetry already revised and corrected, of which he corrected again, or cut out the half, when he judged it suitable. And there was no appeal from his criticism. His Poet had to go back to versify it afresh.

A slightly different account is found in the first published proceedings of the Académie Royale des Inscriptions et Belles-Lettres, in effect a sub-committee of the Académie Française which was given an independent status as the official authority on matters of mythological correctness and symbolical designing.[10] It was among its express functions to suggest to court artists subjects appropriate for allegorical treatment and the proper disposition of these subjects. We read that 'when Quinault was directed to work for the king in the production of Tragedies in music, His Majesty directly commanded him to consult with the Academy.' This consultation was more than a mere revision of the poetic text, though such revision evidently occurred. The actual choice of subjects reflected the policy of the Academy, whose suggestions in the matter were accepted by both Quinault and Lully; and this policy was itself in more or less responsive continuation of the first Academy of Baïf, of Ronsard and of their colleagues of the Pleiad or associated with it.

To that extent (by no means, of course, to the original extent), the policy remained a Neoplatonic policy, and the choice of subject a Neoplatonic choice. For though the history of the French academies themselves was not continuous, the persistence of their ideas was very marked, as several contemporary authors were at pains to convey. Buti's choice of mythological subjects, and Lully's also until his *Amadis* in 1684, suggests as much. What Quinault represents of literally academic tradition is therefore two-fold. He maintained a certain classical dignity and restraint, expressed in lucid plots and consistent characters, and worded in felicitous verse based on the stately alexandrine metre but with considerable modifications towards shorter lines and more variable patterns. He also inherited at least some potential influence from that noble Neoplatonic vision of art as a veil which half reveals in the very act of half concealing deeper meanings.

One hostile critic of French opera was Saint-Évremond;[11] but his strictures were written in London where he would have heard only selections from Lully. Most contemporary spectators considered, quite truly, that Quinault and Lully triumphed where Perrin and Cambert had no more than fumbled; and that this triumph was in the best classical tradition.

THE FRENCH CONVENTION

In considering French opera, then, as it arose about midway through the baroque period and persisted through the remainder of that period with no very substantial modification, we find a blend of classical tradition with imaginative originality which resulted in a limited but, within its limits, uncommonly consistent and felicitous species of operatic convention. Like the *opera seria* of its Italianate contemporaries, French opera has the defects of its virtues; but these virtues are emphatically operatic virtues, and we may well agree with the familiar assumption of the times, that in opera only the French and the Italian counted. What Lully contributed to French opera was doubtless more original and imaginative than what Quinault contributed; but it was entirely appropriate to the symmetry and the lucidity and the implied inwardness of Quinault's verse and Quinault's images. When we turn to Lully's music, we may be inclined to find its most striking originality and its most subtle imagination in the melodic outline of his recitative, so flexible in its rhythm and so assured in its attachment both to the verbal contours and to the verbal meanings.

The flexibility of the French recitative is to some extent actually notated by very frequent changes of time-signature, sometimes indicating a change in the speed of the unit of measurement, sometimes merely a nuance in the accentuation. Some Italian composers (for example, Cavalli, as we saw when considering his *Ormindo*) used similar changes of time-signature in recitative; but this dropped out of later Italian recitative, becoming by then a distinction of the French idiom. Some of the tempo problems to which this notation gives rise have now been definitively solved,[12] and there is no doubt at all that the intention is to let the singer follow the verbal rhythms as they would be in spoken declamation, rather than as a musical measure might inflect them if taken literally. 'For recitatives, the movement is arbitrary and it is the words which decide it', Henri-Louis Choquel[13] confirmed as late as 1759; nearer to Lully's time, in 1694, Charles Masson[14] wrote that in operatic recitative, 'he who beats the Measure is obliged to follow the voice', and in 1701 Sébastien de Brossard[15] spoke of 'a manner of Singing which holds as much of *Declamation* as of *Song*, as if one *declaimed* in *singing*, or as if one *sang* in *declaiming*, hence where one has more attention to expressing the *Passion* than to following exactly a timed measure. . . one has the liberty to alter the beats of this measure, and make some longer or shorter than others. . .' That recalls the Italian Berardi,[16] with his 'singing one speaks, and speaking one sings'; but it was the French way too, as Le Cerf de la Viéville informs us by quoting Lully as having spoken to the same effect—indeed as having put it with a certain exaggeration.

The passage in question comes in a discussion of the degree of ornamentation proper to his music, which makes it clear that while in the airs and duets, on the one hand, Lully would tolerate and perhaps enjoy the moderate but free embellishments which Lambert taught his singers; in the recitative on the other hand, Lully would not tolerate any embellishment at all beyond the customary little ornaments (trills, slides, mordents, appoggiaturas) more or less taken for granted (but in recitative, not many even of these). 'No embellishment!', Lully is quoted as exclaiming; 'my Recitative is only made for speaking, I want it to be absolutely plain.' Then the discussion continues: 'He wanted it so plain, said the Countess, that it is claimed that he went to shape it at the theatre (*à la Comédie*) on the accents (*tons*) of La Chanmêlé. He heard La Chanmêlé declaim, remembered the accents, then gave them the grace, the harmony and the degree of strength which they should have in the mouth of a Singer, to fit to the music to which he adapted them in this manner.'[17] No wonder that the line flows so mellifluously along; no wonder that it is responsive to each least turning of the sense and each least inflection of the sound of these classical but impassioned verses of Quinault's dramas. It was designed to combine, as Italian opera no longer greatly scrupled to combine, the eloquence and immediacy of the spoken theatre with the vocal felicities of opera. French opera was persistently directed towards dramatic expressiveness at a time when Italian opera was increasingly directed toward vocal expressiveness: but not until Mozart, perhaps, was the balance held quite so evenly again as once before it had been by Monteverdi.

Apart from Lully's recitative, which may sometimes be monotonous but is seldom perfunctory, there is in his music, and particularly in his harmony, a sort of inspired obviousness which may not be of the same stature as Handel, but is in this respect of the same kind. Lully's great choruses are symmetrical and mainly homophonic, stemming as they do from the much earlier (but cruder) experiments in *musique mesurée à l'antique*. They are often of an impressive spaciousness and power, and move us by their very solidity and shapeliness. Lully's overtures, again, are sincere and majestic in their slow openings, vigorous and inventive in their lively continuations. His dances are elegant and inventive, ranging from sprightly gigues, charming menuets and sentimental sarabandes to long and diversified chaconnes or passacailles. We can almost always predict which way the harmony is going, and even the surprises lie within an assured convention. But this relative predictability (which in Lully very seldom becomes banal) brings its own exhilaration. Everything falls out so exactly right. Lucidity in music could barely go further. It only sounds obvious when it has been done, of course; the talent which can do it is by no means obvious. It is done by setting up very firm expectations, and never finally disappointing them even when diverting them for a few measures in order to satisfy them the more conclusively by some cadence deliberately postponed. The contrasts introduced in this and other ways are not extreme, but they are sufficient. The musical depiction of character and situation is for the most part reticent; but the touch is sure, and there is more inwardness of feeling than the easy manner and the mostly smooth texture ostensibly reveal.

Still waters run deep. There is more evident excitement in Rameau; but also more self-consciousness and more sense of artifice. Where Rameau may sound on occasion almost a little too well-contrived, Lully nearly always sounds natural and at his ease. Much of what is best in Rameau came down to him from Lully. Their great length is somewhat against them today, and to cut out entire scenes (rather than distort them by shorter and more arbitrary excisions) is I think acceptable. But it is nevertheless the cumulative impression which can build up so movingly, and we have to allow Lully his native spaciousness. We have hardly begun to give him his due as yet in modern times; but his service in launching French opera was worthy of his contemporary reputation. With all his limitations, Lully is a great figure in the history of music.

XIX
Love and Glory

❧❦❧

A CHIVALRIC FANTASY

An excellent example of the methods of Quinault and Lully at their maturest is *Amadis de Gaule*,[1] performed at the Paris Opéra in 1684. The intention had been to perform this opera, for which the king chose the subject, at Versailles that year, but that was precluded by the death of the queen; the performance at Versailles only occurred in 1685.

The story of *Amadis* is the first of those used by Quinault and Lully which derives not from mythology but from a romance of chivalry. This romance survives only in a Castilian (i.e. Spanish) text, the earlier sources of which have not been satisfactorily established. Three books of the romance are mentioned in the second half of the fourteenth century, probably in a Spanish though possibly in a Portuguese version. In the first printed edition known and extant, published at Saragossa in 1508, four books appear, the last generally accepted as being by de Montalvo, who claims to have arranged and revised the first three books from 'the ancient originals'. There is some possibility that the author of the version there revised may have been João de Lobeira, who was a Gallician knight known to have been at the Portuguese court between 1258 and 1285. Behind the extant Spanish and the conjectured Portuguese recensions, however, there certainly stands some substantial material which derives either from the French cycle of Round Table romances, or from prior common sources; but whether as a translation or as a compilation cannot be stated.

The extant work (Saragossa, 1508) is a prose epic on feudal premisses, skilfully narrated, and abounding in heroic adventure and romantic enchantment: a work to which Cervantes referred as 'the best of all books of this kind which have ever been written'. Its influence on the literature and even on the social conventions of the sixteenth and seventeenth centuries was very considerable; and we may see it as an interesting commentary on the fantasies and make-believe current at the French court that this remarkable romance should have been selected for the first French opera libretto on a subject other than strictly mythological.

There are, indeed, mythological themes embedded in much of the early chivalric literature, wherever its more primitive strata remain in evidence. In the Celtic cycles there are tales of a decidedly mythological princeling, Amadis, who showed his archetypal quality by starting as an illegitimate infant exposed at birth, and thus set apart from more ordinary mortals; but he was rescued to fulfil the hero's role, conquering both kings and wizards, and ending up as the successful suitor of an English princess whom he first encountered on a magic island.

By the time we come to Quinault's libretto, the setting apart and the primitive symbolism are reduced to a much more sophisticated scenario. It is certainly romantic and chivalric and beset by enchantments both hurtful and helpful; but nevertheless it is much more of an agreeable fantasy and much less of an obsessive vision than the fierce originals. After a brilliant Overture in what was by then the standard French pattern (majestic opening, lightly fugal continuation, sometimes—though not here—with further majestic recapitulation or dance forms) we find ourselves in just such an enchanted forest, of no specific place or time, as has served so many poets for a symbolic embodiment of wishful thinking and blissful illusion, when the mood is pastoral and Arcadian, as for the moment it is; but also of unseen danger and bemused wandering, when the same imagery takes on its darker aspect. We see a fantastic company: Alquif, a benevolent enchanter, his consort Urgande, a benevolent enchantress, and their attendants. Stranger yet, we catch them in the fixed attitudes of no normal sleep; for the enchanters are themselves under an enchantment, from which, however, we watch them in the very next moment emerging. It is a wonderful opportunity for a producer to make effective visual theatre; and both the poetry and the music are conducive to it. (See Plate XVI.)

After a few measures of serene orchestral introduction, the voices of Urgande and Alquif are superimposed over the same music in homophonic duetting: 'the spell is broken; let us awake.' At that, the attendants also wake up and intersperse similarly homophonic phrases, in four-part harmony, to the same words. With further duetting and chorusing, still entirely homophonic and with orchestral doubling for the choruses, but with continuo support for the soloists (together or alone), the leisurely prologue flows on to inform us that 'when Amadis was lost, we were compelled by sadness to conceal ourselves in these groves; a spell of deep enchantment made our eyes to close, until fortune restored the fate of the world to one who shall be still more renowned, still more glorious'—and here we are to imagine not only the actors but the audience turning their admiring glances towards the monarch thus transparently flattered, Louis XIV, as he sits there drinking it all in and having no difficulty whatsoever in taking the expected reference to himself. 'It is he who has taught the rulers of the kingdoms in the great art of warfare; it is he who has taught them the true way to rule.' And as they sing, they dance to show their delight in waking and returning to life and movement. To enhance the symbolism, 'the statues which support the pavilion', and which are evidently attached to some of the elaborate stage mechanisms, 'carry it up in flight', leaving more space for the figures of the dance as the divertissement thus plausibly provided for follows its appointed course. And not only is the singing and the dancing provided for by the scene; the scene is provided for by introducing characters who will take part at the proper time in the main action of the piece; for this is one of those Prologues forming the opening scene of the ensuing drama. We shall see these benevolent magicians again at a subsequent crisis, and be very glad to welcome them.

A DARK FOREST OF MISUNDERSTANDING

To supply a Prologue for Act I, we are instructed by the stage-directions to repeat the opening Overture of the opera; whereupon we meet in Scene i the two tenor heroes, Amadis and his natural half-brother Florestan, and learn that Oriane, the soprano heroine beloved of Amadis, is repudiating him—as it turns out, owing to a suspicion, which we are to suppose is groundless, that he is being unfaithful to her. There comes up a general discussion of the twin themes, Love and Glory, of all others the most typical of the current preoccupation of French literature and French etiquette. Florestan is now seen with his soprano heroine, Corisande, and evidently these two are at present on terms of mutual happiness (Scene ii). But Oriane enters (Scene iii) to complain of the 'new conquest' made, she insists, by Amadis, and when Florestan reports that Amadis has protested his distress at her unwarranted coldness, she dismisses that as 'an artifice'. Corisande comments rather tritely that 'at least a great heart, when it changes, should change without disguise'. We are evidently in for one of those stubborn misunderstandings on which baroque opera—even, as it now seems, French baroque opera—so thrives. The texture, hitherto mainly an alternation of solo and duet in flexible recitative, thickens to a three-part ensemble; then in Scene iv, on no very urgent excuse, there is a 'March for the Combat at the Lists', and with full orchestra including trumpet and drums (they have independent parts notated) we surge into the finale of the Act, as the combat proceeds and the victors bring their trophies to Oriane. The chorus sing her praises broadly, the dancers display themselves brilliantly, the March loudly returns, and we are left in no doubt about the importance of the ballet to such a finale, no matter whether the action is thereby forwarded or not.

Act II has a Prelude in slow 2-time leading in Scene i directly into an eloquent recitative whose first ten bars use the same bass, after which the progressions are free though similar. We hear the soprano Arcabonne, a malevolent enchantress, telling her brother the bass Arcaläus, a malevolent enchanter, the story of her rescue from a fearsome monster by an unknown hero who strangely drew her heart; to which Arcaläus replies that 'love is but a vain error', and that she has a heart made only for anger. She is not so sure about this now; for, she sings, 'I no longer know my heart.' But with a very little persuasion he has her again duetting with him of vengeance against a hero of whom they do know, though she has no knowledge of ever having seen him. This hero is Amadis, who has recently killed another brother of hers, Ardan. As she retires into the forest, at Scene ii, Amadis wanders in, lost in more senses than one; Arcaläus, after warning his evil demons to prepare for action, also retires without being seen. Now this pair of hurtful magicians are evidently the counterparts or opposite aspects of the helpful pair, whose voices are the same (soprano and bass), and whose functions are identical except in carrying a positive instead of a negative sign. As characters of fantasy, they all four include suggestions of the parental figures. Magic itself is commonly a way of expressing (and for primitive people, of explaining) events and forces which are so hidden in the unconscious that their effects are evident but not their causes. We may expect some surprises from these awesome beings.

In Scene iv, Amadis, now left alone, sings to a beautiful texture of five-part strings that most famous of Lully's arias, 'Bois épais': 'Gloomy wood, redouble your shadows; you cannot be too dark for my sorrows; you cannot be too dense to hide my unhappy love.' The forest which was so agreeably enchanted in the Prologue has turned menacing now that Amadis has lost his way in it; and here Quinault surely had it in mind to recall that yet more famous dark wood, that *selva oscura* in which Dante found himself 'in the middle of the journey of our life. . .because the straight way was lost.' But soon in Scene v another lost character appears. It is Corisande. For a while each sings of the cruelty of destiny without noticing the other, although we hear them jointly in harmonious duet as they get nearer to each other across the stage. Then in astonished recognition they exchange their sad stories. It seems that Florestan, though in all simplicity of heart, really has gone off to rescue an unknown damsel, supposedly in distress, and as a result has fallen into a trap set for him by that sinister Arcaläus. Amadis at once wants to get started to the rescue, merely pausing to

enquire which way to go; and on the instant, there is Arcaläus con-
fronting him fiercely for Scene vi, the chief matters of which are an
angry exchange of recitative and a splendid invocation by Arcaläus of
his supporting demons.

In Scene vii the demons come rushing on to attack Amadis in a
mimed ballet which is here not only appropriate but necessary to the
action. (See Plate XVII.) Making no impression upon his spirited
defence, they cunningly transform themselves into nymphs and
shepherds. 'No, no', sing the seeming nymphs in three-part harmony,
'to close your defences safely, you must not be open to love!' But, of
course, being an operatic hero, Amadis is open to love, and gullible
into the bargain. Thus when one of the nymphs takes the appearance
of his beloved Oriane, he falls at once into the delusion and follows her
bemusedly off-stage.

Another victim, then, of the malevolent enchanter. Or should we
put it that Amadis is more truly the victim of his own confusion?
Amadis would not have fallen so easily if in some part of himself he
had not been all too eager to fall. I have the same feeling about this as I
have in general about the pastoral idyll. I think the notion of a lost but
blissful Arcadia connects with our perennial temptation to grasp at
anything which looks like the mothered state we really needed in early
childhood, yet must increasingly relinquish on the way to adult independence if we are to approach any sort of inner maturity and wholeness in later life. When a woman beckons, or seems to beckon, it is
hard not to project on to her that regressive yearning. No actual
woman can fulfil it. But a man may spend his life passing from one
woman to another in the unavailing search for what really can only be
found and in some manner confronted within himself. By letting
himself follow this fancied Oriane, Amadis, on the unconscious level
which the magic implies, is being just as unfaithful to the actual
Oriane as she has all along suspected. He is also being unfaithful to his
real self.

A DARK PRISON OF THE SPIRIT

We are now instructed that the Gigue of the Prologue will serve as
entr'acte before Act III. The chorus comes into its own at the rise of the
curtain for Scene i. Part of it is in the role of prisoners 'chained and shut
into a dungeon'; the other part is in the role of their jailers. After the
orchestra has introduced them, the lamenting prisoners sing of their
longing for death, in linked suspensions worthy of Carissimi; the
bullying jailers interject brief but forceful phrases; Florestan and
Corisande exchange sad greetings at being re-united only in their
fetters. For Scene ii, Arcabonne 'carried in the air by the demons

descends into the ruined palace' and promises a speedy release in death, to which the prisoners reply in further four-part harmony that 'to die is more welcome than to endure this terrible life'. The jailers return with: 'you will be released from your agony soon, very soon; you are going to die.' It is a scene of rich sonority and very considerable feeling, in which the simplicity of rhythm inherited by the choral writing from lingering recollections of the old *musique mesurée* is turned by the strength of the harmony to powerful account. There follows a touching duet from Florestan and Corisande, each asking to be killed in place of the other, but the villainness cries out: 'No! too much blood cannot be shed to avenge the death of my brother', from which we learn at least what ostensible motive lies behind so much vindictiveness.

Now, to a most sinister orchestral passage, Arcabonne approaches what we discover to be her brother Ardan's tomb, and thus addresses his shade: 'you who but a little while ago were buried in this tomb, and who living were a terror to all, receive this blood which my fury is shedding to offer you.' Then as she hears some strange groaning from within the tomb, her recitative grows more disconnected. Scene iii is a splendid set piece as the shade (a baritone part of which we would have liked to hear more) rises to sing an air of extraordinarily sustained and melancholy power, accompanied by rich five-part harmony from the orchestra. To our surprise and her terror, he announces: 'Ah! You have betrayed me, false sister.' Then, more weakly, 'I descend, the daylight hurts me'; and very powerfully again, on his top E natural, 'for to punish you for your weakness, it is on Hell that I rely.' This he repeats with diminishing force as he does indeed descend. We shall find shortly that what he really means (though neither she nor we are yet aware of it) is that she is *going* to betray him—and in this he seems to hint that, being a ghost, he shares the usual foreknowledge of his eerie species, because coming up as he does from somewhere in the unconscious, he has no regard for time, and takes a premonition for no different from an actuality. But he has made his point. It is not a long scene, and it was in a well established operatic tradition; but it is uncommonly good of its kind, and an excellent example of Lully's mastery of the apparently conventional effects which he had a rare genius in carrying to more than conventional effectiveness.

Arcabonne has only just time to repeat that nothing shall prevent her from carrying out her vengeance, before in Scene iv her chief enemy, Amadis, is flung in chains upon the stage. And even as she raises her dagger to dispatch him, she sees that he is the hero who saved her from the monster, as she has already described to Arcalaüs in our hearing at the beginning of the second act. It is a momentous confrontation, and evidently a turning-point, as that prescient ghost foresaw. It has been well suggested[2] in connection with Henry James that a ghost in art as in dreams and actual hallucinations may stand less for an unappeased grievance than for an unlived potentiality. Unfinished business in desperate need of attention might be one way of putting it. The unfinished business here may be some hazardous but potentially liberating encounter with the darker aspect of a man's own feminine underside. For as soon as Amadis takes it in that, so far from killing him, Arcabonne is offering him any boon he likes to ask, he asks for the liberation of the prisoners.

Out they dance into the free light of day, rejoicing our hearts with ballet and chorus not merely apt to the situation, but comprised in it. The more brilliant the lighting here and the more jubilant the dancing, the more the simple symbolism will impinge, almost as in *Fidelio* when the prisoners first pour out; and our sense of liberation here likewise holds a promise though not yet a fulfilment. For Amadis is still retained, as if his liberation requires some further working out. The encounter shows both positive and negative potentialities in what is evidently as yet an ambiguous situation. (See Plate XVIII.)

One of the airs from the ballet is to serve as *entr'acte*. Scene i of Act IV reveals 'an agreeable island'—but insidiously so, since we now see the dark magicians in consultation. Fourteen agitated measures in the orchestra introduce an exchange of recitative in which Arcaläus tells Arcabonne: 'by my enchantments Oriane is captured', for whom Amadis lives. 'You cannot punish her too much!' is the immediate answer; but when Arcaläus proposes to do this by showing Oriane 'the body of her Amadis who falls a victim to your revenge', the answer is a grievous sigh, followed by a dialogue of which the words are not less compact than the recitative carrying them is expressive.

Protracted as its total length may be, a Lully opera can move with exemplary swiftness when the situation requires it. Arcaläus: 'I hear you sigh! You do not dare to speak. Can these be the sighs that your hatred breathes?' Arcabonne: 'You are lucky that you need not even dream of it, only to hate and be avenged. Alas! In the enemy himself I have found the unknown man I love.' Arcaläus: 'To increase your torment you must see the lovers happy in marriage!' Arcabonne: 'Ha! I had rather a thousand times that both of them should perish.' Arcaläus: 'Can I rely on you again?' Arcabonne: 'You can rely on jealous love. It is more cruel than hatred'—and forthwith their magic goes out against Amadis, so that he seems to die. But magic is never quite what it seems to be. All that we can with some assurance infer is that the inner situation is growing critical.

In Scene ii, Oriane is heard lamenting her helpless state, from which Amadis, if he were not, as she is still convinced, unfaithful, would by all the conventions of romantic chivalry be actively engaged in rescuing her. In Scene iii, Arcaläus comes to taunt her with the proud boast that he has captured Amadis, which she merely regards as

impossible. Oriane: 'no one can conquer him and that you know!'
Arcaläus: 'ah, so that is how you hate him!' And then in Scene iv she
sees the seeming corpse of Amadis, and with the utmost revulsion of
feeling she sings: 'so my anger was fatal to him', and resolves to join
him in death. She faints away and becomes another seeming corpse for
the hurtful magicians to gloat over in Scene v.

And then, at this darkest hour, somehow the hurt itself calls up its
healing opposite, and help arrives. Most fortunately for our human
species, there seems to be in the psyche, just as much as in the body, a
certain disposition for a damaged condition to mobilize its own remedy. Too one-sided a conscious attitude may evoke in our dreams and
our fantasies powerful images of an opposite tendency, which, if our
intuitions can take some sort of a hold of them, may help to put us into
better balance. Or if the situation is too unfavourable for that, then the
unconscious may force a crisis or even a breakdown, as the best hope
of loosening up the block in the personality which is keeping back
some urgently needed development.

Our two heroes here have certainly got themselves into a crisis, and
their heroines likewise. The rather naïve Florestan and his Corisande
seem to have been let out of it again, and also the anonymous prisoners; but from the more complex couple (rather like Tamino and
Pamina in *The Magic Flute*, or Mark and Jenifer in *The Midsummer
Marriage*), something further in token of growth of character is perhaps required. But if that is so, they must on some level have been
doing better than they knew, or they would not have been open to the
new turn of events which now to all appearances comes of its own
accord.

THE ANSWERING GLOW

We see a remarkable stage contraption, which is a sort of boat provided by the mouth of an unusually capacious serpent or dragon, and
which is bringing in the benevolent enchanters of that long distant
Prologue: Alquif, Urgande and their fantastic train. One such monster has already been killed off-stage by Amadis in rescuing Arcabonne; and we may again feel astonished by the ambivalent connection
and mutual complementariness of the opposing forces. There seems
to be a polarity in the psyche so far down as we can detect at all; but
ultimately the opposing forces may not be different. It may be that the
force polarized is all one force, and that what it really consists of is the
glorious force of life itself. (See Plate XIX.)

There is a glory in the music now, as a majestic introduction in the
orchestra invites a décor and a choreography and a stage lighting to
match. Many hundreds of candles would be illuminating the scene.

And in molten recitative, Urgande starts to explain herself. 'I rule by my laws Hell, Earth and Sea. Without anyone knowing where I am, I journey through the world; and I know secrets that the Gods have not shown yet to any eyes but mine. Take care, take care to know Urgande, know and accept.' And at once the complementary pair of opposing magicians assent: 'we shall accept a spirit stronger than our own'. Both pairs then repeat these solo comments in homophonic duets. The forces of light gather themselves into 'the vessel of the great Serpent', and surround themselves with flames; the dark forces, notwithstanding their good resolution, surround themselves with demons flying up from Hell, who are combated by others flying down from Heaven; for after all there must be a ballet, and certainly no one could complain here of any deficiency either in the machinery or in the spectacle. A trumpet tune from Act III serves as *entr'acte*.

But what is it in the psyche which might thus be symbolized; which commands secrets not yet revealed to consciousness; and which nevertheless we shall do well intuitively to know and accept? It would seem to be that completer self at the centre of us, that totality of our being which, in so far as we manage to know and accept it, can make sense of our lives. Certainly a man's inner component of femininity can help to mediate on these levels, and a woman's inner component of masculinity likewise; for our own deeper levels are by no means easy of access, and every fairy-tale has its trials and its ordeals to be undergone before the reward is reached, and its powerful figures to help the adventurers, or to hinder them, or to help them by hindering them enough for them to test and strengthen their own need and capacity for independence.

The reward in a fairy-tale always, I think, includes in its symbolism some such inner growth of character towards greater consciousness and maturity. It includes finding not only literally and biologically a mate, but also imaginatively and psychologically an experience of the contra-sexed component within oneself. Both these can be steps towards completer living, but the second is the more essential in the long haul. Treasure, too, can relate, literally, to material prosperity; but still more significantly can it relate, symbolically, to an access of consciousness and maturity. It is the same with myths and rituals of rebirth, of initiation, or of the sacred marriage. They all give form, religious or legendary but in any case intuitive, to some sort of a perennial search within the psyche of ordinary people as well as of poets and of prophets. What is being sought is wholeness. That is the basic human scenario. We are animals and more than animals. We have good impulses and bad ones. We are pulled this way and that, but there is something in us which seeks for some sort of inward reconciliation and acceptance, as Urgande here presents it. This seems to be an archetypal goal, however much obscured by our unavoidable wrong turnings along the way, in course of which it is all too possible to get lost to oneself entirely. But when Dante got lost in his dark wood, he got out again with one of the finest of all poetic masterpieces.

Such consummate achievements are indeed very rare; but it is very common to search for wholeness under one projected activity or another, and although the goal must remain for ever unattainable, it is certainly approachable. Initiation is the image for it which is used deliberately in *The Magic Flute*, and likewise in *The Midsummer Marriage*, where Michael Tippett knew very well what he was intending to convey in renewing the ancient symbols of the four-fold ordeal by earth and water, air and fire, and of the sacred marriage at the climax of it. After that, his hero and heroine found themselves able to get married in a perfectly normal and literal manner, such as rejoices our hearts at the happy endings of so many romantic stories. But I think that we rejoice all the more because of the wider implications which our intuitions are at the same time picking up.

In *Amadis* here, there are hints of death and rebirth; there are parent figures to help and hinder as the situation requires; there is a royal union to catch subliminal echoes of the sacred marriage; there are philosophical reflections and well-earned rejoicings to sum it all up. The real reversal of fortunes having already occurred, Act V has little to add to the drama though plenty to the divertissement. In Scene i, Urgande, undisputed now in her helpful leadership, brings on the company of 'loyal lovers'. In Scene ii, Amadis and Oriane share the delight of one another's recovery at least from seeming death. First Oriane laments in very grievous recitative at being brought back to life only to confront her utter loss; then before her eyes Amadis also revives; next they mingle solos and duets of growing melodiousness, culminating in a sort of homophonic air together.

In Scene iii, Urgande formally unites and blesses the happy couple; in Scene iv, a splendid *symphonie* starts off the general celebrations in dance and song. There is the customary long Chaconne, ranging through full five-part harmony for orchestra, light three-part passages for wind, vocal solos, small ensembles and big choruses, the ground-bass and the dance continuing the while. 'Understand what has happened, our choice will be right; choose but rightly, our hearts are committed for life; cease to fear, love that which we have chosen; grieve no more, grief with love goes not in season.' Two-directional sentiments, as it seems to me, and equally felicitous on the obvious erotic level and on the veiled symbolic level. 'Love will be angry if we give way to despair'; and indeed despair is life-denying. 'Let our senses delight, our joy is innocent'; and certainly unguilty sensuality is life-enhancing. 'Let our hearts keep good faith worthy of our delight; let us sing our delight in the glory of love; let us accept the faith that we have chosen; we who have suffered grief in our loving shall be rewarded for our faithfulness to love's command.' It reminds me just a little of Shakespeare's 'This above all: to thine own self be true, And it must follow, as the night the day, Thou canst not then be false to any man'.[3] For I seem to sense in this radiant scene some wider resonance, some triumph not only of love but of life, some awe and wonder and release such as comes to us in fine moments of artistic experience.

I am not sure whether Quinault and Lully intended that wider resonance, as I am sure that Rinuccini, Chiabrera and Striggio intended it. We should need to know more about those crucial meetings with the French Academy, where scenarios were discussed and symbolic imagery was chosen. What overtly Neoplatonic recollections had come down from Ronsard and his still respected school? What reliance remained upon Giraldi and Cartari and Conti, whose Neoplatonic popularizations were still being printed in the seventeenth century, together with newer treatises like the impressive *De Idolatria Liber* of Dionysius Vossius first published at Amsterdam in 1641 and often reissued, or *Mystagogus Poeticus, or the Muses Interpreter* by Alexander Ross at London from 1647? I am not aware of any such direct connection as that of Cartari with the Florentine interludes of 1589, or of Conti with *Circe* in 1581. But I would go so far as to say that these early French librettos are compatible with a Neoplatonic implication. The images persisted long after the philosophy narrowed to a few special groups such as the Cambridge Platonists or eccentric talents such as Coleridge. Images persisting from force of habit can still be symbolically effectual.

I am, perhaps, more interested at this stage in the possibilities of intuitive and to some extent traditional symbolism, such as I believe may insinuate itself more or less spontaneously into any imaginative product of the human psyche. There are many subliminal associations and elusive channels of communication, such as have been increasingly explored of late by art historians and literary critics. Coleridge, who was himself unusually alert to these possibilities and put them to excellent use in his own poetry, became the subject of that pioneering study by John Livingston Lowes, *The Road to Xanadu*, which was published at Boston and New York in 1927, since when the savants of the Warburg Institute in London and some other workers have pursued this line of thought. It is as yet less familiar to musicians, but I believe it may be just as promising in our direction.

I have suggested throughout this book that our subliminal associations with archetypal imagery may be one way of accounting for certain features of the operatic libretto which have long been a source of some bewilderment. An operatic scenario can seem so bizarre, yet add up with its music to so convincing a totality in the theatre. I think that we must all the time be catching subliminal resonances which are anything but bizarre, and which reflect common areas within our nature where although we are not the same we may be very much alike. We sense some glow of visionary truth; and there is that within us which responds as with an answering glow.

It seems obvious that our responses to a work of art are not in the main rational. An opening of doors and windows upon our own potentialities for inner illumination would be more my way of putting it. The light and the warmth brought by that experience are what I mean here by an answering glow.

Ex. 22. Lully, Amadis, *Paris, 1684, samples of the French idiom in opera: (a) slow opening to the French overture, as notated; (b) approximately as it might be played; (c) quick continuation in loosely imitative texture; (d) and (e) duet somewhat recalling the opening of the overture, and next taken up by the chorus; (f) French recitative, from Act I, Scene iii (melodious but almost unornamented—at Lully's personal insistence); (g) French aria, from Act II, Scene iv (relatively simple, but appropriate for some ornamentation—in the style originally brought from Italy and taught with Lully's approval by his father-in-law Lambert); (h) French chorus, from the prison scene at the start of Act III, Scenes i-ii (mainly homophonic, but capable of great expressiveness in the broad manner)—realizations mine:*

g)

Bois é – pais, re – dou – ble ton om-bre. Tu ne sau – rais être as-sez som-bre

[Dark wood, redouble your shade. You cannot be too sombre]

h)

[Not too slow]

Ciel! Ô Ciel! Quel sup-pli-ce! Hé – las! Ciel! Ô Ciel! Quel sup-pli-ce! Hé – las!

[Heaven! O heaven! What torment! Alas!]

And so French opera arose, out of Italian opera and yet apart from it. So too, in essence, French opera remained until Traetta and Jomelli and Gluck, learning between them as much from Rameau as from Handel and Hasse, brought these two baroque traditions into contact again, to lead on through Mozart towards the latter and more familiar half of our operatic history. For Mozart stands at the middle point, in date as well as in his assimilation and transformation of most of what was going on around him at the time. Not until Wagner, however, did opera evolve full cycle round, in that different idiom, to its original conception as drama flexibly and continuously unfolding in words and music. And with Wagner, myth came to the front again, and symbolical interpretation is not only a possibility but a necessity of the case. As indeed in some measure perhaps it always is.

APPENDIX
Opera and the Calendar

DIFFERENCES IN THE CALENDAR

So closely consecutive were the events immediately leading to the rise of opera, and so hotly disputed were the actual priorities, that we may wish to consider certain complexities in the calendar, which have been very troublesome for many previous periods of history, and which remain important for the late renaissance and early baroque periods when it comes to allotting the credit in this competitive arena. The complications which concern us here fall into two classes: those resulting from the uneven application of the Gregorian reform, in 1582, of the Julian Calendar; and those resulting from the various dates on which the New Year was treated as beginning at different times and places.[1]

JULIAN (OLD STYLE) TO GREGORIAN (NEW STYLE)

A reform of the calendar is needed whenever small discrepancies between the physical year and the calendar year have accumulated to substantial dimensions, so that seasonal events no longer correspond sufficiently with their official dates.

The physical year can itself be calculated from certain slightly different observations, one of which is the apparent yearly motion of the stars through the night sky, and another of which is the apparent yearly motion of the sun through the day sky. By taking an average of the differences caused by very small discrepancies in the actual motion of the earth, the mean tropical solar year is calculated astronomically to be 365 days, 5 hours, 48 minutes and 46.51 seconds; and this calculation has provided an important standard of reference, though not quite the most exact at which it is now possible to arrive by electronic time measurement derived from periodic vibrations in quartz crystals.

There was a successful reform of the calendar under Julius Caesar in 46 B.C. The astronomical calculations on which this reform (resulting in the Julian or Old-Style Calendar) was based were substantially accurate; but their application treated as negligible a discrepancy as to the lunar month (taken as 235 lunations in 19 Julian solar years, which they exceed by about one and a half hours), and as to the solar year (taken as 365.25 days, which gave a civil year 11 minutes and 14 seconds longer than the mean tropical solar year).

The Julian Calendar added (intercalated) one day (intercalary day) to each fourth year (the bissextile year or leap-year, of which the number is exactly divisible by four). This took good care of the gross error of maintaining each year at 365 days; but the lesser error was not negligible over a long period. Thus the Spring Equinox, observed as 25 March in the Julian Calendar in 46 B.C., had by the time of the Council of Nicaea in A.D. 325 receded to 21 March, and this was recognized in the ecclesiastical calculations then established by which Easter, the movable feast on which the other movable feasts of the Christian year depend, is conditioned by the phases of the moon in that lunar month which includes the Spring Equinox.

As the same error further accumulated down the centuries, the need for a reform of the Julian Calendar was repeatedly recognized. Various tentative initiatives were made; but not until the Council of Trent, at its last session in 1563, were instructions given to Pope Gregory XIII which resulted in his Papal Bull of 1582, instituting the Gregorian or New-Style Calendar.

The Gregorian Calendar retained the intercalary day once in four years, with a most ingenious modification to correct its cumulative inaccuracy. The intercalary day is itself omitted from three centenary years out of four. Thus just as one year in four is a leap-year, but the other three are not, so one century in four observes the normal centennial leap-year, but the other three do not. This keeps the civil year in correspondence with the solar year with an error approximately of one day in 35 centuries; and though further refinements of intercalation have been proposed, none has so far been adopted.

Unfortunately for historians, this admirable Gregorian reform of the calendar was instituted with a complication which was not astronomically necessary, but was thought to be ecclesiastically necessary in order to avoid disturbing the date observed by the Council of Nicaea in A.D. 325 for the Spring Equinox, i.e. 21 March, on which the hallowed calculations for deciding the date each year of Easter depended; and that in spite of the irrationality and inconvenience by which Easter may by these calculations fall more than a month apart in different years.

By the time of the Gregorian Calendar of 1582, the actual Spring Equinox, because of the continued accumulation of the error in the

Julian Calendar, had receded a further ten days, to 11 March. By a forceful rather than judicious operation, it was brought back to 21 March. In March of 1582, Pope Gregory XIII officially abolished the Julian Calendar (thereafter known as Old Style) and substituted the Gregorian Calendar (thereafter known as New Style). The unwanted ten days were, with due notice given, deemed to be deleted: the day after 4 October 1582 was deemed to be 15 October.

Thus the Gregorian reform had two purposes. There was the improvement of intercalation with the primary purpose of bringing the civil year more closely into accord with the solar year: a desirable purpose successfully achieved. There was the deletion of ten days with the secondary purpose of restoring the Spring Equinox, and with it the calculations for Easter, to the same relationship with the calendar as had obtained at the Council of Nicaea: a less desirable purpose, and less successfully achieved in that the traditional presumptions relating the lunar year to the solar year were thrown further out of line by the very fact of the improved intercalation.

There is an unavoidable element of fiction in all sufficiently practicable presumptions relating lunations to years; and the astronomical equinox actually being variable from year to year, this element of fiction also extends to any fixed official dating of the Spring Equinox itself. For these reasons, there were at the time advocates of a new method of calculating Easter by astronomical observations instead of fictional calculation; but the advocates of the traditional calculations were strong enough to retain these at least in form, and therefore the ten days had to be deleted in order to preserve the form.

It was not a purpose of the Gregorian reform to establish a uniform beginning to the year on 1 January; but nevertheless this was a natural association, since the Roman usage was such at the time of the reform. Thus the adoption of Gregorian Calendar and of 1 January as the beginning of the year might (though they did not have to) coincide, as for example they did in England, although not in Scotland.

If all countries had adopted the Gregorian Calendar simultaneously, and with it a uniform beginning of the year on 1 January, the passing complication of the ten deleted days would have been a trivial irritation to historians compared with the lasting simplification and the improved accord with the astronomical year. But this did not happen.

Broadly speaking, the Catholic countries accepted the Gregorian Calendar on the appointed day of 5 October 1582 (Italy, Spain, Portugal), or within that year (France by deleting the ten days after 9 December 1582), or at or near the transition into the following year (Catholic Germany and the Catholic Low Countries with Holland and Zeeland, by deleting the last ten days of 1582 and thus going ten days early into 1583; Austria and Catholic parts of Switzerland in mid-January, 1584). Poland followed at the end of 1585; Hungary in 1587.

Protestant Denmark assented in 1582 with certain reservations. But most Protestant countries, preferring as the saying went to be out of accord with the sun rather than in accord with Rome, held back for a century or more: Protestant Germany did not follow until 1700, and with a distinct manner of calculating Easter astronomically; Sweden and most Protestant parts of Switzerland then or not long after, the last however not until 1811; while the Orthodox Church continued outside, and in Russia the Gregorian Calendar was not accepted until the Soviet régime, in 1917.

We have also to remember that between 1790 and 1806, Revolutionary France substituted for the Gregorian Calendar a succession of confusedly astronomical calculations, culminating in a Republican Era begun as from the Autumn Equinox which fell on the same date as the proclamation of the Republic, 22 September 1792; although this Republican Calendar fell out of all but the most official use some years before its official abolition on 11 *nivòse an XIV*, i.e. 1 January 1806. Thereafter France recognized, as before, the Gregorian Calendar, which indeed had never been quite out of common employment.[2]

In Great Britain, the acceptance of the Gregorian Calendar was provided for by the Calendar (New-Style) Act of 1750; but by that time, the reformed manner of intercalating the corrective days, i.e. of calculating leap-years, had caused the difference between Old Style and New Style to be not ten days, but eleven. Prior to 1700, the leap-years coincided; but 1700, although a leap-year in Old Style, was deliberately arranged not to be a leap-year in New Style, as part of the method of improving the continued accuracy of the calendar. This occurred also in 1800. As a consequence, the difference, which was eleven days in the eighteenth century, was twelve days in the nineteenth century. At the present time, it is thirteen days.

The Calendar (New-Style) Act of 1750 in Great Britain therefore provided for the change to Gregorian datings by deleting the eleven days between 2 September and 14 September 1752 (i.e. the day following the 2nd was deemed to be the 14th). The Gregorian refinement for modifying future leap-years at the century intervals was also accepted; and at the same time, the start of the legal year (as opposed to the civil or common-practice year) was moved back from 25 March to 1 January beginning with 1751. This had already been effected in Scotland from 1600.

ADJUSTING OLD-STYLE DATINGS TO MODERN USAGE

When translating (Julian) Old-Style dating into (Gregorian) New-Style dating, that is to say into our ordinary modern dating, we have to allow for ten days' difference up to and including 1700; thereafter for eleven days' difference up to and including 1800; thereafter for twelve days' difference up to and including 1900; thereafter for thirteen days' difference up to and including (N.B.!) 2100.

For dates falling within these ambiguous days, historians often use a notation in the form, e.g. 1650/51, implying that a document or an event then dated, e.g. 5 January 1650, must now be taken as 5 January 1651, if we wish to meet the assumptions of the ordinary modern reader who might otherwise be put a year out in his interpretation.

To adjust Old-Style dating to New-Style dating (where no local complications occur), for all (Julian) Old-Style datings from 1 January to 10 January (1582 to 1700), or to 11 January (1701 to 1800) or to 12 January (1801 to 1900) or to 13 January (1901–2100): *add one year.*

LOCAL (OLD STYLE) TO UBIQUITOUS (MODERN STYLE)

Local complications occur where at certain times and places the year has been treated as beginning on different dates, i.e. other than 1 January according to the usage now general. The chief such divergent usages are those mentioned below; there were, however, others, and investigation into this extremely difficult topic is by no means yet completed.

An old-style beginning to the year may be found in combination either with an Old-Style (Julian) Calendar, or with a New-Style (Gregorian) Calendar. Since the difference here may be rather of months than of days, we have to be still more careful to make any necessary adjustments.

YEAR BEGINNING 1 JANUARY

The Roman civil year in antiquity began on 1 January; and this obtained widely under the spread of the Roman Empire, but gave place to a great variety of local usages as Roman civilization declined and withdrew.

Thus in France, 1 January was still current under the Merovingians of the fifth century A.D., and is found later concurrently with other usages. In a few places, 1 January remained throughout the middle ages; but in most, either an older dating (e.g. 1 March) returned or a Christian festival (e.g. Christmas or Easter) supervened.

During the sixteenth century, there was a widespread recrudescence of 1 January. The Holy Roman Empire, Spain, Portugal and the Low Countries went over to 1 January from around the middle of the sixteenth century; Prussia, Denmark and Sweden from 1559; France, from between 1564 and 1580 in various regions, but in the main from 1568; Scotland from 1600, but England and Ireland not until 1752; Russia not until 1725; Venice for the civil year in private affairs, from about 1520, but for the official and legal year, not until the fall of the Republic in 1797 (and in practice, civil dating *more veneto*, Venetian old style, is often found, very inconsistently and confusingly, at least throughout the seventeenth century); Tuscany (including Florence, so important in our operatic studies) not until 1750.

But for certain purposes, 1 January continued to be regarded as the first day of the year at all periods and places: the astronomical year was always reckoned from 1 January; calendars and almanacs have traditionally taken January for the first month of the year; part of the ecclesiastical calculations relevant to Easter (the golden number, the domenical letter) have always changed on 1 January (Kalends of January).

Because 1 January is officially the festival of the Circumcision of Christ, the usage of beginning the year on 1 January is sometimes known as the Style of the Circumcision.

Because beginning the year on 1 January is normal modern-style dating, no adjustment is necessary in this respect.

YEAR BEGINNING 1 MARCH

The Roman religious year in antiquity began on 1 March; and this may also have been an ancient Germanic usage, and one brought by the Franks to France, where traces of it are found in the Merovingian period (5th cent. A.D.), and sporadically later.

The year beginning on 1 March had very restricted subsequent importance, except that it was retained as the official and legal year (not after about 1520 in theory, though often in practice, as the civil year, which after about 1520 began on 1 January) by Venice until the fall of the Republic in 1797. The usage of beginning the year on 1 March is therefore widely known as the Venetian Style or *mos venetus*.

To adjust Venetian old-style dating to modern-style dating, for all dates from 1 January to 28 or 29 February: *add one year.*

YEAR BEGINNING WITH THE SPRING EQUINOX

This beginning, reckoned as 21 or 22 March, was used in Russia from the eleventh century A.D. up to 1725; for all dates between 1 January and 20 or 21 March: *add one year.*

YEARS BEGINNING 25 MARCH AS
THE ANNUNCIATION

Two different styles began the year on 25 March, as the day of the Annunciation to the Virgin Mary of the Incarnation of Christ (Lady Day), for which the abbreviation *ab Inc. (ab Incarnatione*, from the Incarnation) may (but will not necessarily) appear in documents so dated.

The Incarnation chronologically preceded the Nativity, and presumably for this reason, one such style began the year from 25 March *previous* to that beginning on 1 January.

But 25 March previous is much farther than 25 March subsequent from 1 January; and perhaps for that reason, the other style began the year on the 25 March *subsequent* to that beginning on 1 January.

YEAR BEGINNING 25 MARCH (PREVIOUS)

The year beginning on 25 March previous to 1 January was used in some Tuscan cities, including Pisa, Pistoia and Siena, and even by the chancellery of some popes of the twelfth century A.D. But at Pisa, this style of dating (taking as the beginning of the year the Annuciation *previous* to 1 January) remained in use until 1750; and for this reason, it is most commonly called Pisan Style or *calculus Pisanus*.

In Pisan style, the year began nine months and seven days *before* modern style. To adjust Pisan old-style dating to modern-style dating, for all dates from 25 March to 31 December: *subtract one year*.

YEAR BEGINNING 25 MARCH (SUBSEQUENT)

The year beginning on 25 March subsequent to 1 January was of very great medieval and renaissance importance, particularly in parts of Italy and above all of Tuscany; in parts of France, and above all of mid-France; in England, Ireland and Scotland; and in a much smaller degree, it was also used elsewhere. Florence and some other parts of Tuscany retained this style of dating (taking as the beginning of the year the Annunciation *subsequent* to 1 January) until 1750; and for this reason, it is most commonly called Florentine Style or *calculus Florentinus* (but also *stilus Treverensis, mos curiae Lausannensis*, and exceptionally, *mos Gallicanus*). It gave place to 1 January in France during the reforms around 1564. It remained in England and Ireland until 1752, but in Scotland only until 1600.

In Florentine Style, the year began two months and twenty-four days *after* modern style. To adjust Florentine old-style dating to modern-style dating, for all dates from 1 January to 24 March: *add one year*.

YEAR BEGINNING WITH EASTER

The year beginning with one of the days (most usually Holy Saturday) of Easter was also of great medieval and renaissance importance, particularly in France from the twelfth or thirteenth century onwards (also Lorraine, Cologne, Liège and parts of Belgium and Holland), so that it became commonly known as French style, *stilus Francicus* or *mos Gallicanus* (also *mos Coloniensis*, or by the terms *anno a Resurrectione* or *a Paschate*). With the adoption around 1564 of 1 January in France, the importance of this style of dating from Easter soon fell away.

Since Easter is a movable feast, the adjustment of Easter datings to modern-style datings has to be separately calculated for any one year in question: the rules for doing this are very complicated, but they will be found admirably set out by A. Giry in his very practical *Manuel de Diplomatique*.[3]

The extreme variation in Easter is thirty-five days in either direction, thus allowing a year varying from 330 to 400 days, in which the last ten days of March and the first ten days of April may appear twice, or not at all. It is a tribute to the sanctity of this great festival rather than to the utility of such French old-style dating that the year beginning with Easter should have retained so long and extensive an employment. When the date of Easter has been determined, for dates within the year but prior to this date: *add one year*.

YEAR BEGINNING WITH THE AUTUMN EQUINOX

This beginning, in a misplaced attempt to be scientific, was reckoned as (Gregorian) 21, 22, 23 or 24 September, according to astronomical calculations of the Autumn Equinox by observation at the meridian of Paris for each individual year, in France under the Republican Calendar, officially from 1793 to 1805 inclusive. The years were numbered I, II, etc. of the Republican Era, but with some confusion as to the months of 1793 before 21 September (first allotted to year II, then to year I; year II of the Republican Era thus became 22 September 1793 to 20 September 1794, etc.). The months themselves were reorganized at 30 days, and re-named; 5 (in leap years, 6) supplementary days completed the year. Weeks were replaced by three divisions (*décades*) of ten days to each month. Days were of ten hours, hours of 100 minutes and minutes of 100 seconds, Republican style.

To translate datings in the French Republican Calendar into

Gregorian (normal modern-style) datings, it is again necessary to know the conditions obtaining for the year in question, since the date of its beginning depended upon the variable factor of the sun's apparent passage across the equinoctial point of the celestial equator. Giry[4] gives the necessary information and instructions, and he also prints a complete Table of Concordance between the Republican and Gregorian Calendars, 1793–1805. Best advice here: *look it up in Giry.*

YEAR BEGINNING WITH CHRISTMAS

The year beginning with Christmas was of great antiquity, and of continuing importance throughout the middle ages—even in some localities throughout the renaissance. The medieval usage was strong in papal Rome, in the rest of Italy and in the Empire; up to the Norman Conquest or occasionally later in England and Ireland; in France, the usage persisted (or reappeared) in many districts into the late renaissance, especially Dauphiné (whence one term, *style Delphinal*, for the Christmas beginning, as opposed to *style de France* for the Easter beginning); in many parts of Germany and of German-speaking Switzerland likewise, up to the second half of the sixteenth century; in Spain and Portugal, during the renaissance up to the sixteenth century. The term *Anno ab Nativitate* might be used of it.

In the Style of the Nativity or Christmas style, the year began seven days *before* modern style. To adjust Christmas old-style dating to modern-style dating, for all dates from 25 to 31 December: *subtract one year.*

OLD DATINGS IMPORTANT TO OPERA

Of the numerous old-style datings, those important for the study of opera are (i) Old Style in its particular sense of Julian, as opposed to New Style in its particular sense of Gregorian: especially in Protestant Germany (till 1700) and England (till 1752); and (ii) those old-style datings, in the general sense, which take for the beginning of the year the day of the Annunciation (25 March) subsequent to 1 January: especially Florentine old-style dating (till 1750), and the equivalent year (Lady Day beginning) in England (till 1752); also, for official and legal and in practice often for common purposes, Venetian old style which takes for the beginning of the year 1 March (till 1797).

DIFFERENCES IN THE TIMES OF DAY AND NIGHT

So far as I am aware, no historic issues concerning the rise of opera depend upon the hour of the day or night at which a performance began or ended. But Thomas Walker has drawn my attention privately to the fact that the hour assumed to be the first hour of the day or the night, from which the numbering of the subsequent hours was therefore taken, also varied. Not only was this different at different dates and places; it might also differ with the season. The first hour of darkness or of lightness, if taken as the start of the diurnal cycle, does not, of course, remain a constant excepting at the Equator; it is therefore possible to encounter hours of variable length, in the manner more ordinarily associated with antiquity. As a result of these variables, entertainments described in contemporary reports as lasting to the second or third or fourth hour of the night may not imply such nocturnal habits as might otherwise appear. A general study of this problem is needed in connection with early opera, and meanwhile it has to be borne in mind that possibilities of misunderstanding can occur requiring at least a precautionary investigation of the case in question.

DATES FOR CARNIVAL

Carnival is a period of jubilation before the putting aside at Lent of flesh for food (Lat. *carnem levare*), and has varied widely by local custom. The most common date of commencement for Italy was 17 January (feast of S. Antonio); for many localities, 2 February (Candlemas); for France and the greater portion of Western Europe, Christmas, New Year's Day or Epiphany. For Sicily, Epiphany; for the Tyrol, Epiphany or Candlemas. Epiphany was mostly 6 January, the following day being a common commencement of Carnival.

Notes

❦❧

References given below in the form: See Ch. I, n.1, etc., are to notes in this present book.

Chapter I

1. See especially Joseph Kerman, *Opera as Drama*, New York, 1947; and on the relation between opera and oratorio, Winton Dean, *Handel's Dramatic Oratorios and Masques*, London, 1959, and his letter to the *Musical Times*, Aug. 1978.
2. See Richard Wagner, letters to Liszt, 25 Nov. 1850, and to Röckel, 23 Aug. 1856; also the famous letter to Röckel of 25 Jan. 1854; also *Oper und Drama*, Leipzig, 1852 (preface dated 1851), esp. II, 3 (*Gesammelte Schriften*, Vol. 4, p. 81); and 'Religion und Kunst', in *Bayreuther Blätter*, 1880–81, esp. the opening sentence (*Gesammelte Schriften*, Vol. 10, p. 275).

Chapter II

1. The standard work is George E. Mylonas, *Eleusis and the Eleusinian Mysteries*, Princeton, 1961. A depth-psychologist's study is C. Kerényi, *Eleusis, Archetypal Image of Mother and Daughter*, New York, 1967.
2. A standard work in English is W. K. C. Guthrie, *Orpheus and Greek Religion*, London, 1935; Ivan M. Linforth, *The Arts of Orpheus*, Berkeley, 1941, is highly perceptive and informative; Walter Wili, 'Die Orphischen Mysterien und der Griechische Geist', in the *Eranos Jahr-Buch*, XI, 1944, pp. 61–105, is psychologically also insightful. For information in depth, however, and for comprehensive references to the classical and post-classical sources as well as secondary sources available at the time of writing, see the long and magnificent article *s.v.* Orpheus by Otto Gruppe in W. H. Roscher, ed., *Ausführliches Lexicon der griechischen und römischen Mythologie*, 8 vols., Leipzig, 1884–1937. Virgil, *Georgic* 4, 454–503, and Ovid, *Met.* 10, 1–73, are familiar versions; and see Conon, *Narr.*, 45, 2; Apollodorus, *Bibl.*, 1, 3, 3; Pausanias, 9, 30, 5–6; Fulgentius, *Myth.*, 3, 10. See also J. B. Friedman's most interesting *Orpheus in the Middle Ages*, Cambridge, Mass., 1970.
3. Lucius Apuleius, *Metamorphoses*, XI, 23.
4. Pseudo-Dionysius, *De coelesti hierarchia*, II, 3. See R. T. Wallis, *Neoplatonism*, London, 1972; and the articles 'Neoplatonism' by A. Harnack and J. M. Mitchell in the 11th ed. (1910–11), and 'Platonism and Neoplatonism' by A. H. Armstrong in the 15th ed. (1974) of the *Enc. Brit.*
5. Aristotle, *Met.*, and *De Coelo* (e.g. ii, 9 on the harmony of the spheres).
6. Dante Alighieri, *Divina Commedia*, I, 1–3.
7. The *Vita Nuova* (implying both 'Young Life' and 'New Life', as the contents make evident) was probably completed by 1300, and was first printed at Florence in 1576: it contains the story of Dante's love for Beatrice and sonnets upon it, with prose comments, and ends with the famous vision of her instructing him to glorify her celestial transformation.
8. *Inferno*, IX, 61–3.

9. Giovanni Boccaccio, *Genealogia deorum gentilium*, Venice, 1472, ed. Vincenzo Romano, Bari, 1951, Bk. XIV, Ch. 7.

10. Nesca A. Robb, *Neoplatonism of the Italian Renaissance*, London, 1935, is a sound introduction, particularly valuable for its translations and discussions of Neoplatonic poetry, including Michelangelo's. On the broader intellectual climate, a most important and definitive study is B. Weinberg, *A History of Literary Criticism in the Italian Renaissance*, Chicago, 1961, and a useful and informative one is Baxter Hathaway, *The Age of Criticism: The Late Renaissance in Italy*, Ithaca, N.Y., 1962. See also n. 11 below.

11. The standard work is Paul Oscar Kristeller, tr. Virginia Conant, *The Philosophy of Marsilio Ficino*, New York, 1943—a superb study.

12. Frances A. Yates, *Giordano Bruno and the Hermetic Tradition*, Chicago, 1964, is magnificent on the inner meanings and Neoplatonic uses of Hermetic, Cabalistic and other esoteric writings, including magic and astrology as symbolic carriers for psychological intuitions. Her latest study as I write is *The Occult Philosophy in the Elizabethan Age*, London, 1979. D. P. Walker, *Spiritual and Demonic Magic from Ficino to Campanella*, London, 1958, is just as interesting on a similar range of topics, again stressing the deliberately psychological interpretation of them in Neoplatonic writings of the period; in particular, the symbolism of the supposed Orphic doctrines is brought out, and also the central symbolism of the sun in this and other connections. Indeed a fascinating line of enquiry, and closely relevant to our modern interest in depth-psychology.

13. C. G. Jung, *Zwei Schriften über Analytische Psychologie*, 1928/43, Engl. tr. R. F. C. Hull, *Coll. Wks.*, Vol. 7, London, 1953, as *Two Essays on Analytical Psychology* (the essays were extensively revised). Other works by Jung of relevance to this present book in its Neoplatonic aspects include *Symbole der Wandlung*, 1912/52, tr. as *Symbols of Transformation*, in Vol. 5, 1956 (this is the greatly revised version of the *Psychology of the Unconscious*, the early work which established Jung's independent reputation); *Die Psychologie der Übertragung*, 1946, tr. as *The Psychology of the Transference*, Vol. 16, 1954 (an outstanding investigation especially relevant here for the symbolical imagery of alchemy in its psychological implications); *Psychologie und Alchemie*, 1944, tr. as *Psychology and Alchemy*, Vol. 12, 1953 (a further rich source for mythological symbols); *Aion*, 1951, tr. as *Aion: Contributions to the Symbolism of the Self* in Part II of Vol. 9, entitled *Archetypes and the Collective Unconscious*, 1959 (a work central to Jung's developed conceptions). For Michelangelo and his Neoplatonic representations, see Erwin Panofsky, *Studies in Iconology: Humanist Themes in the Art of the Renaissance*, London and New York, 1939. For a very advanced interpretation of *The Magic Flute* on partly esoteric and partly psychological premisses, see Jocelyn Godwin, 'Layers of Meaning in *The Magic Flute*', *Mus. Quart.*, LXV, 4, Oct. 1979.

14. Philo, I, 5; Dionysius Halicarnassiensis, *Is.*, 11; Cicero, *Att.* 16, 3, 1; Varro, *De Re Rust.*, 3, 5, 8; Juvenal, 2, 7; Martial, 7, 11 and 12, 69; Pliny minor, *Ep.* 5, 10; the word was still uncommon in later antiquity (3rd cent. B.C. to 4th cent. A.D.), but see e.g. Macrobius, *Sat.*, 7, 14; found in Plotinus, 5, 1, 4; Proclus in his commentary on Plato's *Republic* (*In Remp.*, 2, 296 K); Pseudo-Dionysius, *Mys. Th.*, 428A, *De dir. nom*, II, 6; the *Corpus Hermeticum*, ed. Scott, II, 140, 22.

15. See, for Jung's sources and general concepts, the excellent summary and discussion by Iolande Jacobi, tr. R. Mannheim as *Complex Archetype, Symbol*, London, 1942, rev. ed. 1959.

16. For example, *Rep.* X, 595ff.

17. Especially *Pol.*, 1340B–1342B; *De anima*, 407B–408A; and the late, unfinished *Poetics*, 1447Aff. (quotations from IX and XXV). The *De Poetica* (Poetics) of Aristotle was first given a renaissance translation by Lorenzo Valla in 1498 and became of vastly increasing influence through the sixteenth century.

18. *Tutti le Lettioni di Giovanni Battista Gelli, Fatte da lui nella Accademia Fiorentina*, Florence, 1551, [Sig. Aa₂]. And see Ch. IX, n. 20.

19. The collected works were published as *Marsilii Ficini Opera Omnia* at Basel in 1561; there is a facsimile of the edition of Basel, 1576, edited, with introduction, by Paul Oscar Kristeller (see also n. 11 above). All page references here and later in this book are to this facsimile: here, the references are to pp. 255ff.; 263ff.; 20; 241ff.; 250ff.; 209; 208; 241ff.; 399; 638. In comparing psychological with physiological behaviour-patterns, a valuable text-book is Aubrey Manning, *An Introduction to Animal Behaviour*, London, 1967, 2nd ed. 1972, which includes the interesting statement (p. 150) that 'all behaviour has an inherited basis, but strictly speaking it is only a potentiality which is inherited'—as Ficino also put it. This applies to our experience of the archetypes both in a Neoplatonic and in a Jungian context.

20. Pico della Mirandola, a great disputant, an expounder of the Cabala, a qualified opponent of astrology, and at one time in danger for heretical opinions, ended his short life under the influence of Savonarola. His works were edited by his nephew Giov. Fran. Pico and published two years posthumously at Bologna in 1496. References here are to the *Commento*, III, xi, 9, ed. Garin, p. 580; and *De hominibus dignitate*, ed. Garin, p. 162.

Chapter III

1. See Ernst Hans Gombrich's brilliantly suggestive 'Botticelli's Mythologies, a Study in the Neoplatonic Symbolism of his Circle', *Journ. of the Warburg and Courtauld Institutes*, VIII, 1945, pp. 7–60; and more generally his *Art and Illusion: a Study in the Psychology of Pictorial Representation*, London, 1972; also Aby Warburg, *Sandro Botticelli's 'Geburt der Venus' und 'Frühling'*, Leipzig, 1893 (in *Gesammelte Schriften*, Leipzig and Berlin, 1932); also Erwin Panofsky's powerful *Studies in Iconology: Humanist Themes in the Art of the Renaissance*, London and New York, 1939, climaxing with the Neoplatonic elements in Michelangelo. Edgar Wind, *Pagan Mysteries in the Renaissance*, London, 1958, 2nd enlarged ed., London, 1967, is a seminal study on the element of Neoplatonic symbolism in all the arts of that period, with especial attention to painting. An earlier study of great value in the same direction is Jean Seznec, *La survivance des dieux antiques*, London, 1940, tr. Barbara Sessions as *The Survival of the Pagan Gods*, New York 1953. A further investigation is Don Cameron Allen, *Mysteriously Meant: the Rediscovery of Allegorical Interpretation in the Renaissance*, Baltimore, 1970. A. Grafton, 'On the Scholarship of Politian and Its Context', *Journ. of the Warburg and Courtauld Institutes*, XL, 1977, pp. 150–88, shows him pioneering a stricter scholarly discipline far in advance of his day and very valuable to the course of humanist studies. But the great modern pioneer of this approach to renaissance art by way of its symbolical contents was Aby Warburg (who gave its name to the Warburg Institute); his highly important writings (including that mentioned above in this note) may be consulted most conveniently in the *Gesammelte Schriften*, Leipzig and Berlin, 1932. See also Ch. II, n. 12.

2. The sources and the early variants of the Orpheus legend will be found briefly discussed by Maurice Bowra, 'Orpheus and Eurydice', *Classical Quarterly*, New Series II (July-Oct. 1952), pp. 113–26. For the Orphic mysteries and doctrines, see Ch. II, n. 2. On the attitude of Ficino and his Neoplatonic circle, of which Poliziano was so prominent a member, to Orphic traditions, see especially D. P. Walker's valuable article, 'Orpheus the Theologian and Renaissance Platonists', *Journ. of the Warburg and Courtauld Institutes*, XVI, 1953, pp. 100–20. For the relevance to Ficino's circle of the pastoral drama *Orfeo* by Poliziano (who was so intimate a member of it) see Edgar Wind, *Pagan Mysteries in the Renaissance*, London, 1958, esp. p. 163 of the enlarged ed. of 1967. For a good modern text and discussion of this *Orfeo*, see Angelo Poliziano, *La Favola di Orfeo*, ed. Giosue Carducci, Bologna, 2nd ed., 1912. Of the three surviving manuscript versions, the first two are in Carducci, with a good commentary on their probable dates.

The second version, which must date from after 1480, is entitled *Orphei Tragoedia*, and is not certainly by Poliziano: the differences are considerable, though the poem is substantially the same. I have not seen the third version. Alfred Einstein, in *The Italian Madrigal*, Princeton, 1949, ed. of 1971, p. 34, following a confusion made by a nineteenth-century copyist, misattributed some of the music for this play (none of which survives) to 'a certain Germi'; he is a ghost composer who should now be gently laid to rest. Nino Pirrotta, *Li due Orfei, da Poliziano a Monteverdi*, Turin, 1969, is as lively as this author's distinguished best, and includes a discussion of many related *intermedi*, but regards Poliziano's *Orfeo* as a 'proto-opera', which implies a different definition of opera from mine. The last portion is in effect an Italian version of Pirrotta's chapter, 'Early Opera and Aria', in *New Looks at Italian Opera, Essays in Honor of Donald Grout* ed. Wm. W. Austin, Ithaca, N.Y., 1968, pp. 39–107. Important for the Neoplatonic connection is J.B. Friedman, *Orpheus in the Middle Ages*, Cambridge, Mass., 1970.

3. See n. 1 above.
4. See n. 2 above and Ch. II, n. 2.
5. The dress of Thracian bacchanals was made of the skin of the fox (βασσάρα); hence the title of the lost *Bassarids* (Βασσάραι) by Aeschylus, for which see Ch. XI, n. 49.
6. For example, Natale Conti, *Mythologiae*, Venice, 1567, ed. of Venice, 1581, pp. 505ff.
7. In the *Vita Nuova*: see Ch. II, n. 7.
8. Plato, *Symp.* 179D, where Orpheus is shown only a wraith of his Euridice, because he lacked the courage really to die for her like Alcestis for Admetus. And see *Rep.* 620a.
9. Marsilio Ficino, *Opera Omnia*, ed. of Basel, 1576, p. 119; see Ch. II, n. 19.
10. *Poetics*, Vi, 1449b, 27.
11. See B. Weinberg, *A History of Literary Criticism in the Italian Renaissance*, 2 Vols., Chicago, 1961, Vol. II, pp. 1074–105.
12. John Bettley, 'North Italian *Falsobordone* and its Relevance to the early *Stile Recitativo*', *Proc. of the Roy. Mus. Ass.*, Vol. 103, 1976–7 (publ. 1978), pp. 1–18.
13. Pierre de Ronsard, *Works*, ed. H. Vaganay, Paris, IV, 1924, p. 159.
14. Sir John Harrington, *Orlando Furioso in English Heroical Verse*, London, 1591 — with 'A Preface, or rather a brief Apologie of Poetrie' (in *Elizabethan Critical Essays*, ed. G. Gregory Smith, II, Oxford, 1904).
15. Jon A. Quitsland, 'Spenser's *Amoretti VIII* and Platonic Commentaries on Petrarch', *Journ. of the Warburg and Courtauld Institutes*, XXXVI, 1973, pp. 256–76, is most valuable altogether on Spenser's Platonism under both Italian and French influences.
16. John Bunyan, *The Pilgrim's Progress from this world, to That which is to come; Delivered under the Similitude of a Dream. . .*, London, 1678, prefatory poem.
17. Among a very large number of books searching into the inner meaning of music and the other arts, from a wide variety of viewpoints, are William Coker, *Music and Meaning*, New York, 1972 — highly intelligent on a behaviourist approach; John Dewey, *Art as Experience*, Chicago, 1934 — something of a classic; Gordon Epperson, *The Musical Symbol*, Chicago, 1967 — a musician's elaboration of Langer's approach, for which see below; Ernst Hans Gombrich, *Art and Illusion: a Study in the Psychology of Pictorial Representation*, London, 1972 — a radical investigation; and his *Symbolic Images: Studies in the Art of the Renaissance*, London, 1972 — from a Neoplatonic angle; Arthur Koestler, *The Act of Creation*, New York, 1964 — a creative vision indeed though with blind spots due to overlooking the archetypal dimension; I. A. Richards, *Practical Criticism*, London, 1964 — philosophically interesting (more so than his provocative study with R. Ogden, *The Meaning of Meaning*, London, 1932); Susanne K. Langer, *Philosophy in a New Key: Study in the Symbolism of Reason, Rite and Art*, Harvard, 1957 — decidedly a

breakthrough; and her *Reflections on Art*, New York, 1961—an intensification of the above; Terence McLaughlin, *Music and Communication*, London, 1970—a suggestive essay on broadly post-Freudian and post-Jungian lines; Jacques Maritain, *Creative Intuition in Art and Poetry*, New York, 1953—oddly inconclusive but valuable for many passing insights; Wilfrid Mellers, *Caliban Reborn: Renewal in Twentieth-Century Music*, New York, Evanston and London, 1967—suggestive on music's underside; Leonard B. Meyer, *Emotion and Meaning in Music*, Chicago, 1956—the most tenacious search, based on a theory of cumulative associations whose only weakness lies in taking them too much as 'accidental' and too little as archetypal, and his *Music, the Arts and Ideas*, Chicago, 1968—a still more persistent and minute enquiry; in a class of its own is John Livingston Lowes, *The Road to Xanadu*, Boston and New York, 1927—justly famous for its brilliant investigation into every discoverable association conscious or unconscious working in the mind of Coleridge especially when writing *The Ancient Mariner*, and again only deficient in not realizing how richly these incidental associations linked up with archetypal images; Anton Ehrenzweig, *The Hidden Order of Art: a Study in the Psychology of Artistic Imagination*, Berkeley and Los Angeles, 1967—an excellent example both of the limitations and of the strengths of post-Freudian analysis; that profoundly suggestive though inconclusive study, rightly famous, Edmund Wilson's *The Wound and the Bow*, London, 1941; and two anthologies, *Art and Psychoanalysis*, ed. William Phillips, New York, 1957—mainly Freudian and in part of much suggestiveness—and *The Creative Process*, ed. Brewster Ghiselin, Berkeley, Calif., 1952—a very remarkable assortment of mainly perceptive essays from various angles of approach. My own largely post-Jungian study, *Wagner's 'Ring' and Its Symbols: the Music and the Myth*, London, 1963, still strikes me as holding some points of interest. For a massive and very impressive new study of the physiological links between mind and matter, see J. Z. Young, *Programs of the Brain*, Oxford, 1978. See also Anthony Storr's important *Dynamics of Creation*, London, 1977.

18. References as at Ch. I, n. 2.
19. Goethe to Eckermann, in Richard Friedenthal, *Goethe: His Life and Times*, London, 1965, p. 493.
20. Thomas Carlyle, *Sartor Resartus*, Boston, 1836 (first with poor success in *Fraser's Magazine*, 1833–4), ed. P. C. Parr, Oxford, 1913, p. 159.
21. Plato, *Phaedrus*, 246ff. has the famous comparison of the soul pulled by two horses of opposite temperament and controlled with difficulty, if at all, by the charioteer.
22. Ronsard: see n. 13 above.

Chapter IV

1. Wolfgang Osthoff, *Theatergesang und darstellende Musik in der italienischen Renaissance (15. und 16. Jahrhundert)*, 2 vols., Tutzing, 1969, is a detailed, comprehensive and invaluable study in text and music of pre-operatic theatre music. An excellent specialized study is John P. Cutts, *La Musique de scène de la troupe de Shakespeare*, Paris, 1959; and a more general one of much insight is F. W. Sternfeld, *Music in Shakespearian Tragedy*, London, 1963; see also John H. Long, ed., *Music in English Renaissance Drama*, Lexington, 1968. A new stage of research is represented by two reports edited by Maria Teresa Muraro, *Studi sul teatro veneto fra rinascimento ed età barocca*, Florence, 1971, and *Venezia e il melodramma nel seicento*, Florence, 1976, with distinguished contributions from Bruno Brizi, Marie-Françoise Christout, William Holmes, Giovanni Morelli, and with Thomas Walker, Pierluigi Petrobelli and others continuing through the seventeenth century.
2. For one variant see C. R. Baskerville, *The Elizabethan Jig*, Chicago, 1929.
3. Leo Schrade, *La Représentation d'Edipo Tiranno*, Paris, 1960.
4. Leeman Perkins, 'Mode and Structure in the Masses of Josquin', *Journ. American*

Musicological Soc., XXVI, 2, 1973, pp. 189–239, is interesting on the transition from modal to key tonality. See also James Haar, 'False Relations and Chromaticism in Sixteenth-Century Music', *Journ. American Musicological Soc.*, XXX, 3, Fall 1977. An outstanding study is Edward E. Lowinsky, *Tonality and Atonality in Sixteenth-Century Music*, Berkeley and Los Angeles, 1961.

5. Henricus Glareanus, *Dodecachordon*, Basel, 1547.
6. John Bull, *Ut re mi*, Fitzwilliam Virginal Book, Cambridge, I, 183; Alfonso Ferrabosco the Younger, *Ut re mi*, Christ Church, Oxford, MS 2, à 4 at f.80, à 5 at f.138; etc. But already in Josquin the cycle of fifths was used: see James Haar, 'False Relations and Chromaticism in Sixteenth-Century Music', *Journ. American Musicological Soc.*, XXX, 3, Fall 1977.
7. For a good discussion see Cecil Adkins, ed., *L'Amfiparnaso . . . with Historical and Analytical Essays*, Chapel Hill, N.C., 1977.
8. For an enthusiastic account of the earliest surviving Welsh music for the harp and its full two-handed vertical harmony, see Arnold Dolmetsch, in *The Consort*, June 1934, and 'Translations from the Penlynn Manuscript of Ancient Harp Music', Vol. I, Llangefni, 1937. For a more restrained account, see Peter Crossley-Holland, in *Grove's Dict. of Music and Musicians*, 5th ed. London, 1954, Vol. III, p. 399, cols. 1–2, and Vol. IX, p. 135, col. 2 to p. 136, col. 1. See also Thurston Dart, 'Robert ap Huw's Manuscript . . .', *Galpin Soc. Journ.* XXI, March, 1968.

Chapter V

1. Among the numerous primary and secondary sources for the Italian interludes of the sixteenth century are [Baccio Baldini], *Discorso sopra la masquerata della genealogia . . .*, Florence, 1566; Howard Mayer Brown, 'Psyche's Lament: Some Music for the Medici Wedding in 1565', in *Words and Music: the Scholar's View . . . in Honor of A. Tillman Merritt*, ed. Laurence Berman, Cambridge, Mass., 1972, pp. 1–27, and his important *Sixteenth-Century Instrumentation: the Music for the Florentine Intermedii*, [Rome], 1973; Robert L. Weaver, 'Sixteenth-Century Instrumentation', *Mus. Quart.*, XLVII 1961, pp. 363–78; Federico Ghisi, *Feste musicali della Firenze Medicea (1480–1589)*, Florence, 1939; Henry Kaufmann, 'Music for a Noble Florentine Wedding (1539)', in *Words and Music . . .*, ed. Laurence Berman, Cambridge, Mass., 1972, pp. 161–88; Angelo Ingegneri, *Della poesia rappresentativa e del modo di rappresentare le favole sceniche*, Ferrara, 1598; [Christofano Malvezzi], *Nono Parte. Intermedii et Concerti . . .*, Venice, 1591 (for the 1589 interludes); Andrew C. Minor and Bonner Mitchell, *A Renaissance Entertainment: Festivities for the Marriage of Cosimo I, Duke of Florence, 1539 . . .*, Columbia, Miss., 1968; A. d'Ancona, *Le origini de teatro italiano*, 2 vols., Turin, 1891 (a basic study); A. M. Nagler, *Theatre Festivals of the Medici, 1539–1637*, Yale, 1964 (the standard work on plots, scenery and machinery, but has not much on music); Bastiano de' Rossi, *Descrizione dell' apparato e degl' Intermedi . . .*, Florence, 1589; Leo Schrade, 'Les Fêtes du mariage de Francesco dei Medici et de Bianca Cappello', in *Les Fêtes de la renaissance*, I, Paris, 1956, pp. 107–44; Jean Seznec, 'La Masquerade des dieux à Florence en 1566', *Mélanges d'archéologie et d'histoire*, LII, 1935, pp. 224–43; Angelo Solerti, *Musica, ballo e drammatica . . .*, Florence, 1905 (documents relating to the Medici court); Oscar G. Sonneck, 'A Description of A. Striggio's and F. Corteccia's Intermedi "Psyche and Amor", 1565', in his *Miscellaneous Studies in the History of Music*, New York, 1921; D. P. Walker, ed., *Les Fêtes de Florence (1589), I, Musique des intermèdes de la Pelegrina*, Paris, 1963 (with excellent notes by Federico Ghisi, D. P. Walker and J. Jacquot); D. P. Walker, 'La Musique des intermèdes florentins de 1589 et l'humanisme', in *Les Fêtes de la renaissance*, I, Paris, 1956, pp. 133–44; Aby Warburg, 'I Costumi teatrali per gli intermezzi de 1589', in *Atti del' Accademia del R. Istituto Musicale di Firenze*, Florence, 1895; also in his *Gesammelte Schriften*, Leipzig and Berlin, 1932, pp. 259–300; this shows how deliberately Bardi set out to depict here 'one of the

most profound allegories of Plato'. The survey of theatrical music leading towards opera in August Wilhelm Ambros, *Geschichte der Musik*, IV, Leipzig, 1909, 3rd ed. rev. and enl. by Hugo Leichentritt, pp. 161–346, is remarkably comprehensive. Cesare Molinari, *Le nozze degli dei, un saggio sul grande spettacolo italiano nel seicento*, Rome, 1968, is interesting in connecting Bardi's Interludes of 1585/6 with Ripa, Cartari and other expositions of Neoplatonic thought. A very fine article, in the front line of our advancing knowledge, is Iain Fenlon, 'Music and Spectacle at the Gonzaga Court, *c.*1580–1600', *Proc. of the Roy. Mus. Ass.*, Vol. 103, 1976–7 (publ. 1978). Nino Pirrotta, *s.v.* 'Intermedium' in MGG, is excellent: see also *Enc. della spettacolo*, VI, Rome, 1959.

2. The standard work is Margaret M. McGowan, *L'Art du Ballet de Cour en France, 1581–1643*, Paris, 1963; but a mass of fascinating background information and discussion will be found in Frances Yates, *The French Academies of the Sixteenth Century*, London, 1947 — a splendid book though not primarily musical. See also: Balthasar de Beaujoyeulx, ed., and others, *Circe ou le Ballet comique de la royne*, Paris, 1582, tr. and introd., Carol and Lander MacClintock, [n. p.], 1971; Giacomo Alessandro Caula, *Baltazarini e il 'Ballet Comique de la Royne'*, Florence, 1964; Catherine de Parthenay, ed. and introd. Raymond Ritter, *Ballets Allégoriques en Vers, 1592–3*, Paris, 1927; Henry Prunières, 'Ronsard et les fêtes de cour', *Revue Musicale*, V, (May 1924), pp. 27–44, and *Le Ballet de Cour en France avant Benserade et Lully*, Paris, 1914; Julien Tiersot, 'Ronsard et la musique de son temps', *Sammelbände der Internationalen Musikgesellschaft*, IV (1902–3), pp. 70–142.

3. See A. M. Nagler, *Theatre Festivals of the Medici, 1539–1637*, Yale, 1964, p. 120.

4. See under Howard Mayer Brown and Oscar Sonneck in n. 1 above.

5. Lucius Apuleius, *Metamorphoses* (2nd cent. A.D., popularly known as *The Golden Ass*), Books IV–VI. There is a Jungian study of the tale by Erich Neumann, *Amor and Psyche*, New York, 1956.

6. Giovanni Boccaccio, *Genealogiae deorum gentilium*, Venice, 1472, ed. V. Romano, Bari, 1951, I, p. 259.

7. Pico della Mirandola, *Opera*, Venice, 1519, ff. 18v–19r.

8. See Liddell and Scott, *Lexicon, s.v.* Ψυχή, p. 2026 col. 2 in ed. of Oxford, 1968.

9. See under Baldini and Seznec in n. 1 above.

10. For an excellent overview of the *study* of ancient mythology from antiquity down to the present day, see Otto Gruppe, *Geschichte der klassischen Mythologie . . .*, Leipzig, 1921.

11. Baccio Baldini: see n. 1 above.

12. Jean François Champollion, *Sur l'écriture hiératique*, Paris, 1821.

13. Lawrence F. Bernstein, 'The "Parisian Chanson": Problems of Style and Terminology', *Journ. of American Musicology*, XXXI, 2, Summer 1978, pp. 193–240.

14. See for the general situation Frances Yates' pioneering study, *The French Academies of the Sixteenth Century*, London, 1947, whose range of topic and of vision is so much wider than its title suggests; and D. P. Walker's excellent article, 'The *Prisca Theologia* in France', *Journ. of the Warburg and Courtauld Institutes*, XVII, 1954, pp. 204–59. Also Jean Seznec, 'Les manuels mythologiques italiens et leurs diffusions en Angleterre à la fin de la renaissance', in *Mélanges d'archéologie et d'histoire*, Paris, 1933; and Guy Demerson's very long and valuable *La Mythologie classique dans l'oeuvre lyrique de la 'Pléiade'*, Geneva, 1972.

15. The edition of 1565 will be found in the collected works, ed. G. Cohen, [Paris], 1950, II, pp. 997ff.

16. Marin Mersenne, *Harmonie universelle*, 2 parts, Paris, 1636–7, 'Traitez de la Voix, et des Chants', p. 179; and see n. 18 below.

17. The most thorough study is D. P. Walker's unpublished thesis, 'Vers et musique mesurés à l'antique' (1940), Bodleian Lib., Oxford. Daniel Heartz, '*Voix de ville*: Between Humanist Ideals and Musical Realities', in *Words and Music: the Scholar's View . . . In Honor of A. Tillman Merritt*, ed. Laurence Berman, Harvard, 1972,

pp. 115–35, is valuable and relevant. And see Claude Le Jeune, *Airs*, Paris, 1608, ed. D. P. Walker, Vol. I, Introd. by François Lesure and D. P. Walker ('Part I of the Premier Livre'), Rome, 1951.

18. Marin Mersenne, *Harmonie universelle*, 2 parts, Paris, 1636–7: see the Introd. by François Lesure to the facsimile of the copy in Bibl. des Arts et Métiers, 3 vols., Paris, 1963. Mersenne's discussion of poetic scansion and rhythm in their relation to music comes in Pt. IV, pp. 374ff. of the 'Traitez des Consonances . . .'; see also pp. 170ff. and esp. p. 179 of the 'Traitez de la Voix . . .'.

19. Sir Thomas Elyot, *The Boke named the Governour*, London, 1531, ed. H. H. S. Croft, 2 vols., London, 1880, ed. of 1967, p. 239. The reference to 'Tulli' is Cicero, *De Officiis*, Lib. 1, cap. 43.

20. The authoritative study is Allardyce Nicoll, *Stuart Masques and the Renaissance Stage*, London, 1937. Enid Welsford, *The Court Masque*, Cambridge, 1927, is now a little dated, but E. J. Dent, *The Foundations of English Opera*, Cambridge, 1928, preserves like so much of his more distinguished writings a remarkably enduring value. Willa McClung Evans, *Ben Jonson and Elizabethan Music*, London, 1929, has plenty of valuable detail, and the benefit of a new Preface (mainly bibliographical) to the facsimile edition, New York, 1965. The following are valuable on Ben Jonson from various angles of approach: David Fuller, 'The Jonsonian Masque and Its Music', *Music and Letters*, LIV, No. 4, Oct. 1973, pp. 440ff.; Allan H. Gilbert, *The Symbolic Persons in the Masques of Ben Jonson*, Durham, 1948; Paula Johnson, *Form and Transformation in Music and Poetry of the English Renaissance* (better on the poetry than the music, but philosophically interesting), New Haven and London, 1972; Enid Welsford, 'Italian Influence on the English Court Masque', *Mod. Lang. Rev.*, XVIII, 1923, pp. 934ff; Andrew J. Sabol, 'New Documents on Shirley's Masque, "The Triumph of Peace"', *Music and Letters*, XLVII, Jan. 1966, pp. 10–26; a most impressive and scholarly volume is Andrew J. Sabol, ed., *Four Hundred Songs and Dances from the Stuart Masque*, with full annotations and introduction, Providence, Rhode Island, 1979; Jean Seznec, 'Les manuels mythologiques italiens et leur diffusions en Angleterre à la fin de la renaissance', in *Mélanges d'archéologie et d'histoire*, Paris, 1933; Alan Levitan, *The Life of Our Design: the Jonsonian Masque as Baroque Form*, dissert., Princeton, 1964; John C. Meagher, 'The Dance and the Masques of Ben Jonson', *Journ. of the Warburg and Courtauld Institutes*, XXV, 1962, pp. 258–77—bringing out the Neoplatonic implications, especially in regard to the theories of measured poetry, music and dance, and more generally to the humanist union of the arts; see also Barbara C. Garner, 'Francis Bacon, Natalis Comes [i.e. Natale Conti] and the Mythological Tradition', *Journ. of the Warburg and Courtauld Institutes*, XXXIII, 1970, pp. 264–91—showing the debt of Bacon's rather disappointing *De Sapientia Veterum*, London, 1609, to Conti's *Mythologiae* of Venice, 1567, of which the opening premiss of Bk. X is 'all the dogmas of philosophy are to be contained in fables': see n. 24 below; and Murray Lefkowitz' admirably discussed *Trois masques à la cour de Charles Ier d'Angleterre*, Paris, 1970. Also Sarah Thesiger, 'The *Orchestra* of Sir John Davies and the Image of the Dance', *Journ. of the Warburg and Courtauld Institutes*, XXXVI, 1973, pp. 277–304. See also n. 14 above.

21. Pierre de Ronsard, *Oeuvres Complètes*, ed. H. Vaganay, Paris, 1924, p. 80; and see n. 14 above.

22. Consult for this personage Giacomo Alessandro Caula, *Baltazarini e il 'Balet comique de la royne'*, Florence, 1964. See also n. 2 above.

23. Balthasar de Beaujoyeulx, ed., and others, *Circe ou le Balet comique de la royne*, Paris, 1582; facs. Turin, 1965; tr. with an excellent introd., Carol and Lander MacClintock, [n.p.], 1971.

24. Natale Conti (Natalis Comes), *Mythologiae sive Explicationis fabularum libri decem*, Venice, 1567. The prior edition sometimes attributed to 1551 is now thought not to have existed. The reference for the quotation in my text here is to Bk. VI, Ch. vi, '*De Circe*'—in the ed. of Venice, 1581, which I have used here, pp. 374–80.

25. See Ch. II, n. 9.
26. See Ch. III, n. 13.
27. See Catherine de Parthenay, ed. and introd. Raymond Ritter, *Ballets allégoriques en vers, 1592–3*, Paris, 1927, p. 17.
28. *Symp.* 189e ff. An alchemical elaboration of the hermaphrodite in connection with the sacred marriage is found in the *Rosarium philosophorum*, Frankfurt, 1550, of which the symbolism is extensively and illuminatingly discussed by C. G. Jung in *The Psychology of the Transference*, for which see Ch. II, n.13. Also discussed in relation to Wagner's use of transformation by fire and water in my *Wagner's 'Ring' and Its Symbols*, London, 1963, pp. 269ff.
29. Ed. of Venice, 1581, p. 377.
30. *Circe*, Paris, 1582, pp. 74–6.
31. Ed. of Venice, 1581, p. 378.
32. Ed. of Venice, 1581, p. 379.
33. *Eth. Nic.*, II, ii–iv.
34. Barbara Russano Hanning, 'The Influence of Humanist Thought and Italian Renaissance Poetry on the Formation of Opera', Ph.D. diss., Yale, 1968. See also her valuable article, 'Apologia pro Ottavio Rinuccini, *Journ. American Musicological Soc.*, XXVI, 2, Summer 1973, pp. 240–62; an interesting but inconclusive criticism of it by Gary A. Tomlinson, 'Ancora su Ottavio Rinuccini', id. XXVIII, Summer 1975, pp. 351–6; and her very able reply, id. XXIX, Fall 1976, pp. 501–3.
35. Cesare Molinari, *Le nozze degli dei, un saggio sul grande spettacolo italiano nel seicento*, Rome, 1968.
36. See Alfred Einstein, *The Italian Madrigal*, 3 vols., Princeton, 1949, II, p. 730.
37. See Ch. V, n. 1, esp. Malvezzi, Rossi, Walker, Warburg.
38. *Rep.*, X, 614ff.
39. Ovid, *Metamorphoses*, I, 150.
40. London, Theatre Museum.
41. *Imagini*, 2nd ed., Venice, 1571, p. 304: see note 42 below.
42. Lilio Gregorio Giraldi (Giraldus), *De deis gentium varia et multiplex historia . . .*, Basel, 1548; Vincenzo Cartari, *Le Imagini, con la spositione de i dei de gli antichi*, Venice, 1556 (the second edition of Venice, 1571, first included the numerous engravings by Bolognino Zaltieri; the nature, number and quality of illustrations in subsequent editions varies); for Conti, see n. 24 above.
43. Dante, *Paradiso*, IV, 40–45.
44. Ovid, *Metamorphoses*, Bk. V.
45. Plato, *Laws*, II, 653ff.

Chapter VI

1. Sarah Jane Williams, *Journ. Amer. Musicological Soc.*, XXI, 3, 1968, pp. 251–7.
2. Howard Mayer Brown, 'Fantasia on a theme by Boccaccio', *Early Music*, V, 3, July 1977, pp. 324–39.
3. Pietro Bembo, *Gli Asolani*, Venice, 1505, in *Opere in Volgare*, ed. Mario Marti, Florence, 1961, pp. 14ff.
4. Baldassare Castiglione, *Il libro del cortegiano*, Venice, 1528, tr. Sir Thomas Hoby as *The Courtyer. . .*, London, 1561, ed. W. H. D. Rouse, London, [1928], pp. 61ff.
5. Gioseffo Zarlino, *Le istitutioni armoniche*, Venice, 1558, in *Tutte l'opere*, I, Venice, 1589, p. 92; elsewhere in IV, 32; Plato, *Republic*, 398d.
6. Michael Kelly, *Reminiscences*, London, 1826, I, p. 119.
7. Article in *Grove V, Supplementary Volume*, London, 1961, p. 147.
8. Paul Collaer, 'Lyrisme baroque et tradition populaire', in *Les Colloques de Wegimont*, IV, Paris, 1963, pp. 109–30.
9. Alfred Einstein, *The Italian Madrigal*, Princeton, II, 1949 (see Ch. 11 and Ch. 12)

included examples: there is an important study of the genre in Carol MacClintock's fine *Giaches de Wert*, [n.p.], 1966, esp. pp. 165ff. (see also pp. 178ff., 198ff.); and Claude V. Palisca not only traces the connection but is extremely interesting on improvised singing within traditional patterns in his valuable article, 'Vincenzo Galilei and Some Links between "Pseudo-Monody" and Monody', *Mus. Quart.*, XLVI, 3, July 1960, pp. 344–60. Further material on the precedents of the reciting style will be found in Otto Kinkeldey, *Orgel und Klavier in der Musik des 16. Jahrhunderts*, Leipzig, 1910, Ch. 6 (a classic in its own right); in Federico Ghisi, 'La tradition musicale des fêtes florentines et les origines de l'opéra', *Musique des intermèdes de "La Pelegrina"*, ed. D. P. Walker, Paris, 1963, pp. xi–xxii; and best of all, in Wm. V. Porter, 'The Origins of the Baroque Solo Song: A Study of Italian Manuscripts and Prints from 1590 to 1610', dissertation, Yale University, 1962. A monumental study is Warren Kirkendale, *L'Aria di Fiorenza*, Florence, 1972.

10. Plato, *Republic*, III, 398ff.; and see Liddell and Scott *s.v.* λογός, esp. VIII on p. 1059 in ed. of 1968. See also *Rep.*, III, 400 D ff., for a parallel passage.

11. Dean T. Mace, 'Pietro Bembo and the Literary Origins of the Italian Madrigal', *Mus. Quart.*, LV, 1, Jan. 1969, pp. 65–86.

12. The most relevant parts of Bembo's discussion will be found in Pietro Bembo, *Prose . . . della volgar lingua*, Venice, 1525, ed. Mario Marti, Padua, 1955, pp. 73ff.

13. Of Dante's Latin treatise, *De vulgari eloquentia*, two books only exist out of the four intended. An Italian translation by Trissino was published at Vicenza in 1529; the Latin original first at Paris in 1577. The work as it stands is both long and detailed, and of much interest.

14. There is an uncommonly interesting discussion (showing some French influence) of the problems of setting English words to operatic music in the preface to John Dryden's unsuccessful opera, *Albion and Albanus*, London, 1685.

15. Letter to Marc-André Souchay, 15 Oct. 1842.

16. Gioseffo Zarlino, *Istitutioni armoniche*, Venice, 1558, IV, 32; Thomas Morley, *Plaine and Easie Introduction to Practicall Musicke*, London, 1597, pp. 177ff.

17. William Byrd, *Gradualia*, I, London, 1605, Epistola Dedicatoria.

18. Zarlino, III, 71; Galilei, pp. 88ff.; Morley, pp. 177ff.; and see n. 16 above.

19. See an excellent article by Olga Termini, 'The Transformation of Madrigalisms in Venetian Operas of the later Seventeenth Century', *Music Review*, Feb. 1978, pp. 4–21.

20. Claude Palisca, 'The Alterati of Florence, Pioneers in the Theory of Dramatic Music', in *New Looks at Italian Opera, Essays in Honor of Donald Grout*, ed. Wm. W. Austin, Ithaca, N.Y., 1968, pp. 9–38. See also Edmond Strainchamps, 'New Light on the *Accademia degli Elevati* of Florence', *Mus. Quart.*, LXII, 4, Oct. 1976, pp. 507–35—valuable on this rather later body, one of whose members, however, was Rinuccini.

21. Girolamo Mei, ed. with an invaluable commentary by Claude Palisca, as *Letters on Ancient and Modern Music*, [n.p.], 1960.

22. Pietro de' Bardi's letter was published as part of Ch. 9 of the 'Trattato della musica scenica' by Giovanni Battista Doni, the Roman musicologist and historian; this was written around 1635, and was included with others of his collected writings by A. F. Gori in 2 vols. as *Lyra Barberina* and *De' trattati di musica*, Florence, 1763. An English translation of the letter will be found in Oliver Strunk, ed. and tr., *Source Readings in Music History*, New York, 1950, pp. 363ff.; the original Italian is most easily consulted in Angelo Solerti, *Le Origini del melodramma*, Turin, 1903, pp. 143–7. See also Nino Pirrotta, tr. Nigel Fortune, 'Temperaments and Tendencies in the Florentine Camerata', *Mus. Quart.*, XL, 2, April 1954, pp. 169–89; and especially Claude Palisca, 'The "Camerata Fiorentina": a Reappraisal', *Studi Musicali*, I, 2, 1972, pp. 203–34, which is a masterly study and a reappraisal indeed.

23. For the date of Corsi's death, see Edmond Strainchamps, 'New Light on the

Accademia degli Elevati of Florence', *Mus. Quart.*, LXII, 4, Oct. 1976, pp. 507–35. For Bardi's and Corsi's friendship, see John Walter Hill, 'Oratory Music in Florence', *Act. Mus.*, LI, 1979, i–ii.

24. See Claude Palisca, 'Musical Asides in the Diplomatic Correspondence of Emilio de' Cavalieri', *Mus. Quart.*, XLIX, July 1963, pp. 339–55; also Palisca and Pirrotta in n. 22 above.
25. See n. 21 above.
26. *Lyra Barberina*, II, *Trattati di musica*, Florence, 1763, pp. 233–48: see n. 22 above.
27. See n. 10 above.
28. Aristotle, *Politics*, VIII, 1340a.
29. Zarlino, *Sopplimenti*, Venice, 1588, VII, xi.
30. The term used by Girolamo Frescobaldi in the preface to his *Toccate*, Rome, 1615, 2nd ed. of 1615/16.
31. See n. 22 above.
32. For a sample of something perhaps near to it, see Claude Palisca, 'The "Camerata Fiorentina": a Reappraisal', *Studi Musicali*, I, 2, 1972, pp. 203–34.
33. Giulio Caccini, *Nuove musiche*, Florence, 1602. The title-page has 1601, which may have been meant as Florentine Old-Style dating for 1602; but even so, it is not correct, since we are told in a printer's note that owing to delays in the printing, the actual publication was after and not before 25 March. The reverse of the title-page gives 1602, the correct date on either system. Caccini's dedication is dated 1 February 1601; and this is certainly Florentine Old-Style dating for 1602. The ecclesiastical *licenzia de Superiori* is dated the last of June 1602. The imprimatur is dated 1 July 1602, and that is therefore the earliest month at which publication can have occurred. The licence to print is dated 1 June 1602; but in view of the dates given for the *licenzia de Superiori* and the imprimatur, we can only suppose that this is a mistake for July. On the last page, the date 1602 appears; but there is a sort of smudge which shows that this has been altered on the plate from 1601. In short, 1601 (whether actually or as Florentine Old-Style dating for 1602) was originally intended; but unforeseen factors (which included the death of Caccini's father) delayed publication until 1602 (on either style of dating). The date on the title-page should have been but was not altered; the date on the last page was correctly altered. Thus the date 1601 is wrong on any calculation. The right date is 1602. The best modern edition by far is by Wiley Hitchcock, Madison, 1970, including an excellent translation of the very difficult Italian of Caccini's important preface, and many extremely musicianly comments. It should perhaps be mentioned here that Giulio Caccini's *Nuove Musiche* of Florence, 1614, is not a second impression or a second edition of his *Nuove musiche* of 1602, but a separate work: see Wiley Hitchcock, 'Caccini's "Other" *Nuove musiche*', *Journ. American Musicological Soc.*, XXVII, No. 3, 1974, pp. 438–60. For the reciting style itself, see William V. Porter, 'The Origins of the Baroque Solo Song: A Study of Italian Manuscripts and Prints from 1590 to 1610', dissertation, Yale Univ., 1962, a most detailed and perceptive investigation; Nigel Fortune, 'Italian Secular Song from 1600 to 1635: the Origins and Development of Accompanied Monody', dissertation, Gonville and Caius, Cambridge Univ., 1953, is a very comprehensive survey, and his 'Italian Secular Monody from 1600 to 1635', *Mus. Quart.*, XXXIX, 1953, pp. 171–95, is a condensed account, both excellent; Jan Racek, *Stilprobleme der italienischen Monodie*, Prague, 1965, is a study of great scholarship and insight (in Czech as *Italská monodie. . .*, Prague, 1945). The poetry is very well discussed in Carlo Calcaterra, *Poesia e Canto*, Bologna, 1951, Ch. IV.
34. See Ch. XIV, n. 15 for research on this opera. Its ending is in some question.

Chapter VII

1. There is a good discussion of the term, in all its confusions and ambiguities, in

John H. Baron, 'Monody: a Study in Terminology', *Mus. Quart.*, LIV, 4, Oct. 1968. For the history and the style of monody, see also Ch. XVI, n. 6.
2. Plato, *Laws*, 764D–E.
3. Diomedes, 492K, 489K.
4. Isidorus, *Orig.* 6, 19, 6.
5. Giovanni Battista Doni, *Compendio del trattato de' generi e de' modi della musica*, Rome, 1635, p. 68.
6. Pietro della Valle, 'Della musica dell' età nostra', letter dated 16 Jan. 1640, Rome, in Angelo Solerti, *Origini*, Turin, 1903, pp. 148ff.; see p. 154.
7. G. B. Doni, ed. A. F. Gori, *Trattati*, II, Florence, 1763, pp. 29–30; see Ch. VI, n. 22.
8. See Ch. VI, n. 33.
9. See Ch. VI, n. 30.
10. Giovanni Maria Artusi, . . . *delle imperfettioni della moderna musica*, Venice, I, 1600, II, 1603. The controversy has been brilliantly explained by Claude Palisca, and further pursued by Jerome Roche, Nigel Fortune and Denis Stevens, in several chapters of the *The Monteverdi Companion*, ed. Denis Arnold and Nigel Fortune, London, 1968.
11. In G. F. Malipiero, *Claudio Monteverdi*, Milan, 1930, pp. 291–4. The recipient of this letter was Doni: see D. Stevens, *Letters of Claudio Monteverdi*, London, 1980, pp. 412ff.
12. Sig. C4. See Claude Palisca, 'Marco Scacchi's Defence of Modern Music (1649)', in *Words and Music . . . in Honor of A. Tillman Merritt*, ed. Laurence Berman, Cambridge, Mass., 1972, pp. 189–235.
13. Aristotle, *Pol.*, 1340a.
14. Miles Coverdale, *Goostly psalmes and spirituall songs*, London, [?1539], preface.
15. Erasmus, letter commenting on Corinthians, XIX, 19.
16. Queen Elizabeth's *Injunctions* of 1559, Article 49.
17. Claudio Monteverdi, cited by his brother Giulio Cesare Monteverdi in his annotations to Claudio Monteverdi's *Scherzi musicali*, Venice, 1607.
18. See n. 17 above.
19. Giovanni Maria Artusi, *L'Arte del contrapunto*, Venice, I, 1586, II, 1589, etc. And see n. 10 above.
20. For the remarkable and until recently unsuspected extent to which lightly but genuinely polyphonic madrigals continued to be composed and published and therefore doubtless performed, see Gloria Rose, 'Polyphonic Italian Madrigals of the Seventeenth Century', *Music and Letters*, XLVII, 1966, p. 153.
21. [Ercole Bottrigari], *Il Desiderio, overo De' concerti di varii strumenti musicali*, Venice, 1594, p. 9. Carol MacClintock's translation with commentary, [Rome], 1962, is excellent. For the contemporary meanings and uses of the term concerto, see David Boyden's definitive article, 'When is a Concerto not a Concerto', *Mus. Quart.*, XLIII, April 1957, pp. 220–32.
22. Michael Praetorius, *Syntagma musicum*, 3 vols., Wittenburg and Wolfenbüttel, 1614–20, III, Wolfenbüttel, 1618 (nearly all surviving copies 1619), p. 4.
23. Claudio Monteverdi, *Madrigali guerrieri et amorosi*, Venice, 1638.
24. Robert L. Weaver, 'The Orchestra in Early Italian Opera', *Journ. of the American Musicological Soc.*, XVII, Spring 1964, pp. 83–9, makes good though conservative use of the scanty material; Gloria Rose, 'Agazzari and the Improvising Orchestra', JAMS, XVIII, 3, 1965, carries the investigation to more adventurous conclusions, and is of great interest. See Ch. XI, n. 8; also n. 7, esp. for Tarr and Walker, of fundamental interest for the early operatic orchestra.

Chapter VIII

1. Angelo Solerti, 'Laura Guidiccioni Lucchesini ed Emilio de' Cavalieri', *Rivista Musicale Italiana*, IX, 1902, pp. 797–829; and see Federico Ghisi's valuable intro-

duction to D. P. Walker's admirable discussion and edition of the *Musique des intermèdes de 'La Pelegrina'*, Paris, 1963, pp. xi–xxii.

2. Baldassare Castiglione, *Il libro del cortegiano*, Venice, 1528 (but already finished by 1514), ed. B. Maier, Turin, 1955, p. 124.

3. Nino Pirrotta, 'Early Opera and Aria', in *New Looks at Italian Opera*. . ., ed. Wm. W. Austin, Ithaca, N.Y., 1968, p. 54.

4. Giulio Caccini, *Nuove musiche e nuova maniera di scriverle*, Florence, 1614, preface repr. in A. Solerti, *Origini*, Turin, 1903, pp. 72–5; see esp. p. 75. There is a most valuable discussion of the characteristics of Caccini's style in Claude V. Palisca, *Baroque Music*, Englewood Cliffs, N.J., 1968 (in the Prentice-Hall History of Music).

5. Severo Bonini, MS 2218, Bibl. Riccardiana, Florence, partially repr. in A. Solerti, *Origini*, Turin, 1903.

6. Privately communicated.

7. The Italian text is most readily available in Solerti, *Origini*, Turin, 1903, pp. 143–7. The full English translation by Strunk, ed., *Source Readings*, New York, 1950, pp. 363–6 (or in the separate Vol. III, New York, 1965, pp. 3–6) is satisfactory though not quite literal.

8. In *Trattati di musica*, ed. A. F. Gori, Florence, 1763, II, ix, p. 22; see Ch. VI, n. 22. The extracts in Solerti, *Origini*, Turin, 1903, pp. 195–221, are all of the greatest possible interest.

Chapter IX

1. The libretto as, at the same time, a literary form in its own right and a constituent part of opera, has itself formed the subject of a considerable literature. Oscar Sonneck's classic *Library of Congress Catalogue of Opera Librettos printed before 1800*, Washington D.C., 1914, is a rich mine of comment and information. Alfred-Camille Wotquenne, *Catalogue de la Bibliothèque du Conservatoire royal de musique de Bruxelles*, 4 vols., Brussels, 1898–1912, remains a monument of scholarship; Claudio Sartori, *Catalogo dei libretti d'opera italiani stampato fino al 1800*, a working tool of the highest importance, in preparation but now available in xerox form from Ann Arbor, Mich. (Milan, 1973–). E. J. Dent's article *s.v.* 'Libretto' in *Grove V*, London, 1954, Vol. V, pp. 223–30, remains an invaluable introduction. Patrick J. Smith, *The Tenth Muse, a historical study of the opera libretto*, New York, 1970 (but the very idea that there could be a tenth Muse!) is the book rather of a critic than of a trained scholar, and in addition is tiresomely written; but, after an unsound start, the commentary becomes most interesting and informative. Carlo Calcaterra, *Poesia e canto, studi sulla poesia melica italiana e sulla favola per musica*, Bologna, 1951, is extremely relevant and helpful; Aldo Caselli, *Catalogo delle opere liriche pubblicate in Italia*, Florence, 1969, though not wholly complete or correct, is most valuable; Ulderico Rolandi, *Il libretto per musica attraverso i tempi*, Rome, 1951, is mainly descriptive and very useful all through from the 16th to the 20th centuries, and particularly good on Zeno, Metastasio and Calzabigi; there is a valuable bibliography. Andrea Della Corte, *Drammi per musica allo Zeno*, 2 vols., Turin, 1958, is dogged by carelessness or misfortune, for example in jumbling up alternate passages from *both* endings of Striggio's and Monteverdi's *Orfeo* of 1607, evidently taken from Angelo Solerti's reliable and important *Gli Albori del melodramma*, Milan/Palermo/Naples, [1903–4], where the text as printed by Striggio is given *separately* from the text (in footnotes) as set by Monteverdi. But this same Andrea Della Corte contributes an interesting introduction to his own edition of O. Rinuccini, *Drammi per musica: Dafne, Euridice, Arianna*, Turin, 1926. Barbara Russano Hanning, 'Apologia pro Ottavio Rinuccini', *Journ. of the American Musicological Soc.*, XXVI, 2, Summer 1973, pp. 240–62, is particularly valuable on the poetic forms of the interludes and the early librettos, and the principles of their musical setting. For later baroque opera, Robert Freeman is

remarkably interesting in his 'Opera Without Drama: Currents of Change in Italian Opera, 1675 to 1725, and the Roles Played Therein by Zeno, Caldara and Others', Ph.D. dissertation, Princeton Univ., 1967, though the first words of his title are perhaps a little extreme; and Cuthbert Girdlestone, *La Tragédie en musique (1673–1750) considérée comme genre littéraire*, Geneva, 1972, is characteristically detailed and authoritative, especially on Quinault. Even better on Quinault is Etienne Gros, *Philippe Quinault*, Paris, 1926. Peter Conrad, *Romantic Opera and Literary Form*, Berkeley, 1978, is not very sound; but Gary Schmidgall, *Literature as Opera*, London, 1978, though a little less sound on the music than on the words, is a most serious and valuable discussion of the problem in general. For a detailed view of Venetian librettos at one point, see Karl Leich, *Girolamo Frigimelica Robertis Libretti (1694–1708)*, Munich, 1972.

2. William V. Porter, 'Peri and Corsi's *Dafne*: Some New Discoveries and Observations', *Journ. American Musicological Soc.*, XVIII, 2, 1965, pp. 170–96: a key article, including valuable references to the further literature. Oscar Sonneck's pioneering entry *s.v. Dafne*, in his classic *Library of Congress Catalogue of Opera Librettos*, Washington D.C., 1914, I, pp. 339–45, is still very well worth consulting. And see especially Federico Ghisi, *Alle fonti della monodia*, Milan, 1940, pp. 10ff. F. W. Sternfeld, 'The First Printed Opera Libretto', *Music and Letters*, LIX, 2, April 1978, pp. 121–38, is a most valuable study of the libretto of *Dafne* in its various states (including a new discovery) and the probable performances of the opera. Yves F.-A. Giraud, *La Fable de Daphné*, Geneva, 1969, discusses well the *Dafne* librettos of Rinuccini and Busenello.

3. To be seen in the Theatre Museum, London.

4. In the Florentine MS, Codex 704 (*olim* 8750), Bibl. du Conservatoire Royal de Musique, Brussels.

5. For a discussion of these, see Gary A. Tomlinson, 'Ancora su Ottavio Rinuccini', *Journ. American Musicological Soc.*, XXVIII, Summer 1975, pp. 351–3.

6. Barbara Russano Hanning, paper, 'The Laurel of Victory: A Context for Rinuccini's *Dafne*', read to the Sixth Intern. Congress on Musical Iconography, New York, Spring 1978, publication pending.

7. See Ch. V, nn. 24 and 42.

8. Natale Conti, *Mythologiae*, Venice, 1567, ed. of Venice, 1581, pp. 227–43: see Ch. V, n. 24.

9. Cicero, *De Natura Deorum*, Bk. III.

10. Giordano Bruno, *De gli eroici furori*, I, ii, 349. Compare Heraclitus, Fragm. 67. And see Ch. XI, n. 13.

11. Carl Gustav Jung, *Erinnerungen, Träume, Gedenken. Aufgezeichnet und herausgegeben von Aniela Jaffé*, Zürich and Stuttgart, 1962; transl. Richard and Clara Winston as *Memories, Dreams, Reflections*, [London], 1963, pp. 249–52.

12. Natale Conti, *Mythologiae*, Venice, 1567, ed. of Venice, 1581, p. 377: see Ch. V, n. 24.

13. Plato, *Symp.*, 187A.

14. Plato, *Symp.*, 201D ff.

15. Francesco di Zanobi Cattani da Diaceto, *De Amore*, probably 1508 but published posthumously, Venice, 1561, Bk. II, Ch. i.

16. See Pico della Mirandola, *Commento*, in *Opera Omnia*, Venice, 1572, I, p. 96 and pp. 735ff.: see Ch. II, n. 20.

17. Baldassare Castiglione, *Il libro del cortegiano*, Venice, 1528, IV, lxii, 486; and see Ch. VI, n. 4.

18. Plato, *Symp.*, 180D ff.

19. Titian, 'Venus Blindfolding Cupid', Borghese Gallery, Rome. See Edgar Wind, *Pagan Mysteries in the Renaissance*, London, 1958, 2nd enlarged ed. of 1967, esp. pp. 78–80.

20. Pompeo della Barba, Lecture to the Florentine Academy, April, 1548, in *Esposizione d'un sonetto platonico, fatto sopra il primo effetto d'amore che e il separare l'anima dal*

corpo de l'amante, dove si tratta de la immortalita de l'anima secondo Aristotile, e secondo Platone . . ., Florence, 1549, p. 14: the title alone is very instructive, with its reference to Aristotle's view of the immortality of the soul and Plato's, seen as fundamentally compatible. See also Eugenio Garin, 'Aristotelismo e Platonismo del Rinascimento', *La Rinascità*, Anno 2, Florence, 1939.

21. Giordano Bruno, *Eroici furori*, Part II, Dialogo 1, in *Opere italiene*, ed. G. Gentile, 1925–7, II, pp. 307–519; tr. L. Williams, London, 2 vols., 1887–9, II, p. 30 (the poem is in Vol. II, p. 447; the translation in Vol. II, p. 28).
22. Ficino, ed. of Basel, [1576], p. 1793; see Ch. II, n. 19.
23. 1 Cor. 15:31.
24. See Ch. V, nn. 30 and 31.
25. See n. 6 above; also Ch. V, n. 34.
26. Dante, *Purgatorio*, XVII, 104–5.
27. Dante, *Convivio*, III, ii, 3 and 9.
28. Plato, *Phaedrus*, 252D and 255D.
29. Pico della Mirandola, *De ento et uno*, V, ed. Garin, p. 414, the Orphic Fragment there quoted being Kern 82; and see n. 16 above and Ch. II, n. 20.
30. Ficino, ed. of Basel, [1576], p. 1911; see Ch. II, n. 19.
31. See n. 10 above.
32. Ronsard: see Ch. III, n. 13.

Chapter X

1. See, on this aspect, Silke Leopold's valuable article, 'Das geistliche Libretto im 17. Jahrhundert zur Gattungsgeschichte der frühen Oper', *Die Musikforschung*, 31, Heft 3, July-Sept., 1978, pp. 245–57.
2. See Ch. III, n. 16.
3. Margaret Johnson, 'Agazzari's *Eumelio*, a "Dramma Pastorale" ', *Mus. Quart.*, LVII, 8, July 1971, pp. 491–505.
4. W. K. C. Guthrie, *Orpheus and Greek Religion*, London, 1935, 2nd ed., 1952, p. 31; and Euripides, *Alcestis*, lines 355ff.
5. Francesco Petrarca, *Rime*, CCXLV, l.9.; that the sonnet was taken as describing 'divine' rather than sensual love, at least for the initiated, is made plain in the sixteenth-century edition entitled *Il Petrarcha con l'espositione de M. Giovanni Andrea Gesualdo*, Venice, 1533: see ed. of Venice, 1573, pp. 263ff. And see Ch. XI, n. 17.
6. Ficino, ed. of Basel, [1576], p. 119; see Ch. II, n. 19.
7. See Ch. V, nn. 30 and 31.
8. Marco da Gagliano, *Dafne*, perf. Mantua, 1608, publ. Florence, 1608, preface.
9. Claude V. Palisca, 'The First Performance of "Euridice"', repr. New York, 1964, from the *Twenty-Fifth Anniversary Festschrift* of Queen's College, City University of New York. A particularly interesting comparison of Peri's style with Caccini's will be found in Howard Mayer Brown, 'How Opera Began: an Introduction to Jacopo Peri's *Euridice* (1600)' in *The Late Italian Renaissance, 1525–1630*, ed. Eric Cochrane, London, 1970, pp. 401–43.
10. Michelangelo Buonarrotti the younger, *Descrizione delle felicissimi nozze* . . ., Florence, 1600.
11. See n. 10 above.
12. See Howard Mayer Brown under n. 9 above.
13. See Ch. VI, nn. 22 and 26; also Ch. VII, n. 5.
14. Modena, Archivio di Stato, Cancelleria Ducale, Carteggio degli ambasciatori Estense, Firenze; quoted in A. Solerti, *Musica, ballo e drammatica*, Florence, 1905, p. 23.
15. Claude V. Palisca, 'The First Performance of "Euridice"', p. 8; see n. 9 above.
16. Memorie, Florence, Archivio di Stato, Filza Strozziana XXVII, f. 41; quoted in Solerti, op. cit., p. 25, n. 1.

17. Re-quoted by Solerti, ibid., from E. Costa, 'Le nozze di Enrico IV re di Francia con Maria de' Medici', *Rassegna Emiliana*, I, 188, pp. 113–14.

18. Modena, Archivio di Stato, Cancell. ducale, Carteggio di ambasciatori e agenti estensi a Firenze; quoted in Solerti, op. cit., p. 27, note.

19. Venice, Archivio di Stato, Dispacci da Firenze, 1600, f.a. XVa; quoted in Solerti, ibid.

20. Florence, Archivio di Stato, VI, f. 221; quoted in Solerti, op. cit., p. 26, n. 2.

21. Caccini, *Nuove musiche*, Florence, 1602, p. 19.

22. Florence, Archivio di Stato, Carte Strozziane, CVIII, f. 26; quoted in Solerti, ibid.

23. Quoted in Solerti, op. cit., pp. 34, 38, 66–67.

Chapter XI

1. Raffaello Gualterotti, *Feste . . .*, Florence, 1579, p. 20.

2. Thomas Morley, *Plaine and Easie Introduction to Practicall Musicke*, London, 1597, p. 35.

3. [C. Malvezzi], *Nono Parte. Intermedii e concerti fatti per la commedia . . .*, Venice, 1591, p. 10. See D. P. Walker, in *Les Fêtes de Florence (1589), I, Musique des Intermèdes de la Pelegrina*, ed. Federico Ghisi, D. P. Walker and J. Jacquot, Paris, 1963, esp. p. xxxviii.

4. Francesco Rasi has also been suggested: see a letter from Tim Carter and David Butchart to the *Musical Times* of May 1977. But see Domenico de' Paoli, *Claudio Monteverdi*, Milan, 1945, p. 106: here, Magli is confidently assumed, but there is certainly some confusion in the matter. In recent times, Magli has been described as a castrato. This seems to be a late nineteenth-century conjecture taken over by de' Paoli (and thereafter repeated by others) from Antonio Bertolotti, *Musici alla corte dei Gonzaga in Mantova dal secolo XV al XVIII*, Milan, [1890], who described Gio. Gualberto as a castrato and a pupil of Caccini, but cited no evidence; he did, however, cite a letter showing that Magli was his last name, as well as two others proving the pleasure taken by the Duke (especially) and others in Magli's performances in 'the *favola* sung at our Academy' (pp. 86ff.). The title role of Monteverdi's *Orfeo* really settles the point about the voice by being notated in the tenor clef, since this clef so far as I know was not (like the treble clef) subject to octave transposition. See also, more generally, a good article by Denis Arnold, 'Monteverdi's Singers', *Mus. Times*, Oct. 1970, pp. 982–5.

5. Leo Schrade's very lively and interesting *Monteverdi*, New York, 1950, is a little outmoded in its outlook now; Hans Redlich, *Claudio Monteverdi: Leben und Werk*, Olten, 1949, Engl. tr. by Kathleen Dale, London, 1952, remains significant; Denis Arnold, *Monteverdi*, London, 1963, is admirably dependable and intelligent. *The Monteverdi Companion*, ed. Denis Arnold and Nigel Fortune, London, 1968, contains much that is of value. Anna Amalie Abert's *Claudio Monteverdi und das Musikalische Drama*, Lippstadt, 1954, is important; so is Wolfgang Osthoff, *Das dramatische Spätwerk Claudio Monteverdis*, Tutzing, 1961—a splendidly close and careful study; there is great value in Domenico de' Paoli, *Claudio Monteverdi*, Milan, 1945.

6. [Federico Follino], *Compendio della sontuose feste . . .*, Mantua, 1608.

7. See Anthony Baines, 'The Evolution of Trumpet Music up to Fantini', *Proc. of the Roy. Mus. Ass.*, Vol. 101 (1974–5), pp. 1–9, for an excellent brief survey, with bibliographical references which include an account by Michael Praetorius, *Syntagma musicum*, Wolfenbüttel, 1619, iii [*sic* for III, 1618], 172. Edward H. Tarr and Thomas Walker, 'Die Verwendung der Trompete in der italienischen Oper des 17. Jahrhunderts', *Hamburger Jahrbuch für Musikwissenschaft*, Hamburg, 1978, is of the first importance.

8. This difficult and important topic will be brought up again; but some of the relevant literature may be mentioned here as follows. Taddeo Wiel, *I codici*

musicali contariniani del secolo XVII nella R. Biblioteca di San Marco in Venezia, Venice, 1888 (available in a facsimile reprint, Bologna, n.d.), gives a meticulous account, opera by opera, of the holdings in this famous seventeenth-century collection of manuscripts, and a careful reading of it already yields much instructive information, both on their many gaps and on their intermittent mention of various instruments. An important study is still Gloria Rose, 'Agazzari and the Improvising Orchestra', *Journ. American Musicological Soc.*, XVIII, 3, 1965, pp. 382–91. See also Denis Arnold, '"L'Incoronazione di Poppea" and its Orchestral Requirements', *Mus. Times*, CIV, 1963, pp. 177ff.; R. L. Weaver, 'The Orchestra in Early Italian Opera', *Journ. American Musicological Soc.*, XVII, 1964, pp. 83–9; J. A. Westrup, 'Monteverdi and the Orchestra', *Music and Letters*, XXI, July 1940, pp. 230–45; Stuart Reiner, 'La vaga Angioletta (and others)', *Analecta musicologica*, Band xiv, 1974, p. 54; Jane Glover, *Cavalli*, London, 1978; Thomas Walker, part of article *s.v.* 'Opera' in *The New Grove*, London, 1980; Lorenzo Bianconi and Thomas Walker, 'Production, Consumption and Political Function of 17th-Century Opera', paper at the Berkeley Conference of the International Musicological Society, 1977 (in preparation) — an important study; and for the relevant social and economic factors, H. C. Wolff, *Die venezianische Oper in der zweiten Hälfte des 17. Jahrhunderts*, Berlin, 1937, and Simon Towneley Worsthorne's valuable *Venetian Opera in the Seventeenth Century*, Oxford, 1954.

9. See Ingegneri, Malvezzi, Rossi, Walker (twice), and Warburg in Ch. V, n. 1 — esp. Walker's ed. of Paris, 1963.
10. Pindar, *Pyth.*, 4, 177. For *aurea aetas*, Ovid, Met., 1, 89.
11. Giordano Bruno, *De umbris idearum*, Paris, 1582, II, i, 20, Intentio G.; Frances Yates, *Giordano Bruno and the Hermetic Tradition*, Chicago, 1964, p. 155.
12. In antiquity, the legend of Orpheus in this improbable role of crypto-theologist can be traced, for example, through Plato (*Symposium*, 179D), Aristophanes (*Frogs*), Virgil (*Georgics*, IV), Ovid (*Metamorphoses*), Horace (*Ars Poetica*), etc. The half-jesting, half-philosophical cult of Orpheus by Ficino and his circle is discussed by Edgar Wind, *Pagan Mysteries in the Renaissance*, London, 1958, enl. ed. 1967, where he suggests (p. 163) that Poliziano's *Orfeo* may have been connected with it. See Ch. III, n. 2.
13. This Heraclitan doctrine *deum esse diem et noctem*, that God is day and night, will be found recalled, and in these actual words, by Theodore Marcile in Bartolomeo Delbene, *Civitas Veri*, Paris, 1609, pp. 244ff. (dedication dated 1585).
14. Ficino, ed. of Basel, [1576], p. 86; see Ch. II, n. 19.
15. Conti, *Mythologiae*, ed. of Venice, 1581, p. 241.
16. See n. 13 above.
17. Francesco Petrarca, *Rime*, CCXLV, 'Due rose fresche', line 9. For a Neoplatonic explanation, see Giovanni Andrea Gesualdo, *Il Petrarcha con l'espositione di M. Giovanni Andrea Gesualdo . . .*, Venice, 1533, pp. 263ff. in ed. of Venice, 1573. Jon A. Quitslund, 'Spenser's *Amoretti VIII* and Platonic Commentaries on Petrarch', *Journ. of the Warburg and Courtauld Institutes*, XXXVI, 1973, pp. 256–76, is excellent on the Neoplatonic interpretations of Petrarch during the later renaissance, and includes many valuable references to the sources. Dante was interpreted just as Platonically, as these studies show. Here, Gesualdo's *espositione* makes it particularly plain that the love described in the sonnet is to be taken not merely as sensual but divine.
18. Donald Grout, 'The Chorus in Early Opera', in *Festschrift Friedrich Blume*, ed. Abert and Pfannkuch, Kassel, 1963, p. 159.
19. *Homeric Hymn*, iii, 300ff.
20. Publius Vergilius Maro, *Georgics* (30 B.C.), IV, lines 456ff.; also *Ecl.*, IV, 57.
21. Dante, *Inferno*, III, 9.
22. See n. 4 above.
23. Conti, *Mythologiae*, ed. of Venice, 1581, p. 237.

24. Snorri Sturluson, *The Younger or Prose Edda*, tr. A. G. Brodeur, New York, 1916, London ed., 1929, pp. 143ff.
25. Poliziano, *Orfeo*, first version, line 259; second version, lines 269 and 294.
26. Rinuccini, *Euridice*, lines 460ff. and 503ff.
27. C. Kerényi, *Eleusis, Archetypal Image of Mother and Daughter*, New York, 1967, p. 138. This book is important for what follows; see also C. G. Jung and C. Kerényi, tr. R. F. C. Hull, *Essays on a Science of Mythology*, New York, 1949, and as *Introduction to a Science of Mythology*, London, 1950 (English *Coll. Works* of Jung, Vol. 9, part 1); and the very sceptical but magnificent study by George E. Mylonas, *Eleusis and the Eleusinian Mysteries*, Princeton, 1961. And see Ch. II, n. 15.
28. Plato, *Symp.*, 179D.
29. Angelo Poliziano, *Omnia Opera*, Venice, 1498, p. 310.
30. Ficino, ed. of Basel, [1576], p. 493; see Ch. II, n. 19.
31. Ficino, ed. of Basel, [1576], p. 1327; see Ch. II, n. 19.
32. Sappho, *Lyrica*, 40.
33. Poliziano, *Orfeo*, first version, line 306; second version, line 341.
34. Boccaccio, *Genealogia*, V, xii.
35. Conti, *Mythologiae*, ed. of Venice, 1581, p. 505; see Ch. V, n. 24.
36. Following Mythog. Vatic. 3, 8, 20.
37. Dante, *Purgatorio*, XXIV, 58–60.
38. See Ch. III, n. 1.
39. Plotinus, *Enneads*, VI, ix, 9; IV, viii, 3.
40. Ficino, ed. of Basel, [1576], p. 663; see Ch. II, no. 19.
41. See Ch. X, n. 4.
42. Plato, *Symp.*, 179D.
43. Conti, *Mythologiae*, ed. of Venice, 1581, pp. 504ff.; see Ch. V, n. 24.
44. Pausanias Periegata, 9, 30, 5.
45. Gelous Apollodorus, Rh., 1, 2, 3.
46. Source appears to be Pausanias, 9, 30, 5–6.
47. Sources appear to be Pausanias, 9, 30, 5, and Diogenes Laertius, proomin. 5.
48. Conon Historicus, *Narr.*, 45, 2.
49. Given in Hans Joachim Mette, *Die Fragmente der Tragödien des Aischylos*, Berlin, 1959, pp. 29–30; and see Ch. III, n. 5.
50. For the evidence, see esp. cols. 1110ff. in Roscher's *Lexicon, s.v.* Orpheus—for which see Ch. II, n. 2. The closeness of Apollo and Dionysus with each other, and with Orpheus, Artemis, Hecate, Hermes and others in their chthonic or under-worldly aspects, is also brought out in some detail.
51. Friedrich Wilhelm Nietzsche, at his best in this connection, in his early and brilliant though typically speculative and inconsistent *Die Geburt der Tragödie aus dem Geiste der Musik*, 1872.
52. According to Ovid, *Amores*, III, 9, 21ff. and some others (including the scholiast on Pindar, 313 Boeckh), Orpheus was the son of Apollo; Pindar himself, frag-ment 139 B4, and most subsequent authorities make him the son of Oiagros; but the scholiastic references cited in n. 49 above actually state on the authority of Aeschylus that Orpheus called Apollo, not Dionysus, the greatest god, in his anger at which Dionysus sent his Bassarids (Maenads) to dismember Orpheus.
53. See Ovid, *Met.* 2, 219, and 10, 1–73; see also n. 52 above.
54. Diadorus, 4, 25.
55. Dante, *Paradiso*, I, 19–21.
56. Plato, *Phaedrus*, 244.
57. Lucian, *Adversus Indoctum*, 11–12. According to Phanocles on Orpheus, 5, the lyre was buried with the head.
58. A reproduction of a vase painting showing the head of Orpheus with two bystanders, one of whom is taking down its prophecy in writing, will be found at

Col. 1178 in Otto Gruppe's article *s.v.* Orpheus in Roscher's *Lexicon*, for which see Ch. II, n. 2.

59. No. 89 in Jacob and Wilhelm Grimm, *Fairy-Tales*, Berlin, 1812–15.
60. Philostratos, *V. Ap.*, 151.
61. Plutarch, *Is. Os.*, 35.
62. See Euripides, Fr. 477, Fr. 480 by Macrob. I, 18, 6, and the Orphic Hymn 52, 11.
63. Heraclitus, Fragm. 14.
64. Hippolytus, *In Neaeram*, LIX, 21.
65. Diadorus, 4, 55.

Chapter XII

1. Even allowing amply for the customary elements of exaggeration, this is a very large audience in a very large theatre, and by no stretch of the imagination suitable circumstances for a chamber-scale performance. It is notable that Federico Follino, an eye-witness of the festivities and a generally reputable reporter, gives the higher estimate in his *Compendio della soutuose feste* . . ., Mantua, 1608.
2. See Follino in n. 1 above.
3. Bacchylides, *Odes*, 16.
4. Early sources are somewhat scanty, and Plutarch, *Theseus*, though a little late (A.D. ?46–*c.*120), is much our best ancient authority; the more primitive layers appear in certain evident affinities with Hercules.
5. Monteverdi to Striggio, dated Venice, 9 Dec. 1616.
6. Follino, *Compendio della sontuose feste*. . ., Mantua, 1608, p. 30.
7. Letter dated 29 May 1608 (quoted in Angelo Solerti, *Gli albori del melodramma*, Milan/Palermo/Naples, [1903–4], I, 99.
8. *Il terzo libro della musica di Claudio Monteverde. . . fatta spirituale da Aquilino Coppini*, Milan, 1609, dedication.
9. G. B. Doni, 'Trattato della musica scenica', *c.*1635, *Trattati*, II, 25; quoted in Solerti, *Origini*, Turin, 1903, p. 213.
10. J. A. Westrup, 'Monteverdi's "Lamento d'Arianna"', *Music Review*, I, 1940, pp. 144–54. The manuscript in Luigi Rossi's hand is British Museum (now British Library), London, Add.MS. 30491; the other manuscript is Bibl. Nazionale, Florence, cod. Magl. XIX, 114.
11. Monteverdi, *Il sesto libro de madrigali*, Venice, 1614.
12. Monteverdi, *Selva morale e spirituale*, Venice, 1640 on title-page, but dedication is dated 1 May 1641.
13. Severo Bonini, Bibl. Riccardiana, Florence, MS. 2218, *c.*1650, f. 87v; quoted in Solerti, *Origini*, Turin, 1903, p. 139.
14. See n. 6 above.
15. G. P. Rinuccini, *Poesie*, Florence, 1622, preface.
16. Iain Fenlon, 'Music and Spectacle at the Gonzaga Court, *c.*1580–1600', *Proc. of the Roy. Mus. Ass.*, Vol. 103, 1976–7 (pub. 1978).
17. See Ch. VIII, n. 8.
18. Preface to Part II.
19. Wolfgang Osthoff, 'Monteverdis "Combattimento" in deutscher Sprache und Heinrich Schütz', in *Festschrift Helmuth Osthoff*, Tutzing, 1961, pp. 195–227. And see Fabio Fano in his interesting comparison, '*Il Combattimento di Tancredi e Clorinda* e *L'Incoronazione di Poppea* di Claudo Monteverdi', in *Studi sul teatro veneto fra rinascimento ed età barocca*, Florence, 1971, pp. 346–71.
20. See n. 22 below.
21. See n. 22 below.
22. For the French masques and ballets, see Henry Prunières, *Le Ballet de cour en France avant Benserade et Lully*, Paris, 1914; Margaret M. McGowan, *L'Art du ballet de cour en France, 1581–1643*, Paris, 1963; and Marie-Françoise Christout, *Le ballet de cour de Louis XIV, 1643–1672*, Paris, 1967. For the English masques, see Allardyce

Nicoll's authoritative *Stuart Masques and the Renaissance Stage*, London, 1937; E. J. Dent's still classic *Foundations of English Opera*, Cambridge, 1928; for examples, see Thomas Campion, *Description of a Masque*. . ., 1607 (at the wedding of Lord Hayes), and Murray Lefkowitz, *Trois masques à la cour de Charles Ier d'Angleterre*, Paris, 1970 (an excellent study); for the music, David Fuller, 'The Jonsonian Masque and Its Music', *Music and Letters*, LIV, 4, Oct. 1970, pp. 440ff., and Alan Levitan, 'The Life of Our Design: the Jonsonian Masque as a Baroque Form', Ph.D. diss., Princeton, 1964 (esp. on the reciting style in Ferrabosco); for the dance in relation to French theories of 'measured' poetry and music and to the humanist union of the arts generally, John C. Meagher, 'The Dance and the Masques of Ben Jonson, *Journ. of the Warburg and Courtauld Institutes*, XXV, 1962, pp. 258–77; for a brilliant study of the relationship between Italian choreography and French choreography at their most elaborate and extensive, see Iain Fenlon, 'Music and Spectacle at the Gonzaga Court, *c.*1580–1600', *Proc. of the Roy. Mus. Ass.*, Vol. 103, 1976–7 (publ. 1978); for the Neoplatonic significance of the poetic and visual images in Ben Jonson and others, see D. J. Gordon, *England and the Mediterranean*, Oxford, 1945; his 'Hymenaei: Ben Jonson's Masque of Union', *Journ. of the Warburg and Courtauld Institutes*, VIII, 1945, pp. 107–45; and his crucial article, 'The Imagery of Ben Jonson's *The Masque of Blacknesse* and *The Masque of Beauty*', in *Journ. of the Warburg and Courtauld Institutes*, VI, 1943, pp. 122–41, showing close parallels in Ben Jonson with Giraldi, Conti, Cartari, Ripa, Valeriano etc.; for a reasoned application, by Francis Bacon in his *De Sapientia Veterum*, London, 1609, of Conti's premiss that 'all the dogmas of philosophy are to be contained under [the form of] fables (Natalis Comes, i.e. Natale Conti, *Mythologiae*, Venice, 1567, X, first premiss), see Barbara Carman Garner, 'Francis Bacon, Natalis Comes and the Mythological Tradition', *Journ. of the Warburg and Courtauld Institutes*, XXXIII, 1970, pp. 264–91. See also Douglas Bush, *Mythology and the Renaissance Tradition in English Poetry*, Minneapolis, 1932, 2nd rev. ed., 1963; and DeWitt T. Starnes and Ernest William Talbot, *Classical Myth and Legend in Renaissance Dictionaries*, Chapel Hill, North Carolina, 1955 (just what its title promises and very valuable). For the thought of Giordano Bruno and his considerable influence on English Neoplatonism in the late sixteenth and early seventeenth centuries, see Frances A. Yates, *Giordano Bruno and the Hermetic Tradition*, Chicago, 1964. See also Ch. V, n. 14. For the stage-craft so important in court ballets and masques, see Hellmuth Christian Wolff, *Oper: Szene und Darstellung von 1600 bis 1900*, in the series *Musikgeschichte in Bildern*, ed. Heinrich Besseler and Max Schneider, Band IV, Lieferung 1, Leipzig, [1968]; Margarete Baur-Heinhold, tr. Mary Whittall, with photos by Helga Schmidt-Glassner, *Theater des Barock*, London, 1967; P. Bjurström, *Giacomo Torelli and Baroque Stage Design*, Stockholm, 1961 (very good and detailed); N. Sabbatini, *Pratica di fabricar scene, e machine ne' teatri*, Ravenna, 1638 (an important source); G. Moynet, *La Machinerie théâtrale*, Paris, 1893; Donald Grout, 'The "Machine" Operas', *Bulletin of the Fogg Museum of Art*, Harvard Univ., Cambridge, Mass., IX, 5, 1941; François Lesure, *L'Opéra classique français, XVIIe et XVIIIe siècles*, Geneva, 1972 (including costumes). A useful catalogue including early Italian and Italianate opera in Vienna is Anton Bauer, *Opern und Operetten in Wien. . .von 1629 bis zur Gegenwart*, Graz/Cologne/Vienna, 1955; see also Franz Hadamowsky, 'Barocktheater am Wiener Kaiserhof, mit einer Spielplan, 1625–1740', *Jahrbuch der Gesellschaft für Wiener Theaterforschung* 1951/52, publ. 1955, pp. 7–117.

Chapter XIII

1. See Stuart Reiner's very interesting article, 'Vi sono molt'altre mezz'Arie', in *Studies in Music History: Essays for Oliver Strunk*, ed. Harold Powers, Princeton, 1968.
2. See n. 4 below.

3. Agostino Agazzari, *Del sonare sopra'l basso con tutti li stromenti*, Siena, 1607 (there is a facsimile, Milan, 1933; another, Bologna, 1969; and an English translation in Oliver Strunk, ed. and tr., *Source Readings in Music History*, New York, 1950, pp. 424–31; and the text was relayed to German readers of the early seventeenth century by Michael Praetorius, *Syntagma musicum*, III, Wolfenbüttel, 1618— most surviving copies 1619—Ch. VI). Pietro della Valle, 'Della musica dell' età nostra', letter written at Rome dated 16 Jan. 1640, printed in A. Solerti, *Origini*, Turin, 1903, pp. 148ff.—an independent explanation confirming Agazzari. G. B. Doni, 'Trattato della musica scenica', written at Rome about 1635, printed in *Trattati di musica*, ed. A. F. Gori, Florence, 1763, II, pp. 110–13 and p. 24 of the Appendix (actually a prior draft of the Treatise). And see Ch. XI, n. 8.
4. Simon A. Carfagno, 'The Life and Dramatic Music of Stefano Landi with a Transliteration and Orchestration of the Opera *Sant' Alessio*' is a four-volume dissertation, Univ. of California, Los Angeles, 1960.
5. John Milton, letter to Lucas Holstensius, dated Florence, 30 March 1639. And see Stuart Reiner, 'Collaboration in *Chi soffre speri*', *Music Review*, XXII, 1961, pp. 265–82.
6. M. de Lionne, letter to Mazarin, 27 Feb. 1642, quoted by Henry Prunières, *L'Opéra italien en France avant Lully*, Paris, 1913, p. 27.
7. Rome, Vatican Library, MS Barb. lat. 4387; autograph attribution maintained by Gloria Rose, private communication.
8. See, for example, Act I, Scenes x–xii, and Act II, Scene xvii.
9. See Livio Niso Galvani, *I teatri musicali di Venezia*, Milan, 1879, Introd.; Simon Towneley Worsthorne, *Venetian Opera in the Seventeenth Century*, Oxford, 1954, Ch. I.; and esp. Angelo Solerti, 'I rappresentazioni musicali di Venezia dal 1571 al 1605', *Riv. Mus. It.*, ix, 1902, p. 503.
10. See Thomas Walker, 'Gli errori di "Minerva al Tavolino"', in *Venezia e il melodramma nel seicento*, Florence, 1976, with regard to a surviving piece.
11. Simon Towneley Worsthorne, *Venetian Opera in the Seventeenth Century*, Oxford, 1954, 2nd ed., 1968, is very good and well documented; Livio Niso Galvani, *I teatri musicali di Venezia*, Milan, 1879, and Ludovico Zorzi and others, *I teatri pubblici di Venezia (secoli XVII–XVIII)*, Venice, 1971, are richly informative; Taddeo Wiel, *I codici musicali Contariani. . .*, Venice, 1888, and where relevant, E. Vogel, *Bibliothek der gedruckten weltlichen Vocalmusik italiens aus den Jahren 1500–1700*, Berlin, 1892, are invaluable; so is A. Loewenberg, *Annals of Opera, 1597–1940*, 2 vols., Cambridge, 1943, 2nd revised ed., Geneva, 1955, if used with some caution; see also the valuable article, P. Petrobelli, '"L'Ermiona" di Pio Enea degli Obizzi ed i primi spettacoli d'opera veneziani', *La Nuova Musicologia Italiana*, Quad. della Rass M Vol. 3, Turin, 1965; Christine J. Day's informative 'The Theater of SS. Giovanni e Paolo and Monteverdi's *L'Incoronazione di Poppea*', *Current Musicology*, No. 25, 1978, pp. 22–38; Jane Glover's admirable *Cavalli*, London, 1978; G. Moynet, *La Machinerie théâtrale*, Paris, 1893; N. Sabbatini, *Pratica di fabricar scene, e machine ne' teatri*, Ravenna, 1638 (ed. Elena Povolada, Rome n.d.—with good commentary); Christoforo Ivanovich, *Minerva al Tavolino*, Venice, 1681 (a decidedly unreliable but important contemporary witness and reporter, on whom see Thomas Walker, as at n. 10 above); a most valuable recent study is Nicola Mangini, *I teatri di Venezia*, Milan, 1974. And see Lorenzo Bianconi and Thomas Walker, 'Dalla *Finta pazza* alla *Veremonda*: storie di Febiarmonici', *Rivista Italiana di Musicologia*, Vol. X, 1975, pp. 379–454; and Giovanni Morelli and Thomas Walker, 'Tre controverie intorno al San Cassiano', in *Venezia e il melodramma nel seicento*, Florence, 1976. Also Giovanni Carlo Bonlini, *Le glorie della poesie e della musica. . .di Venezia*, Venice, [1730]; Antonio Groppo, *Catalogo di tutti i drammi per musica. . .di Venezia dall' anno 1637*, Venice, [1745].
12. See Donald J. Grout, 'The Chorus in Early Opera', *Festschrift Friedrich Blume*, ed. Abert and Pfannkuch, Kassel, 1963, pp. 151–61, an insightful article.

13. e.g. by Donald Grout, *A Short History of Opera*, New York, 1947, 2nd ed., 1965, p. 80; but contrast S. T. Worsthorne, *Venetian Opera in the Seventeenth Century*, Oxford, 1954, p. 83.

14. Evelyn, *Diary*, ed. E. S. de Beer, Vol. II, Oxford, 1955, p. 449.

15. *Ercole in Lidia*, composed by Giovanni Rovetta, on a libretto by Maiolino Bisaccioni (libretto publ. Venice, 1645). But there are problems concerning the date and circumstances, for which see Lorenzo Bianconi and Thomas Walker, 'Dalla *Finta pazza*' (as at n. 11 above), p. 416, n. 154.

16. See Murray Lefkowitz' admirable study, *Trois masques à la cour de Charles Ier d'Angleterre*, Paris, 1970. Whitelocke's description was not published until his *Memorials of the English Affairs*, London, 1682, but his earlier account and notes also survive.

17. Venezia, Archivo di Stato, Scuola Grande di S. Marco, Busta 194, Account book of 1658, verso of letter T ff.; Conte attinenti al gu: Marco Faustini, fol. 268; see Denis Arnold, ' "L'Incoronazione di Poppea" and its orchestral requirements', *Musical Times*, CIV, Jan. 1963, pp. 176–8; Lorenzo Bianconi and Thomas Walker, 'Production, Consumption and Political Function of 17th-Century Opera', as at Ch. XI, n. 8.

18. *Le nouveau mercure galant. . .au mois de avril de l'année 1679*, Paris, 1679, pp. 66–7, 71. But see Bianconi and Walker in n. 17 above.

19. Taddeo Wiel, *I codici Musicali Contariniani. . .*, Venice, 1888.

20. Bibl. Marc., Venice, 9879.

21. Alexandre Toussaint de Limojon, *La Ville et la république de Venise*, Paris, 1680.

22. See Jurgen Eppelsheim's invaluable study, *Das Orchester in den Werken Jean-Baptiste Lullys*, Tutzing, 1961, esp. pp. 150ff.

23. François Maximilien Misson, *Nouveau voyage d'Italie fait en l'année 1688*, The Hague, 1691.

24. See n. 22. The most up-to-date and in general convincing discussion comes in Edward Tarr and Thomas Walker, 'Die Verwendung der Trompete in der italienischen Oper des 17. Jahrhunderts', *Hamburger Jahrbuch für Musikwissenschaft*, Band 3, 1978.

Chapter XIV

1. Letter from Monteverdi, probably to Striggio, 1 May 1627, No. 89 in G. F. Malipiero, *Claudio Monteverdi*, Milan, 1930, pp. 249–51: see p. 250.

2. Vienna, Nationalbibl., 1876.

3. For a definitive study of the sources, see Wolfgang Osthoff, 'Zu den Quellen von Monteverdis *Ritorno di Ulisse in patria*', *Studien zur Musikwissenschaft*, XXIII, 1956, pp. 67–78; for samples of the controversy, see Emil Vogel, *Vierteljahrschrift für Musikwissenschaft*, III, 1887, pp. 403ff.; Robert Haas, *Denkmäler der Tonkunst in Österreich*, Vol. 57, Vienna, 1922, and his full commentary *Studien zur Musikwissenschaft*, IX, 1922, pp. 3ff. The last word is to be found in the good sense and solid arguments of Wolfgang Osthoff's splendid study, *Das dramatische Spätwerk Claudio Monteverdis*, Tutzing, 1960, pp. 181ff., but the book should be consulted in full.

4. The partial draft of Gloria Rose's book on the chamber cantata, left unfinished at her death, is in the keeping of the Barber Institute of Fine Arts, University of Birmingham, England, where it is available to students together with a considerable collection of her unpublished notes. It is hoped that this material may be completed and prepared for publication by whoever wishes to undertake this rewarding assignment. Her chapter, 'The Italian Cantata of the Baroque Period', in *Gattungen der Musik. . .Gedankschrift Leo Schrade*, ed. Max Haas et al., Bern, 1973, pp. 655–77, is an original and valuable short study.

5. Leo Schrade, *Monteverdi*, New York, 1950, p. 349; Guetano Giordano, *Intorno al Gran Teatro. . .in Bologna*, Bologna, 1855, p. 62.

6. Homer, *Odyssey*, Books XIII to XXIII.
7. Wolfgang Osthoff, *Das dramatische Spätwerk Claudio Monteverdis*, Tutzing, 1960, p. 183.
8. Venice, Biblioteca Nazionale Marciana, MSS It. IV, 439: 9963. For some of the problems of this opera, see Osthoff as at n. 7 above, also his 'Neue Beobachtungen. . .' in *Musikforschung*, XI, 1958; and Chiarelli as at n. 15 below.
9. Naples, Biblioteca del Conservatorio di Musica 'S. Pietro e Majella', 49^ 2.7.
10. Tacitus, *Annals*, xii-xvi; Suetonius, *Lives of the Caesars: Nero*; also Dio Cassius, *Epit.* lxi-lxiii, and Zonaras, *Ann.* xi.
11. Tacitus, *Ann.*, xiii, 12–20.
12. Suetonius, loc. cit. in n. 10 above.
13. Samuel Johnson, *The Plays of William Shakespeare* [edited with] *Notes by Sam Johnson*, London, 1765, preface.
14. No. 6 in Jacob and Wilhelm Grimm, *Fairy-Tales*, Berlin, 1812–15.
15. See Alessandra Chiarelli, 'L'Incoronazione di Poppea o Il Nerone: Problemi di filologia testuale', *Rivista Italiana di Musicologia*, Vol. IX, 1974, pp. 117–51.
16. See Lorenzo Bianconi and Thomas Walker, 'Dalla *Finta pazza* alla *Veremonda*: storie di Febiarmonici', *Rivista Italiana di Musicologia*, Vol. X, 1975, pp. 379–454.
17. Conti, *Mythologiae*, ed. of Venice, 1581, p. 241.
18. See Ch. V, n. 28.

Chapter XV

1. Allardyce Nicoll, *The World of Harlequin*, Cambridge, 1963, is a standard work on the dramatic contexts; Nino Pirrotta, 'Commedia dell' arte and Opera', *Mus. Quart.*, XLI, 1955, pp. 305–24, is an important article; K. M. Lea, *Italian Popular Comedy: a Study in the Commedia dell' arte, 1560–1620*, 2 vols., Oxford, 1934, is a most extensive and valuable study; and there is a doctoral dissertation at the University of Cologne, 1970, by Lisolette de Ridder, 'Der Anteil der Commedia dell' Arte an der Entstehungs- und Entwicklungsgeschichte der komischen Oper', stronger on the texts than on the music. Irène Mamcarz, *Les Intermèdes comiques italiens au XVIIIe siècle en France et en Italie*, Paris, 1972, is very long indeed, but virtually all on the texts, with very little on the music and that little somewhat unreliable.
2. See Lorenzo Bianconi and Thomas Walker, 'Production, Consumption and Political Function of 17th-Century Opera', paper at the Berkeley Conference of the Int. Musicological Soc., 1977, in preparation—n. 138 of typescript.
3. A notable pioneering study was Egon Wellesz, 'Cavalli und der Stil der venetianischen Oper von 1640–1660', in *Studien zur Geschichte der Wiener Oper*, Vienna, 1913, pp. 1–103. Henry Prunières, *Cavalli et l'opéra vénitien au XVIIe siècle*, Paris, 1931, though quite short, is a remarkably perceptive study and remains of great value for its stylistic examination. Gordon F. Crain, 'Francesco Cavalli and the Venetian Opera', *Opera*, XVIII, June 1967, pp. 446–51, is popular but accurate and very interesting. David Swale, 'Cavalli: the "Erismena" of 1655', in *Miscellanea Musicologica: Adelaide Studies in Musicology*, Vol. 3, Adelaide, 1968, pp. 145–70, is a very interesting close-up. A very up-to-date and excellent survey, both for scholarship and for musicianly insight, is Jane Glover, *Cavalli*, London, 1978; it has a valuable bibliography.
4. Information privately communicated by Thomas Walker, but is in his article *s.v.* 'Cavalli' for *The New Grove*, London, 1980. Also consult Jane Glover's excellent *Cavalli*, London, 1978.
5. Bibl. Marc., Venice, Cod. It., IV-368, N. 9892.
6. Ellen Rosand, 'L'Ormindo travestito in Erismena' in *Journ. Amer. Musicological Soc.*, XXVIII, 1975, pp. 268–91.
7. Bibl. Marc., Venice, Cod. It., IV-353, N. 9877.

8. See the text and bibliography of R. Donington, *Interpretation of Early Music, New Version*, London, 1974, for more on this difficult and interesting topic.

Chapter XVI

1. Egon Wellesz, 'Zwei Studien zur Geschichte von der Oper im 17 Jahrhundert', in *Sammelbände der internationalen Musikgesellschaft*, XV, 1913, pp. 124–54, tr. by Patricia Kean in *Essays on Opera*, London, 1950, pp. 54–81; W. C. Holmes, 'Giacinto Andrea Cicognini's and Antonio Cesti's *Orontea* (1649)' in *New Looks at Italian Opera: Essays in Honor of Donald J. Grout*, ed. Wm. Austin, Ithaca, N.Y., 1968, pp. 108–32, and 'Cesti's "L'Argia": An Entertainment for a Royal Court', *Chigiana*, XXVI-XXVII, Florence, 1971, pp. 35–52. J. Victor Crowther, 'The Operas of Cesti', *Music Review*, XXXI, May 1970, pp. 93–113, is briefly descriptive of the nine surviving operas, with an undocumented and unreliable sketch of the life. Carl B. Schmidt, 'Antonio Cesti's *La Dori*: A Study of Sources, Performance Traditions and Musical Style', *Rivista Italiana di Musicologia*, Vol. X, 1975, pp. 455–98, is highly reliable, and in fact is one of the most informative and important essays on an individual opera of the mid 17th century, throwing in addition considerable light on the composer.
2. See Holmes in n. 1 above; but also Thomas Walker, 'Gli errori di *Minerva al Tavolino*', in *Venezia e il melodramma nel Seicento*, ed. M. T. Muraro, Florence, 1977, at p. 14ff.; *Orontea*, ed. Wm. Holmes, Wellesley Coll., 1973, survives in four MSS: Rome, Bibl. del Cons. Naz. di S. Cecilia (Rsc); Rome, Bibl. Apost. Vat., Chigi Q. V. 53 (Rvat); Parma, Bibl. del Cons., Bibl. Palatina (PAc); Cambridge, Magdalene Coll., Pepysian Lib. 2210 (Cmc).
3. See Schmidt in n. 1 above.
4. See Wellesz in n. 1 above; and the important article by Carl B. Schmidt, 'Antonio Cesti's *Il pomo d'oro*: a Re-examination of a Famous Hapsburg Court Spectacle', *Journ. American Musicological Soc.*, XXIX, 3, Fall 1976, pp. 381–412, in which among many points of interest the rediscovery of portions of the lost Acts III and V is described.
5. See Ch. XIII, n. 18.
6. See Gloria Rose, 'The Italian Cantata of the Baroque Period', in *Gattungen der Musik in Einzeldarstellungen: Gedenkschrift Leo Schrade*, ed. Max Haas *et al.*, Bern and Munich, 1973, pp. 655–77—a model of clarity and accuracy. The connection of the chamber cantata with the existing tradition of monody is admirably brought out by Nigel Fortune's dissertation 'Italian Secular Song from 1600 to 1635: the Origins and Development of Accompanied Monody' (Gonville and Caius Coll., Univ. of Cambridge, 1953); or see his shorter 'Italian Secular Monody from 1600 to 1635', *Mus. Quart.*, XXXIX, 1953, pp. 171–95; and his splendid chapter, 'Solo Song and Cantata', in *The New Oxford History of Music*, Vol. IV, London, 1968, pp. 155ff. Jan Racek, *Stilprobleme der italienischen Monodie*, German ed., Prague, 1965, is a major study of the greatest excellence (in Czech as *Italská monodie. . .*, Prague, 1945). For the baroque view of chamber cantata as the essence of the form, and of the public cantata (e.g. in J. S. Bach) as really a species of motet, see Johann Mattheson, *Der vollkommene Capellmeister*, Hamburg, 1739, Pt. II, Ch. 13, Sect. 26ff. (pp. 214ff.).
7. Giacomo Antonio Perti, *Cantate morali, e spirituali*, Bologna, 1688, preface.
8. See Ch. XII, n. 13.
9. Angelo Berardi, *Ragionamenti musicali*, Bologna, 1681, p. 136.
10. For the long period of transition from continuous opera towards number opera, the two volumes of Hugo Goldschmidt, *Studien zur Geschichte der italienischen Oper im 17. Jahrhundert*, Leipzig, 1901 (facs. ed. Wiesbaden, 1967), remain a work of pioneering value. Donald Jay Grout, in his highly dependable *Short History of Opera*, New York, 1947, 2nd ed., 1965, is as always indispensable. Simon Towneley Worsthorne, *Venetian Opera in the Seventeenth Century*, Oxford, 1954,

2nd ed., 1968, and Hellmuth Christian Wolff, *Die Venezianische Oper in der zweiten Hälfte des 17. Jahrhunderts*, are very important on that most flourishing of mid-baroque operatic centres. The growing eminence of Naples is traced by William P. Stalnaker in a Ph.D. dissertation, 'The Beginnings of Opera in Naples', Princeton Univ., 1968, and is the subject of an admirable study (including a good bibliography) by Michael F. Robinson, *Naples and Neapolitan Opera*, Oxford, 1972; very detailed light on one phase of this growth is thrown by Lorenzo Bianconi and Thomas Walker, 'Dalla *Finta Pazza* alla *Veremonda*: storie di Febiarmonici', *Rivista Italiana di Musicologia*, Vol. X, 1975, pp. 379–454, one of the most impressive of recent articles on opera both for informative detail and perceptive new thinking. Robert L. Weaver, 'Opera in Florence: 1646–1731', in *Studies in Musicology: Essays. . .in Memory of Glen Haydon*, ed. James W. Pruett, Chapel Hill, N.C., 1969, pp. 60–71, and Carolyn Gianturco, 'Evidence for a Late Roman School of Opera', *Music and Letters*, LVI, 1, Jan. 1974, pp. 4ff., keep these great schools well in the picture; for the abortive English opera of the Restoration, Edward J. Dent, *Foundations of English Opera*, Cambridge, 1928, remains important, though since supplemented by Eric Walter White, *The Rise of English Opera*, London, 1951; for the significant though eventually eclipsed Hamburg school, Hellmuth Christian Wolff's *Die Barockoper in Hamburg*, Wolfenbüttel, 1957, is the best introduction, but see also George J. Buelow's perceptive and informative article, 'Opera in Hamburg 300 Years Ago', *Musical Times*, Jan. 1978, pp. 26–8; and more generally Renate Brockpähler, *Handbuch zur Geschichte der Barockoper in Deutschland*, Emsdetten, Westf., 1964—giving detailed and very valuable information town by town. Good samples of special studies include: Heinz Hess, *Die Opern Alessandro Stradellas*, Leipzig, 1966; Carolyn M. Gianturco, 'Caratteri stilistici delle opere teatrali di Stradella', *Rivista Italiana di Musicologia*, VI, 1971, pp. 211–45; Edward J. Dent's classic, *Alessandro Scarlatti*, London, 1905, New Impression with preface and additional notes by Frank Walker, London, 1960; David Poultney, 'Alessandro Scarlatti and the Transformation of Oratorio', *Mus. Quart.*, LIX, 4, Oct. 1973, pp. 584–601 (excellent on the relationships between oratorio and opera)—and in that connection, E. Smither, *A History of the Oratorio*, 2 Vols., Chapel Hill, N.C., 1978, and another classic, Winton Dean, *Handel's Dramatic Oratorios and Masques*, London, 1959; Zelm Laus, *Die Opern Reinhard Keisers: Studien zur Chronologie, Überlieferung und Stilentwicklung*, Munich, 1975; Rosamund Drooker Brenner, 'Emotional Expression in Keiser's Operas', *Music Review*, Aug. 1972, pp. 224–32; Eulan van Brooks, 'Richard Keiser and his Opera *Fredegunda*', a very thorough and interesting M.A. thesis, Denton, Texas, 1966; Andrew D. McCredie, 'Christopher Graupner as Opera Composer', in *Miscellanea Musicologica: Adelaide Studies in Musicology*, Vol. I, Adelaide, March 1966, pp. 74–116; and of especial interest on word-setting, D. T. Mace, 'Musical Humanism, the Doctrine of Rhythmus, and the Saint Cecilia Odes of Dryden', *Journ. of the Warburg and Courtauld Institutes*, XXVII, 1964, pp. 251–92. A fundamental study is Robert Lamar Weaver and Norma Wright Weaver, *A Chronology of Music in the Florentine Theater, 1590–1750*, Detroit, 1978; another is Lorenzo Bianconi, 'Funktionen des Operntheaters in Neapel bis 1700. . .', in *Colloquium Alessandro Scarlatti, Würzburg 1975*, ed. Wolfgang Osthoff and Jutta Ruile-Dronke, Tutzing, 1979, pp. 13–116.

11. Venice, Bibl. Marc., Cod. It. IV-460, N. 9984.
12. Paris, Bibl. Nat., Rès. 2692 (1–2).
13. Paris, Bibl. Nat., D. 11,897.
14. Paris, Bibl. Nat., D. 11,902 (1–3).

Chapter XVII

1. See Ch. V, n. 23.
2. See Le Cerf de la Viéville, *Comparaison de la musique italien et de la musique française*,

3 Parts, Brussels, 1704–6, reprinted in Jacques Bonnet's *Histoire de la musique*, Amsterdam, 1725, esp. pp. 182ff. See also Ch. XVIII, n. 9.

3. Marin Mersenne, *Harmonie universelle*, 2 Parts, Paris, 1636–7, II, vi, 356, and 'Livre Premier de la Voix', p. 40. For Mersenne's humanist approach, see also Dean T. Mace, 'Marin Mersenne on Language and Music', *Journ. of Music Theory*, XIV, Spring 1970, pp. 2–34.

4. André Maugars, *Response faite à un curieux sur le sentiment de la musique d'Italie, escrite à Rome. . .1639*, Paris, 1639.

5. See esp. P. Bjurström, *Giacomo Torelli and Baroque Stage Design*, Stockholm, 1961, and Thomas E. Lawrenson, *The French Stage in the XVIIth Century: A Study in the Advent of the Italian Order*, Manchester, 1957; and see Ch. XII, n. 22. Much pictorial and other evidence will be found in François Lesure's valuable *L'Opéra classique français, XVIIe et XVIIIe siècles*, Geneva, 1972.

6. A good sampling will be found in Mabel Dolmetsch, *Dances of England and France, 1450–1600*, London, 1949, and *Dances of Italy and Spain, 1400–1600*, London, 1954. Sources include Thoinot Arbeau, *Orchésographie*, Langres, 1588; Fabritio Caroso, *Il ballarino*, Venice, 1581, and *Nobiltà di dame*, Venice, 1600; Cesare Negri, *Le grazie d'amore*, Milan, 1602, new ed. as *Nuove inventioni di balli*, Milan, 1604; Marin Mersenne, *Harmonie universelle*, Paris, 1636–7, 'Traitez de la voix, et des chants', pp. 170ff.; Raoul Auger Feuillet, *Chorégraphie ou l'art de décrire la danse. . .*, Paris, 1699.

7. Henry Prunières, *L'Opéra italien en France avant Lully*, Paris, 1913, is quite indispensable here as elsewhere; and more directly, his important *Le Ballet de cour en France avant Benserade et Lully*, Paris, 1914. Marie-Françoise Christout, *Le Ballet de cour de Louis XIV, 1643–1672*, Paris, 1967, is a most valuable and detailed study. See also Anthony R. James, *French Baroque Music from Beaujoyeulx to Rameau*, London, 1973, and Robert M. Isherwood, *Music in the Service of the King: France in the Seventeenth Century*, Ithaca, N.Y., and London, 1973.

8. Johann Joachim Quantz, *Versuch. . .die Flöte traversiere zu spielen* (Essay on Playing the Transverse Flute), Berlin, 1752, XVIII, 53.

9. Florence State Archives, Mediceo 5425, f. 221; quoted in Prunières, op. cit. in n. 7 above, p. 61.

10. Quoted in Prunières, op. cit. in n. 7 above, p. 375.

11. *Gazette de France*, 1645, p. 1180; quoted in Prunières, op. cit. in n. 7 above, p. 74.

12. Rome, Bibl. Vat., Chigi, Q V 39.

13. Letter from Bagni, Rome, Vatican Archives, *Nuziatura di Francia*, 95; quoted in Prunières, op. cit. in n. 7 above, p. 103n.

14. Archivio di Stato di Modena, Francia Amb. fila 109; quoted in Prunières, op. cit. in n. 7 above, p. 381.

15. *Gazette de France*, 8 May 1647; quoted in Prunières, op. cit. in n. 7 above, p. 109n.

16. Venice, Bibl. Marc., Cod. It. IV, 359, N. 9883.

Chapter XVIII

1. Philip H. Kennedy, 'The First French Opera: the Literary Standpoint', *'Recherches' sur la musique française classique*, VIII, 1968, pp. 77–88.

2. For the French academies of the seventeenth century, see Frances Yates, *The French Academies of the Sixteenth Century*, London, 1947, where she fortunately carries her splendid story through to the age of Louis XIV. Bernard Champigneulle, *L'Âge classique de la musique française*, Paris, 1946, is useful more generally. Marcelle Benoit, *Versailles et les Musiciens du Roy, 1661–1733* (heavily documented in *Musiques de cour, chapelle, chambre, écurie, 1661–1733*), Paris, 1971, conveys a large quantity of detailed information. Henry Prunières, 'Lully and the Académie de Musique et de Danse', *Mus. Quart.*, XI, Oct. 1925, is valuable.

3. From the considerable literature, the following stand out: Henry Prunières, *Lully*, Paris, 1910; Lionel de la Laurencie, *Lully*, Paris, 1911; Wilfrid Mellers,

Jean-Baptiste Lully, in *The Heritage of Music*, ed. Hubert Foss, III, London, 1951, pp. 32–52—brief but insightful; see also his valuable *François Couperin and the French Classical Tradition*, London, 1950.

4. M. Pelisson, *Les Comédies-ballets de Molière*, Paris, 1914; Julien Tiersot, *La Musique dans la comédie de Molière*, Paris, [1918]; F. Böttger, 'Die Comédie-Ballets von Molière und Lully', dissertation, Berlin, 1931. See also J. Ecorcheville, *Corneille et la musique*, Paris, 1906, and Richard A. Oliver's very substantial study, 'Molière's Contribution to the Lyric Stage', *Mus. Quart.*, XXXIII, 3, July 1947, pp. 350–64; and Henry Prunières, 'La Fontaine et Lully', *La Revue Musicale*, II, 1921, pp. 97–112.

5. See Le Cerf de la Viéville, as under Ch. XVII, n. 2, p. 188. See also n. 9 below.

6. Cuthbert Girdlestone, *La Tragédie en musique (1673–1750) considérée comme genre littéraire*, Geneva, 1972, is long and detailed, especially on Quinault, for whom see also Fr. Lindemann, 'Die Operntexte Quinaults', dissertation, Leipzig, 1904, and Etienne Gros, *Philippe Quinault*, Paris, 1926—a particularly full and sympathetic study. Meredith Ellis, 'The Sources of Jean-Baptiste Lully's Secular Music', *Recherches sur la musique classique française*, VIII, Paris, 1968, pp. 89–130, is uncommonly helpful in tracing the musical texts. For the succession to Lully, Lionel de la Laurencie, *Rameau*, Paris, 1926, and Paul-Marie Masson's magnificent study, *L'Opéra de Rameau*, Paris, 1930, are standard works.

7. Aristotle, *Poetics*, 1415A, 35, suggests the desirability of one action; 1449B, 12ff., the desirability of keeping the time within twenty-four hours if possible, though as he points out the early Greek tragedies did not; place was added in 1570 by Castelvetro in his edition of the *Poetics*, on the general grounds of Aristotle's insistence on 'probable' action.

8. [N. Boindin], *Lettres historiques sur tous les spectacles de Paris*, II, Paris, 1719, p. 88.

9. Le Cerf de la Viéville, in J. Bonnet, *Histoire de la musique*, here quoted from ed. of Amsterdam, 1725, pp. 195ff.; but this much pirated passage stems from Le Cerf's *Comparaison de la musique italienne et de la musique française*, Brussels, 1704–6, and also appears in a slightly shorter form (but otherwise verbally almost identical) in [Nicolas Boindin], *Lettres historiques sur tous les spectacles de Paris, Second partie*, Paris, 1719, pp. 87ff. The *Histoire de la musique* was itself begun by Abbé Bourdelot, continued by Pierre Bonnet, completed and published by Jacques Bonnet; first pub. Paris, 1715—but Vols. 2–4 of the Amsterdam eds of [?1721], 1725 and 1726 are a reprint of the *Comparaison* of Le Cerf. Hence the slightly involved presentation of the present reference. One small difference is that Boindin has Quinault and Lully both take the choice of subjects to the king.

10. See n. 2 above, esp. Yates, pp. 301ff.

11. Charles Marguetel de Saint-Denis, Seigneur de Saint-Évremond, 'Sur les Opéra à Monsieur le Duc de Bouquinquant [Buckingham]', apparently 1677, publ. in *Oeuvres meslées*, Tome XI, Paris, 1684. For the text and its very complicated history, see Saint-Évremond, *Oeuvres en Prose*, ed. René Ternois, 4 vols, Paris, 1662–9, Vol. 2, pp. 195–8, and Vol. 3, pp. 127–64.

12. Wolf, R. P., 'Metrical Relationships in French Recitative of the Seventeenth and Eighteenth Centuries', *Recherches sur la musique classique française*, Vol. XVIII, 1978, p. 29. And see Robert Donington, *The Interpretation of Early Music, New Version*, London, 1974, pp. 643–50.

13. Henri-Louis Choquel, *La musique rendue sensible*, Paris, 1759, 2nd ed., Paris, 1762, pp. 109ff.

14. Charles Masson, *Nouveau traité des règles de la composition de la musique*, Paris, 1697, p.6.

15. Sébastien de Brossard, *Dictionnaire des termes*, Paris, 1701; [enl. ed. as] *Dictionaire [sic] de musique*, Paris, 1703, *s.v.* RECITATIVO.

16. See Ch. XVI, n. 9.

17. Le Cerf de la Viéville, as under n. 9 above, p. 188.

Chapter XIX

1. In the excellent collected edition of Lully by Henry Prunières, Vol. III of the operas. The Bibliothèque Nationale at Paris has a copy of the folio score of 1684 (Vm? 73) among other editions.
2. Saul Rosenzweig, 'The Ghost of Henry James', in *Art and Psychoanalysis*, ed. William Phillips, New York, 1957, p.89.
3. William Shakespeare, *Hamlet*, I, iii, 78.

Appendix

1. An excellent account of the scientific and mathematical problems of the Calendar will be found *s.v.* Calendar in Vol. 3 of the fifteenth edition of the *Enc. Brit.* (Chicago, London etc., 1973), by Colin Alistair Ronan and others. But all standard works of reference tend to be uncommonly elusive on the more intractable aspects of the practical problems for the historian caused by the astonishingly variable methods of dating early documents and events. Much the best account readily available, and as lucid as the subject allows, will be found in a book of wide scope and unfailing practicality: A. Giry, *Manuel de diplomatique*, Paris, 1894, pp. 83–314. For those with a real taste for the monumental, there are the eight fabulous volumes of chronological investigation prepared by the indefatigable Benedictines, *L'Art de vérifier les dates*, Paris, 1783. Of fundamental assistance is Adriano Cappelli, *Cronologia, cronografia e calendario perpetuo*, Milan, 1905, 2nd ed. 1930, repr. 1960.
2. For the very considerable complications and inconsistencies of the French Republican Calendar, see Giry, op. cit. in n. 1 above, pp. 169–73.
3. Giry, op. cit. in n. 1 above, pp. 131–58.
4. Giry, op. cit. in n. 1 above, pp. 169–72, p. 173.

Select Bibliography

The following list represents my initial selection from the enormous literature. Many of the works listed include, of course, their own Bibliographies: Donald Grout's, for example, in his *Short History of Opera*, occupies well over two hundred pages, and is especially to be recommended for this wide coverage. In my own quite extensive Notes above there will be found, grouped according to the many and various subjects treated in my text, a much larger quantity of bibliographical information on both the primary and the secondary sources relating to those subjects severally. The Notes are numbered by chapters throughout the book, and are linked to the text by these numbers in the usual way; but it is also possible to track down any author mentioned in the Notes, as well as in the text, by means of the Index.

For the reader wishing to pursue much further reading relevant to a given subject, it seemed better to group my suggestions and comments in this more or less logical fashion, rather than to comment systematically on those books which appear alphabetically by author's name in the list below, although in some cases I have also added information there about their contents, or a word or two of special recommendation or reservation. For readers merely wishing to check a bibliographical reference where the author's name is already known, the alphabetical arrangement below is an obvious convenience. For intensive study, my numbered Notes are the place to look. Entries which for whatever reason I failed to consult in time will be found added in a Postscript on p. 361.

LIST OF ABBREVIATIONS

Act. Mus.	Acta musicologica
AnMc	Analecta Musicologica
CMc	Current Musicology
JAMS	Journal of the American Musicological Society
JMT	Journal of Music Theory
Mf	Die Musikforschung
MGG	Die Musik in Geschichte und Gegenwart
ML	Music and Letters
MMA	Miscellanea Musicologica (South Australia)
MQ	Musical Quarterly

MR   Music Review
MT   Musical Times
PRMA   Proceedings of the Royal Musical Association
RIM   Rivista Italiana di Musicologia
RMCF   Recherches sur la musique classique française
RMI   Rivista Musicale Italiana
SMw   Studien zur Musikwissenschaft

Abert, Anna Amalie, *Claudio Monteverdi und das musikalische Drama*, Lipp-stadt, 1954.
Adkins, Cecil, ed., *L'Amfiparnaso: A New Edition of the Music with Historical and Analytical Essays*, Chapel Hill, N.C., 1977.
Ambros, August Wilhelm, *Geschichte der Musik*, IV, Leipzig, 1909, 3rd ed. rev. and enl. by Hugo Leichentritt, pp. 161–346.
Ancona, A. d', *Le origini del teatro italiano*, 2 vols., Turin, 1891. (A basic study.)
[Anon.], *Li sontuosissimi apparechi, trionfi, e feste* . . . , Florence, Ferrara and Venice, 1589.
Anthony, James R., *French Baroque Music from Beaujoyeulx to Rameau*, London, 1973.
Apollonio, M., *Storia del teatro italiano*, Florence, 1950.
Arnold, Denis, *Monteverdi*, London, 1963.
—— 'Monteverdi's Singers', MT, Oct. 1970, pp. 982–5.
—— and Nigel Fortune, eds, *The Monteverdi Companion*, London, 1968.
—— and ——, eds, *Italian Baroque Opera*, in preparation.
Artusi, Giovanni Maria, . . . *delle imperfettioni della moderna musica*, Venice, 1600. *Seconda parte* . . . , Venice, 1603. (Has the celebrated attack on Monteverdi.)
Austin, Wm. W., ed., *New Looks at Italian Opera: Essays in Honor of Donald J. Grout*, Ithaca, N.Y., 1968.
[Baldini, Baccio], *Discorso sopra la masquerata della genealogia* . . . , Florence, 1566.
Barba, Pompeo della, *Espositione d'un sonetto platonico, fatto sopra il primo effetto d'amore che e il separare l'anima dal corpo de l'amante, dove si tratta de la immortalita de l'anima secondo Aristotile, e secondo Platone* . . . , Florence, 1549.
Barnard, Mary, *The Mythmakers*, Athens, Ohio, 1966. (Good on the element of fun in myth.)
Baron, John H., 'Monody: a Study in Terminology', MQ LIV 4 (Oct. 1968).
Baskerville, C. R., *The Elizabethan Jig*, Chicago, 1929.
Baur-Heinhold, Margarete, *Theater des Barock*, photos by Helga Schmidt-Glassner. Engl. tr. Mary Whittall, London, 1967. (Staging.)
Beaujoyeulx, Balthasar de, ed., *et al.*, *Circe ou le balet comique de la royne*, Paris, 1582. Facs. Turin, 1965. Tr. and introd. Carol and Lander MacClin-tock, [n.p.], 1971. (Account of the performance of 1581, with allegorical interpretations.)
Bembo, Pietro, *Dialoghi degli Asolani*, Venice, 1505. (Probably begun in 1495. Tales of cultured court life, with deliberately Neoplatonic under-tones. A model for Castiglione's *Book of the Courtier*.)
——*Prose nelle quali si ragiona della volgar lingua*, Venice, 1525.

Benoit, Marcelle, *Versailles et les Musiciens du Roy, 1661–1733*, Paris, 1971. (Information.)

—— ed., *Musiques de cour, chapelle, chambre, écurie, 1661–1733*, Paris, 1971. (Documents.)

Bernstein, Lawrence F., 'The "Parisian Chanson": Problems of Style and Terminology', JAMS XXXI, no. 2 (Summer 1978), pp. 193–240.

Bertoletti, A., *Musici alla corte dei Gonzaga in Mantova dal secolo XV al XVIII . . .* , Milan, 1890.

Bettelheim, Bruno, *The Uses of Enchantment: The Meaning and Importance of Fairy Tales*, London, 1976. (A basic post-Freudian study.)

Bettley, John, 'North Italian *Falsobordone* and its Relevance to the early *Stile Recitativo*', PRMA, Vol. 103 (1976–7) (but published 1978), pp. 1–18.

Bianconi, Lorenzo, 'Funktionen des Operntheaters in Neapel bis 1700 und die Rolle Alessandro Scarlattis', *Colloquium Alessandro Scarlatti, Würzburg 1975*, ed. Wolfgang Osthoff and Jutta Ruile-Dronke, Tutzing, 1979, pp. 13–116. (A fundamental study.)

—— and Thomas Walker, 'Dalla *Finta pazza* alla *Veremonda*: storie di Febiarmonici', RIM, X, 1975, pp. 379–454. (Important on early opera at Naples.)

—— and ——, 'Production, Consumption and Political Function of 17th-Century Opera'. Paper at the Berkeley Conference of the International Musicological Soc., Sept. 1977 (in preparation).

Bjurström, P., *Giacomo Torelli and Baroque Stage Design*, Stockholm, 1961. (Good and detailed.)

Boccaccio, Giovanni, *Genealogia deorum gentilium*, Venice, 1472. [Actual title: *Genealogiae deorum gentilium secundum Johannem Boccatium*. Venetiis, 1472. Autograph (lost) *c.* 1350. Copy made late 1370 or early 1371. Thereafter unauthorized copies. A second autograph copy still being revised by Boccaccio at the time of his death in 1375.] Ed. Vincenzo Romano, Bari, 1951. (The source of many enterprises.)

Bonlini, G. C., *Le glorie della poesie e della musica . . . di Venezia*, Venice, [1730].

Böttger, F., 'Die Comédie-Ballets von Molière und Lully', Diss., Berlin, 1931.

Bowra, C. M., 'Orpheus and Eurydice', *Classical Quarterly*, New Series II (July–Oct. 1952), pp. 113–26. (Varying sources and versions, including the 'happy ending'.)

Boyden, David, 'When is a Concerto not a Concerto?'. MQ XLIII (April 1957), pp. 220–32.

Brenner, Rosamund Drooker, 'Emotional Expression in Keiser's Operas', MR (Aug. 1972), pp. 224–32.

Brizi, Bruno, 'Teoria e prassi melodrammatica di G. F. Busenello e "L'Incoronazione di Poppea" ' in *Venezia e il melodramma nel seicento*, ed. M. T. Muraro, Florence, 1976, pp. 51–74. (Good on poetic detail.)

Brockpähler, Renate, *Handbuch zur Geschichte der Barockoper in Deutschland*, Emsdetten, Westf., 1964. (Valuable information, town by town.)

Brooks, Eulan van, 'Richard Keiser and his Opera *Fredegunda*', M.A. thesis, Denton, Texas, 1966.

Brown, Howard Mayer, 'How Opera Began: an Introduction to Jacopo Peri's *Euridice* (1600)', in *The Late Italian Renaissance, 1525–1630*, ed. Eric Cochrane, London, 1970, pp. 401–43.

—— 'Psyche's Lament: Some Music for the Medici Wedding in 1565' in

Words and Music: the Scholar's View . . . in Honor of A. Tillman Merritt, ed. Laurence Berman, Cambridge, Mass., 1972, pp. 1–27.

—— *Sixteenth-Century Instrumentation: The Music for the Florentine Intermedii*, [Rome], 1973. (A most detailed and musicianly study, including the actual instruments and the manner of their use—has especial reference to the intermedii of 1589 and reproduces the Buontalenti settings.)

—— *Music in the Renaissance*, Englewood Cliffs, New Jersey, 1976.

Buelow, George J., 'Opera in Hamburg 300 Years Ago', MT (Jan. 1978).

Buonarrotti, Michelangelo, *Descrizione delle felicissimi nozze della Christianissima Maestà di Madama Maria Medici Regina di Francia e di Navarra*, Florence, 1600.

Byrd, William, *Gradualia*, I, London, 1605. (Has the important Epistola Dedicatoria.)

Caccini, Giulio, *Nuove musiche*, Florence, 1602. [Title page 1601 is in error since the imprimatur is dated 1 July 1602, which is thus the earliest possible date and cannot even be Florentine Old-Style 1601, which ended 25 March.] (For the important preface. The ed. by Wiley Hitchcock, Madison, 1970, has a valuable introduction and notes, together with his excellent translation. Caccini's *Nuove musiche* of Florence, 1614, is a different work.)

Calcaterra, Carlo, *Poesia e canto, studi sulla poesia melica italiana e sulla favola per musica*, Bologna, 1951.

Cametti, Alberto, *Il Teatro di Tordinona poi di Apollo*, 2 vols., Tivoli, 1938. (Includes good source material.)

Campion, Thomas, *Description of a Masque*, London, 1607.

Cappelli, Adriano, *Cronologia, cronografia e calendario perpetuo*, Milan, 1905; 2nd ed. 1930; repr. 1960; 3rd ed. Milan, 1969. (Compact.)

Carfagno, Simon A., 'The Life and Dramatic Music of Stefano Landi with a Transliteration and Orchestration of the Opera *Santa' Alessio*', Diss., 4 vols., Univ. of California, Los Angeles, 1960.

Caroso da Sermoneta, Fabritio, *Nobiltà di dame*, Venice, 1600.

Cartari, Vincenzo, *Le Imagini, con la spositione de i dei de gli antichi*, Venice, 1556. (Long and solid, and particularly rich in pictorial illustrations—though not in the first edition, and different in different subsequent editions.)

Caselli, Aldo, *Catalogo delle opere liriche pubblicate in Italia*, Florence, 1969. (Has inevitably some mistakes and omissions.)

Castiglione, Baldassare, *Il libro del cortegiano*, Venice, 1528. Written by 1514. Tr. Sir Thomas Hoby, as *The Courtyer of Count Baldassar Castilio done into Englyshe by Thomas Hoby*, London, 1561.

Caula, Giacomo Alessandro, *Baltazarini e il 'Ballet comique de la royne'*, Florence, 1964.

Cavalieri, Emilio de', *Rappresentatione di anima, et di corpo*, Rome, 1600. (With Guidotti's informative preface.)

Cavallino, S., *Raccolta di tutti le solennissime feste . . .*, Rome, 1589.

Champigneulle, Bernard, *L'Âge classique de la musique française*, Paris, 1946.

Chiarelli, Alessandra, 'L'Incoronazione di Poppea o Il Nerone: Problemi di filologia testuale', RIM, Vol. IX, 1974, pp. 117–51.

Christout, Marie-Françoise, *Le Ballet de cour de Louis XIV, 1643–1672*, Paris, 1967. (A valuable and detailed study.)

—— 'L'Influence venitienne exercée par les artistes italiens sur les premiers spectacles à machine montés à la cour de France durant la Régence (1645–1650)', in *Venezia e il melodramma nel seicento*, ed. M. T. Muraro, Florence, 1976.

Coker, Wilson, *Music and Meaning*, New York, 1972. (Nearer to behaviourist than to depth psychology, but as such highly intelligent.)

Conti, Natale [Natalis Comes], *Mythologiae sive explicationis fabularum libri decem*, Venice, 1567 [ed. cited for 1551 appears not to have existed]. (The acknowledged source of the *Balet comique de la royne*.)

Crain, Gordon F., 'Francesco Cavalli and the Venetian Opera', *Opera*, XVIII (June 1967), pp. 446–51. (Succinct and interesting.)

Cutts, John P., *La Musique de scène de la troupe de Shakespeare*, Paris, 1959. (Excellent.)

Davies, Sir John, *Orchestra or a Poeme of Dauncing Judicially proving the true observation of time and measure, in the Authenticall and laudable use of Dauncing*, London, 1596. (Has a strongly Neoplatonic tendency.)

Day, Christine J., 'The Theater of SS. Giovanni e Paolo and Monteverdi's *L'incoronazione di Poppea*', CMc, No. 25 (1978), pp. 22–38.

Dean, Winton, *Handel's Dramatic Oratorios and Masques*, London, 1959. (A classic of practical musicology.)

Demerson, Guy, *La Mythologie classique dans l'oeuvre lyrique de la 'Pléiade'*, Geneva, 1972. (A major study.)

Dent, Edward J., *Alessandro Scarlatti*, London, 1905; New Impression with preface and additional notes by Frank Walker, London, 1960.

——*Foundations of English Opera*, Cambridge, 1928.

——'Libretto', in *Grove's Dictionary of Music and Musicians*, 5th ed. (ed. Eric Blom), London, 1954, Vol. V, pp. 223–30. (Valuable.)

Dewey, John, *Art as Experience*, Chicago, 1934.

Doni, Giovanni Battista, 'Trattato della musica scenica' [*c.*1635] and other collected writings, ed. A. F. Gori in 2 vols., *Lyra Barberina* and *De' trattati di musica*, Florence, 1763. (Long extracts in Angelo Solerti, *Origini*, Turin, 1903, pp. 186–228; is one of our main historical sources.)

—— *Compendio del trattato de' generi e de' modi della musica*, Rome, 1635. (Summary for unpublished book; but a sequel, *Annotazioni sopra il Compendio*, was published, Rome, 1640.)

—— *De praestantia musicae veteris*, Florence, 1647.

Dryden, John, *Albion and Albanus*, London, 1685. (Music by Grabu. The preface by Dryden is of great interest.)

Ecorcheville, J., *Corneille et la musique*, Paris, 1906. (Attitude to opera.)

Ehrenzweig, Anton, *The Hidden Order of Art: a Study in the Psychology of Artistic Imagination*, Berkeley and Los Angeles, 1967. (Post-Freudian and excellent in that kind.)

Einstein, Alfred, *The Italian Madrigal*, 3 vols., Princeton, 1949.

Ellis, Meredith, 'The Sources of Jean-Baptiste Lully's Secular Music', RMCF VIII (Paris, 1968), pp. 89–130.

Elyot, Sir Thomas, *The Boke named the Governour*, London, 1531.

Eppelsheim, Jurgen, *Das Orchester in den Werken Jean-Baptiste Lullys*, Tutzing, 1961. (Admirable.)

Epperson, Gordon, *The Musical Symbol*, Chicago, 1967. (Post-Langerian.)

Evelyn, John, *Diary*, ed. E. S. de Beer, Oxford, 1955. (Has the important reference to Venetian opera, on p. 449 of the ed. cited here.)

Fano, Fabio, '*Il Combattimento di Tancredi e Clorinda e L'Incoronazione di*

Poppea di Claudio Monteverdi', in *Studi sul teatro veneto fra rinascimento ed età barocca*, Florence, 1971, pp. 346–71.

Fenlon, Iain, 'Music and Spectacle at the Gonzaga Court, *c.*1580–1600', PRMA, Vol. 103, 1976–7 (publ. 1978). (Excellent.)

Ficino, Marsilio, Coll. works as *Marsilii Ficini opera*, Basel, 1561. Facs. of ed. of Basel, [1576], ed. Paul O. Kristeller, New York, 1959.

[Follino, Federico,] *Compendio della sontuose feste. . .*, Mantua, 1608. (For the Mantuan Festivities of 1608, including Monteverdi's *Arianna*.)

Fortune, Nigel, 'Italian Secular Monody from 1600 to 1635', MQ XXXIX (1953), pp. 171–95. (Excellent.)

—— 'Italian Secular Song from 1600 to 1635: the Origins and Development of Accompanied Monody', Diss., Gonville and Caius, Univ. of Cambridge, 1953.

—— 'Solo Song and Cantata' in *The New Oxford History of Music*, Vol. IV, London, 1968, pp. 155ff.

Freeman, Robert, *Opera Without Drama: Currents of Change in Italian Opera, 1675 to 1725, and the Roles Played Therein by Zeno, Caldara, and Others*, Ph.D. diss., Princeton Univ., 1967.

—— ed. and contr., *The Florentine Intermedi of 1589*, B.B.C., London, 1979.

—— 'Apostolo Zeno's Reform of the Libretto', in JAMS XXI No. 3 (Fall 1968), pp. 321–41.

Friedman, J. B., *Orpheus in the Middle Ages*, Cambridge, Mass., 1970.

Fuller, David, 'The Jonsonian Masque and Its Music', ML LIV 4 (Oct. 1973), p. 440ff. (Valuable.)

Gagliano, Marco da, *Dafne*, Florence, 1608. (With Gagliano's important preface.)

Galilei, Vincenzo, *Dialogo. . .della musica antica, e della moderna*, Venice, 1581. (The polemic against vocal polyphony.)

Galvani, Livio Niso, *I teatri musicali di Venezia*, Milan, 1879.

Garin, Eugenio, 'Aristotelismo e Platonismo del Rinascimento', *La Rinascità*, Anno 2, Florence, 1939.

Gérold, Théodore, *L'Art du chant en France au XVIIe siècle*, Strasbourg, 1921. (Important.)

Gesualdo, Giovanni Andrea, *Il Petrarcha con l'espositione di M. Giovanni Andrea Gesualdo. . .*, Venice, 1533 and many eds. (Typical of the Platonic *Espositioni*—was known to Spenser.)

Ghisi, Federico, *Feste musicali della Firenze medicea (1480–1589)*, Florence, 1939.

Gianturco, Carolyn M., 'Caratteri stilistici delle opere teatrali di Stradella', RIM VI (1971), pp. 211–45.

—— 'Evidence for a Late Roman School of Opera', ML LVI 1 (Jan. 1974), pp. 4ff. (i.e. late 17th cent.)

Giraldi, Lilio Gregorio [Giraldus], *De deis gentium varia et multiplex historia. . .*, Basel, 1548. (Weighty and elaborate, especially on mythological 'attributes'.)

Giraud, Yves F.-A., *La Fable de Daphné. . .*, Geneva, 1969. (Immensely impressive as literary history; includes the Rinuccini-Peri *Dafne*, but is quite out of date and unacceptable on the musical issues.)

Girdlestone, Cuthbert, *La Tragédie en musique (1673–1750) considérée comme genre littéraire*, Geneva, 1972. (Good and detailed, especially on Quinault.)

Giry, A., *Manuel de Diplomatique*, Paris, 1894. (Pp. 83–168 are on problems of dating and the Calendar: invaluable.)

Glover, Jane, *Cavalli*, London, 1978. (Excellent.)

—— 'The Peak Period of Venetian Public Opera: The 1650's', PRMA, 102 (1975–6), pp. 67–82.

Godwin, Jocelyn, 'Layers of Meaning in *The Magic Flute*', MQ LXV 4 (Oct. 1979). (Includes much unusual insight.)

Goldschmidt, Hugo, *Studien zur Geschichte der Italienischen Oper im 17. Jahrhundert*, 2 vols., Leipzig, 1901. Facs. Wiesbaden, 1967. (Of pioneering importance.)

Gombrich, Ernst Hans, 'Botticelli's Mythologies, a Study in the Neoplatonic Symbolism of his Circle', *Journ. of the Warburg and Courtauld Institutes*, VIII (1945), pp. 7–60.

—— *Art and Illusion: a Study in the Psychology of Pictorial Representation*, London, 1972. (A classic of practical aesthetics.)

—— *Symbolic Images: Studies in the Art of the Renaissance*, London, 1972.

Grafton, A., 'On the Scholarship of Politian and Its Context', *Journ. of the Warburg and Courtauld Institutes*, XL (1977), pp. 150–88.

Groppo, Antonio, *Catalogo di tutti i drammi per musica recitati ne' teatri di Venezia dall' anno 1637 all' anno presente 1745*, Venice, 1745.

Grout, Donald Jay, *A Short History of Opera*, New York, 1947, 2nd ed. 1965. (The best general survey; has an encyclopedic Bibl.)

—— 'The Chorus in Early Opera', *Festschrift Friedrich Blume*, ed. Abert and Pfannkuch, Kassel, 1963, pp. 151–61.

Gruppe, Otto, Article s.v. 'Orpheus (u. Euridice)' in W. H. Roscher, ed., *Ausführliches Lexicon der griechischen und römischen Mythologie*, 8 vols. Leipzig, 1884–1937. (The most comprehensive scholarly presentation, with references to the classical and post-classical primary sources together with many secondary sources.)

—— *Geschichte der klassischen Mythologie. . .während der Neuzeit*, Leipzig, 1921. (Supl. to Roscher's *Lexicon*, for which see under Roscher.)

Guthrie, W. K. C., *Orpheus and Greek Religion*, London, 1935.

Haar, James, 'False Relations and Chromaticism in Sixteenth-Century Music', JAMS XXX 3 (Fall 1977).

Hamm, Charles, *Opera*, Boston, 1966. (A highly intelligent composer's view of opera.)

Hanning, Barbara Russano, 'The Influence of Humanist Thought and Italian Poetry on the Formation of Opera', *Studies in Musicology*, Ann Arbor, 1979. (An important original contribution.)

—— 'Apologia pro Ottavio Rinuccini', JAMS XXVI 2 (Summer 1973), pp. 240–62. (See above.)

Harrington, Sir John, *Orlando Furioso in English Heroical Verse*, London, 1591. [With 'A Preface, or rather a Briefe Apologie of Poetrie': this Preface is in *Elizabethan Critical Essays*, ed. G. Gregory Smith, II, Oxford, 1904.]

Hathaway, Baxter, *The Age of Criticism: The Late Renaissance in Italy*, Ithaca, N.Y., 1962.

Heartz, Daniel, '*Voix de ville*: Between Humanist Ideals and Musical Realities', in *Words and Music: the Scholar's View. . .In Honor of A. Tillman Merritt*, ed. Laurence Berman, Harvard, 1972, pp. 115–35. (Union of poetry and music.)

Hess, Heinz, *Die Opern Alessandro Stradellas*, Leipzig, 1966.

Hill, John Walter, 'Oratory Music in Florence: I, *Ricercar Cantando*, 1583–1655; II, At San Firenze in the Seventeenth and Eighteenth Centuries', *Act. Mus.*, LI, 1979, i–ii. (Includes light on Bardi's and Corsi's relationship.)

Hinks, Roger, *Myth and Allegory in Ancient Art*, London, 1939.

Hitchcock, H. Wiley, 'Caccini's "Other" *Nuove musiche*', JAMS XXVII 3 (1974), pp. 438–60. (And see Caccini.)

Holmes, William C., 'Cesti's "L'Argia": An Entertainment for a Royal Court', *Chigiana*, XXVI–XXVII (Florence, 1971), pp. 35–52.

Isherwood, Robert M., *Music in the Service of the King: France in the Seventeenth Century*, Ithaca, N.Y., and London, 1973.

Ivanovich, Cristoforo, 'Memorie teatrali di Venezia', *Minerva al tavolino*, Venice, 1681, pp. 369–453.

Johnson, Margaret F., 'Agazzari's *Eumelio,* a "Dramma Pastorale"', MQ LVII 8 (July 1971), pp. 491–505.

Johnson, Paula, *Form and Transformation in Music and Poetry of the English Renaissance*, New Haven and London, 1972. (Is best on the poetry.)

Jung, Carl Gustav, *Erinnerungen, Träume, Gedenken von C. G. Jung. Aufgezeichnet und herausgegeben von Aniela Jaffé*, Zürich and Stuttgart, 1962. Tr. Richard and Clara Winston as *Memories, Dreams, Reflections,* [London], 1963. (For primitive sun-worship and very much else besides.)

Kaufmann, Henry W., *The Life and Works of Nicola Vicentino*, Amer. Inst. of Musicology, [n.p.], 1966. (Brilliant.)

—— 'Music for a Noble Florentine Wedding (1539)', in *Words and Music: the Scholar's View. . .in Honor of A. Tillman Merritt*, ed. Laurence Berman, Cambridge, Mass., 1972, pp. 161–88. (Has translation and music.)

Kennedy, Philip H., 'The First French Opera: the Literary Standpoint', RMCF VIII (1968), pp. 77–88.

Kerényi, C., *Eleusis, Archetypal Image of Mother and Daughter*, New York, 1967.

—— and C. G. Jung, tr. R. F. C. Hull, *Essays on a Science of Mythology*, New York, 1949, and as *Introduction to a Science of Mythology*, London, 1950 (in Jung, *Coll. Wks.*, Vol. 9, part 1).

Kerman, Joseph, *Opera as Drama*, New York, 1947. (Uneven but magnificent.)

Keyte, Hugh, 'From de' Rossi to Malvezzi: Some Performance Problems', *The Florentine Intermedi of 1589*, B.B.C., London, 1979, pp. 27–31.

Klingender, Francis, *Animals in Art and Thought*, London, 1971. (Enchanting, with both Freudian and Jungian insights.)

Koestler, Arthur, *The Act of Creation*, New York, 1964. (In many respects, though not quite in all, a highly perceptive and creative vision indeed.)

Kristeller, Paul Oscar, *The Philosophy of Marsilio Ficino*, tr. Virginia Conant, New York, 1943.

Lajarte, Théodore de, *Bibliothèque musicale du Théâtre de l'Opéra*, 2 vols., Paris, 1878. Facs., Hildesheim, 1969.

Langer, Susanne K., *Philosophy in a New Key: Study in the Symbolism of Reason, Rite and Art*, Harvard, 1957. (Justly celebrated.)

—— *Reflections on Art*, New York, 1961.

Laurencie, Lionel de la, *Lully*, Paris, 1911.

—— *Rameau*, Paris, 1926.

Laus, Zelm, *Die Opern Reinhard Keisers: Studien zur Chronologie, Überlieferung und Stilentwicklung*, Munich, 1975.

Lavallière, Louis César de La Baume Le Blanc, *Ballets, opéra, et autres ouvrages lyriques. . .*, Paris, 1760.

Lawrenson, Thomas E., *The French Stage in the XVIIth Century: A Study in the Advent of the Italian Order*, Manchester, 1957. (Staging and machinery.)

Lea, K. M., *Italian Popular Comedy: a Study in the Commedia dell' Arte, 1560–1620*, 2 vols., Oxford, 1934.

Lefkowitz, Murray, *Trois masques à la cour de Charles Ier d'Angleterre*, Paris, 1970. (An excellent study.)

Leich, Karl, *Girolamo Frigimelica Robertis Libretti (1694–1708)*, Munich, 1972. (A most intensive monograph.)

Lesure, François, *L'Opéra classique français, XVIIe et XVIIIe siècles*, Geneva, 1972. (With pictures etc. of theatres, stage designs, and costumes; important.)

—— *Musik und Gesellschaft im Bild: Zeugnisse der Malerei aus sechs Jahrhunderten*, tr. from Fr. by A. M. Gottschick, Kassel, 1966; Eng. tr. by D. and S. Stevens as *Music and Art in Society*, University Park, Pa., and London, 1968.

—— *Claude le Jeune et musique mesurée*, tr. E. Gianturco and H. Rosenwald, *s.v.* Walker, *Musicians and Poets of the French Renaissance*, New York, 1955.

Levitan, Alan, 'The Life of Our Design: the Jonsonian Masque as Baroque Form', dissert., Princeton, 1964. (Valuable on the Italian influence.)

Lewis, Anthony, and Nigel Fortune, eds., *New Oxford History of Music*, Vol. V, 'Opera and Church Music, 1630–1750', London, 1975.

Lindemann, Fr., 'Die Operntexte Quinaults', dissert., Leipzig, 1904.

Linforth, Ivan M., *The Arts of Orpheus*, Berkeley, 1941. (Thorough and critical on the Orphic cult.)

Loewenberg, Alfred, *Annals of Opera, 1597–1940*, 2 vols, Cambridge, 1943; 2nd ed. rev., Geneva, 1955. (A splendid standby.)

Long, John H., ed., *Music in English Renaissance Drama*, Lexington, 1968.

Lowes, John Livingston, *The Road to Xanadu*, Boston and New York, 1927. (A pioneering classic on subliminal association in the arts.)

Lowinsky, Edward E., *Tonality and Atonality in Sixteenth-Century Music*, Berkeley and Los Angeles, 1961. (An important investigation and hypothesis.)

MacClintock, Carol, *Giaches de Wert*, [n.p.], 1966. (Detailed and valuable.)

McCredie, Andrew D., 'Christoph Graupner as Opera Composer', MMA, Vol. 1. Adelaide, March 1966, pp. 74–116.

Mace, Dean T., 'Musical Humanism, the Doctrine of Rhythmus, and the Saint Cecilia Odes of Dryden', *Journ. of the Warburg and Courtauld Institutes*, XXVII (1964), pp. 251–92. (Interesting on word-setting.)

—— 'Pietro Bembo and the Literary Origins of the Italian Madrigal', MQ LV 1 (Jan. 1969), pp. 65–86. (Suggestive.)

—— 'Marin Mersenne on Language and Music', JMT XIV (Spring 1970), pp. 2–34.

McGowan, Margaret M., *L'Art du ballet de cour en France, 1581–1643*, Paris, 1963. (A highly intelligent and detailed study.)

McLaughlin, Terence, *Music and Communication*, London, 1970. (Suggestive on post-Freudian and post-Jungian lines.)

Malvezzi, Cristofano, *Intermedii et concerti. . .*, Venice, 1591. (For the 1589 interludes.)

Mamcarz, Irène, *Les intermèdes comiques italiens au XVIIIe siècle en France et en Italie*, Paris, 1972. (Good on the librettos.)

Manelli, Francesco, *La Delia o sia La sera sposa del sole*, Venice, 1639. (Has the interesting Allegoria.)

Mangini, Nicola, *I teatri di Venezia*, Milan, 1974. (A detailed study theatre by theatre.)

Manning, Aubrey, *An Introduction to Animal Behaviour*, London, 1967, 2nd ed. 1972. (Physiology and psychology related.)

Maritain, Jacques, *Creative Intuition in Art and Poetry*, New York, 1953. (Heady but visionary.)

Marshall, Robert L., ed., *Studies in Renaissance and Baroque Music in Honor of Arthur Mendel*, S. Hackensack, N.J., 1974.

Masson, Paul-Marie, *L'Opéra de Rameau*, Paris, 1930. (A standard work.)

Mazzocchi, Domenico, *La Catena d'Adone*, Venice, 1625. (With the Allegoria at the end.)

Meagher, John C., 'The Dance and the Masques of Ben Jonson', *Journ. of the Warburg and Courtauld Institutes*, XXV (1962), pp. 258–77. (Neoplatonic implications.)

Mei, Girolamo, ed. Claude Palisca, *Letters on Ancient and Modern Music*, Amer. Inst. of Musicology, [n.p.], 1960. (Important.)

Mellers, Wilfrid, *François Couperin and the French Classical Tradition*, London, 1950. (Excellent.)

—— 'Lully' in *The Heritage of Music*, ed. Hubert Foss, 3 vols., London, 1951, Vol. III, pp. 32–52.

—— *Caliban Reborn: Renewal in Twentieth-Century Music*, New York, Evanston, and London, 1967. (Suggestive on music's underside.)

Mersenne, Marin, *Harmonie universelle*, 2 pts., Paris, 1636–7. Facs. introd. F. Lesure, 3 vols. Paris, 1963. (For Mersenne's discussions of the relationship of words and music, see Dean T. Mace.)

Meyer, Leonard B., *Emotion and Meaning in Music*, Chicago and London, 1956. (A most powerful attempt.)

—— *Music, the Arts and Ideas*, Chicago, 1968. (A worthy sequel.)

Miller, Nancy S., *The Venetian Operas of Giovanni Maria Pagliardi*, M.A. thesis, Columbia Univ., 1967.

Minor, Andrew C., and Bonner Mitchell, *A Renaissance Entertainment: Festivities for the Marriage of Cosimo I, Duke of Florence, in 1539; An Edition of the Music, Poetry, Comedy, and Descriptive Account, with Commentary*, Columbia, Miss., 1968. (With much good background material.)

Misson, François Maximilien, *Nouveau voyage d'Italie fait en l'année 1688*, The Hague, 1691.

Mitchell, Ronald E., *Opera Dead or Alive*, Madison and London, 1970. (Chiefly on production.)

Molinari, Cesare, *Le nozze degli dei, un saggio sul grande spettacolo italiano nel seicento*, Rome, 1968. (Links Bardi's interludes of 1585/6 with Ripa, Cartari and Neoplatonic thought.)

Monteverdi, Claudio, *Letters*, tr. and ed. Denis Stevens, London, 1980.

Monteverdi, Giulio Cesare, Annotations to Claudio Monteverdi's *Scherzi musicali*, Venice, 1607. (For the celebrated First and Second Practice.)

Morelli, Giovanni, and Thomas Walker, 'Tre controversie interno al San Cassiano', in *Venezia e il melodramma nel seicento*, ed. M. T. Muraro, Florence, 1976.

Muraro, Maria Teresa, 'Venezia' in *Enciclopedia dello spettacolo*, Rome, IX, 1962.

—— ed., *Studi sul teatro veneto fra rinascimento ed età barocca*, Florence, 1971.

—— ed., *Venezia e il melodramma nel seicento*, Florence, 1976.

Mylonas, George E., *Eleusis and the Eleusinian Mysteries*, Princeton, 1961.

Nagler, A. M., *Theatre Festivals of the Medici, 1539–1637*, Yale, 1964. (Plots, scenery, machinery, with many illustrations.)

Neumann, Friedrich-Heinrich, *Die Ästhetik des Rezitativs*, Strasbourg/Baden-Baden, 1962.

Nicoll, Allardyce, *Stuart Masques and the Renaissance Stage*, London, 1937.

—— *The World of Harlequin*, Cambridge, 1963.

Oliver, Richard A., 'Molière's Contribution to the Lyric Stage', MQ XXXIII 3 (July 1947), pp. 350–64.

Orrey, Leslie, *A Concise History of Opera*, London, 1972. (Tells a very good story.)

Osthoff, Wolfgang, 'Zu den Quellen von Monteverdis *Ritorno di Ulisse in patria*', SMw XXIII (1956), pp. 67–78.

—— 'Neue Beobachtungen zu Quellen und Geschichte von Monteverdis *Incoronazione di Poppea*', Mf XI (1958), pp. 129–38.

—— *Das dramatische Spätwerk Claudio Monteverdis*, Tutzing, 1960. (Excellent.)

—— 'Monteverdis "Combattimento" in deutscher Sprache und Heinrich Schütz', in *Festschrift Helmuth Osthoff*, Tutzing, 1961, pp. 195–227.

—— *Theatergesang und darstellende Musik in der italienischen Renaissance (15. und 16. Jahrhundert)*, 2 vols., Tutzing, 1969. (A most thorough study of theatre music pre-opera.)

Palisca, Claude V., 'Girolamo Mei: Mentor to the Florentine Camerata', MQ XL (1954), pp. 1–20.

—— 'Vincenzo Galilei and Some Links between "Pseudo Monody" and Monody', MQ XLVI 3 (July 1960), pp. 344–60.

—— 'Musical Asides in the Diplomatic Correspondence of Emilio de' Cavalieri', MQ XLIX (July 1963), pp. 339–55.

—— 'The First Performance of "Euridice"', in *Queen's College. . .Twenty-Fifth Anniversary Festschrift*, ed. A. Mell, New York, 1964, pp. 1–23.

—— *Baroque Music*, Englewood Cliffs, N.J., 1968. (Good on early opera.)

—— 'The Alterati of Florence, Pioneers in the Theory of Dramatic Music', in *New Looks at Italian Opera, Essays in Honor of Donald Grout*, ed. William W. Austin, Ithaca, N.Y., 1968, pp. 9–38.

—— 'The "Camerata Fiorentina": a Reappraisal', *Studi Musicali*, I, 2 (1972), pp. 203–34. (Masterly.)

—— 'Marco Scacchi's Defence of Modern Music (1649)', in *Words and Music: the Scholar's View. . .in Honor of A. Tillman Merritt*, ed. Laurence Berman, Cambridge, Mass., 1972, pp. 189–235.

Panofsky, Erwin, *Studies in Iconology: Humanist Themes in the Art of the Renaissance*, London and New York, 1939. (A pioneering classic of mythological interpretation.)

Parthenay, Catherine de, *Ballets allégoriques en vers, 1592–3*, ed. and introd. Raymond Ritter, Paris, 1927. (Neoplatonic images for diplomatic purposes.)

Pavoni, G., *Diario. . .delle feste celebrate. . .*, Bologna, 1589.

Pelisson, M., *Les comédies-ballets de Molière*, Paris, 1914.

Peri, Jacopo, *L'Euridice*, Florence, 1601. (With Peri's important preface.)

Perkins, Leonard, 'Mode and Structure in the Masses of Josquin', JAMS XXVI 2 (1973), pp. 189–239. (Interesting on the transition from modal to key tonality.)

Petrobelli, Pierluigi, ' "L'Ermiona" di Pio Enea degli Obizzi ed i primi spettacoli d'opera veneziani' in *Quaderni della Rassegna musicale*, III (1965), pp. 128ff.

—— 'Francesco Manelli—documenti e osservazioni' in *Chigiana*, XXIV (Nuova Serie, 4) (1967), pp. 43–66.

Pirrotta, Nino, tr. Nigel Fortune, 'Temperaments and Tendencies in the Florentine Camerata', MQ XL 2 (April 1954), pp. 169–89. (Itself a little tendentious but of fascinating interest.)

—— '*Commedia dell' arte* and Opera', MQ XLI (1955), pp. 305–24.

—— 'Teatro, scene e musica nelle opere di Monteverdi' in *Claudio Monteverdi e il suo tempo*, ed. R. Monterosso, Verona, 1968. (Especially on the two divergent endings to the *Orfeo* of 1607.)

—— *Li due Orfei, da Poliziano a Monteverdi*, Turin, 1969.

—— 'Intermedium', MGG, Lief. 56, Col. 1310ff.

—— and Elena Povoledo, 'Intermezzo' in *Enciclopedia dello Spettacolo*, VI, Rome, 1959.

Poliziano, Angelo [Politian etc.] (i.e. Ambrogini), *La favola di Orfeo*, ed. Giosue Carducci, Bologna, 2nd ed. 1912. (Three MS versions exist, of which the first two are in Carducci's ed., with a discussion of the possible dates: 1472 used to be accepted, but probability now is about 1478; latest possible date is 1483. The 2nd version must date from after 1480; it is entitled *Orphei tragoedia*, and is not certainly by Poliziano. The differences are considerable but the poem is substantially the same in both these versions. I have not seen the third version.)

—— *Omnia opera Angeli Politiani*, Venice, 1498.

Porter, William V., 'Peri and Corsi's *Dafne*: Some New Discoveries and Observations', JAMS XVIII 2 (1965), pp. 170–96. (A crucial article.)

Poultney, David, 'Alessandro Scarlatti and the Transformation of Oratorio', MQ LIX 4 (Oct. 1973), pp. 584–601. (Relation of oratorio and opera.)

Powers, Harold, ed., *Studies in Music History: Essays for Oliver Strunk*, Princeton, 1968.

Prunières, Henry, *Lully*, Paris, 1910.

—— *L'Opéra italien en France avant Lully*, Paris, 1913. (Indispensable.)

—— *Le Ballet de cour en France avant Benserade et Lully*, Paris, 1914. (Invaluable.)

—— 'Lully and the Académie de Musique et de Danse', MQ XI (Oct. 1925), pp. 528–46.

—— *Cavalli et l'opéra vénitien au XVIIIe siècle*, Paris, 1931.

Quitslund, Jon A., 'Spenser's *Amoretti VIII* and Platonic Commentaries on Petrarch', *Journ. of the Warburg and Courtauld Institutes*, XXXVI (1973), pp. 256–76. (Valuable for Platonic and Aristotelian interpretations of Dante, Petrarch etc.)

Racek, Jan, *Italská monodie. . .*, Prague, 1945; and Ger. ed. as *Stilprobleme der italienischen Monodie*, Prague, 1965. (A profound study.)

Redlich, Hans, *Claudio Monteverdi: Leben und Werk*, Olten, 1949; Engl. tr. Kathleen Dale, London, 1952.

Reiner, Stuart, 'Vi sono molt'altre mezz'Arie' in *Studies in Music History: Essays for Oliver Strunk*, ed. Harold Powers, Princeton, 1968.

—— 'La vaga Angioletta (and others)', AnMc, Band xiv (1974), p. 54. (Includes much excellent background.)

Richards, I. A., *Practical Criticism*, London, 1964.

Ridder, Lisolotte de, 'Der Anteil der Commedia dell' Arte an der Entstehungs- und Entwicklungsgeschichte der komischen Oper', doctoral dissert. Univ. of Köln, 1970.

Rinuccini, Ottavio, *Drammi per musica: Dafne, Euridice, Arianna*, ed. Andrea Della Corte, Turin, 1926. (The first librettist of opera.)

Ripa, Cesare, *Iconologia*, Rome, 1593. Reprinted Hildesheim and New York, 1970.

Robb, Nesca A., *Neoplatonism of the Italian Renaissance*, London, 1935.

Robinson, Michael F., *Opera before Mozart*, London, 1966. (Popular but of good quality.)

—— *Naples and Neapolitan Opera*, Oxford, 1972. (Excellent.)

Rolandi, Ulderico, *Il libretto per musica attraverso i tempi*, Rome, 1951. (Good on Zeno, Metastasio, Calzabigi.)

Ronsard, Pierre de, *Abrégé de l'art poétique français*, Paris, 1560. Ed. of Paris, 1565, is in *Works*, ed. Gustave Cohen, [Paris], 1950, II, p. 997.

Rosand, Ellen, 'Aria as Drama in the Early Operas of Francesco Cavalli' in *Venezia e il melodramma nel seicento*, ed. M. T. Muraro, Florence, 1976, pp. 75–96.

——, 'Comic Contrast and Dramatic Unity: Observations on the Form and Function of Aria in the Operas of Francesco Cavalli', MR XXXVII (1976), pp. 92–105.

—— 'Francesco Cavalli in Modern Edition', CMc, No. 27, 1979, pp. 73–83. (Relates the actual experience of making one.)

Roscher, W. H., ed., *Ausführliches Lexicon der Griechischen und Römischen Mythologie*, 8 vols., Leipzig, 1884–1933. (Especially *s.v.* 'Orpheus (u. Euridice)'—article by Otto Gruppe.)

Rose, Gloria, 'Agazzari and the Improvising Orchestra', JAMS XVIII 3 (1965).

—— 'Polyphonic Italian Madrigals of the Seventeenth Century', ML XLVII (1966), p. 153. (Shows their continued popularity.)

—— 'The Italian Cantata of the Baroque Period' in *Gattungen der Musik. . .Gedenkschrift Leo Schrade*, ed. Max Haas *et al.*, Bern and Munich, 1973, pp. 655–77. (Excellent.)

Rossi, Bastiano de', *Descrizione dell' apparato e degli' Intermedi. . .*, Florence, 1589.

Sabol, Andrew J., 'New Documents on Shirley's Masque "The Triumph of Peace"', ML XLVII (Jan. 1966), pp. 10–26.

—— ed., *Four Hundred Songs and Dances from the Stuart Masque*, Providence, Rhode Island, 1979.

Saint-Évremond, Charles Marguetel de Saint-Denis, Seigneur de, *Oeuvres meslées*, Tome XI, Paris, 1668. (Has the Letter on Opera to the Duke of Buckingham: see Saint-Évremond, *Oeuvres en prose*, ed. René Ternois, 4 vols., Paris, 1662–9, Vol. 2, pp. 195–8, and Vol. 3, pp. 127–64.)

Sartori, Claudio, *Catalogo dei libretti d'opera italiani stampato fino al 1800*, Milan, 1973– [xerox copies from Ann Arbor, Mich.].

Schmidgall, Gary, *Literature as Opera*, London, 1978. (A valuable attempt to connect words and music.)

Schmidt, Carl B., 'Antonio Cesti's *La Dori*: A Study of Sources, Performance Traditions and Musical Style', RIM X (1975), pp. 455–98.

—— 'Antonio Cesti's *Il pomo d'oro*: A Re-examination of a Famous Hapsburg Court Spectacle', JAMS XXIX 3 (Fall 1976), pp. 381–412. (Portions of Acts III and V rediscovered.)

Schrade, Leo, *Monteverdi*, New York, 1950.

—— 'Les Fêtes du mariage de Francesco dei Medici et de Bianca Cappello', in *Les Fêtes de la renaissance*, I, Paris, 1956, pp. 107–44.

Selfridge-Field, Eleanor, *Venetian Instrumental Music from Gabrieli to Vivaldi*, Oxford, 1975.

Seznec, Jean, 'Manuels mythologiques italiens et leur diffusion en Angleterre à la fin de la renaissance' in *Mélanges d'archéologie et d'histoire*, Paris, 1933.

—— 'La Masquerade des dieux à Florence en 1566', *Mélanges d'archéologie et d'histoire*, LII (1935), pp. 224–43.

—— *The Survival of the Pagan Gods* (in French as *La Survivance des dieux antiques*, London, 1940), tr. Barbara Sessions, New York, 1953. (Important.)

Shearman, John, 'The Florentine *Entrata* of Leo X, 1515', *Journ. of the Warburg and Courtauld Institutes*, XXXVIII (1975), pp. 136–54.

Silke, Leopold, 'Das geistliche Libretto im 17. Jahrhundert zur Gattungsgeschichte der frühen Oper', Mf 31, Heft 3 (July–Sept. 1978), pp. 245–57.

Smith, Patrick J., *The Tenth Muse, a historical study of the opera libretto*, New York, 1970.

Smither, H. E., *A History of the Oratorio: I, The Oratorio in the Baroque Era, Italy, Vienna, Paris; II, The Oratorio in the Baroque Era, Protestant Germany and England*, Chapel Hill, N.C., 1978. (Valuable.)

Solerti, Angelo, 'Laura Guidiccioni Lucchesini ed Emilio de' Cavalieri', RMI IX (1902), pp. 797–829.

—— *Origini del melodramma*, Turin, 1903. (Prints extensive source material.)

—— *Gli Albori del melodramma*, 3 vols., Milan/Palermo/Naples, [1903–4]. (Preface is dated 1903–4.) (Prints librettos.)

—— *Musica, ballo e drammatica. . .*, Florence, 1905. (Documents relating to the Medici court.)

Sonneck, Oscar, *Library of Congress Catalogue of Opera Librettos printed before 1800*, 2 vols., Washington D.C., 1914. (A classic of its kind.)

—— 'A Description of A. Striggio's and F. Corteccia's Intermedi "Psyche and Amor", 1565', in *Miscellaneous Studies in the History of Music*, New York, 1921.

Stalnaker, William P., Jr., 'The Beginnings of Opera in Naples', Ph.D. dissert., Princeton Univ., 1968.

Starnes, DeWitt T., and Ernest William Talbot, *Classical Myth and Legend in Renaissance Dictionaries*, Chapel Hill, N.C., 1955.

Steinbeck, Dietrich, 'Die Oper als theatralische Form', Mf XX 3 (1967), pp. 252–62. (Good on inner *v.* outer realities.)

Sternfeld, F. W., *Music in Shakespearian Tragedy*, London, 1963. (Valuable.)

—— 'Intermedi and the Birth of Opera', *The Florentine Intermedi of 1589*, B.B.C., London, 1979, pp. 10–16.

—— 'The First Printed Opera Libretto', ML LIX 2 (April 1978), pp. 121–138.

Stevens, Denis, tr. and ed., *The Letters of Claudio Monteverdi*, London, 1980. (With excellent commentaries.)

Storr, Anthony, *The Dynamics of Creation*, London, 1972. (Goes a very long way in.)

Strainchamps, Edmond, 'New Light on the *Accademia degli Elevati* of Florence', MQ LXII 4 (Oct. 1976), pp. 507–35. (Excellent.)

Strong, Roy, *Splendour at Court: Renaissance Spectacle and Illusion*, London, 1973. (Especially valuable on the importance of political allegory.)

Strunk, Oliver, ed. and tr., *Source Readings in Music History*, New York, 1950. (Has opened doors and windows for countless students.)

Swale, David, 'Cavalli: the "Erismena" of 1655', in MMA, Vol. 3, Adelaide, 1968, pp. 145–70.

Taille, Jacques de la, *Manière de faire des vers en français comme en grec et en latin*, Paris, 1573. (But written 1562).

Teicher, Anna, 'The Spectacle of Politics', *The Florentine Intermedi of 1589*, B.B.C., London, 1979, pp. 17–21.

Termini, Olga, 'The Transformation of Madrigalisms in Venetian Operas of the later Seventeenth Century', MR (Feb. 1978), pp. 4–21.

Testi, Flavio, *La musica italiana nel seicento*, [I] *Il Melodramma*, Milan, 1970. (Largely borrowed, esp. from T. Wiel.)

Thesiger, Sarah, 'The *Orchestra* of Sir John Davies and the Image of the Dance', *Journ. of the Warburg and Courtauld Institutes*, XXXVI (1973), pp. 277–304. (Dance as a metaphor for harmonious order.)

Tiersot, Julien, *La Musique dans la comédie de Molière*, Paris [1918].

Toussaint de Limojon, Alexandre, *La Ville et la république de Venise*, Paris, 1680.

Valeriano, Giovanni Pierio Bolzani, *Hieroglyphica, sive de sacris aegyptiorum literis commentarii*, Basel, 1556. (The most important of its rather dubious kind. The ed. of Basel, 1575, is fuller; many later eds. including Frankfurt, 1678. Numerous small woodcuts and a very learned if abstruse text.)

Valle, Pietro della, 'Della musica dell' età nostra', letter written at Rome, dated 16 January 1640, repr. in A. Solerti, *Origini*, Turin, 1903, pp. 148ff. (Valuable.)

Walker, D. P., 'Vers et musique mesurés à l'antique', unpublished thesis in Bodleian Library, Oxford, 1940. (An important study.)

—— 'Orpheus the Theologian and Renaissance Platonists', *Journ. of the Warburg and Courtauld Institutes*, XVI (1953), pp. 100–20.

—— 'The Prisca Theologia in France', *Journ. of the Warburg and Courtauld Institutes*, XVII (1954), pp. 204–59. (Important.)

—— 'La Musique des intermèdes florentins de 1589 et l'humanisme' in *Les Fêtes de la renaissance*, I, Paris, 1956, pp. 133–44.

—— *Spiritual and Demonic Magic from Ficino to Campanella*, London, 1958.

—— ed., *Les Fêtes de Florence (1589), I, Musique des intemèdes de 'La Pelegrina'*, with notes by Federico Ghisi, D. P. Walker and J. Jacquot, Paris, 1963.

Walker, Thomas R., 'Gli errore di "Minerva al Tavolina"', in *Venezia e il melodramma nel seicento*, ed. M. T. Muraro, Florence, 1976. (And see under Bianconi, Morelli. Valuable work.)

Wallis, R. T., *Neoplatonism*, London, 1972. (Hellenistic, not renaissance.)

Warburg, Aby, 'I costumi teatrali per gli intermezzi de 1589' in *Atti dell' Accademia del R. Istituto Musicale di Firenze*, Florence, 1895, and in *Gesammelte Schriften*, Leipzig and Berlin, 1932, pp. 259–300. (Has pictures reproduced from *I disegni di Bernardo Buontalenti*, and a valuable discussion of the Platonic elements.)

—— *Gesammelte Schriften*, Leipzig and Berlin, 1932. (A great pioneer of symbolical interpretation.)

Weaver, Robert L., 'Sixteenth-Century Instrumentation', MQ XLVII (1961), pp. 363–78. (Highly informative.)

—— 'The Orchestra in Early Italian Opera', JAMS XVII (Spring 1964), pp. 83–9. (Perhaps a little conservative, but makes excellent use of our all too scanty material.)

—— 'Opera in Florence: 1646–1731', *Studies in Musicology: Essays in the History, Style and Bibliography of Music in Memory of Glen Haydon*, ed. James W. Pruett, Chapel Hill, N.C, 1969, pp. 60–71.

—— and Norma Wright Weaver, *A Chronology of Music in the Florentine Theater, 1590–1750*, Detroit, 1978.

Weinberg, B., *A History of Literary Criticism in the Italian Renaissance*, Chicago, 1961. (A definitive study.)

Weisstein, Ulrich, ed., *The Essence of Opera*, London, 1964. (Translations and comments are not reliable; selection admirable.)

Wellesz, Egon, *Essays on Opera*, various dates around 1910; tr. Patricia Kean, London, 1950. (Pioneering studies.)

Welsford, Enid, 'Italian Influence on the English Court Masque', *Modern Language Review*, XVIII (1923), pp. 934ff.

Westrup, J. A., 'Monteverdi's "Lamento d'Arianna"', MR I (1940), pp. 144–54.

—— 'The Nature of Recitative', in *Proc. Brit. Acad.*, XLII (1956).

White, E. W., *Rise of English Opera*, London, 1951.

Wiel, Taddeo, *I codici musicali Contariniani del secolo XVII nella R. Biblioteca di San Marco in Venezia*, Venice, 1888. (Minute and valuable.)

Wili, Walter, 'Die Orphischen Mysterien und der griechische Geist', *Eranos Jahr-Buch*, XI (1944), pp. 61–105.

Wilson, Edmund, *The Wound and the Bow*, London, 1941. (Pioneering.)

Wind, Edgar, *Pagan Mysteries in the Renaissance*, London, 1958; 2nd ed. enlarged, London, 1967. (A seminal study.)

Wolff, Hellmuth Christian, *Die Venezianische Oper in der zweiten Hälfte des 17. Jahrhunderts*, Berlin, 1937.

—— *Die Barockoper in Hamburg*, Wolfenbüttel, 1957.

—— chairman of Round Table on 'Die Beziehungen zwischen Oper, Oratorium und Instrumentalmusik der Barockzeit' in *Bericht über den Neunten Internationalen Kongress Salzburg 1964* (of the Int. Musicol. Soc.), II, Basel, 1966, pp. 212–25.

—— *Oper: Szene und Darstellung von 1600 bis 1900* (in the series *Musikgeschichte in Bildern*, ed. Heinrich Besseler and Max Schneider, Band IV, Lieferung 1), Leipzig, [1968]. (Décor, stage machinery etc.)

Worsthorne, Simon Towneley, *Venetian Opera in the Seventeenth Century*, Oxford, 1954; 2nd ed., 1968. (Splendid.)

Wotquenne, Alfred-Camille, *Catalogue de la Bibliothèque du Conservatoire royal de musique de Bruxelles*, 4 vols., Brussels, 1898–1912.

Yates, Frances A., *The French Academies of the Sixteenth Century*, London, 1947. (Magnificent.)

—— *Giordano Bruno and the Hermetic Tradition*, Chicago, 1964.

Young, J. Z., *Programs of the Brain*, Oxford, 1978. (In the front of its kind.)

Zarlino, Gioseffo, *Le istitutioni armoniche*, Venice, 1558. (Of the first importance and in no way the reactionary of Galilei's caricature.)

Zorzi, Ludovico, et al., *I teatri pubblici di Venezia (secoli XVII–XVIII)*, Venice, 1971. (Documentary notes.)

—— *The Occult Philosophy in the Elizabethan Age*, London, 1979.

POSTSCRIPT

New Grove. *The New Grove Dictionary of Music and Musicians*, ed. Stanley Sadie, 20 vols., London, 1980. This was not available in time to use for the present book, but a small sampling of the most relevant articles appears below, together with other important publications.

Anthony, James R., 'Lully', *New Grove*, Vol. 11, pp. 314–29.

Arnold, Denis (text and bibliography) and Elsie M. Arnold (work-list), 'Monteverdi', *New Grove*, Vol. 12, pp. 514–34.

Brown, Howard Mayer, ed., *Italian Opera, 1660–1770*, New York, 1976–. (Invaluable series of facsimile scores and librettos.)

—— 'The Geography of Florentine Monody', *Early Music*, Vol. 9, No. 2, April 1981, pp. 147–68.

Grout, Donald J., *Alessandro Scarlatti: An Introduction to his Operas*, Berkeley, 1979.

—— 'Opera' in part, *New Grove*, Vol. 13, pp. 544–647.

—— general ed., *The Operas of Alessandro Scarlatti*, Harvard, 1974–, Vol. I, *Eraclea*, ed. Grout, 1974, Vol. II, *Marco Attilio Regolo*, ed. Joscelyn Godwin, 1975, both with excellent introductions by Grout.

Heartz, Daniel, 'Opera' in part, *New Grove*, Vol. 13, pp. 544–647.

Hitchcock, Wiley H., 'Caccini', *New Grove*, Vol. 3, pp. 576–81.

Nutter, David, 'Intermedio', *New Grove*, Vol. 9, pp. 258–69.

Palisca, Claude, 'Cavalieri', *New Grove*, Vol. 4, pp. 20–3.

Porter, William V., 'Peri', *New Grove*, Vol. 14, pp. 401–5.

Sadie, Stanley, 'Opera' in part, *New Grove*, Vol. 13, pp. 544–647.

Walker, Thomas R., 'Cavalli', *New Grove*, Vol. 4, pp. 24–34.

—— 'Opera' in part, *New Grove*, Vol. 13, pp. 544–647.

Index

꙳ꙮ꙳

Compiled by Terence A. Miller, ACP

Page numbers in italics include verbal or musical quotations and examples, those in bold type denote more important references.